Adobe® Premiere® Pro
STUDIO TECHNIQUES WITHDRAWN

Jeff I. Greenberg
with Tim Kolb, Christine Steele, and Luisa Winters

Adobe

Adobe® Premiere® Pro Studio Techniques

Jeff I. Greenberg, Tim Kolb, Christine Steele, and Luisa Winters

Adobe Press

www.adobepress.com

This Adobe Press book is published by Peachpit, a division of Pearson Education.
For the latest on Adobe Press books, go to www.adobepress.com.

To report errors, please send a note to errata@peachpit.com

Acquisitions Editor: Karyn Johnson
Project Editors: Rebecca Gulick, Karyn Johnson
Copy Editor: Anne Marie Walker
Production Editor: Katerina Malone
Technical Editor: Maxim Jago
Proofreader: Liz Welch
Composition: Danielle Foster
Indexer: Valerie Haynes Perry
Cover Design: Charlene Charles-Will
Cover Illustration: Alicia Buelow

ISBN-13: 978-0-321-83997-8
ISBN-10:   0-321-83997-8

Contents

Foreword   vi

Introduction   viii

Chapter 1 Editing in Adobe Premiere Pro 1
Format Agnostic   3
Transcode Is a Dirty Word   12
Mercury Engine   14
Creative Cloud   16
System Design   23
Overview of a Workflow   36
Order of Learning   40

Chapter 2 Setup and Organizing   47
Optimized Setup   48
Interface Nuances   58
Media Setup Outside of Adobe
    Premiere Pro   66
Project Setup   70
Import   85
Organization   97
Suite Relations   104
Media Setup Summary   118
Speech and Script Technologies   118

Chapter 3 Editing Techniques   125
Editing Essentials   127
Timeline Finesse   160
Basic Trimming   180
Advanced Timeline Editing   200
Advanced Workflows   217
Multi-camera Editing   222

Chapter 4 Professional Audio   235
Listening Environment   237
Gain and Levels   240
Timeline Interface   244
Mixing Sound   250
Mixers and Submixes   260
Audio FX   265
Adobe Audition   276

Chapter 5 Advanced Compositing
             and Effects   283
Adobe Premiere Pro Effects
    Processing   285
Fixed and Standard Effects   286
Animating Effects   287
One Effect Multiple Approaches   290

Saving Effect Presets   299
The Warp Stabilizer   300
Using the Title Designer   304
Keying and Compositing   315
Opacity Blend Modes   322
Dynamic Link   327

Chapter 6 Color Correction   331
Plan Your Time Wisely   333
Goals of Color Correction   333
Understanding Light   335
Color Correction Interface Setup   340
Process: What to Do First?   351
Fundamental Color Correction
    Effects   351
Common Primary Corrections   357
Common Secondary Corrections   368
Practical Shot Matching   377
Saving and Reusing Effects   380
Looks   380
Legalizing Video   387
Direct Link with Adobe SpeedGrade   388
Minimalist Adobe SpeedGrade   391
Minimalist Adobe SpeedGrade   391

Chapter 7 Exporting Strategies   407
Understanding Architectures and
    Codecs   409
Getting Output Right   415
Common Outputs   420
The Export Media Dialog Box   420
Final Output   426
h.264 Distribution Outputs   431
Smart Compression Tips   434
Outputting a Still Frame   435
Queue Button   436
Adobe Media Encoder   437
Mastering Presets and Settings   442
Automating Adobe Media Encoder   450

Chapter 8 Workflow Management   453
Protect Your Assets   454
Organizing for Post   456
Postproduction Planning   463
Exporting Media   475
Archiving a Project   477

Index   482

About the Authors

Jeff I. Greenberg

Jeff I. Greenberg has nearly two decades of experience as a Postproduction consultant and Master Instructor (trainer for other trainers) for Adobe, Apple, and Avid, specializing in the areas of editorial, workflow, compositing, sound, color grading, and compression.

Consistently voted as one of the top seminar speakers/interviewers, audiences' feedback includes depth of subjects covered, approachability, and student-centered teaching that helps keep them up to date on industry standards. Jeff teaches seminars at events such as NAB, IBC, CES, and Inter BEE. He's the chair for the Editors Retreat, an annually held exclusive getaway for editors.

Jeff is a published author of several books on the subject of editing and postproduction, including *An Editor's Guide to Adobe Premiere Pro* (Peachpit, 2012). Jeff writes for various blogs and creates training materials for Lynda.com and macProVideo.com. He's happy to talk to you about consulting and helping you find solutions for your training needs at his company J Greenberg Consulting (www.JGreenbergConsulting.com).

Tim Kolb

Tim Kolb has spent nearly 30 years in video production in a variety of roles, including director, DP, videographer, editor, compositor/visual effects artist, and even some time as a software product manager. Tim is an Adobe Premiere Master Instructor and an Adobe Certified Instructor. His writing credits include books and articles for trade magazines and websites, and he is the technical editor for *Adobe Premiere Pro Classroom in a Book* (Adobe Press, 2014). Recognition for his production work includes multiple American Advertising Awards, Tellys, International Television Association honors, a Chicago Film Festival Hugo, and an Emmy.

Christine Steele

Christine Steele has edited film and video for Disney, Paramount, Warner, Pixar, Showtime, Frontline, MSNBC, Electronic Arts, VH1, ABC, and PBS. She edited *Air Racers 3D*, which is now screening in IMAX theaters worldwide.

Christine also produces documentaries and music videos. She served as the Postproduction Supervisor and Supervising Editor for Paramount's feature documentary *talhotblond*, now available on Netflix and Amazon.com. She also supervised the postproduction of *Free Radio* for VH1 and worked as lead editor for all episodes of the Animated TV show *Da Jammies*. Christine won a ProMax award for editing promos for ABC's *Desperate Housewives*.

An Adobe Master Trainer and content creator who enjoys the art of storytelling, Christine Steele uses moving pictures and sound to inspire others. She is currently editing a documentary series for PBS using Adobe Premiere Pro.

Luisa Winters

Luisa Winters is an Adobe Premiere Master Instructor, an Adobe Certified Instructor, and an Apple Certified Trainer. She is an accomplished videographer, editor, 3D animator, and graphics designer. Her compositions have been seen on broadcast TV as well as in private video productions. She has created and edited scores of video and web projects for dozens of corporate, government, and educational, commercial, and private clients. An accomplished nonlinear editor and instructor, Luisa has conducted training sessions and master classes for Adobe After Effects, Photoshop, Adobe Premiere Pro, Flash, Dreamweaver, Captivate, and Encore DVD.

Luisa has led sessions and workshops in almost every U.S. state and in several countries across the world. She has been a featured speaker at NAB every year since 2005 and has been a featured instructor for Government Video Expo, DV Expo, CES, and PMA.

About the Technical Editor

Maxim Jago

Maxim Jago is a filmmaker, award-winning film scriptwriter, teacher, stage presenter, communications consultant, and the author or co-author of multiple books and courses, including *Adobe Premiere Pro Classroom in a Book* (Adobe Press, 2014) and *Adobe Premiere Pro: Learn by Video* (Adobe Press and Peachpit, 2014). He is an Adobe Master Trainer, Grass Valley Master Trainer, Avid Certified Instructor, and the creator of the ESP Teaching System, which helps make complex technologies more accessible and meaningful for creative minds. As well as speaking at conferences internationally, Maxim has been published in magazines, has been quoted in books on film production, and has taught media production all around the world. His training company is 123 Training (123training.co.uk), and his filmmaker website is www.maximjago.com.

Foreword

When I wrote *Adobe Premiere Pro 2.0 Studio Techniques* back in 2006, the landscape of nonlinear editing, not to mention the technology in the film and video business, was nothing like it is today. There were few HD video cameras, formats like DigiBeta and DVCam were still considered standard and acceptable delivery formats, and HDV was a thing. There was little discussion of 4k, and RED was the color of the Adobe logo. It's amazing to reflect on how much has changed in the last seven years and mostly all for the better and benefit of the users and artists.

Ironically, the end of 2006 marked a major career turning point for me as I partnered with my friends Mike "Mouse" McCoy and Scott Waugh as the CTO and head of postproduction for our company, Bandito Brothers.

In a very real way, the edited component of Bandito Brothers was born and raised in Adobe Premiere Pro. The techniques I described in the previous volumes were used day in and day out as part of our post workflow. Having learned the application inside and out, we created and ran an efficient and contained postproduction pipeline that gave us complete control of all the projects we edited. We mixed and matched every format we could get our hands on, and developed a language and style that represented who we were, which now serves as the visual foundation of who we are.

While we remain deep in technology and the latest and greatest tools, Adobe Premiere Pro is still an integral part of our postproduction pipeline. With the recent Creative Cloud version of Adobe Premiere Pro, the buzz around the industry is no longer about Avid or Final Cut Pro but finally about our old friend Adobe Premiere Pro.

The principal idea of the *Studio Technique* series is to thrust you deeper into ideas and advanced methods of working with the tools. Lessons guide you down a path to get to a destination. But along the way you learn a bunch of tricks that make you more proficient in not only the end result, but in the details of getting there—quicker methods to complete tasks, shortcuts, workflow tips, and ways to make your content look better and your flow be more efficient.

When I wrote the previous volumes of this series, it was just me and my own collective experience. With this latest volume, readers now have the luxury of learning from a bevy of experts and professionals to create an even more dynamic and broader range of techniques that are essential to honing your skills.

At the end of the day, the tool does not make the artist. The work is made meaningful by the passion that goes into it and the content that carries it. Honing your skills and perfecting your craft enables you to get closer to creating exactly what is in your head to the best of your abilities. For me, becoming an expert in Adobe Premiere Pro was a means to fulfilling a lifelong dream of making movies, telling stories, and being a part of something I believed in. I trust that this latest volume will ensure you safe travel along your own journey and help you understand Adobe Premiere Pro in new and more powerful ways. It's exciting when your old friend gets better with age.

—Jacob Rosenberg

Jacob Rosenberg is a Director and the CTO of Bandito Brothers in Culver City, California. His directorial debut film, Waiting for Lightning, *was released in 2012 by Samuel Goldwyn Films.*

Introduction

Jeff I. Greenberg

On This Rare Occasion Please Read the Introduction

If you've picked up this book, we want to encourage you to look through its contents and discover the techniques that will put you further on the path to becoming an advanced user of Adobe Premiere Pro.

In this *Studio Techniques* book, it's assumed you've used Adobe Premiere Pro and that you're no longer a novice. Maybe you've never used every Adobe tool, but you've acquired footage and edited and delivered output. We expect that some of you have read the *Adobe Premiere Pro Classroom in a Book* or equivalent, and others may have been using Adobe Premiere Pro for years.

We also assume that you understand the concepts of real-world delivery schedules, clients who are unreasonably demanding, and headache-producing market pressures. Perhaps you even have friends and family that you're able to spend time with occasionally.

The pressures that an editor is under today seem much greater than a decade ago when concepts such as "offline editor only," "picture lock," and a reasonable delivery schedule ruled the day. Nowadays, footage is being thrown at the busy editor from every direction, clients often don't make up their minds (although they truly never have!), and there's constant pressure to always be upgrading software and hardware.

This book gives you the advanced tips and techniques that can make your workflow smoother and your editing faster. It includes techniques that could literally take months or *years* to discover on your own.

What makes this book extraordinary is that it's not a "how to" use Adobe Premiere Pro book; rather, it dives into practical, real-world techniques used by editors working in the trenches with the software every day and teaching others to use it as well. Not only do the four authors who wrote this book earn their living as editors working day-to-day in film, television, and video postproduction, but they also have been "blessed" by Adobe and made Adobe Premiere Pro Master Instructors. This gives them the distinction of teaching instructors and Adobe Certified Experts on how to teach Adobe Premiere Pro to others in the Adobe way.

Hitting a Moving Target

One of the best features of Adobe Creative Cloud is the flexibility it gives Adobe to roll out an update, which is fantastic as a user. But it's *not so great* for an author, especially when a chapter has been finished and put to bed. Major changes can wreak havoc with your sanity and sleeping patterns when you wake up in the middle of the night screaming because much of what you've written must be revised. This book has been written as much as possible in a *general* way—not specifically tied to a particular version. And as significant updates that affect the content occur, they'll be addressed with errata on the web page with the downloadable files (see "A Note About Downloadable Content").

A Note About Overlap

All of the authors had quite a bit of freedom to write about concepts they felt were important to the techniques they were writing about, *even* if there was some overlap. For you, the advantage of this overlap is that it can help you understand the "why" behind the techniques—sometimes from multiple points of view. For example, it's valuable to remap the keyboard. Hearing the reason for it from an editorial point of view is different than hearing it from a colorist's point of view.

How This Book Works

For the most part, each chapter is readable in isolation. When necessary, other relevant chapters are referenced. While trying to maintain a similar style, authors were given the liberty to write in their own voice. Multiple authors provide the flexibility for different viewpoints in editorial and a faster writing process. Any of these authors are skilled enough to have written the entire text!

We offer you loads of gems throughout the book in Tips (something cool) and Notes (something to watch out for), but many are also scattered throughout the text.

You'll know *some* of the techniques discussed in this book, but I can assure you that you won't know all of them. Yes, in some cases you might be able to jump through a chapter quickly, but if you're weak in a given chapter's topic, we highly recommend a deep read. The following sections provide a brief overview on each chapter.

▶ Chapter 1: "Editing in Adobe Premiere Pro" discusses some of the specific functionality that makes Adobe's nonlinear editor nimble and quick in this all-too-soon to be 4k world. Topics include what makes Adobe Premiere Pro so special, and what differentiates a consumer camera and a cinema camera.

The chapter also explains that you should give special attention to hardware system design, performance monitoring, and the order in which you may want to approach using and learning the tools in Adobe Creative Cloud.

▶ Chapter 2: "Setup and Organizing" offers wonderful tips on how to best set up Adobe Premiere Pro and your media *prior* to starting a project. If you create and build a Common Media folder with a preconfigured project, you'll be able to start new projects faster that are optimized to your system. You'll learn to adjust preferences to improve working with Adobe Premiere Pro as well as learn how to set up caches throughout Adobe Creative Cloud applications. And if you're a narrative- or transcript-based editor, be sure to check out the section "Speech and Script Technologies" at the end of the chapter.

▶ Chapter 3: In "Editing Techniques," Christine Steele gives you great insights on how to edit smarter and faster with some power techniques. And just because you've been editing for years doesn't mean you should skip the "Editing Essentials" section. The techniques provided for three-point editing and replace editing could change the way you work! If trimming mystifies you, there are loads of details about the different ways you can trim efficiently. If you're a razor blade and delete editor, this information will open up new ways to work.

▶ Chapter 4: In "Professional Audio," Luisa Winters helps demystify the audio workflow process by describing smart techniques in order of process—from adjusting prior to the edit to using sophisticated submixing and audio FX. She also explains the methods of performing noise reduction and fixing clipped audio in Adobe Audition.

▶ Chapter 5: Tim Kolb takes a very practical approach to effects in "Advanced Compositing and Effects," showing you how you can think "outside the box." The techniques he shows are very much about the type of play you often do to get an effect to work. He starts with some simple elements and builds on them to create more complex effects.

▶ Chapter 6: "Color Correction" helps you understand the way light and video scopes work. Many examples are provided, and also included is a generalized recipe on which order to adjust the Three-Way Color Corrector. Shot matching and Secondaries are explored as well to help you do everything possible directly within Adobe Premiere Pro. Extend your knowledge outside of Adobe Premiere Pro by moving your material to Adobe Speed-Grade and back with this quick usable crash course on its interface.

▶ Chapter 7: "Exporting Strategies" is about unlocking some of the cool techniques in Adobe Premiere Pro and Adobe Media Encoder. Some great presets are built right in the chapter, which should help you get an idea of what to adjust when you want to tweak the presets in both tools.

▶ Chapter 8: Workflow is always difficult to write about because no two work-flows are identical. And if you're reading about a workflow that doesn't apply to you, it can be difficult to find what's important. In "Workflow Management," Tim Kolb approaches workflow by giving you specific techniques that aren't obvious, which are guided by his years of experience working with Adobe Premiere Pro.

What's Not in This Book

We tried to include as much varied content as we could that represented the other video-related tools in Adobe Creative Cloud. But this is mostly an Adobe Premiere Pro book. However, Adobe Premiere Pro doesn't exist in a vacuum, so we included the key details that are necessary to know about the other video-based applications.

Here are some items that you won't find in the book:

▶ **No tape-based techniques.** We know you're saying, "But I still use tape." We're not in any way, shape, or form saying you shouldn't use tape. In fact, the authors romantically wish they were still using tape.

Most of the situations we've been in in the last five years or so have been tapeless worlds, which is the reason we didn't include any material about tape-based work.

▶ **Only the key Adobe Creative Cloud applications.** Yes, we're huge fans of the entire Adobe tool set, but although tools like Adobe Illustrator, Adobe Bridge, Adobe InDesign, and Adobe Dreamweaver have loads of value, they're not linchpins of video editing.

A Note About Downloadable Content

Not every chapter has media. Chapters 1, 2, 7, and 8 *do not* contain projects. Chapter 2 has a script and clip to use with the speech recognition section, and a template of folders to help you organize your own projects. Chapters 3, 4, 5, and 6 have complete projects and media that you can download that work with specific examples from the text. Chapter 6 also has two broadcast legal looks to use in Adobe Premiere Pro with the Lumetri filter. Chapter 7 has a surprise! I've build the presets from the chapter for download as well.

Throughout this book, you'll see examples of scenes that are used to demonstrate various concepts and techniques. The downloadable content includes a wide variety of corresponding media clips that you can use as a playground for experimenting with the techniques discussed.

At the back of this book is a card with an access code. To access the files, please follow these steps.

1. On a Mac or Windows computer, go to www.peachpit.com/redeem and enter the code at the back of your book.

2. If you do not have a Peachpit.com account, you will be prompted to create one.

3. The download files will be listed in the Lesson & Update Files tab on your Account page.

4. Click the file links to download them to your computer.

This process may take some time to complete, depending on the speed of your computer and Internet connection.

Note that if updates to this book are posted, those updates will also appear on your Account page at www.peachpit.com.

Special Thanks

As the lead author, the only real power I get to abuse is lavishing thanks upon others. Without these people, this book would have never have happened. There are so many people to thank that even narrowing down the number to what you see here was difficult.

This is an indulgence, but here is a personal note from me (Jeff) to you the reader: If you find *anything* in this book that makes your life easier (and there should be lots!) and if you ever meet any of these wonderful people, take a moment and let them know! Writing, like editing, is done in a small room with what often feels like only negative feedback.

My Co-authors

This book has been a massive effort. During the writing major life forces were at work, which make book writing all that more difficult. Let me start by thanking each of my co-authors and their families. I'm sorry I had to take so much of their time:

Christine Steele. When Christine signed on to write about editing, I tried to warn her about how much work goes into writing a chapter. She amazingly managed to fit in the writing in addition to a new project she's editing for PBS.

Luisa Winters. Luisa was a superstar, writing a great chapter on audio and turning it around remarkably fast during her busy schedule. I've worked with

Luisa for years, so the result was no surprise given her knowledge base and her professional skills.

Tim Kolb. Tim contributed so much technical knowledge to the book. His chapter on workflow really ties down some small nuances that I've never seen before in print.

Maxim Jago. Maxim is the unofficial co-author of this book. He agreed to do the technical edit, and luckily for us he went far and beyond. Maxim even wrote several sections in a couple of chapters. I absolutely couldn't have shepherded this book without my friend Maxim on board.

Shawn Lamb. Thank you for your extra work early on in the audio chapter.

Peachpit Press

Relationships between authors and publishers are always rocky. Deadlines are always in the front of the publisher's mind and keep authors awake at night. My thanks go out to the following Peachpit crew:

Karyn Johnson. Karyn's cool head prevailed, especially toward the end of the deadline when the doors inevitably come off the machine.

Rebecca Gulick. I would not have taken this role and the book wouldn't have happened if it wasn't for Rebecca. She was a rock for me, especially in the early days of the book. Thank you so much!

Anne Marie Walker. This is the third book you've copyedited for me. I hope I'm not the only author ever to tell you this: I'm stunned at how much better my writing sounds because of your deft hand.

Adobe

And then there are those people inside the walls. Thanks to all those who work at Adobe and help fools like me rave about what I love (and on occasion what drives me crazy!):

Michelle Gallina. I know you're now off in Adobe After Effects land, but this book and the Master Trainer program wouldn't exist without you! You are my favorite person at Adobe, and I am indebted to you for your help and support.

David Helmly. So many times there was a minor question or some obscure switch I needed help with, and time after time you've been there for me.

Mitch Wood. I should print and frame the massive email of answers you've helped with and send you a photo! Thank you so much.

Additionally, the Adobe people that I absolutely, positively have to thank for all their support include Bill Roberts, Al Mooney, Meagan Keane, Steve Ford, Patrick Palmer, Dennis Radeke, Todd Kopriva, Kevin Monahan, Jason Levine, Colin Smith, Anita Engleman, Ellen Wixted, and Leonard Rosenthol.

Friends and Colleagues

Of course, I'd like to thank the rest of the Master instructors as well, particularly my friends Abba Shapiro and Rich Harrington who helped Adobe start the program.

William Robinson (Robbie) Carman for your wisdom, guidance, and sanity (yeah, Catherine too).

Stu Bass for a quick insight into how his episodic TV projects are set up.

Ben Kozuch and Jeff Rothberg, and everyone at FMCTraining.

Those people who are near and dear to my soul: Dorn Hetzel, Gabeba Baderoon, Yossy Tessone, Jack Reilly, Jeff and Jen Smith, Jeff and Holly Preston, and Rich Frumer.

My Family

Isn't it terrible that family comes last all too often?

First, to Amy, my wife: I love you so very much. You've been my sanity and my beacon of hope at some downtimes while cranking out this book. I hear you loud and clear about publishing and deadlines.

To my daughter Sophia, although you're too young to read this, later in life you'll laugh as you see photos of you hidden in this book. Dada loves you.

It's important that I mention of course my close family: Scott, Rachelle, Morgan, and Maddox; Al and Dee; Roger, Elanna, Jesse, Juillette, and Gabrielle; Steven, Avra, Jake, Sam, and Nate; Charles and Amy. Now you'll have to own a copy of the book.

1

Editing in Adobe Premiere Pro

Author: Jeff I. Greenberg

Film editing is now something almost everyone can do at a simple level and enjoy it, but to take it to a higher level requires the same dedication and persistence that any art form does.

—Walter Murch

Editing in Adobe Premiere Pro

At one point this chapter was called the "New Method of Editing," except it's not new. It's about three or four years old and was introduced in CS5. What is the "new" way of editing? It's a pair of ideas that basically mean *the tools should get out of your way*:

▶ Just drop your footage in a project and edit.

▶ Use whatever tools you feel are best for the job.

Once upon a time you were limited by the video formats you could use. If your tool didn't support it, you had to jump through hoops to get the footage to work (see "Transcode Is a Dirty Word" later in this chapter.)

You shouldn't be *forced* to work in a specific frame rate or frame size, or be limited to just broadcast frame sizes. You should be able to output for broadcast as well as for digital signage (where the video is vertical), museum installations (nearly every one is custom), and mobile devices.

And the workflow you choose or build should wrap around tools you're familiar with. In fact, you should use whatever tools from Adobe you prefer and use other companies' tools where you feel appropriate. Adobe Premiere Pro has fantastic interoperability with other third-party tools, whether it's a Digital Audio Workstation (DAW), a compositor, or a color correction suite, even though Adobe provides all of these.

The beautiful thing? As content creators, we shouldn't care. Use what you need. Pick a format. Pick an output. Don't neglect planning and testing, and make sure your pipeline works; your tools shouldn't stand in your way.

Best of all, Adobe Premiere Pro packaged in an interface that's recognizable to editors. It's the common 2-up editing interface, with a Timeline that feels familiar.

The biggest hurdle for you the editor, is picking up the depth and the techniques that are available in Adobe Premiere Pro, beneath the immediate surface—that's what this book is about.

This chapter explores some of the areas that are more abstract, like the overview of the general workflow in Adobe Creative Cloud, and progresses to concrete subjects, like choosing appropriate hardware.

Format Agnostic

In a given year I see at least ten formats that come from hundreds of cameras: XDCam, P2 cards (**Figure 1.1**), Red R3d files, and even footage from iPhones and other smartphones.

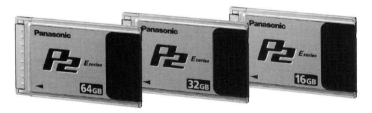

Figure 1.1 P2 cards are one of the key digital formats used in Electronic News Gathering (ENG).

Traditionally, trying to make all these pieces fit have caused editors major headaches. In fact, I believe there's someone sitting in a room right now making up a new format just to give editors more headaches.

The message I'm trying to relay is to stop sweating. When I encounter a new format, I just throw it at Adobe Premiere Pro. So far, it's almost always worked. And if it doesn't work now, I know the next Adobe Premiere Pro update will make it work.

This flexibility doesn't stop at cameras. It extends to other nonlinear editors (NLEs) through XML and AAF. For this reason, Adobe Premiere Pro is the hub that intersects with my camera and all my software.

TIP

It's all too common for productions to want to use prosumer cameras. Although they're not optimum for professional work, Adobe Premiere Pro handles their files beautifully. Just be sure to hold the cameras sideways!

Any Camera Format

There are three generalized camera types: prosumer, professional, and cinema. I use the term generalized because the distinction between these formats *used* to be very black and white. Now, it's a gray haze because some of these cameras can cross boundaries.

Therefore, it's crucial to know which formats you have to work with. Each type has different advantages and limitations.

Prosumer cameras

No longer are there consumer cameras. Everything *can* be used on professional productions. Therefore, everything is prosumer.

The idea that I can use my iPhone (**Figure 1.2**) or iPad to shoot glorious 1080 video is both wonderful and maddening at the same time. It's become almost a bad joke that on set a client can use his cell phone and shoot video just to give you an alternate shot (or give an opinion of what he envisions the shot should be).

What makes a prosumer camera *prosumer* is mostly the small sensor size and high compression of the video. Uncompressed video eats about 6 GB per minute. But that same 6 GB can capture about an hour of video on my iPhone. The best camera can be the camera in your pocket because it goes with you anywhere and everywhere. That's the beauty of these prosumer cameras.

Figure 1.2 The easiest camera to shoot with is the one you have in your pocket.

The other limitation of prosumer cameras, aside from compression, is that they have a very small chip, which affects how they capture light and focus. The chip creates all sorts of struggles in low-light situations to capture a decent image. More often than not, these cameras end up producing lots of noise.

Professional cameras

As with prosumer cameras, professional cameras typically shoot HD, but they have a couple of different features that make them attractive to the pro market.

The footage they capture is less compressed. In many ways, the less compressed the footage is, the easier it will be to edit, color correct, and output. Sometimes you have the ability to change lenses on these cameras, and the lenses are engineered with a higher grade of glass, meaning that you can shoot cleaner, sharper images with the added benefit of adjustable apertures and f-stops (**Figure 1.3**).

They may also have features like jam sync of timecode (making two cameras' clocks exactly match, which is fantastic for multicam shoots), zebra striping (in-camera exposure awareness), and possibly some input adjustment of metadata like essence marks (essentially clip markers made by some cameras while shooting). Such features make these cameras "run and gun" devices—perfect for everyday use and ENG.

Figure 1.3 Professional cameras have critical features that place them in a class above consumer/ prosumer cameras.

Cinema cameras

The hallmarks of a cinema camera are that these cameras can produce formats idealized for postproduction with less compression, such as Avid's DNxHD and Apple's ProRes, and some can deliver raw sensor data.

Cameras in this category often shoot greater than HD (2k, 4k, and beyond), which provides the flexibility of being able to deliver footage at these higher resolutions or just in HD and reframe the content as needed (**Figure 1.4**).

Figure 1.4 The RED Scarlet-X shoots 5k on a sensor that's greater in size than a frame of 35mm film.

Cinema cameras may not be as flexible or optimized for "run and gun" shooting. For example, it may be necessary to capture dual sound—sound on the camera and on an outboard device—and then sync both in post. These cameras require much more customization; not just to the camera body. Lenses, battery packs, SSD (solid state drive) storage systems, camera mounts, and device acquisition systems (such as the AJA Ki Quad Pro) are all items that will increase your costs in addition to the camera body.

Often, when a cinema camera is used on a shoot, there's additional on set support, such as a DIT (Digital Imaging Technician) and possibly an on set editor and/or colorist to assist with the image.

Tape-based cameras

Because of the debate about the inclusion of tape-based cameras in this book, sadly, little will be mentioned about them.

Each author loved the permanence of tape (or film!). But realistically, in the past five years the amount of tape we've worked with has been nearly nil. So, this book won't cover much tape-based information because the industry has moved away from it.

File-based camera flexibility

Every camera type mentioned previously is now primarily file based, storing data on a card or a chip, not on a video tape. Video tape has this nasty limitation of forcing you to work in real time.

A unique ability in Adobe Premiere Pro is that you can check the cards from these cameras while on set. It's not a file listing, but it gives you a chance to view the actual footage.

Handling cards (such as P2, CF cards, or SD cards) on set is commonly done by a DIT who does this sort of work and more (including backing up and checking the files for consistency). However, all too frequently this job gets lumped with the tasks of a DP or assistant editor.

The ability to quickly check a card and hoverscrub (where you hover over a clip and scrub to preview the clip) for content allows for the quick analysis and checking of the card content, ensuring that the footage looks good before the media is copied and the card is reformatted for reuse.

Using the Media Browser to preview media

Because it's all too common to encounter editors who aren't aware of the Media Browser, it's worth mentioning and describing here. You can find the Media Browser in the default workspace in the lower-left panel (**Figure 1.5**).

If you're not familiar with the Media Browser, this is an epiphany because you can browse a card *visually*.

In Adobe Premiere Pro's Media Browser (which is essentially the same as Adobe Prelude's Ingest panel) is a view of the

Figure 1.5 The Media Browser (maximized here due to the accent (`) key), is the fastest way to look at a card.

media. Merely navigate to the card (on the left side of the Media Browser are the Volumes on your system), and the card contents become available to you visually as thumbnails.

You can hoverscrub these clips (pass your mouse over the clip), and the thumbnail changes to show different sections of the clip. Double-clicking the thumbnail will place the clip in the Source Monitor *but not add it to your project!* This is a great way to view the clip using the JKL keys and other playback tools.

Unless you drag it into the Project panel or Timeline, this clip, which is living out on a card, *isn't part of your project* and yet can be played back full screen.

And you can *edit* directly from the card. The obvious *danger* is if you eject the card, the media is gone. But this concept of being able to view media on a *live card* is *fantastic!*

Adobe Prelude, a dedicated tool in Adobe Creative Cloud, is discussed in Chapter 2, "Setup and Organizing" and Chapter 8, "Workflow Management." Prelude can view clips as well as do a more important step: It can handle your file-based media correctly by ensuring that a copy is made.

Now that you've seen how flexible Adobe Premiere Pro is with media (more about this in Chapter 2), it's worth looking at other NLE interoperability.

Final Cut Pro

It's likely that Adobe Premiere Pro isn't your primary editorial tool. Even if it is, clients may come to you with projects from Apple's Final Cut Pro (**Figure 1.6**) that they would like continued or revised.

Because of XML (eXtensible Markup Language), it's possible to import a project from Final Cut Pro into Adobe Premiere Pro and relink it to the QuickTime files (if you have them).

This ability to export XML exists for Apple's Final Cut Pro version 7 and earlier. If you're utilizing Final Cut Pro X, you'll need a tool from Intelligent Assistance to convert the XML from Final Cut Pro X to the XML of Final Cut Pro 7 so it's compatible with Adobe Premiere Pro.

TIP

In the Program or Record Monitor, pressing Ctrl+` (accent key) will fill the screen with the video. Over and over again you'll see the accent key (`) mentioned in this book. It's probably the most useful feature because it enables you to maximize a panel when you mouse over it.

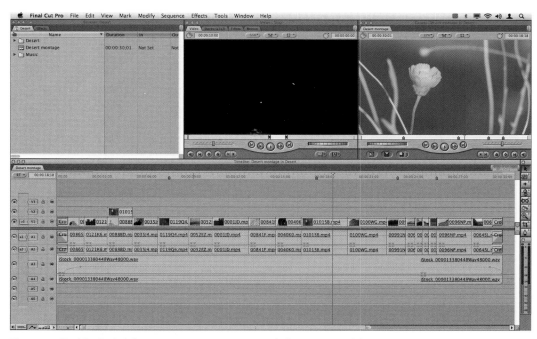

Figure 1.6 Final Cut Pro's ability to export XML permits cross-platform interoperability.

Export XML

When you export an XML file from Final Cut Pro, it's important to be aware of a couple of possible speed bumps:

▶ Make sure that all your media is connected prior to your XML export.

▶ Be aware of any camera codecs that need rewrapping into QuickTime, such as XDCam and clips from P2 cards.

▶ If you're working with Final Cut Pro X, you'll need translation software to make the XML file more compatible.

What translates?

The elements that translate to Adobe Premiere Pro include clips (including multiclips), dissolves, most transfer modes, scale, crop, rotation, opacity, audio keyframes, several audio filters, and several video filters (including the Three-Way Color Correctors).

The elements that don't translate are mostly "generated," such as titles, generators, and motion elements.

After importing an XML file, a report is generated if errors occurred. This Final Cut Pro Translation report is a text file. Double-click it to open it and show the names of the clips and timecodes of where errors occurred.

Media considerations

QuickTime media is the architecture of all the video media that comes from Final Cut Pro. QuickTime is installed on all Macs and merely needs to be installed on a Windows computer. Apple's own professional codec, ProRes, is readable on both platforms but only writable on the Macintosh.

To relink clips and sequences, simply select everything in a project and choose File > Relink Media.

One issue you need to be aware of is *rewrapped* media. File-based media from XDCam and P2 cards are normally natively stored in the MXF (Materials eXchange Format) architecture, which is a rich media architecture and is similar to QuickTime in that there are different codecs available within the MXF container. Final Cut Pro ingests these files by taking them out of MXF and rewrapping them as QuickTime files. This is an issue because these codecs have to be licensed to use. If you do not have Final Cut Pro installed on your system, you're not licensed to use these codecs in QuickTime.

On a Mac, owning any of the Apple ProApps (Compressor, Motion, Final Cut Pro X, or Logic) grant the system a license to use these codecs.

On Windows, it's necessary to purchase a license from Calibrated Software. It has several packages that will add the appropriate licensed codecs to QuickTime, making the rewrapped media available to QuickTime.

Avid

Importing from Avid Media Composer (**Figure 1.7**) is limited to a single sequence (not a project like Final Cut Pro). What's exciting about the Adobe Premiere Pro CC release is the licensing of Avid's DNxHD codec. All Avid media is now available to Adobe Premiere Pro.

TIP

Do you need to bring bins across from an Avid sequence? Build sequences of all the clips in a bin on a single sequence, and then export the AAF for the sequence that represents the bin.

Figure 1.7 AAF exports from Avid Media Composer, Symphony, and Newscutter can translate to Adobe Premiere Pro but only on a sequence-by-sequence basis.

Export AAF

When you export an AAF from Avid Media Composer, you need to do a few things first:

▶ Make sure you select the Edit Protocol in the Export dialog.

▶ Set Media to Link if you want to link to the existing media.

▶ Set Media to Consolidate to copy existing media. The best place for media to be copied is in a folder in the same location as the AAF file.

▶ Convert Audio Sample Rate to Project so all of your audio is a single sample rate.

The following should be tested prior to exporting to avoid problems:

▶ Mixed frame rates

▶ Clips linked via Avid Media Access (AMA)

What translates?

The clips and tracks import without a problem. Key items like cross dissolves and audio clip gains also come across cleanly.

Media considerations

Media support from Avid Media Composer is very robust: It's possible for Adobe Premiere Pro to reconnect to AMA media, file-based MXF (such as XDCam and P2), and DNxHD; the latter is new in Adobe Premiere Pro.

Less certain for successful sequence/media transfers are situations with mixed media sizing (SD in HD projects) and mixed frame rates.

Transcode Is a Dirty Word

Transcoding video refers to the process of re-encoding video files to an architecture + codec that your NLE can handle or can handle with less stress on your system.

For example, many NLEs have struggled with h.264 files (regardless of containers such as QuickTime, MTS, or MXF) because of the very lossy nature of this distribution codec (**Figure 1.8**). Some editorial systems can't handle them. Some formats suffer and drop frames so heavily that editing is difficult or unrealistic.

TIP

Place your media caches on your fastest storage, preferably on a USB 3 or a Thunderbolt connected SSD drive. More about this in detail in Chapter 2.

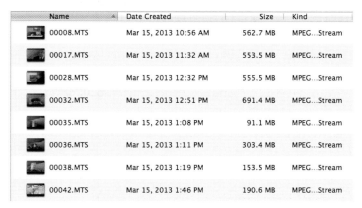

Name	Date Created	Size	Kind
00008.MTS	Mar 15, 2013 10:56 AM	562.7 MB	MPEG...Stream
00017.MTS	Mar 15, 2013 11:32 AM	553.5 MB	MPEG...Stream
00028.MTS	Mar 15, 2013 12:32 PM	555.5 MB	MPEG...Stream
00032.MTS	Mar 15, 2013 12:51 PM	691.4 MB	MPEG...Stream
00035.MTS	Mar 15, 2013 1:08 PM	91.1 MB	MPEG...Stream
00036.MTS	Mar 15, 2013 1:11 PM	303.4 MB	MPEG...Stream
00038.MTS	Mar 15, 2013 1:19 PM	153.5 MB	MPEG...Stream
00042.MTS	Mar 15, 2013 1:46 PM	190.6 MB	MPEG...Stream

Figure 1.8 This is a directory of MTS – MPEG Transport Stream files. Here they're h.264 wrapped in the MPEG architecture. Many NLEs struggle or require multiple steps to use this type of media, often forcing editors to transcode.

Some formats, such as R3D files that contain RAW information from the camera sensor, ask your system to push large amounts of data, making it difficult for playback. Transcoding used to be common in these situations. But Adobe Premiere Pro handles these formats without transcoding due to the Mercury Playback Engine (see the section "Mercury Engine" later in this chapter).

So, why transcode? One of Adobe Premiere Pro's strengths is that you should just be able to import and edit!

Every Format Should Import

Adobe Premiere Pro can import any and every video format. Part of the advantage of Adobe Creative Cloud is the ability for Adobe to rapidly implement new formats as they become available. While writing this book, Adobe in fact improved these capabilities. For example, Adobe added the ability to import the format from RED Dragon sensor footage.

To Transcode or Not to Transcode

Although transcoding is considered evil, there are two great reasons to transcode: performance and portability:

▶ **Performance.** Some formats, even on the best hardware, stress out a system, particularly heavily compressed h.264 video and larger formats with high data rates (2k and above media, such as RED R3d or ArriRaw). On older hardware transcoding may be a *necessity* to get any decent playback at all. Multicam editing, especially beyond four streams, may also stress a system enough that transcoding may help.

 The best transcoding choice for performance is to use a postproduction codec (as long as you have the bandwidth), such as Avid's DNxHD (DNxHD 145 or 220) or Apple's ProRes (ProRes 422 or HQ).

▶ **Portability.** Whether it's to share the project with another editor or have the flexibility of working on a laptop on an airplane, the idea of making a "smaller" version of the video is generically called *proxy* or *offline* editing. The easiest way to make smaller media files is by choosing a codec/data rate combination that is low (such as DNxHD 36 or ProRes Proxy) and that is optimized for postproduction and provides an adequate enough picture.

 At the very end of the edit, you'll need to relink the sequence to the full quality footage.

If you're working in a news/fast turnaround environment, it's ideal to select Use Previews in the Export Media dialog. This option forces Adobe Premiere Pro to use previews (lower-quality processing) for faster output.

Proper Media Handling

The golden rule when you're working with various file-based media is to organize it outside of Adobe Premiere Pro. It's crucial to have copies of your media. Linking to clips that are on media cards is dangerous, because it's likely the cards will be ejected and reformatted.

See the section "Start Organized and Sleep at Night" in Chapter 2.

Mercury Engine

The Mercury Playback Engine (MPE) is the technology that permits the real-time acceleration of formats and effects in Adobe Premiere Pro. The key elements that power this technology include:

▶ **64-bit architecture.** This moves more data through the computer's CPU and can address more RAM compared to 32-bit architectures.

▶ **Multithreading.** Tasks can be broken down into smaller jobs and doled out to multiple cores on each CPU.

▶ **RAM.** Utilize as much RAM as the system has, shared between multiple applications. Be sure to have 2 to 3 GB of RAM per core (see the section "System Design" later in this chapter.)

▶ **Video card.** Some effects and processing are accelerated and offloaded from the CPU (a general processor) to the GPU (Graphical Processing Unit), which is optimized to process video (some cards have over 100 cores and some over 1000!). The right types of video card (CUDA and Open CL) with at least 1 GB of RAM are vital to obtain this acceleration.

Leveraging the MPE

The key to maximizing the capabilities of the MPE is twofold: one part is in your system design (mentioned later in this chapter); the other part is how you choose to do your workflow.

Most of the MPE benefits are invisible. You can't see how the Mercury Playback Engine permits areas that just "work" like processing footage that might have needed transcoding.

The ideal strategy is to select only accelerated effects (marked in **Figure 1.9**) in the Effects panel. Certain items, such as scaling, deinterlacing, blending modes, and color space conversions, also benefit from using the right video card.

Don't render (Adobe calls the render files *Previews*) unless you absolutely need to. Often, footage and effects will play back without needing any rendering at all—*even if the Timeline has a red line!* An exception to this would be workflows that have crucial time-based deliverables—usually same day productions, such as news. It's devastating to discover that output will take longer than you expected because of extra rendering that was left for processing until the output stage.

Turn on the dropped frame indicator (**Figure 1.10**) in the Settings menu on the Program Monitor. You'll see a green light to the right of the timecode as long as playback is working. If you encounter a problem, the light will turn yellow. Mousing over the dropped frame indicator shows you how many frames were dropped.

When playback is sluggish, that's a sign to take one of three actions:

▶ **Drop the video resolution.** Adobe Premiere Pro's default is to play back at half (½) resolution. For HD and SD sizes, the only option is to drop the Playback Resolution to ¼ (**Figure 1.11**). When you pause the video, Adobe Premiere Pro will still show the full resolution of the image. Even at ¼ resolution, the image was still decent. It's not like you're doing a one-to-one pixel mapping on your screen. The video has been reduced to "fit," so why would you calculate those pixels for playback? If you work on a sequence that's greater than HD, such as 2k from an Arri Alexa, you'll unlock more resolution choices, such as ⅛ and ¹⁄₁₆.

▶ **Build renders (previews).** Consider building renders. Just press the Return (Enter) key on your keyboard. Once the preview is created, it'll be played instead of the individual original media. Any change will require new previews to be created.

▶ **Consider transcoding.** See the earlier sidebar "To Transcode or Not to Transcode."

TIP

Consider rendering Adobe After Effects compositions in Adobe Premiere Pro's Timeline. Although the Dynamic Link feature is fantastic for making changes, the playback depends on Adobe After Effects having cache files for the composition. By rendering in Adobe Premiere Pro, you reduce the strain on your system.

Figure 1.9 Using accelerated effects maximizes the playback of effects by offloading complex calculations to the GPU—a dedicated processor for graphics.

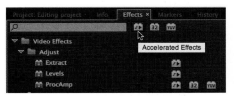

Figure 1.10 The dropped frame indicator is green, indicating no dropped frames.

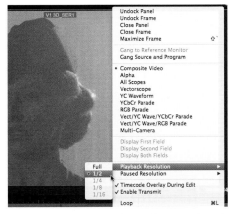

Figure 1.11 Playback resolution choices are based on the size of the sequence.

CUDA or Open CL Architecture

Originally, Adobe optimized systems for cards that supported CUDA architecture (developed by nVidia), which allowed offloading of pixel pushing from the CPU to the video card that was optimized for graphics. Some cards have over 100 CPUs.

After CUDA, Adobe implemented Open CL (a similar technology supported by ATI/AMD). It doesn't matter which technology you adopt, as long as you choose a card that supports one of these two architectures.

Mercury Transmit I/O

The Mercury Transit architecture allows Adobe Premiere Pro to "transmit" the Mercury Engine processing to output cards (used for monitoring or tape output).

Do you have an output card? If so, you'll get all the great acceleration on output (a feature that earlier versions of Adobe Premiere Pro did not have). This technology is applicable *only* if you have an output card or breakout box (**Figure 1.12**), such as the those from AJA, Black Magic Designs, BlueFish, or Matrox. Given that some of these devices are less than $300 (like the AJA T-Tap), professional editors consider this sort of outboard monitoring (*especially* for color correction) a mandatory addition.

It's crucial that you make sure your GPU and the specific type of I/O you're using are supported by the Mercury Engine.

Figure 1.12 Breakout cards and boxes permit the professional evaluation of video on studio monitors (not to be confused with a regular LCD or LED flat panel). The AJA IO 4k will handle 4k and Ultra HD over Thunderbolt 2.

Greater than HD

At one point HD was a dream to most editors, and SD was the standard. Today, everyone shoots in HD (they might look at SD in their archives). If larger formats, such as 2k, 3k, 4k, and above, aren't on your radar, they *will* be on your competitors' radar. And the MPE is what will power this greater than HD future. See the section "System Design" to get insights on how and what to buy to utilize these technologies.

Adobe Creative Cloud

In May of 2013, Adobe switched from a perpetual licensing model (physical boxes) to a Software as a Service (SAS) model.

The major benefit of Adobe Creative Cloud is obvious: Get every major Adobe tool, and download what you need from a selection of nearly 20 different tools spanning video photography, print, and web (**Figure 1.13**).

Although some people just buy Adobe Premiere Pro, nearly everyone we've met has chosen the Creative Cloud package, giving them more tools than they know what to do with.

The access to so many tools is amazing (and a little overwhelming); it's worth noting that there are some practical benefits beyond *just* the software.

Sync Settings

Adobe has added the capability to synchronize settings, such as your preferences and keyboard shortcuts. This capability is tied to your Adobe ID and is probably the most valuable *professional* benefit for editors. Your customizations are saved, *and* they can be transferred from system to system.

When you sit down on *your* system, you want it to be *exactly* adjusted the way you want. But what if you need to work on someone else's system? Or what if you want to use Adobe Premiere Pro on a second system (see the section "Two Licenses")? What if you need to reset your settings? Sync Settings enables you to do all of these tasks easily.

When you launch Adobe Premiere Pro, you'll see that Sync Settings to Adobe Creative Cloud is part of the Welcome dialog, as shown in **Figure 1.14** on the next page.

On a Mac, the Sync Settings is located in the Premiere Pro menu; on Windows it's in the Edit menu. Initially, it's the login for the Adobe ID that was used to install the software.

From the Creative Cloud, Sync Settings uploads and downloads your personalized adjustments on a per application setting. These settings include:

▶ **Preferences.** Almost all the preferences, ranging from the General category through the Trim settings.

▶ **Workspace Layouts.** The unique way you customize the arrangement of the different windows and panels.

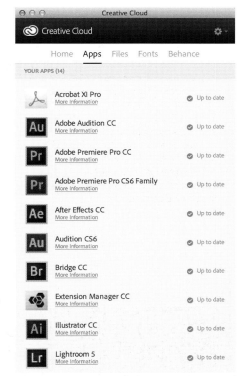

Figure 1.13 The Creative Cloud application runs in either the menu bar of OS X or the system tray in Windows. It's the heart of installing applications, managing fonts, and identifying what was installed or modified in Adobe Creative Cloud.

▶ **Keyboard Shortcuts.** Any keyboard adjustments are also capable of being synced.

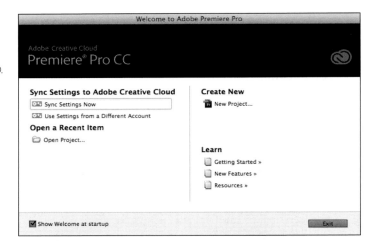

Figure 1.14 Signing into the Adobe Creative Cloud account permits you to sync key settings. The account sign in can be the owner's Adobe ID, a different user, or even a "free" Adobe ID. When signed in, the user's email will appear here.

Not everything is synced. The most important items that are ignored are *cache files* (which speed up some media handling), because they're always going to be unique to your local system.

Multi-user systems are still commonly found in many facilities, where two editors share the same machine and often the same logon. The Adobe Creative Cloud settings are *initially* tied to the license, but don't have to be.

Sync doesn't rely on ownership of Adobe Creative Cloud

It's possible to create an Adobe ID *without* buying or downloading anything. You do get some storage space (2 GB) and a couple of other features as a "free user" of the Creative Cloud.

So starting a free membership grants you an Adobe ID. With that ID you can sync your preferences. To sign up, go to http://creative.adobe.com and choose Get started (**Figure 1.15**).

If you're a working freelancer and you don't own Creative Cloud (and even if you do), this ID allows you to transfer settings via the Internet from location to location. Just re-

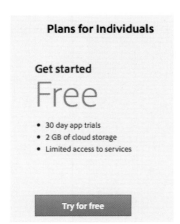

Figure 1.15 This free method of acquiring an ID permits users to easily transfer their favorite settings without being tied to the purchase of Adobe Creative Cloud.

member to sign out when you're finished. You don't want someone else updating or changing your keyboard!

Key preferences

Some users constantly tweak their settings. It's important that if you fall into this category, you *save your settings to the Cloud* on a regular basis. When you choose to Sync Settings via the menu, a dialog asks which you want to do, upload or download. You can automate this option via the Preferences, as shown in **Figure 1.16**.

Figure 1.16 By using the drop-down When Syncing menu, Sync Settings allows you to choose what is synced and whether it should be uploaded or downloaded to the current system.

If your facility consists of freelancers or you're working in other situations where users constantly come and go, it's valuable to adjust the Sync Settings to "Automatically clear settings on application quit." Then, when someone quits for the day, that person can reset Adobe Premiere Pro for the next user automatically.

Two Licenses

You can always have multiple installs of Adobe applications, but prior to this release you were limited to running the software on only one machine at a time per license.

Starting with Adobe Premiere Pro CC, you're able to have two *live* licenses. This makes it easy and convenient to work any way you'd like, for example on a Mac and Windows machine, two different machines in an office, or on your work system and home system.

When you sign in to a *third license instance*, Adobe Creative Cloud logs out the other two users.

Frequent Updates

Although nobody (except Adobe) can exactly say when new feature rollouts will occur, they should occur more frequently than boxed software releases. No longer is Adobe tied to 18-month "major" releases.

Prior to the Adobe Creative Cloud release, Adobe (like most software companies) could legally only add major new features to software with major version changes (for the inquisitive, it's the Sarbanes-Oxley Act that created this issue).

With the new subscription model, it's possible for Adobe to quickly react to technological needs, such as new camera formats, bleeding-edge technology innovations, and rapid bug fixes.

Storage Space

Although not included with the initial release of Creative Cloud, Adobe is including 20 GB of desktop-based sync storage (**Figure 1.17**) with versioning and private folder sharing. This will make it easy for users to share and sync projects invisibly between machines or be accessible from a web browser. Additional storage space will be available for purchase.

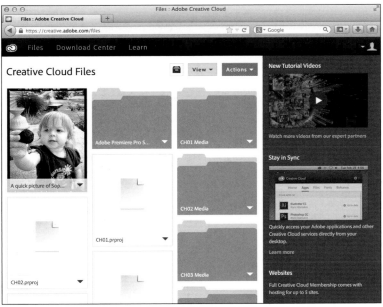

Figure 1.17 The desktop-based sync mimics what's in the Adobe Creative Cloud folder: On the left, the Macintosh folder contains photos, projects, and folders. On the right the same material is synced and available online.

In many ways, this type of storage is the ultimate live backup for projects. Having additional versions of a file will not count against the storage space (unlimited versions are stored for ten days). It's unclear if this will work for Adobe Premiere Pro projects, but it's certain to work for other tools, such as Adobe Photoshop.

Typekit Fonts

You'll have the license to use some 175 plus Typekit fonts for your video, web, and print needs. Getting away from using the default fonts of Helvetica, Arial, Times, and Palatino can *only* be good for your productions.

To access these fonts, use the Adobe Creative Cloud application (**Figure 1.18**) to log into the Typekit website and see the fonts you have access to. The font must be labeled as "desktop" to be used on your system.

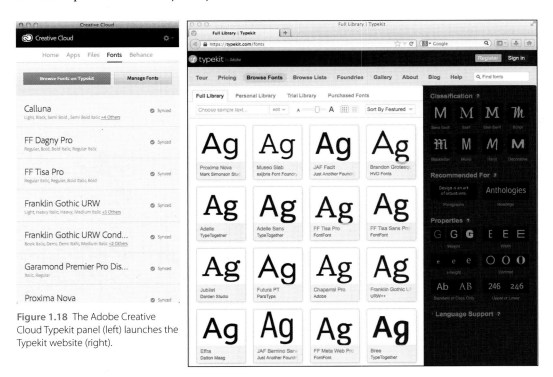

Figure 1.18 The Adobe Creative Cloud Typekit panel (left) launches the Typekit website (right).

Behance /Behance ProSite

Behance is a service that permits the publishing of projects into online portfolios. There is also a professional social network (you can follow and be followed). Publishing your work and discovering others' work can be done from the Adobe Creative Cloud application.

Currently (third quarter 2013), Behance is just available for Adobe Photoshop and Adobe Illustrator documents.

Behance ProSite (**Figure 1.19**) is a full web hosting service with drag-and-drop templates that will help you utilize your uploaded content and create a portfolio driven website in minutes. That content can include your work, additional pages, your resume, and much more.

As with Typekit, currently Behance ProSite is geared more toward those who want to output to print and the web. But we hope to see some expansion into showcasing video directly from Adobe Premiere Pro soon.

Figure 1.19 Behance ProSite used to cost more than $100 a year, but it is now free for Adobe Creative Cloud members.

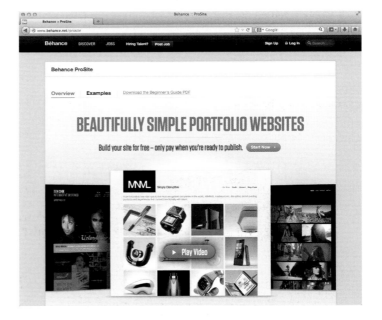

System Design

The most difficult pill to swallow about hardware in the video production industry is how short-lived purchases can be.

To do word processing, I can use a computer from 2007 and it does the same thing as my current system. Technically speaking, I might even be able to use hardware nearly a decade old for word processing.

This is *not* the case with postproduction. If hardware lasts 18 to 24 months, that's ideal. Four years is the *maximum*. Outside of that window of time, the innovations speed the work so significantly that the purchase of new hardware just makes sense.

If performance gains yield a difference of 12 minutes a day, that's an hour a week. That's also *50 hours* a year—a working week's worth of time-savings. This efficiency isn't just for rendering or outputting; it's for everything.

There won't be any holy wars—Mac versus Windows or build it yourself versus a preconfigured box—in this section. The goal here is provide you with valuable information so you can make smart hardware decisions well beyond the publication date of this book.

If the following component sections (**Figure 1.20**) feel overwhelming because of the number of factors to balance, feel free to jump to the section "Too Many Hardware Choices?" later in this chapter.

TIP

Be sure to check Adobe's specification page on Adobe Premiere Pro at www.adobe.com/products/premiere/tech-specs.html before you buy hardware.

NOTES

Never, ever, purchase a system designed at the "minimum" configuration. Although it will work, meeting just the minimum requirements guarantees the worst performance.

Figure 1.20 This Intel motherboard supports Thunderbolt, an interface faster than USB 3.

The essential message I want to convey is *balance*. Buying the best CPU but ignoring the amount of RAM in the machine is equivalent to buying a Ferrari but only being allowed to use two cylinders. I cannot stress enough that each component should be balanced across your system. Just investing entirely in RAM or the fastest CPU will be less effective than balancing both.

One thing is certain; if your motherboard has only USB 2 or FireWire drive connections, it's time to purchase new hardware.

CPU

The CPU is the brain of your system (**Figure 1.21**). It is one of the cornerstones to maximizing the behavior of the MPE. For a balanced system, the critical ingredients are the number of cores (and hyperthreading), cache size, and clock speed.

Here are some general rules when choosing a CPU:

▶ Intel CPUs, particularly the i7 and Xeon CPUs, are the fastest choice for your money today. Pay attention to the latest chipsets. The Haswell architecture chip sets are beginning to become available in desktops and laptops. This architecture is newer than the third generation Ivy Bridge architecture. Those laptops that implement the newer generation will often contain a slower chip (clock speed) than the prior generation for lower power requirements and better battery life—meaning equal or better performance with longer battery life.

▶ The number of cores is more important than clock speed. Hyperthreading is crucial and allows one core to act as two virtual processors.

▶ AMD chips generally won't match Intel performance due to the lack of support of SSE 4.1 (a specific set of instructions that permit the acceleration of data through the chip).

Figure 1.21 A picture of the i7 CPU from Intel.

RAM

Make sure your system isn't starved for RAM (**Figure 1.22**). It should have approximately 2–3 GB per core. Purchasing a system with eight cores *but only* 8 GB of RAM will create a problem in which the cores will be starved for needed RAM.

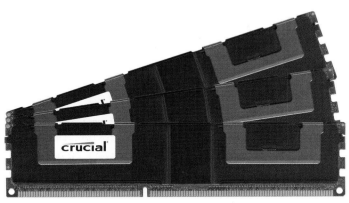

Figure 1.22 Make sure any RAM you purchase has sufficient speed for your system. Two to three gigabytes per core is the minimum. Keep in mind that other tools like Adobe After Effects can quickly use all the RAM in a system.

With multiple CPUs, or cores, many processes occur in parallel. Some processes take longer to finish, and in lower memory situations, the RAM isn't freed up, forcing an individual CPU to wait.

An easy test to determine if your system is starved for RAM is to process some stock effects (nonaccelerated) and check your CPU performance (see "Measuring System Performance" later in this chapter). If your machine is low on RAM, it may be worth trying to disable hyperthreading. Hyperthreading refers to the technology where one core can behave as if it was two (as mentioned in the "CPU" section). By turning off hyperthreading in low RAM situations, it may be possible to achieve better performance, although I'd recommend buying more RAM instead!

For you Apple users out there, the only time Apple updates the video driver is when it does an OS revision (e.g., 10.8.3 to 10.8.4). It's smart to download your video driver directly to have the latest update.

Getting the best performance from RED footage requires at least one RED Rocket board. For laptop users, several companies make a Thunderbolt chassis for a RED Rocket board.

Multiple GPU cards will accelerate export but not playback. This is significant for systems that are intended for use with Adobe After Effects, which can also benefit from multiple video cards.

Laptop users should be aware that you might not be able to upgrade the video card on your laptop. Make sure you purchase the best video card within your budget.

Video Card

The right video card (**Figure 1.23**) is *crucial* for accelerated effects via the MPE. I'd almost go as far as to say that buying a system that supports the MPE is an easy choice to make. This acceleration advantage is one of main reasons for buying Adobe Premiere Pro. So why wouldn't you plan to get a video card that supports it?

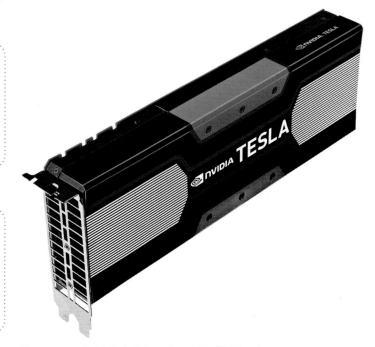

Figure 1.23 nVidia's Tesla K20 card has 5 GB of RAM and 2496 cores.

Make sure the card supports CUDA or OpenCL and that it has at least 1 GB of RAM. If you're working in formats larger than HD, more RAM is a necessity. A 4k frame requires about 510 MB of video RAM.

Video cards have innovations every year. Top-of-the-line cards can be very expensive (over $2000) but can provide maximum acceleration—more than 15x that of a system *without* the card *but only* for certain key effects. It won't necessarily provide acceleration for everything.

Storage

With file-based camera systems being the norm, storage becomes the consumable rather than the video tapes of the past.

Making the right storage choices is just as important as choosing the right processor or the amount of RAM. The biggest need is *speed* but in the right places.

Connections

The drive connection (cable) shouldn't be the bottleneck in your system. Internally, try to connect via the fastest plug on your motherboard. Today, SATA (Serial Advanced Technology Attachment) is the most common internal connection.

Externally, I strongly encourage you to move to USB 3 or Thunderbolt (**Figure 1.24**). Both are faster than most internal connections. At this point (third quarter 2013), I recommend that you divest yourself of hardware that has USB 2 or FireWire because the newer connections are ten or more times faster.

Figure 1.24 Thunderbolt is a new connection from Intel. The protocol can handle 10 Gb/s in a single channel, twice as fast as USB 3 and more than ten times faster than FireWire.

Caches

Configuring caches on the fastest storage possible is vital for making Adobe Premiere Pro as snappy as possible. The connection point (if not internal) is crucial for accessing these cache files; it's best to use USB 3 or Thunderbolt.

Adobe After Effects and Adobe SpeedGrade

In addition to helping you future-proof hardware purchases for Adobe Premiere Pro, there are some extra wrinkles that are worth mentioning if you'll be using the same system for heavy compositing or color correction:

► **Adobe After Effects** can utilize *multiple* video cards as long as they belong to the same CUDA generation (all cards are CUDA 2.0 compatible). This application will utilize as much RAM as it can, with a minimum of 2–3 GB per CPU. A separate cache SSD drive is suggested for its specialized disk cache.

► **Adobe SpeedGrade** is very sensitive to the video card. The GPU delivers most of this application's real-time capabilities and speeds output (beyond the base ability to play footage).

If you want the media to be portable (from system to system), configure the Media Caches (found in the Preferences) with the actual media.

RAID (Redundant Array of Information Disks) is a storage technology where multiple disks are grouped together. Different configurations provide different benefits. See the sidebar "Raid-5 Helps to Maintain Your Sanity."

Objects with moving parts (drives, cars, etc.) break. You can count on it. In fact, you can bet on it happening a day before delivery.

The top choice for fast storage is SSD. An SSD is also ideal for Adobe After Effects. SSDs have no moving parts; their speed is merely just reading and writing to memory chips.

If the cost of an SSD is too high, consider creating a RAID-0 (two or more drives that act as a striped set). Each drive increases the overall speed as it lowers the waiting time for mechanical parts to move the read/write heads.

Media

Speed is a *less important* factor in the straight playback of media. Most drives (USB 2 or FireWire) can play back two streams of media of nearly every HD format short of uncompressed HD.

Redundancy is a more important issue. For the best combination of speed and storage, a RAID-5 (four drives with a section of each for redundancy) provides the best blend of abilities. If one drive dies, nothing is lost.

The alternative is to fully back up every piece of live media on a regular basis. Having a level of redundancy means sleeping well at night knowing your media is safe.

Projects

Projects should be on some cloud-based backup system, like the Creative Cloud's desktop sync. Although this feature is just beginning to roll out while this book is being written, some frequently mentioned Cloud alternatives include Dropbox, and Google Drive, or cloud backups such as CrashPlan or Mozy.

By having your project in the cloud, it's automatically backed up as you work. One caveat (mentioned in detail in Chapter 2) is that you probably don't want your Preview files sitting in the cloud (where they would be *by default*). They can grow quite large and waste space because they're considered temporary.

Raid-5 Helps to Maintain Your Sanity

Expect something to go wrong is a postproduction truism. Most media professionals (that'd be you!) purchase drives as individual units. But this is generally the worst choice you can make. What if a drive dies? You should purchase a second drive to manually duplicate all of your material.

A RAID allows for a more sophisticated joining of drives. Here are the most common types of RAIDs and descriptions of their usage:

▶ **Raid-0** consists of two (or more) drives and stripes (alternates) the data between each drive. This means faster access (because there are two read/write heads rather than one) but at the cost of reliability. If either drive fails, all the data is lost. The advantage of a Raid-0 lies in its speed.

▶ **Raid-1** consists of two drives and writes the data twice, once to each drive. The advantage is pure redundancy. If one drive dies, the other contains all the data. The disadvantage of a Raid-1 is that half of your storage is dedicated to a backup. This is great as a "bulletproof" live mirror but not great from a performance point of view.

▶ **Raid-5** consists of four or more drives (**Figure 1.25**) and stripes them like a Raid-0 (favoring speed), but copies some redundancy information to the other drives. You get nearly the performance of a Raid-0, but if a drive dies, the remaining drives can permit recovery of the lost data. The only real negative is that 33 percent of each drive in a four drive array is lost to redundancy information. A Raid-5 is suggested as the minimum choice for media professionals because it provides nearly the performance of a Raid-0 with the reliability of a Raid-1, sacrificing only one quarter of the total media.

Figure 1.25 A Raid-5 requires at least four drives and a dedicated RAID controller, such as this model from G-Technology.

OS considerations

If you're working on a Macintosh system, the optimal drive format is HFS+. Because most hard drives sold aren't formatted this way, it's a good practice to format a brand-new hard drive on purchase. If you plug an HFS+ drive into a Windows system, a utility called MacDrive allows Windows to read and write to the HFS+ format.

If you're using a Windows system, the optimal drive format is NTFS. Many hard drives come formatted for FAT32, so it's a good practice to reformat a brand-new hard drive on purchase. If you plug an NTFS drive into a Macintosh system, a utility called Paragon NTFS allows a Mac to read and write to the NTFS format.

If you're working cross-platform, the simplest way to work is to format your drives as ExFAT, which will work on both platforms and no third-party software is needed. ExFAT isn't as reliable as HFS+ or NTFS and has some slight overhead, slowing down the speed of a drive's read and write access.

Computer Monitor

Strictly speaking, the computer monitor you use makes no difference whatsoever. Don't confuse a cheap monitor with a *broadcast monitor* (see the sidebar "Real-world Setup" in Chapter 6).

Some editors prefer to use two screens; some prefer very large screens (greater than 1920x1080); and some prefer screens with matte coatings (to avoid distorting black points).

Hardware Monitoring Card

A hardware monitoring card acts as a "black box" connector to transmit the video from your computer to scopes and broadcast monitors (**Figure 1.26**). Although the sidebar "Real-world Setup" in Chapter 6 provides some detail, a hardware output is invaluable for *truly* being able to professionally monitor your playback and connect scopes.

This piece of hardware can actually be a box or a card and is available from companies such as AJA, Black Magic Designs, Bluefish 4444, and Matrox.

Figure 1.26 The AJA T-Tap is one of the most inexpensive ways to perform output monitoring. Plug Thunderbolt into your system and then plug in a broadcast monitor via HDMI or HD-SDI.

Measuring System Performance

Measuring system performance goes beyond just using the Dropped Frame indicator (see the section "Leveraging the MPE" earlier in this chapter). Although it's important to know that you've dropped frames, the more difficult question to answer is *why isn't my system performing well?*

Unfortunately, there is no magic performance tool that will indicate exactly how well *your specific* machine will perform with *your* specific video formats in *your* specific workflow.

But there are tools on Macs and Windows machines that will monitor playback and rendering. By checking these tools while playing back footage (or rendering) you can observe where your bottlenecks may be.

Apple's Activity Monitor

The Activity Monitor (located in your Utilities folder) permits the monitoring of the CPU, RAM, and Disk Activity via tabs at the bottom of the window. It's assumed that you'll look at these tabs (**Figure 1.27**) while you're playing (or rendering) video. The following list describes these tabs in detail:

▶ **CPU.** With the CPU tab active, you can watch the percentage of CPU usage. It can go up to 100 percent per core, so, for example, it's possible to see 600 percent on an eight core system. Adding the floating CPU window (Window> Floating CPU Window > Horizontal [or Vertical]) will display a live bar graph, showing how hard each core is working.

▶ **System Memory.** The item to keep your eye on in this tab is Swap Used. All modern operating systems have relatively unlimited virtual memory. They *page* (write) RAM to the system hard drive when they run out of memory. This slows down your system because it takes time to perform this writing (and later reading) to (and from) your hard drive. Although this is one of the major speed advantages of having your OS run from an SSD, it's optimum to use as little swap space as possible.

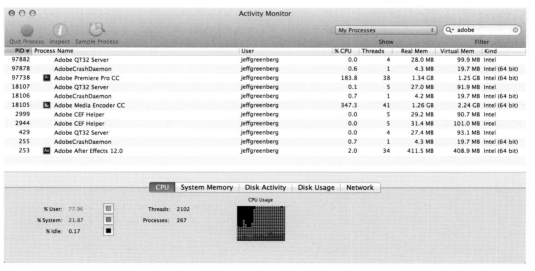

Figure 1.27 The Activity Monitor shown here is being taxed heavily by the simultaneous use of Adobe Premiere Pro and Adobe Media Encoder.

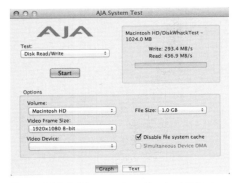

Figure 1.28 A drive speed test, like the AJA System Test, should be used regularly to make sure your system's performance doesn't degrade over time.

▶ **Disk Activity.** It's necessary to use a utility, such as the AJA System Test (**Figure 1.28**) or the Black Magic Disk Speed Test, to max out the read and write speeds your drive can handle. Play back footage in Adobe Premiere Pro and observe the Disk Activity tab. If your drives are nearing their peak speed, they are likely the bottleneck issue.

Window's Resource Monitor

Most users are familiar with the Task Manager (Ctrl+Alt+Del), which has some monitoring capabilities, but a more thorough set of monitoring capabilities is found in the Resource Monitor (**Figure 1.29**).

To start the Resource Monitor in Windows 7, choose Start > All Programs > Accessories > System Tools > Resource Monitor. There's also a button in the Task Manager that brings up the Resource Monitor. The following list explains each tab in more detail:

▶ **Overview.** On the Overview tab are four bar graphs on the right side; each shows system utilization. Watch the CPU, Memory, and Disk Active graphs and see if any graph has filled its display.

Figure 1.29 The Resource Monitor in Windows 7. The tabs along the top allow focusing on how well Windows in performing while under load.

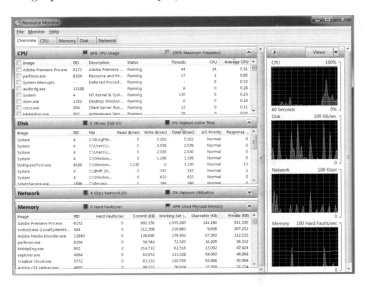

- ▶ **CPU.** With the CPU tab active (not in the overview image), watch the percentage of CPU usage. CPU – Total shows the average usage across all processors. Each processor is individually labeled and measured.

- ▶ **Memory.** Pay attention to the Physical Memory used at the top of the window. If it's over 80%, it's time to add more RAM.

- ▶ **Disk Activity.** It's necessary to use a utility such as the AJA Disk System Test or the Black Magic Disk Speed Test (**Figure 1.30**) to max out the speed of read and write speeds your drive can handle while watching the Peak speed. Then play back footage in Adobe Premiere Pro. If your drives are nearing their peak speed, they are likely the bottleneck issue.

The Resource Monitor has changed a little in Windows 8, but generally the same concepts apply to evaluate machine performance along with the requirement of a speed test utility.

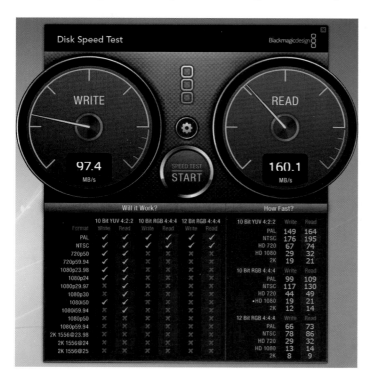

Figure 1.30 On Windows, the Black Magic Disk Speed Test requires you to download one of the drivers for its video software, such as for the line of Intensity output devices. On a Mac, this software can be found in the App store.

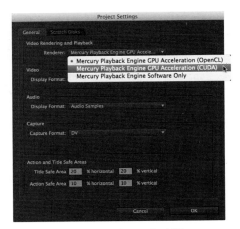

Figure 1.31 When you change the MPE to Software Only, there should be lots of red bars in your Timeline.

Some Apple machines have RAM and video cards permanently soldered to their motherboards, and there may be little or no upgrades possible. Consult http://everymac.com for details on your specific hardware.

GPU card performance

Video card performance is *harder* to measure than disk speed if you have enough RAM. The best way to determine how much assistance your system is getting from the GPU is to *turn off* the GPU and then compare how your system runs when it is *unaccelerated*.

To turn off the acceleration (**Figure 1.31**), choose File > Project Settings, and then choose Software Only from the drop-down menu.

If you don't also see a CUDA or OpenGL choice available, your video card either may not be capable of performing MPE acceleration (make sure you have at least 1 GB of GPU RAM) or your driver may be out of date.

Too Many Hardware Choices?

What if you're not a "do it yourself" sort of user? Perhaps you don't want to build or configure a system, or risk being unsure if you purchased an optimized system.

Consider using a VAR (Value Added Reseller) that specializes in video. There's a certain advantage to being able to buy all of your hardware from a single vendor; the vendor will configure it, possibly set it up, and likely have the associated hardware (such as switchers and black burst generators) that a professional user may need.

On the Apple side, an Apple is an Apple. When you're buying a Mac (**Figure 1.32**) you'll generally buy the same box regardless of whether you purchase it direct or from a reseller. Just be aware that you cannot upgrade many of the Apple products with memory or video cards after the initial purchase.

On the Windows side, HP continues to produce top-of-the-line hardware (**Figure 1.33**) and aggressive systems with specific custom design for professional video users that are also optimized for the Adobe products.

Figure 1.32 Apple's Retina MacBook Pro works well with Adobe Creative Cloud. Just make sure you max out the RAM because there's no changing it after the fact.

Figure 1.33 HP offers optimized products, like the Z820 desktop model (shown here), and mobile workstations, like the 8770w, specifically for pro video needs.

Breathing Life into Old Hardware

The struggle is always to maximize the life of existing hardware equipment. There comes a point when it's not worth upgrading. A system that can work more efficiently just one hour a week (at the very minimum) pays for itself within a year. If you cannot afford new equipment, breathe life into what you already have.

The availability of hardware improvements depend on the system you own. Some motherboards can handle only certain chips. Some video cards may not fit in specific systems. Here are some general tips on what to upgrade and in what order:

- ▶ **SSD.** Getting an SSD for a caching drive and a system drive will make your system seem fast and new.

- ▶ **High-speed external port.** Get a card for your older desktop that allows you to use USB 3 or Thunderbolt.

- ▶ **RAID.** A Raid-0 will provide the fastest performance (at the cost of higher vulnerability). Be sure to have a daily backup when you're using a RAID-0 for media.

- ▶ **Video card.** Get a new GPU. The faster it is and the more RAM it has, the better.

▶ **Correct slot.** When plugging in any GPU or storage card, make sure that it goes in a 16x slot to ensure the best performance. If you're out of slots, consider upgrading your motherboard, if possible.

▶ **Add RAM.** A minimum of 2 GB per core is best. It's possible to experience *degraded performance* when RAM is less than 2 GB.

Overview of a Workflow

The postproduction process mirrors what you can do in Adobe Premiere Pro and the way all the video applications in Adobe Creative Cloud work. With so many tools at your disposal, your workflow can be overwhelming.

So, in parallel, let's walk through the actual process that occurs in production and in postproduction, and explore the options you have while working solely in Adobe Premiere Pro and when working with the alternative tools in the suite.

The Big Picture

It's important to mention that with so many tools at your fingertips, making the best choices as to which to use can be overwhelming to implement as well as to learn.

Table 1.1 outlines the comparison between what Adobe Premiere Pro does intrinsically (nearly everything!) and the general concept of how the other tools fit into a workflow.

The section "Order of Learning," later in the chapter, should provide you with some further insight into the order in which you should learn the tools. Keep in mind that you don't have to master each tool in its entirety to put some features of a tool into operation.

Generally speaking, working in Adobe Premiere Pro will be faster. It's generally faster from creation to output. For example, as you become more skilled in performing audio finishing or color correction, you'll realize that the dedicated tools will have major advantages rather than working entirely in Adobe Premiere Pro.

TABLE 1.1 Production Process in Adobe Creative Cloud

ACTION	ADOBE PREMIERE PRO	OTHER CREATIVE CLOUD APPLICATIONS
Preproduction	No equivalent	Adobe Story permits script writing and preproduction documentation
Ingest	Ingest via the Media Browser	Adobe Prelude to ingest and back up material from card-based media
Editorial	Timeline in Adobe Premiere Pro	No equivalent. Editing should always be performed in Adobe Premiere Pro.
Titling	Built-in titler	Static titles can be built in Adobe Photoshop. Animated titles can be built in Adobe After Effects.
Animation of stills	Keyframe in the Effects Control panel	A linked Adobe After Effects composition allows this type of animation, along with more refined camera moves on stills
Chroma keying	Ultra Keyer Effect	A linked After Effects composition permits more flexible chroma keying through a licensed version of Foundry Keylight
Audio repair	Various effects from the Audio effects category, such as equalizers, compression, and noise reduction	Single clips can be sent to Adobe Audition, which has a larger set of audio effects, visualization of audio via a spectrum view, and superior noise reduction based on taking a "noise sample"
Audio mixing	Adjustment of clip levels, volume level of tracks, and grouping via submixes	Adobe Audition provides an optimized Audio finishing environment and returns a final mix to Adobe Premiere Pro
Color correction	Three-Way Color Corrector and RGB Curves	Adobe SpeedGrade is a full-featured finishing environment with an interface optimized for color correction (including very powerful secondaries and tracking) along with stereoscopic finishing; video output is then laid back in an Adobe Premiere Pro Timeline with finished audio
Output of a digital file	Export media using presets that are shared with Adobe Media Encoder	Adobe Media Encoder permits a deeper set of digital file output controls, permitting background encoding. Adobe Encore CS6 for optical media delivery (see the section "Installing Adobe Encore" at the end of Chapter 7).

As you begin to utilize tools outside of Adobe Premiere Pro, the final quality of the work improves, but it generally takes longer to produce and may possibly increase render times.

A good rule of thumb for a quick turnaround is to use Adobe Premiere Pro. But when you need a specific feature or a higher level of dedicated functionality, that's what the other tools in the suite bring to the table.

Stress-free Start into Other CC Apps

Often, it feels intimidating to consider the number of tools available to you. Although learning each tool provides additional capabilities to editors (you), each interface adds a layer of complexity to the learning curve.

However, some of the tools at your disposal have a *near zero learning curve*. You can just use them for a single function or capability without feeling like you have to learn the entire application.

Adobe Media Encoder for background encoding

Background encoding is probably the first "single use" excursion you should regularly make outside of Adobe Premiere Pro.

Mentioned in detail in Chapter 7, clicking the Queue button (**Figure 1.34**) in the Export Media dialog passes your sequence from Adobe Premiere Pro to Adobe Media Encoder for compression.

The single action you'll need to learn in Adobe Media Encoder is to click the green start button (**Figure 1.35**), which is located at the top right of the Queue window.

Then you can go back to editing your work while Adobe Media Encoder compresses in the background.

Figure 1.34 The Queue button routes the controls from within Adobe Premiere Pro to a dedicated compression tool, Adobe Media Encoder.

Figure 1.35 Adobe Media Encoder has over 400 presets dedicated to making compression easier.

Adobe After Effects for effects and presets

Adobe After Effects can seem fairly daunting. Whereas editing software is horizontal, compositing software is vertical, which changes the feel of the workflow.

To encourage you to use After Effects, I'll emphasize that you can apply an After Effects built-in single effect *or* preset animation to a *single clip* via Dynamic Link. The technique of Dynamic Linking allows you to "try" After Effects by turning it into an *advanced effect engine for Adobe Premiere Pro*. To use this technique:

1. Select a clip on a Timeline.

2. Choose File > Adobe Dynamic Link > Replace with After Effects Composition (**Figure 1.36**).

> **TIP**
>
> Exploring the prebuilt Animation Presets that consist of animated backgrounds, text, shapes, and more in the Effects panel in Adobe After Effects is a must. Some apply directly to a selection (the video you sent from Adobe Premiere Pro). Some require nothing to be selected because they create their own layers.

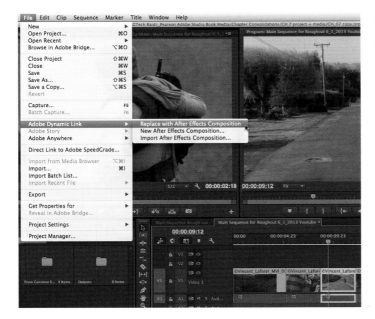

Figure 1.36 Other choices include creating a new Adobe After Effects composition or importing one.

This option generates an After Effects project, which you'll need to save somewhere better than the default location. Chapter 2 covers some best practices for project locations.

Figure 1.37 The Effects & Presets panel in Adobe After Effects looks quite like the equivalent in Adobe Premiere Pro.

Instead of sequences, Adobe After Effects projects contain compositions. Your clip shows up automatically in a composition, with the Timeline visible, ready for you to drag an effect onto the clip.

3. Drag any item from the list in the Effects & Presets panel in Adobe After Effects (**Figure 1.37**) onto your image in the composition window (the main window) to apply the effect. Your Effects controls appear on the left side, which are identical to Adobe Premiere Pro Effects controls.

4. Save your project. Switch back to Adobe Premiere Pro (quitting Adobe After Effects is optional but frees up system resources).

Adobe Audition for noise reduction

Audition has a fantastic *sample-based* noise reduction feature. Although it can't repair audio recorded in a coffee house, it can repair repetitive noises, such as a rumble from a fan or an AC unit, if you provide the application with a sample of the noise.

See the example in the section "Removing Noise" in Chapter 4. The entire noise reduction process can be done in less than five minutes.

Order of Learning

As mentioned earlier, having access to several useful tools can be intimidating, especially because you have everything you could possibly use (and more!) in the Creative Cloud suite. So, in what order should you learn these tools? Maybe it's obvious; maybe it's not.

Here are the two general rules about the order in which you should tackle new software:

▶ **Learn based on similarity/complexity.** Choose an app that is similar to Adobe Premiere Pro to ease learning. Applications with severely different interfaces (such as Adobe SpeedGrade) require a "start from scratch" approach.

▶ **Learn based on need.** Sometimes you'll need a specific feature (like Foundry Keylight, the superior chroma keyer included with Adobe After Effects). The amount of time and difficulty it takes to learn the new tool will be mitigated by the addition of a capability that was weak or nonexistent in Adobe Premiere Pro.

Which to Learn First?

Writing as an educator (rather than an editor), it's easier to learn something that is similar to prior information, like a dialect of a language, rather than learning something completely from scratch, like having to learn a new alphabet.

It's more likely that your needs will dictate which tools you learn and in which order. It's worthwhile to compare your needs against Table 1.1 earlier in the chapter to decide how and where to budget your time.

The following sections provide some *killer* reasons and solutions that make learning specific uses of necessary tools part of your workflow.

Quick to learn

The tools described here share enough interface similarities that they will be the easiest to tackle:

Adobe Media Encoder. Adobe Media Encoder is primarily a utilitarian application and is almost part of Adobe Premiere Pro.

Yes, there's some depth and nuance about how to adjust various codecs, but the preset list enables you create output easily.

You should use its useful background encoding, and given it's utilitarian nature, it's probably the easiest application to learn in the suite. See "Adobe Media Encoder" in Chapter 7 for some advanced techniques, including watch folders.

Adobe Photoshop. It's likely that you already use this industry-standard image manipulation tool. It can perform the obvious of creating titles (with built-in presets for video) and adjusting images for pan/scan moves.

TIP

It's my belief that everyone should always be learning something new and that your brain starts dying when learning stops happening. Every day I try to spend at least 15 minutes trying to chip away at mountains of things I want to learn and need to know.

A lesser-known feature is the ability to work directly with video. Open a video clip directly in Adobe Photoshop and then change the Workspace (Window > Workspace) to Motion. You'll have a full Timeline and access to all of Adobe Photoshop's layers, adjustments, and filters.

When you're finished, choose File > Export > Render Video.

Adobe Prelude. This tool permits the handling of media from file-based cameras and allows you to copy camera media files, back them up to multiple locations, mark and perform some simple editorial *before* transferring your video to Adobe Premiere Pro.

The struggle with card-based media is the need for projects to be organized from the start. The greatest danger is to improperly copy card contents or work directly from the card!

The Ingest window in Prelude (**Figure 1.38**) resembles the Media Browser in Adobe Premiere Pro. Its major difference is its ability to copy (with a check on data integrity, something that OS level file copies do not do!) your card media to one or more locations, helping you to stay organized from the beginning.

Figure 1.38 The Ingest window in Adobe Prelude. Quickly select one or more clips, and then click Ingest to transfer them from your media cards to your system.

Adobe Audition. Adobe Audition shares strong similarities to Adobe Premiere Pro in its track-based layout, mixers, and submixes. It has two interfaces, one for individual clips and a second for multiple tracks.

The first use of Adobe Audition is usually for noise reduction (see Chapter 4) as a clip-based repair. Along with a deeper set of audio effects available, the clip-based editor has analysis tools to analyze and repair at the sample level, and a spectral analysis view along with healing brushes to fix audio based on the audio frequency spectrum (from deep basses through high-pitched whistles).

A full multitrack DAW is used when you send an entire sequence to it by choosing Edit > Edit in Adobe Audition > Sequence in Adobe Premiere Pro. This sends every track and clip to Audition, permitting the use of nondestructive track-based effects and submix features that are very similar to those found in Adobe Premiere Pro (**Figure 1.39**).

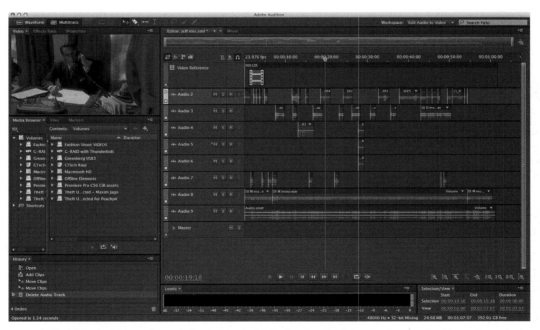

Figure 1.39 Adobe Audition tracks are similar to those in Adobe Premiere Pro. But notice how much of the screen real estate is dedicated to tracks. It's ideal for audio mixing.

NOTES

ADR is also known as looping. The process consists of an actor re-recording his lines in a clean studio. The retiming feature in Adobe Audition does this by retiming the read, not depending on the actor to re-read his lines and match the timing.

Two stand-out features, only available in the Multitrack view are Match Clip Volume and Automatic Speech Alignment. Both are located in the Clip menu in Adobe Audition. Match Clip Volume permits you to quickly select multiple clips and have their volumes match. Automatic Speech Alignment permits you to re-record poor audio *and have the waveform* "retimed" and adjusted to match. This is the equivalent of Automatic Dialog Replacement (ADR).

Require dedicated focus

Some tools aren't as intuitive as others to learn. Usually, that means they have more value, not less. It also means that they probably have more flexibility.

I suggest you make a more dedicated effort to learn these tools because the return will be much higher than learning a tool that's "easy" to jump into. The following two tools—Adobe After Effects and Adobe SpeedGrade—are both learnable but come at a greater cost of time commitment.

Adobe After Effects. This compositing and animation tool has become an important industry standard. Some television animation is built into this tool as well.

What makes Adobe After Effects more difficult to learn is the sheer level of its depth. The following list contains several notable features, but the number of tasks that can be done with Adobe After Effects is nearly endless:

▶ The built-in library of presets and effects are strong standouts. Foundry Keylight, which comes bundled, is an industry standard for performing professional-looking chroma keys.

▶ Text animation is very powerful and has the ability to be quickly animated in or out and comes with over 150 presets, permitting the quick building of kinetic type.

▶ Camera tracking permits the quick interpretation of where the real-world camera was placed; after using this technique, you can create a virtual camera and move objects to match the way the original camera shook or panned.

- The ability to draw masks with freehand Bezier tools allows for the cutting of layers in more complex ways than is possible in Adobe Premiere Pro *and* the idea that an effect can be limited to a portion of a clip based on the mask shape.

- Rotoscoping, the manual drawing of shapes to cut out an object, is painful. After all, that's why you use a chroma key. The RotoBrush tool permits the building of a mask with significantly less effort than drawing shapes by hand because it's based on detecting edges (similar to the way the Magic Wand works in Adobe Photoshop).

Adobe SpeedGrade. This is a full-featured color correction suite that is optimized for sophisticated color correction and stereoscopic (3D) finishing. Where you'll struggle with SpeedGrade is with its interface (**Figure 1.40**).

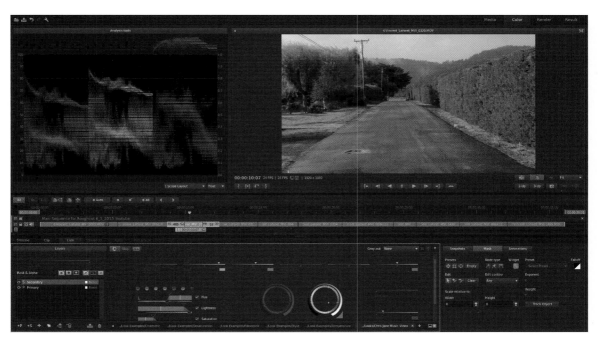

Figure 1.40 Adobe SpeedGrade has powerful new interoperability in its 7.1 release, making it a strong color correction companion to Adobe Premiere Pro.

Whereas Adobe Premiere Pro is optimized for the adjustment of clip length and location, SpeedGrade is optimized for quickly adjusting a shot and moving on to the next.

Powerful secondary effects, such as shape-based vignettes and key-based adjustments, make it quick and easy to adjust flesh tones, skies, and grass without affecting the rest of the image.

A quick, single-click Shot Matching feature allows for the speeding up of getting different camera angles and different cameras to match.

In Chapter 6, "Color Correction," you'll learn how to move an Adobe Premiere Pro project to Adobe SpeedGrade, where to find the scopes and basic color correction tools, and how to work back in Adobe Premiere Pro.

2

Setup and Organizing

Author: Jeff I. Greenberg

Organizing is what you do before you do something, so that when you do it, it is not all mixed up.

—A. A. Milne

Setup and Organizing

A recipe for disaster is setting out to scale a mountain, but instead packing for a trip to the beach. The one question you have to be able to answer is: *Do you know where you're going?*

Regardless of what other people might tell you, editorial endeavors are *nearly always* hard work—scaling a mountain. Although there are some types of projects that have a quick turnaround (such as news-based projects), knowing the point at which you're starting and "packing" correctly ensures the least amount of difficulty in the editorial process.

There's no footage for this chapter; it's far too custom to *your specific* work. Instead I'll cover some of the big (and little) mistakes I see other editors make, as well as cover some key techniques to speed your workflow.

You've been using Adobe Premiere Pro for some time (after all, I know you're not a novice). Let's tweak some of the preferences to create a system that works better than it does now. Then, let's deal with setting up projects and media.

In addition, we'll focus on importing and organizing footage.

Optimized Setup

All default software preferences and layouts for any tool you ever use are ideal for a novice user. But you are not a novice user! And there are some great tweaks to improve the way Adobe Premiere Pro should be running.

Preferences

Adobe Premiere Pro has a variety of preference categories, many of which you never need touch. But when looking through the categories, there were some absolute areas that every author of this book agreed they wanted to adjust.

I won't necessarily cover every choice or every category, but rather discuss those that are most often adjusted from the defaults. The following Preference sections aren't in order, and the media and cache files get their own section because configuring these right is so important!

General

The General preferences (**Figure 2.1**) tend to be the ones you might change more frequently than any of the other categories, so it's best to learn the shortcut key to access the General category, which is Command+comma (Ctrl+comma). Many of these options will be changed for different projects:

TIP

Adobe Premiere Pro doesn't have a keyboard command to open the Preferences; because some of them do get changed regularly, it's smart to map them to a key such as Command+comma (Ctrl+comma).

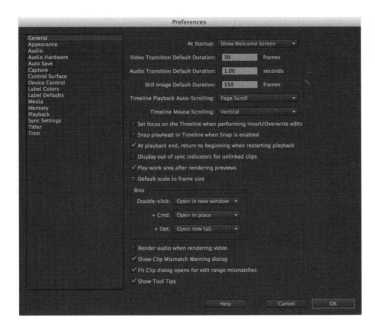

Figure 2.1 The Preferences General category has the most settings that a more experienced editor needs to change.

- ▶ **At Startup.** Most likely you should change this option to Open Most Recent because you'll probably continue to work on today's project tomorrow. One situation where you should leave this at the default is in a multiple user environment. Then each user can switch to the project they're working on.

- ▶ **Video and Audio Transition.** Frankly, the durations of the defaults are too long. Nowadays, 12–15 frames (half a second or less) are a bit better to use.

When adding multiple audio transitions to smooth speech coming from/to silence, change the default transition value to a very small number– close to one tenth of a second (.1).

You can turn on/off the S for snapping even while dragging an element.

When editing, I never, ever turn off linked selections nor unlink clips. Doing this is nearly always a recipe for disaster because it becomes far too easy to break sync. Instead, press the Option (Alt) key to temporarily select just the video or audio of a clip.

▶ **Still Image Default.** Approximately 5 seconds is a good starting place, but this option often gets changed in projects based on need, for example, a series of stills cut to a musical beat. Figure out the beat length in frames and *reimport* your stills.

▶ **Timeline Playback.** Auto-scrolling, *especially* during client review sessions is a super easy way to keep the playhead in the middle of the Timeline. The *sequence* scrolls by the playhead the way that film editorial works. The only drawback is that with this option on, any placement of the playhead away from the center causes a "jump" as the playhead jumps back to the center of the screen.

▶ **Set focus on the Timeline.** If you're a keyboard driven editor, particularly for three-point editing (see Chapter 3), you'll likely want the *Timeline* active, *not* the source, after you make an edit.

▶ **Snap playhead in Timeline.** Although I navigate mostly by using the up and down arrow keys, turning on this option means the playhead jumps *right to* an edit. Toggling Snap is as easy as pressing S.

▶ **Display out of sync indicators for unlinked clips.** I almost never recommend unlinking clips. When you do, the default in Adobe Premiere Pro is to treat them as totally separate elements. Even when I do that I *prefer* this option to be on to make sure I *visually* see if those elements are out of sync.

▶ **Default scale to frame size.** This option is one of the most misunderstood preferences in Adobe Premiere Pro. Its purpose is to scale a clip or a still to match the image size of a sequence using a faster math to reduce the load on your system and in turn limiting the quality of zooming in beyond 100%.

▶ **Bins.** Change Double-click to Open in New Tab. You've probably done this a hundred times: double-clicked on a bin and had a floating window, and then clicked and the window was behind the main interface. Nobody needs a floating window *unless* you're going to tile loads of bins on a *second* display. Why should you hold down a modifier key when you can just set it to behave the way you need?

Smarter Workflows via Default Scale to Frame Size

The Default Scale to Frame Size (Dstfs) can be a confusing switch in Adobe Premiere Pro. Chapter 3 has a more detailed explanation of this feature.

You can take the best advantage of Dstfs any time you have footage that doesn't match the size of your sequence; the most frequent use is on footage that's larger than the sequence size. When Dstfs is on, your system has to do less work. And if you're not taking advantage of the extra information, you probably want to use Dstfs!

Whether it's on or off, Dstfs is set on import. Any time you need to change/reverse this feature after import, select the elements and then choose Modify > Video Options > Scale to Frame size.

It's easiest to envision this technique with 4k video (3880 x 2160) in an HD sequence (1920 x 1080).

When Dstfs is off (the default), every clip comes in at its full size (**Figure 2.2**).

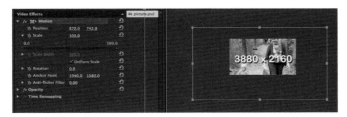

Figure 2.2 This image has access to its full information; when scaled to 100%, it's 3880x2160. To get the whole image to fit in an HD sequence, you'd have to scale it down.

A 4k video file (3880 x 2160) has access to all of its 3880x2160 pixels, which is great because you have all that 4k goodness, making it easy to frame a different section of a clip. But it's more likely that you shot the large format with a framing you liked, meaning you'd have to scale down nearly all of the clips on your Timeline to 50% to get them to fit.

Fortunately, the new Paste Attributes option allows you to just paste the Motion Properties. But you still to have to do this for every shot, which is an inefficient use of your time and system resources at best.

Instead, if you had Dstfs on, every shot that hits the Timeline is scaled to the size of the Timeline (**Figure 2.3**), and 100% is recalibrated to the Timeline size. In this case 100% is 1920x1080.

Figure 2.3 With Dstfs *on*, the image is downsampled; 100% now represents 100% of the sequence size. If you were to increase the Scale parameter of the clip, it would be blowing up a 1920x1080 element *not* a 3880x2160 one.

Edit. Work as you need. *If you need to* reframe a shot or *push in* (scale up), then you'll modify the clip so Dstfs is *off*, returning all that 4k goodness.

Audio

Not much needs to be changed in Audio preferences, but these two options are worth knowing about:

▶ **Play Audio While Scrubbing.** You'll likely either love this option or hate it (I hate it.) So, it's off for me most of the time.

▶ **Automatic peak file generation.** *Most of us* want this switch on unless we're in a rush. When Adobe Premiere Pro first looks at a clip, it generates a waveform from analyzing the audio peaks (hence, a peak file). But what if you're regularly working in a high-speed environment with XDCam, which may have eight audio tracks? You'll need to wait until the peak files are generated. *Or* you can turn off this option completely. Then the only way to create a peak file is to reimport the file.

Memory

Adobe Premiere Pro shares its memory (**Figure 2.4**) with four other applications:

▶ Adobe After Effects   ▶ Adobe Media Encoder

▶ Adobe Prelude   ▶ Adobe Photoshop

If you constantly work with more of them open, *you'll need more RAM than 2–3 GB per core* beyond what Adobe Premiere Pro requires.

Figure 2.4 The more you use other applications (like browsing or email), the more important it is to protect some of your RAM.

It's very important to occasionally check your available RAM as you work, or the RAM reserved for other applications may not be enough or may be too much, depending on what else you have going on while you work. See the section "Measuring System Performance" in Chapter 1.

If you *ever* get a Low Memory Warning alert when rendering, set the Optimize Rendering option for Memory.

Playback

A fantastic adjustment exists with the Playback preference for people who have two screens (even laptops can run a second screen!).

Use your second monitor as a *playback* monitor (**Figure 2.5**). By doing so, you can greatly reduce the size of the Source and Program Monitors on your main screen; all your video will be displayed on your other screen.

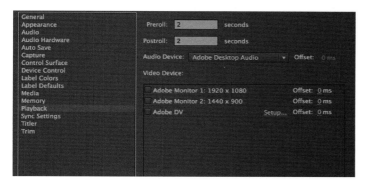

Figure 2.5 If possible, purchase a second monitor that matches or is larger than HD resolutions; you'll be able to see a 1:1 pixel mapping.

However, keep in mind that this is not a broadcast monitor. Although it's a bigger, better picture (and fantastic for client review), it's not a monitor that you should have confidence in its color space.

Sync Settings

With Adobe Creative Cloud's sync capability it's trivial to back up your settings. Even if you don't own Adobe Creative Cloud you can create a free account, and common settings like keyboard and preferences (**Figure 2.6**) can travel with you from system to system (see "Sync doesn't rely on ownership of Adobe Creative Cloud" in Chapter 1).

Figure 2.6 The other portion of Sync is controlled by the Sync Settings menu.

At multiuser facilities two items are important to tweak in Sync Settings:

▶ **When syncing.** Set this to either Ask my preference or Always download. The big danger is accidentally being logged into someone else's user, modifying something, and then *pushing your changes* to their user.

▶ **Automatically clear settings on application quit.** Set this to on if you're at a multiuser facility. Then everyone is forced to log in at the start of their session, and Adobe Creative Cloud will wipe out any changes *except* Media Caches on quit.

Remember that there's a dedicated set of Sync menu choices for further refinement. If you're not signed in to Adobe Creative Cloud, this preference will display in the dialog as Sync Settings; if you are signed in, your email ID will appear (on OS X choose Premiere Pro Menu > Sync Settings; on Windows choose File > Sync Settings).

Trim

Frankly, many editors struggle with trimming. Chapter 3 explains some of the editorial side of trimming.

But as far as the configuration for trimming, quite a bit of trim flexibility is hidden from users to protect them from accidentally trimming when they don't mean to, because trimming can shorten or lengthen footage, which could throw off sync.

Two Trim preferences have some cool features.

▶ **Allow Selection tool to choose Roll and Ripple trims without modifier key.** When you approach an edit point, Adobe Premiere Pro will automatically switch between Ripple and Roll trims depending on which side of an edit your mouse is on.

Often, I'll have this option on because it allows for quick and easy selection of edges of clips, making trims very quick either via dragging or via the keyboard. Just select and trim without switching tools!

- ► **Allow current tool to change trim type of previously selected edit point.** This allows a *single modifier key* (Command [Ctrl]) to switch between the single Red Trim to the single Yellow Trim. Normally, you'd have to deselect the trim and then *reselect* with the modifier key.

Having both of these options on together means you can easily get to an edit point and switch between the various types of trims without a modifier key.

An assembly edit is the first "build" of your Timeline, even before a rough cut. Usually, every clip is a little too long and needs to be adjusted. Having these options on makes it easy to have the type of trim tool you'd like for quick drag-and-drop Timeline trimming.

Everything else

The following Preferences settings are also important to consider. Often, there will be reasons to tweak or adjust some:

- ► **Appearance.** The only selection in this category is how bright or dark you want your interface. I like it a little brighter than the standard gray. *Far more important* is that if you change each Adobe Creative Cloud tool to be a *different gray,* you'll never visually wonder which tool you're in!

- ► **Auto Save.** Change the max to a higher number. But be aware that Adobe Premiere Pro will auto save any time there are unsaved changes, meaning you haven't saved *and* the application is running in the background. Every 15 minutes your unsaved project will be auto saved *again.* Therefore, if you're not editing, save and quit.

- ► **Label Colors.** This may sound nitpicky, but instinctively, I don't know the difference between Cerulean, Iris, and Violet. Renaming the colors to what your brain calls them makes far more sense.

Common Cache Files

Most of the Adobe Creative Cloud video applications utilize some cache files. Many of them overlap with the other applications, using a common cache, mostly for conforming footage. Because Adobe Premiere Pro is our hub, I'll talk about configuring them for optimum efficiency here (**Figure 2.7**). In the section "Suite Relations" later in this chapter is a specific setup for the other most commonly used Adobe tools.

Figure 2.7 The key is to put these caches in a folder on a fast drive. The internal drive is better than the fastest USB 2 drive.

For general understanding, cache files are both critical and unimportant. They are *critical* in that formats like h.264 or formats with compressed audio need a cache file to perform optimally. They are *unimportant* in that these files can be regenerated if needed.

Several considerations are worth taking into account when it comes to cache files:

▶ You want them on fast drives. The whole concept of a cache file is that it's a *quick* reference rather than handling the original media (or having to do a complex computation in real time).

▶ You should discard (delete) the cache files semi-frequently, such as monthly or quarterly. These folders will only grow larger over time.

▶ The Clean option with the cache files removes *only* the caches for those files that aren't online. If you use multiple media drives and forget to mount one, Clean will destroy cache files that you probably want to keep.

▶ Although there's a selection for storing the cache files with the media (based on the idea that you'd have greater flexibility if you move media drives from one station to another), it's advisable not to do this. Corruption still seems to occur a little too frequently.

▶ If you need to move the caches, do so from within Adobe Premiere Pro. When you choose a new location, you'll see the option to move the existing caches.

You can adjust two types of Caches folders in Adobe Premiere Pro: the Media Cache folder and the Media Cache Database folder.

Create an _Adobe Caches folder

In a perfect world you'll use your fast media drives (a RAID-5 or and SSD dedicated for caches) and create a folder called _Adobe Caches. Then target both the Media Cache folder and the Media Cache Database folder in the preferences to this folder. Doing so will keep your caches in a known place and easily accessible (**Figure 2.8**). The default location of your documents folder is necessary to install the software, but it's not a good place for these files *unless* you have loads of room on your boot drive and it's the fastest drive on your system.

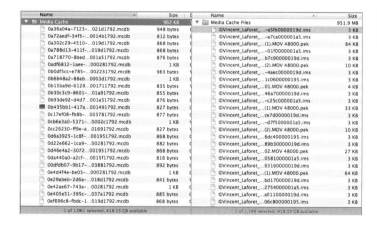

Figure 2.8 Here is just a small sampling of my Cache directories. It's easy to store over 5,000 files in them.

Media Cache files folder

Adobe Premiere Pro automatically creates a folder called Media Cache. This folder contains a series of caches with strange extensions. Here's a decoder ring for most of these files:

▶ **.cfa – Conformed Audio.** All these compressed formats have compressed audio, and Adobe Premiere Pro builds an uncompressed version for them.

▶ **.pek – PEaK files.** These PEaK files are a picture of the peaks that are turned into waveforms.

▸ **.ims – Importer State files.** These files refer to the status of an imported file.

▸ **.mxfassoc - MXF associations.** Some flavors of MXF have media attached; some don't. This cache keeps track of the associations.

▸ **.prmdc – Premiere Metadata Database Cache.** This is a cache for the database.

▸ **.mpegindex – MPEG Index Files.** Some types of MPEG files require their own index.

Media Cache Database folder

Adobe Premiere Pro automatically creates a second folder called Media Cache Database that contains the *databases* for the Media Cache files. This folder is considerably smaller because it contains the database "pointers" to the actual cache files.

The extensions translate to the following:

▸ **.mcdb – Media Accelerator Database.** These Media Common Database files are the heart of the database.

▸ **.prmdc – Premiere Metadata Database Cache.** This is a cache for the database.

Interface Nuances

Although setting up quite a bit of the interface can and should be up to you, there are several adjustments to the interface that nearly every editor does to make life a little bit saner.

Dropped Frame Indicator

The Drop Frame indicator is the first setting I turn on in a brand-new install of Adobe Premiere Pro. It's just too vital to have off.

Figure 2.9 If you've dropped frames, the first course of action is to lower your playback resolution in the Program Monitor's settings menu.

The Drop Frame indicator (**Figure 2.9**) shows you if you've dropped frames (turns yellow) and by mousing over the indicator you'll see how many frames were dropped. It's the difference between thinking your system dropped frames and knowing that it did. One frame isn't serious (it's a system hiccup), but a hundred frames is a different story. The indicator option is located on the Settings menu (wrench) of the Program Monitor.

Dropped frames can result from a variety of causes. Some of the reasons for dropped frames are complex effects (even with Mercury acceleration), your drives can't deliver data fast enough, or your system is overloaded in some other way.

Overlays

The Adobe Premiere Pro release in the last quarter of 2013 had a number of great new features. One of them was the ability to add and customize an Overlay (**Figure 2.10**) on the Source or Program Monitor.

Figure 2.10 Overlays are fantastic ways to add important clip and marker information to the Program and Source Monitors. The yellow "L" in the lower-left corner tells you that the playhead is at the start of a clip.

Information such as timecode, clip names, markers, and even edit point indicators can be configured and displayed for quick recall. This gives you, the editor, the ability to see this information on top of the playing video. It is fantastic for client reviews, but I often like to have it on all the time.

To turn this feature on or off, just right-click on the Source or Program Monitor (usually the Program Monitor). I'd strongly suggest that you consider mapping it to something like Ctrl+O or some other variant of the letter O. Then you can turn it on or off very quickly.

Overlays may need some minor adjustments. The Overlay Settings are available only from the Settings menu (wrench) or the Panel menu.

TIP

The Media Limit indicators add a little extra zebra stripe to the Edit Point indicators. These are great visual indicators for absolute edges clips.

Let's look at two prebuilt configurations and one that might be worth building. It's worth noting that you can save, import, and export in the top right of the Overlay Settings dialog (**Figure 2.11**):

▶ **Editing Overlay preset.** This default preset *generally* works well. It shows Source timecode on the left and markers along the bottom. I'm not a fan of the source timecode for *all the tracks*, just the V1 track. You could change that setting or use the V1 Only Overlay, which is a little cleaner. I prefer the font size a little smaller due to how much space this preset takes up.

▶ **V1 Only Overlay preset.** This shows just the V1 information at the top of the screen. I prefer the font for this a little larger than the default.

▶ **Edit Point and Media Limit indicators.** I love to add an overlay that has the Edit Point indicators along with the Media Limit indicators. This gives me direct visual feedback that I'm at the head (or tail) of a clip, a feature that's missing from Adobe Premiere Pro for everyday editing.

Figure 2.11 The Overlay Settings dialog allows you to configure the Overlay information that appears in specific locations on the screen. Adjust the font or opacity in the lower-right corner.

Buttons

A very controversial opinion/technique is to *get rid of all the buttons*. But I'll guarantee that it'll make you a faster editor.

Adobe Premiere Pro has the ability to customize the buttons at the bottom of the Source or Program panels. Originally, I was going to tell you to add the Safe Margins button; instead, I'll suggest that you get rid of the *all* the buttons (**Figure 2.12**) to get a bigger, better-looking picture. You'll be forced to use the keyboard; the less you move the mouse, the faster you'll be as an editor (note that I didn't say better, just faster).

Figure 2.12 Note the different between the Source Monitor and the Program Monitor. The transport controls were removed from the Program Monitor.

If you work one week without the buttons, you'll never go back.

To eliminate the buttons, go to the settings of either the Source or Program panel and deselect Show Transport Controls. There's not a single button here *you need*. All of the important buttons are already accessible via the keyboard. The only one that I really miss (because it needs to be mapped to the keyboard) is Safe Margins.

Workspaces

All too frequently I watch editors open and close panels to adjust the interface. Every time they adjust some audio, they open the Clip or Audio mixer. If they need the list of markers, they open the Marker panel.

Don't be that editor. Use workspaces.

What makes workspaces *so much better* than just opening and closing panels is simply that they are already mapped to the keyboard.

The first nine workspaces are mappable, and Adobe Premiere Pro handles them *alphabetically*. So if you build one of your own, you may need to be crafty with how you name it (either name it alphabetically or add a number prior to the name to force your favorite workspaces to the top of the list).

Even if you live mostly in two to three workspaces (Editing, Audio, Effects), it's best to map them to the first three workspaces.

How to adjust a workspace

You can drag any panel by its textured tab to any other part of the interface.

When you drag the tab above another panel, you'll see a trapezoid. Click the center and the panel becomes part of that frame. Click one of the four edges to subdivide the panel.

Workspace suggestions

Many of the other chapters suggest some adjustments of the default Workspace layouts. I usually leave most of the defaults as they are. But I'll give you a couple of the little changes (**Figure 2.13**) I like to do to make the interface just a little more editorially friendly:

▶ I often place the meters *above* the Timeline.

▶ I don't *really* need the tools (the icon list that includes items such as the Selection tool and the Razor tool). The keyboard choices you absolutely need to own should be in your head. I do have the tools share some of the space taken up by my meters to help me see *which tool* is currently selected.

▶ If you're working on two screens, *absolutely* use each of the default layouts and build a two-screen version of each.

▶ I generally have two different editorial layouts for two screens: one where the project window takes up the second screen and a different layout where the Time-line takes up the entire second screen.

▶ There's a great hidden panel called Options that should be called Workspace switcher.

▶ I often make the Timecode panel as large as I can get it when I'm with clients. It helps us all see where we are in the edit. Sometimes I'll split the height of the Project panel or Source panel just to give the Timecode panel some real estate.

▶ I love the Markers panel and often display it during complex edits (when I have named markers). It makes navigation a breeze.

▶ Currently, you cannot select individual tabs of a panel from the keyboard. *But you can select different panels* from the keyboard. The default keys—Command+Shift+period (Ctrl+Shift+period) and Command+Shift+comma (Ctrl+Shift+comma)—are super fast. Consider making individual key bins their own panel.

Figure 2.13 This was once the Adobe Premiere Pro Editing 5.5 workspace. The meters were moved over the Timeline, and the tools were docked next to them. The Timecode window is above the Program Monitor so the client can watch on the broadcast monitor. The bottom-left corner was switched to the Marker panel.

Keyboard Mapping

The fastest editors are very keyboard savvy. Keep your left hand on the entire keyboard (yes, you can operate the right side of your keyboard with your left hand) and your right hand on the mouse. Every time you take your hand off the mouse to use the keyboard, you're wasting time. The keyboard *is not* for typing; instead, it's a sophisticated control surface for editorial that allows you to be the fastest editor possible.

Although there are some great default key sets that I'm sure you use, there are numerous adjustments that would permit the keyboard to do *more* for you. For example, if you rarely edit multicam, the keys 0–9 are available for remapping.

Keyboard remapping is very personal. I've seen editors argue about which key belongs where, almost with a religious fervor.

But my one rule is to *pick a key that makes sense.* I set overlay to Ctrl+Shift+O because the other variations on the letter O are used (such as Shift+O to switch to the Out point).

Feel free to take this idea even further: Map keyboards specialized for different types of work; for example, documentary editing is different from promo editing. Or map a specialized keyboard *just* for audio mixing.

How to remap the keyboard

I expect that you already know how to remap the keyboard, but just in case, choose Premiere Pro > Keyboard Shortcuts (Mac OS) or Edit > Keyboard Shortcuts (Windows).

There are presaved keyboards for the following:

▶ **Adobe Premiere Pro Default.** This is the default keyboard. I recommend it over nearly everything else because the software designers tried to optimize the keys based on use.

▶ **Adobe Premiere Pro CS6.** This is great if you're coming from the prior version of Adobe Premiere Pro. Some changes have been made compared to the default keyboard.

▶ **Avid Media Composer.** If you're an Avid Media Composer user, this is the fastest way to jump into Adobe Premiere Pro. There are some things (like Avid's Modes) that don't directly replicate.

▶ **Final Cut Pro 7.0.** If you're an Apple Final Cut Pro 7 (and earlier) user, this keyboard is a close approximation to Final Cut. One of the differences is that Final Cut used multiple key presses; Adobe Premiere Pro does not.

Remapping the keyboard is performed by double-clicking in the field to the right of a command (note the search box at the top). If you pick a key binding that's already in use, you'll be able to choose whether to allow it (or not).

TIP

Holding down Command+Shift (Ctrl+Shift) when opening the Keyboard Shortcuts yields a clipboard button. You can then copy the keyboard and paste it into your text editor of choice, allowing you to search or print all the keys.

Keyboard suggestions

Polled from a number of editors, here are some thoughts about keyboard changes you might want to consider trying:

▶ Set Preferences > General to Command+comma (Ctrl+comma). This mirrors the preferences on the Mac (and a number of Windows apps). Now tasks like adjusting the default transition duration are just a key away.

▶ Try setting the Toggle Source/Program Monitor Focus to Shift+Esc (or Shift+F). It's a quick and easy way to switch back and forth between the Source and Program Monitors.

▶ Map the most common panels to Shift+*a number* if you're not using multicam. Or remap them to a number of your choice *without* the Shift key.

▶ Deselect All is usually Command+Shift+A (Ctrl+Shift+A). But in Adobe After Effects, it's F2. If you're a heavy Adobe After Effects user, it makes way more sense on F2.

▶ Set the Audio Waveform of the Source panel to Shift+W. This allows you to shift the panel to the Waveform for easy audio selections. Then map the Composite Video of the Source to Shift+Q. Yes, this removes the two extend features, but I prefer them on variants of the letter E, not the keys next to it.

▶ Although the search box at the top of the Keyboard Shortcuts is good, you don't always know the name of what you're looking for. Be sure to scroll all the way down to see the possibilities for every panel in Adobe Premiere Pro.

▶ In the Timeline settings are Track Height Presets. It's possible to map them to the keyboard (a powerful way to assign and switch the heights of tracks). But first you need to go to the Timeline Display Settings (the wrench on the Timeline) and choose Manage Presets. From there you can assign Presets to the ten different keyboard slots.

▶ Because the Media Browser is the suggested place to import (see the section "Import" later in this chapter), it's worth swapping the keyboard shortcut for Import and Import from Media Browser. Set the latter to Command+I (Ctrl+I).

Media Setup Outside of Adobe Premiere Pro

The single greatest ongoing battle an editor deals with, *that technically has nothing to do with the actual editorial process*, is dealing with the volume of media that is created and produced for an editorial project.

Let's get this out of the way: Adobe Premiere Pro organizes *only* media it creates—tape-based media and previews. It does *nothing* for imported elements. This likely means that *none of your media is being managed.*

The world has shifted to file-based media from cameras. With this shift, the user, that'd be you, should perform some level of media organization.

Although Adobe Prelude can help corral and back up file-based camera media, it's best to keep everything organized *from the start of a project.* This also means you'll have an easier time backing up and archiving projects.

Start Organized and Sleep at Night

Probably the biggest mistake novice editors make is just importing footage, audio, or stills across drives and folders. I'll bet this has already caused you grief. Instead, collect all media *prior* to importing (linking) to Adobe Premiere Pro and put these assets in a Common Media folder.

Build a project-based Common Media folder template

If you build a set of folders that you can easily duplicate every time you start a project, it will help you *stay organized.*

So, the process is this: Start a project, duplicate the Common Media folder template, and then rename it to match whatever unique method you use to name your projects.

The screen shot in **Figure 2.14** shows a folder list that can store all the pieces of a project in a common location. If you do this, *backing up the entire project* is trivial. Just grab the folder and copy it.

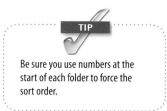

TIP

Be sure you use numbers at the start of each folder to force the sort order.

NOTES

This folder template is available for download. Please see "A note about downloadable content" in the Introduction of this book.

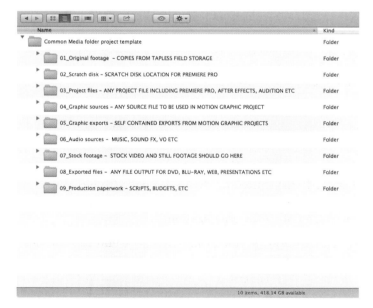

Name	Kind
Common Media folder project template	Folder
01_Original footage – COPIES FROM TAPLESS FIELD STORAGE	Folder
02_Scratch disk – SCRATCH DISK LOCATION FOR PREMIERE PRO	Folder
03_Project files – ANY PROJECT FILE INCLUDING PREMIERE PRO, AFTER EFFECTS, AUDITION ETC	Folder
04_Graphic sources – ANY SOURCE FILE TO BE USED IN MOTION GRAPHIC PROJECT	Folder
05_Graphic exports – SELF CONTAINED EXPORTS FROM MOTION GRAPHIC PROJECTS	Folder
06_Audio sources – MUSIC, SOUND FX, VO ETC	Folder
07_Stock footage – STOCK VIDEO AND STILL FOOTAGE SHOULD GO HERE	Folder
08_Exported files – ANY FILE OUTPUT FOR DVD, BLU-RAY, WEB, PRESENTATIONS ETC	Folder
09_Production paperwork – SCRIPTS, BUDGETS, ETC	Folder

10 items, 418.14 GB available

Figure 2.14 If you're organized prior to editing, you'll never worry that you've misplaced a clip somewhere on your system. Organizing also makes projects a breeze to back up.

Creating a Common Media folder is merely a *good start.* You should still customize your version of this folder in such a way that makes the greatest amount of organizational sense.

Some recommended folders include the following:

▶ **01_Original Footage.** A copy of your original file-based media from your cameras goes in this folder. *Copy the entire* folder structure, not just the individual files. If you use Adobe Prelude (which I'd recommend!), this is the primary destination for your media.

▶ **02_Scratch Disk.** Target any previews (renders) in this location. Optionally, this folder can be emptied prior to backup.

▶ **03_Project Files.** This is where all the project files should be located, including the Adobe Premiere Pro project *along* with project files created by any of the other tools in Adobe Creative Cloud. If you work on complex projects, creating a set of projects inside this folder for the other tools, such as Adobe After Effects or Adobe Audition, would be a good idea as well.

▶ **04_Graphic Sources.** Stills, logos, and any other elements to be imported into Adobe Premiere Pro should go here. Additionally, if anything is built in Adobe After Effects or Adobe Photoshop, those files should be moved here *prior* to import.

▶ **05_Graphic Exports.** Anything generated from Adobe After Effects would go here. Although dynamic linking is powerful, there are some users who additionally create the final render to place back in Adobe Premiere Pro's Timeline.

▶ **06_Audio Sources.** This folder should include any on-set captured audio (such as in dual-capture setups), music, and sound effects.

▶ **07_Stock Footage.** Any purchased materials, such as stock video, stills, or music would go here. Additional nested folders might be warranted. With these assets isolated, it's easy to fill out paperwork necessary for licensing.

▶ **08_Exported Files.** Any export should be named and labeled in such a way that it is obvious what the file is. For more on exporting and specific naming conventions, see Chapter 7.

▶ **09_Production Paperwork.** Any scripts, budgets, PDFs, releases, copies of client communications that would be smart to keep with your project go here.

And that's just a short version of these Common Media folders. It's best to use *too many* than to use too few. Also, don't invent this structure on the fly: Plan, plan, *plan*.

For example, if you're shooting with a cinema camera that has a lookup table (LUT), you should store that LUT with the project. And if you're using multiple LUTs, consider creating a numbered folder that contains them.

If the folder structure described here doesn't work for you, choose a folder structure that does. Believe me, most of your current media headaches will no longer be an issue.

Make Media Backups

Make sure you have a backup of your media! All too often I encounter editorial situations where some type of key footage is gone because a drive has died. And the question I ask is a frightening one: "What kind of liability insurance do you have?"

All camera media should be replicated at least once, preferably in the field, copied immediately from the camera cards.

Editorial systems should be running at RAID-5 (**Figure 2.15**) or some sort of drive system that has a live redundancy.

TIP

PostHaste is a wonderful free, third-party, cross-platform utility on the market at www.digitalrebellion.com that can automatically duplicate and serialize a series of folders like the Common Media folder project template.

Figure 2.15 A RAID-5 has the speed capabilities of a RAID-0 (two or more drives striped as one larger drive) and the redundancy RAID-1 (mirroring).

**What's the Minimum
Number of Backups Necessary?**

The struggle is always how to minimize cost versus the highest degree of data safety.

I suggest at least two copies and likely more. Here is the process I follow:

1. Save a pair of copies from the camera's storage to a set of drives. One set goes to editorial, and the other set sits offsite and remains untouched. Optionally, back up set 2 to an LTO.

2. Copy one set to a RAID-5 that has the Common Media folder structure. Technically at this point, three copies are in play. Backups of any added or created material, such as the project, imported stills, and audio should be performed, possibly to a cloud service.

3. When finished, back up the entire Common Media folder twice to either a pair of hard drives or to an LTO tape.

   If this sounds paranoid, just remember that it's not paranoia if they're out to get you.

And absolutely consider a Linear Tape Open (LTO) drive for long-term storage. These drives are not as fast as the slowest hard drive, but the current version (LTO-6) can contain 2.5 TB in a single cartridge prior to any sort of compression. Tapes are rated for at least 15 years of shelf life along with data verification.

Project Setup

Now that you have the software reconfigured, your caches, and your media setup, you need to address projects.

The following sections really boil down to the idea that if you build a project that represents your work, prepopulated with common bins and elements, you can get a jumpstart on the editorial process by reusing that project. Then you're not reinventing the wheel each time you start a new project.

Optimizing New Projects

When you start a project, you're faced with the dialog shown in **Figure 2.16**, which you've seen before. Of key importance is *not to use the* default project Location setting, which is in your documents folder.

Figure 2.16 The defaults for projects are not where you want to store them. You're better off using a controlled folder collection like the Common Media folder for a project.

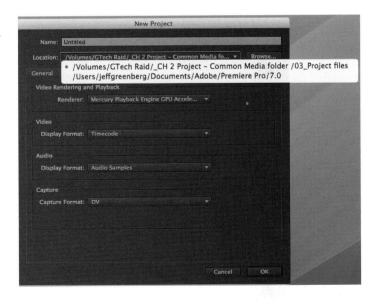

Instead, change the Location to your project's unique Common Media folder's 03_Project Files (Figure 2.16) folder. However, there is one caveat: Changing this location will (by default) also place your preview and auto-save files in the same location. These are all set by default to follow *the project location*, which is great for a novice, but painful once you really start generating media. Leaving these at the defaults will start to fill up your internal drive.

The following sections provide some thoughts on improvements for these default locations.

Captured video and audio

Video and audio is the *only* level of built-in media management that Adobe Premiere Pro does. Choose a known location that will be shared with other nontape-based elements, preferably the 02_Scratch Disk folder in the Common Media folder project template.

Video and audio previews

Although the Mercury Engine technology is amazing, sooner or later you'll need to generate previews. Previews are *less essential* than any other sort of media; they can be regenerated at the cost of *time*.

Look at the Scratch Disks in **Figure 2.17**.

Figure 2.17 Here I've targeted the previews to my RAID-5 (called GTech Raid) and created a folder called _Adobe Previews.

CLOSE-UP

Manually Back Up Projects Separately

Do not rely solely on the Auto Save function. Your projects should also be backed up somewhere else. If you've backed up your raw media to another location, you can rebuild everything if problems arise.

Every day, twice a day (beginning of the day and at lunchtime), manually copy your project to some other location, such as Cloud-based storage that comes with Adobe Creative Cloud! This creates quite a number of project files but provides the greatest flexibility if something goes wrong.

Two thoughts on location:

▶ Probably the best choice is a folder called _Adobe Previews at the root level of your media drive. Each project will automatically generate its own PRV folder, which makes it easy to delete at the end of a project.

▶ An alternate strategy is to target a folder within the Common Media folder for the project. The advantage is that backing up the previews means a level of ease in *restoring* the project including previews in the future. I'm not a fan of this method because like cache files, previews are easily rebuilt.

Project auto save

Hopefully, you'll never need to use an auto-saved version of your project. The only rule is: *Don't have Auto-Save point to the same location or drive as your project.* Instead, use a Cloud-based backup, or store it on your system drive (this is the one exception where this is permitted).

One day your media drive may die. If your project *and* the auto-save version is stored there, *you'll have nothing.* So, the ideal choice is to save to a different physical location.

Choosing the Right Sequence Preset

All too often I'm asked: "Am I using the right sequence preset?" The answer is to consider two major questions that recur at the start of every project:

▶ What type of footage are you (mostly) working with? Likely, this will dictate the type of sequence settings you'll use.

▶ What are you delivering? Most likely it will be an HD size (1080 or 720) that matches your footage, but even when you're working in larger formats (2k and beyond), HD is still the predominant delivery size.

Although it's common to work with more than one format (footage), it's *uncommon* to always work with different formats. Even when this is the case, at the end what you actually have to deliver is often the most important consideration for your sequences.

The dialog in **Figure 2.18** is overwhelming; if you're like most editors, you've tried to pick the sequence preset that closely matches your footage.

Are you worried about what sequence type to choose? Probably not because you likely know one of two tricks to build a sequence that matches your format:

▶ Editing the first clip on any sequence will yield a dialog on a *mismatch*, giving you the opportunity to have Adobe Premiere Pro automatically set up the sequence for you.

▶ Additionally, you can right-click on a clip and choose New Sequence from Clip (or drag a clip to the New Item button on the bottom of the Project panel).

Although both methods work, they reveal a little-known truth: *Sequence types don't matter.*

The great secret concerning sequences

As long as your sequence matches the frame size and frame rate of your clips, Adobe Premiere Pro will work fine. You don't have to make sure your footage matches your rendering codec. You don't have to believe me on this, you can just try it.

What may matter later in your workflow is the Preview codec in the Settings tab. By default, the preview files are ignored (and the Preview codec *doesn't matter*). Everything is directly re-rendered in the final output format, yielding a higher quality output. If you choose to use the render files, then *yes,* the Preview codec *does matter.*

Editing modes

Table 2.1 contains a current list of every editing mode and preview codec combination. Refer to it when you need it. Just remember that as long as your footage matches your Timeline, you can edit!

TABLE **2.1**   Editing Modes

EDITING MODE	FRAME SIZE	PIXEL ASPECT RATIO (PAR)	FIELD ORDER	PREVIEW FORMAT	PREVIEW CODEC
ARRI Cinema	Adjustable	Adjustable	Adjustable	I-Frame Only MPEG	MPEG I-Frame
AVC Intra 100 1080i	1920 x 1080	Square (1.0)	Upper First	I-Frame Only MPEG	MPEG I-Frame
AVC Intra 100 1080p	1920 x 1080	Square (1.0)	Progressive	I-Frame Only MPEG	MPEG I-Frame
AVC Intra 100 720p	1280 x 720	Square (1.0)	Progressive	I-Frame Only MPEG	MPEG I-Frame
AVC Intra 50 1080i	1440 x 1080	HD Anamorphic (1.33)	Upper First	I-Frame Only MPEG	MPEG I-Frame
AVC Intra 50 1080p	1920 x 1080	HD Anamorphic (1.33)	Progressive	I-Frame Only MPEG	MPEG I-Frame
AVC Intra 50 720p	960 x 720	HD Anamorphic (1.33)	Progressive	I-Frame Only MPEG	MPEG I-Frame
AVCHD 1080i Anamorphic	1440 x 1080	HD Anamorphic (1.33)	Upper First	I-Frame Only MPEG	MPEG I-Frame
AVCHD 1080i Square Pixel	1920 x 1080	Square (1.0)	Upper First	I-Frame Only MPEG	MPEG I-Frame
AVCHD 1080p Anamorphic	1440 x 1080	HD Anamorphic (1.33)	Progressive	I-Frame Only MPEG	MPEG I-Frame
AVCHD 1080p Square Pixel	1920 x 1080	Square (1.0)	Progressive	I-Frame Only MPEG	MPEG I-Frame
AVCHD 720p Square Pixel	1280 x 720	Square (1.0)	Progressive	I-Frame Only MPEG	MPEG I-Frame
Canon XF MPEG2 1080i/P	1920 x 1080	Square (1.0)	Upper/Progressive depending	I-Frame Only MPEG	MPEG I-Frame
Canon XF MPEG2 720p	1280 x 720	Square (1.0)	Progressive	I-Frame Only MPEG	MPEG I-Frame
DNxHD 145 1080i	1920 x 1080	Square (1.0)	Upper First	DNX 145 1080i	DNX 145 1080i

TABLE 2.1 *(continued)*

Editing Mode	Frame Size	Pixel Aspect Ratio (PAR)	Field Order	Preview Format	Preview Codec
DNxHD 145 1080p	1920 x 1080	Square (1.0)	Progressive	DNX 120 1080p	DNX 120 1080p
DNxHD 145 720p	1280 x 720	Square (1.0)	Progressive	DNX 60 720p	DNX 60 720p
DNxHD 220 1080i	1920 x 1080	Square (1.0)	Upper First	DNX 220 1080i	DNX 220 1080i
DNxHD 220 1080p	1920 x 1080	Square (1.0)	Progressive	DNX 185 1080p	DNX 185 1080p
DNxHD 220 720p	1280 x 720	Square (1.0)	Progressive	DNX 90 720p	DNX 90 720p
DNxHD 220x 1080i	1920 x 1080	Square (1.0)	Upper First	DNX 220x 1080i	DNX 220x 1080i
DNxHD 220x 1080p	1920 x 1080	Square (1.0)	Progressive	DNX 185x 1080p	DNX 185x 1080p
DNxHD 220x 720p	1280 x 720	Square (1.0)	Progressive	DNX 90x 720p	DNX 90x 720p
DNxHD 36 1080p	1920 x 1080	Square (1.0)	Progressive	DNX 36 1080p	DNX 36 1080p
DNxHD 444x 1080p (RGB 444)	1920 x 1080	Square (1.0)	Progressive	DNX 350 1080p (RGB 444)	
DSLR	adjustable	adjustable	adjustable	I-Frame Only MPEG	MPEG I-Frame
HDV 1080i	1440 x 1080	HD Anamorphic (1.33)	Upper First	I-Frame Only MPEG	MPEG I-Frame
HDV 1080p	1440 x 1080	HD Anamorphic (1.33)	Progressive	I-Frame Only MPEG	MPEG I-Frame
HDV 720p	1280 x 720	Square (1.0)	Progressive	I-Frame Only MPEG	MPEG I-Frame
P2 1080 i/p	1280 x 1080	DVCPro HD (1.5)	Upper/Progressive depending	P2 1080i/p DVCPro HD	DVCPro100
P2 720p	960 x 720	HD Anamorphic (1.33)	Progressive	P2 720p DVCPro HD	DVCPro100
P2 DVCPro NTSC 50	720 x 480	D1/DV NTSC (.9091) or D1/DV NTSC WS (1.2121)	Lower/Progressive depending	P2 DVCPro50	DVCPro50
P2 DVCPro PAL 50	720 x 576	D1/DV PAL (1.094) or D1/DV PAL WS (1.4587)	Progressive	P2 DVCPro50	DVCPro50
QuickTime DV 24p	720 x 480	D1/DV NTSC (.9091) or D1/DV NTSC WS (1.2121)	Progressive	QuickTime DV NTSC	DV25 NTSC
QuickTime DV NTSC	720 x 480	D1/DV NTSC (.9091) or D1/DV NTSC WS (1.2121)	Lower/Progressive depending	QuickTime DV NTSC	DV25 NTSC
QuickTime DV PAL	720 x 576	D1/DV PAL (1.094) or D1/DV PAL WS (1.4587)	Lower/Progressive depending	QuickTime DV PAL	DV25 PAL
RED Cinema	Varies	Square (1.0)	Progressive	I-Frame Only MPEG	MPEG I-Frame
Sony XDCAM EX 1080i	1920 x 1080	Square (1.0)	Upper First	I-Frame Only MPEG	MPEG I-Frame
Sony XDCAM EX 1080p	1920 x 1080	Square (1.0)	Progressive	I-Frame Only MPEG	MPEG I-Frame
Sony XDCAM EX 720p	1280 x 720	Square (1.0)	Progressive	I-Frame Only MPEG	MPEG I-Frame
Sony XDCAM HD 1080p	1440 x 1080	HD Anamorphic (1.33)	Progressive	I-Frame Only MPEG	MPEG I-Frame
Sony XDCAM HD/ EX 1080i (SP)	1440 x 1080	HD Anamorphic (1.33)	Upper First	I-Frame Only MPEG	MPEG I-Frame
Sony XDCAM HD422 1080i/p	1920 x 1080	Square (1.0)	Upper/Progressive depending	I-Frame Only MPEG	MPEG I-Frame
Sony XDCAM HD422 720p	1280 x 720	Square (1.0)	Pro	I-Frame Only MPEG	MPEG I-Frame

Custom editing modes

There is also a custom editing mode choice (**Figure 2.19**), which allows you to adjust and build your own preset based on new formats or a hardware input/output device.

Figure 2.19 Choosing Custom at the top of the Settings tab unlocks the ability to change the Preview File Format.

There are some cool things you can do with custom editing modes (see "Building an Apple ProRes Preset" later in this chapter).

Custom modes have some important wrinkles:

▶ On a Mac the Custom choice is QuickTime and can access QuickTime codecs, even if they are a bad choice.

▶ On Windows the Custom choice is AVI and can access AVI codecs, even if they are a bad choice.

▶ AVI and QuickTime are not cross platform. Switching platforms switches Adobe Premiere Pro to the I-Frame MPEG codec.

Creating a Sequence Template Preset

Going beyond just choosing a sequence type, you should build your own unique presets. By doing so, you'll get a new Custom category in the Sequence list with only the presets you need.

Resave even the built-in preset you commonly use

Even if you use a built-in Adobe Premiere Pro preset for your sequences, you should still save a custom preset (**Figure 2.20**).

Figure 2.20 The Save Preset button.

Then you can ignore the entire preset list except for the unique presets that you need, which are easily located at the bottom of the list (**Figure 2.21**). You'll no longer accidentally create the wrong one!

As a bonus you can add the typical number of tracks and type of audio tracks you need already labeled, ready to go.

Figure 2.21 The Custom category contains the presets you've saved. By resaving the Adobe presets you use most often, you have a shortcut to finding them!

Smart Rendering codecs yield faster exports

It's not for every workflow, but Smart Rendering may be able to accelerate your output (**Figure 2.22**). This can be done with certain codecs by not re-encoding existing material but rather copying it when the output matches the camera codec. For example, you can invoke Smart Rendering when you edit XDCam and output an OP1a MXF file that matches.

Smart Rendering can be fantastic when set up correctly. Matching the footage to the sequence setting will grant you this capability if those two match the output setting.

If some footage doesn't match, it's OK because Adobe Premiere Pro will just handle it normally, but you won't get the benefit of Smart Rendering. Done right this acceleration occurs under the hood.

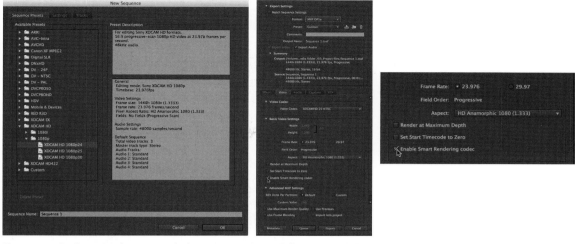

Figure 2.22 For Smart Rendering to work, the sequence settings (left) must match the Export (center) exactly. The switch to Enable Smart Rendering codec (right) must also be selected.

Two general workflows can utilize Smart Rendering:

▶ **Camera cuts only.** You start with some XDCam, edit, and then output XDCam (OP1a MXF). Outputs are super fast because it's just copying the cut points, not re-encoding the video. If you create and render any effects, they'll be I-Frame MPEGs (a different format) and so are automatically encoded. This workflow allows the "cut down" of longer clips exported from a sequence with *no quality loss* because no new encoding has been performed. Anything rendered will have to be encoded.

▶ **An all DNxHD (or ProRes) workflow *including* renders.** This idea is a setup where you start with DNxHD and you intend to finish with DNxHD. You started with it perhaps because you transcoded footage using Adobe Prelude. Because the preview codec matches, you'll be able to accelerate this too.

The following codecs work with Smart Rendering:

▶ DV

▶ DVCProHD

▶ Long Gop 0P1a (XDCam)

▶ AVCIntraframe (MXF)

▶ DNxHD (MXF) OP1a

▶ ProRes (QuickTime)

▶ DNxHD (QuickTime)

With many facilities built around DNxHD or QuickTime ProRes workflows, it becomes valuable to implement this workflow.

You'll see a switch for the Smart Rendering Codec choice on output for all of the preceding formats *except* those built around QuickTime. For those, if you get everything to match, trust Adobe, it works.

Building an Apple ProRes preset

Because Adobe Premiere Pro doesn't come with a preset for ProRes, I'll give you the recipe for how to adjust the sequence settings. This would work for Cineform (cross platform) as well.

1. Choose whichever preset you like. I usually start with an AVC-Intra preset that matches my frame size and frame rate.

2. Go to the Settings tab, and switch the Editing mode to Custom. This allows you to use a different format than the I-Frame MPEG file.

3. Change the Video Preview file format to QuickTime. The Codec drop-down menu will now be available.

4. Match the exact codec of your footage, most often Apple ProRes 422.

Maximum choices in sequence settings

The two Maximum settings (**Figure 2.23**) are set up incorrectly often enough that it's worth giving them their own mention. They're important to set up (and save!) as a part of preset.

Here, these *only affect* the preview (render) files. They're only useful to turn on if you intend to render as you go and use your previews to accelerate your output:

Figure 2.23 These two Maximum options slow down the rendering your previews. Use them only if needed!

▶ **Maximum Bit Depth.** Adobe Premiere Pro handles video in 8-bit depth unless you select this check box. It has benefits in that it doesn't truncate your color correction material. Key elements that will be affected by this are effects that have the 32 bit switch on the Effects panel and 10-bit (and beyond) formats like RED, Alexa, and HDCAM SR. By processing the extra bit depth, Adobe Premiere Pro will handle all of the video data in 32 bits per channel.

▶ **Maximum Render Quality.** Maximum Quality maintains sharpness when you're doing up-converts (from SD to HD) or down-converts (from HD to SD). Be careful with its use; it requires more memory (especially to render).

Tracks

If you look back at the last ten sequences you cut, odds are you used two to three video tracks and somewhere between four and ten audio tracks.

Set up your common audio tracks in the Tracks tab and save a preset for future projects (**Figure 2.24**).

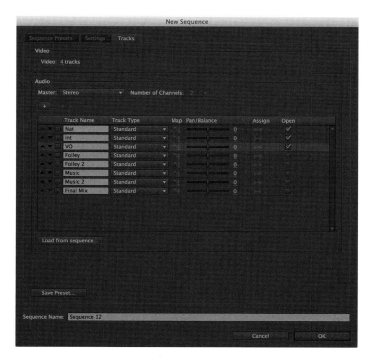

Figure 2.24 If you already have a sequence that has the names and number of audio tracks set up, the "Load from sequence" button will insert them for you. The Open switch will set those tracks larger when starting a new sequence.

For most of us, our standard output is stereo. When adding tracks, most of your needs will be with a standard track. If you place a mono clip there, it'll play equally on both channels; if you put a stereo clip there, it'll take up only one track with two waveforms perfectly panned.

If you're not seeing your track names, you need to increase the vertical height of the tracks.

Take the extra five seconds and name your tracks, such as Narration, VO, SFX, Music, and Music 2. Doing so will create new sequences with these already named. You'll be less likely to make mistakes later when performing audio mixes.

Audio master output

When you create a sequence is the *only time* you can adjust what kind of audio master output you want Adobe Premiere Pro to do. Although sequence types are now adjustable (see "Changing sequence types"), audio master output is the one thing that you cannot change.

To get around this limitation, you would create a new sequence with the correct master output and overwrite your current sequence into that, making sure the Timeline button called "Insert and overwrite sequences as nests or individual clips" (**Figure 2.25**) is *off*.

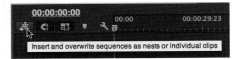

Figure 2.25 Depending on the toggle here, this switch allows you to drag one sequence into another and either get a nest (one clip for the entire sequence) or individual clips.

Multichannel (split channel) masters

It's common in the broadcast world to need to build a master output with more than two channels. Normally, when you have two channels, your output is stereo.

What if you wanted a normal stereo mix but also a "split master" where the voice-over/narrator was on one channel and everything else was on the other channel in the same file?

This sort of output is very common for news:

▶ Listening to only A1+A2 as a "finished" show, ready for air, broadcasters mute the A3 + A4 output.

▶ In a different market, local talent re-records the audio on A3. A4 is the rest of the mix. A1+A2 are never heard. This gives the impression that the local broadcaster created the story.

If you're not familiar with split masters, the idea (regardless of how many tracks you're working with) is to output a stereo mix on A1+A2 but to also output all the narrator elements on A3 and everything else on A4.

Building this master is a little tricky. It requires four channels for output and a special track—the Adaptive track—a track that can route itself to one or multiple outputs.

Again, the four output tracks are two pairs: A1+A2 are a full mix; A3 is just the voice-over/narration (mono); and A4 is everything other than the narration.

Your edit can have as many Input tracks (Timeline tracks) as you like, but here is the basic idea of how to set this up.

1. Start a new sequence with Multichannel Output. For the standard four track split master, you need to give it four outputs (**Figure 2.26**).

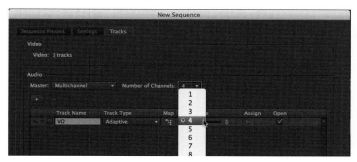

Figure 2.26 You can set a multichannel output to have as many as 32 outputs.

2. Delete all the Audio tracks but one. Change it to an Adaptive track.

3. Change the name of the track to VO. Double-click the Map for the track and Assign Input 1 to Outputs 1 +2 + 3 (**Figure 2.27**). This track needs to be allowed to output to 1+2—that's the stereo mix—but also it needs to output to track 3. VOs are always recorded as a mono element (1 input track); they have no Input 2–4, so we leave these alone.

4. Add any other "main" tracks, like narration, that are meant to match this. Because your last track is an Adaptive track, Adobe Premiere Pro will add a track of the same type, including track mapping.

5. To add the other side of the split, for tracks such as interviews, music, or sound effects (tracks that should be in the A1+A2 mix but should show up on the A4 split) the mapping works like this: Input 1 goes to Outputs 1+4. Input 2 goes to Outputs 2+4 (**Figure 2.28**).

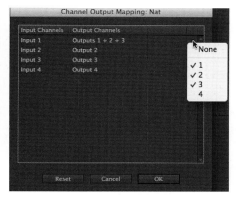

Figure 2.27 The VO track needs to output normally to A1+A2 *but also* to Output A3 for the split master.

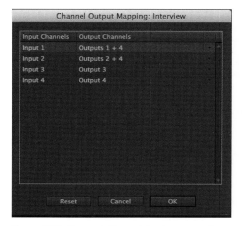

Figure 2.28 Elements like an interview or music need to output normally on 1+2 but should be on the background track of the split master, A4.

Changing sequence types

A new feature for the late 2013 release is the ability to change the Sequence Settings. Anything except the audio mastering is changeable. But even though everything is changeable now, that doesn't mean you should change everything.

You can find this feature by choosing Sequence > Sequence Settings.

You should probably never touch the timebase—the frames per second. Although Adobe Premiere Pro will try to adjust your Timeline for the new speed, it tends to create headaches. It's best to cut your 29.97 Timeline into a 23.98 Timeline rather than just adjust the frame rate.

The biggest item that's worth changing is the codec (**Figure 2.29**), which eases proxy (low resolution/high resolution) workflows.

Figure 2.29 Changing the codec permits the difference between generating proxy quality previews and final quality previews or working between two container types.

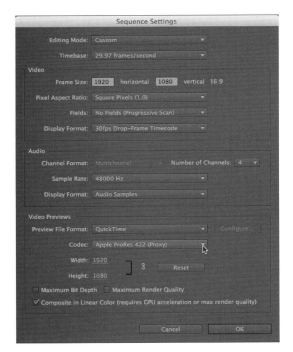

This proxy technique requires two other abilities:

▶ **Create transcoded proxies.** Although in Chapter 1 we looked at the merits of transcoding, it's easy to have Adobe Prelude copy your camera media to one location *while* creating and saving a transcoded copy to a second location. For example, you could copy the RED camera files to a backup drive and transcode to Apple's ProRes Proxy (or DNxHD) at the same time.

▶ **Relink, even between different containers.** The new relink dialog has a powerful feature, which is to *ignore* the file extension. That way you could edit while linked to proxy.mov files but finish utilizing the full quality R3D files.

Building a Master Template

Once you've built a project, targeted everything where you want to store it, and built the right sequence presets, it becomes a better starting point for future projects. Everything is already set correctly!

Place the project (template) in 03_Project Files folder, so when you duplicate the folder structure for a new project, there's already a fresh project sitting there ready to go.

You could even go so far as to prepopulate your project with common bins (see "Common Bins for Every Project") and other common elements.

Just make sure you rename the project prior to starting so the Preview and Auto Save folders create information that exactly matches the name of the project.

Import

You've probably built a number of projects, so you're already familiar with the basics of importing. In this section we need to cover a couple of ideas: why you should focus on the Media Browser, handling dual sound, cinema cameras, and bad clips.

And yes, the biggest rule of importing is to *stay organized* from the beginning.

TIP

There is one case where working with the Import command is better than working with the Media Browser and that is when you just want one specific clip. Don't go to the File menu, don't press Command+I (Ctrl+I); instead, double-click on the background of the project window and you'll bring up an Import dialog.

Media Browser vs. Import

You should stop using the File > Import choice and instead use the Media Browser (**Figure 2.30**) to import your files.

There's really only one reason to use the standard Import command and that is to do an OS level file search.

But if you're working, as this chapter suggests, from a Common Media project folder, you know that all your elements are already in one central place.

Meanwhile, the Import command has several limitations: There is no metadata, it can't handle spanned files, and worst of all, there is no preview/hoverscrub of files.

Figure 2.30 With the Media Browser maximized, it becomes trivial to look at multiple shots quickly—a necessity given the overshooting in the digital age.

Getting the Most Out of the Media Browser

Because the Media Browser is the core for bringing in material, there are a couple of techniques that can add value and mastery to how it works for you.

The first is a recap of the earlier tip: Maximize any window by pressing the accent (`) key to take the Media Browser full screen, which is vital for choosing clips.

Import directly to a bin

Be sure to select a bin *prior* to switching to the Media Browser. Select whichever clips you want to import. Pressing Command+Option+I (Ctrl+Alt+I) imports this selection. Better yet, remap it to Command+I (Ctrl+I). This permits very quick selection and import into Adobe Premiere Pro.

Thumbnail view vs. List view

Both Thumbnail and List views have their advantages. Like many techniques in this book, there isn't a right or wrong choice. In fact, you should try both and see which helps you work smartest (**Figure 2.31**).

The argument for using thumbnails is simple. In the world of hundreds of clips named 001138.MXF, lists of clip names tell you nothing. Using hoverscrub in Thumbnail view permits super fast previews and clip selections.

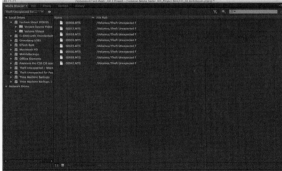

Figure 2.31 The Media Browser views compared: Thumbnail (left) and List (right).

TIP

Double-clicking on a clip does not import it. It permits the clip to be loaded into the Source Monitor but not loaded into the project. Either drag it into the project from the Source Monitor, right-click and choose Import, or edit the clip onto the Timeline to add it to the project.

Figure 2.32 The File Type Display filter looks like a funnel and is found in the top right of the Media Browser.

Figure 2.33 The advantage of professional cameras is the possibility of accessing metadata created in-camera.

You can use the JKL keys to play through the clips, which is fantastic for previewing interview clips (when you don't want all of them) or music and sound effects.

The argument for using List view is the ability to see and select more clips and see metadata, particularly for certain formats and camera metadata, prior to importing.

Filtering by file type

There are times when you'll have a directory of your material with just too many files to make sense of. Perhaps you've saved many Adobe Photoshop files into a directory with some JPEGs and some audio.

The File Type Display filter (**Figure 2.32**) in the upper right of the Media Browser permits you to narrow down busy directories to just a specific format, including camera formats. There are over 35 different file filters available to narrow down what file type you're looking at in the Media Browser!

Directory Viewers

In the top-right corner under the Panel menu of the Media Browser you can choose to Edit Columns and display more (or less) metadata. This could have the potential to be useful. But it really shines when the Directory Viewer drop-down menu is switched to a particular camera type (**Figure 2.33**), such as ARRI raw, Panasonic P2, XDCAM-HD, and everything in between.

Unique for each format, you're able to add other metadata that the camera may or may not supply.

Use Adobe Prelude

In this tapeless world, Adobe Prelude is your camera media capture device. Consider it a "Prelude" to editorial.

Chapter 8 has a section dedicated to using Adobe Prelude. It'll take you less than an hour to get your head around its three major features:

▶ Copying camera media from the card (to the Common Media folder for the project)

- ▶ Backing up camera media to a different location
- ▶ Sending clips (and optionally bins) to Adobe Premiere Pro

Does it do more? Sure. But these three tasks are truly invaluable time-savers in the editing process.

While you're in Adobe Prelude, it's best to organize clips into bins that make sense. Then, when you start in Adobe Premiere Pro, you're ready to edit.

Dual Sound: Merge and Sync Clips

Many cameras with changeable lenses, particularly DSLRs, have been so focused on getting the best picture that their audio is an afterthought. Resourceful productions have learned quickly to resurrect the process used in film—dual capture.

Merge clips based on audio

The merge clips based on audio technique utilizes bad sound on the camera and great sound on an external recorder. Adobe Premiere Pro can "align' the two waveforms, syncing the good sound with the picture. It's best to use a slate (which, of course, you do, right?)

This method doesn't *require* the slate clap, but a slate does help to identify shots if the sound alignment doesn't work.

To process a take, follow these steps.

1. Select the video (with bad audio) and the good audio in the project window.

2. Choose Clip > Merge Clips to access the Merge Clips dialog (**Figure 2.34**).

3. Choose Synchronize Point Audio. Select the channel you want Adobe Premiere Pro to try (usually Track 1).

4. Optionally, Choose Remove Audio From AV Clip. This way the merged clip *only* has the high-quality audio. Do this after you test a couple of clips to make sure there are no sync issues.

Viewing Without Importing

Double-clicking a clip in the Media Browser (or right-clicking and choosing Open in Source Monitor) *doesn't* add the clip to the project. But it does permit you to view a clip, use JKL, mark In/Out points, add markers, and use the maximize feature or the full screen feature (Command+`[Ctrl+ `]), which are fantastic ways to look at footage and even mark it up *prior* to adding it to a project.

The downside is that the original media file is modified. It still has the same creation date, but information like markers or In/Out points are stored in the file, if the file permits it.

Figure 2.34 Merging dual capture sound permits high-quality audio to be captured via a digital recording when a camera can't do professional quality recordings.

Figure 2.35 When dual sync merge doesn't work, the manual method of using a marker (not an In/Out point) is your best bet.

This procedure will yield a new clip with the original video clip's name but with Merged appended to the end of the filename. I usually store these in a bin called Merged Clips.

Merge clips based on other metadata

Sometimes the preceding method just doesn't work. Perhaps the audio was too distorted. Frankly, it doesn't matter. When it doesn't work, you need to help out.

I'll assume that if you're reading this section, you didn't have matching timecode. That leaves us with having to manually add a mark that Adobe Premiere Pro can use to merge and sync the video and audio together.

You'll use the same Merge Clips dialog, but with slightly different selections (**Figure 2.35**).

Having tried all the possibilities, I suggest manually using markers (that I name **Sync Point** on the video clip and the audio clip at the "sync" moment for the merge.

The reason is straightforward: If you use an In point (or Out point), when Adobe Premiere Pro does the merge, that's the spot the clip will start. So, if you actually meant to look for the slate's raw information (the shot, day, take, etc.), it's gone.

Again, I prefer to select Remove Audio From AV Clip so it's only the clean audio on the merged shot.

Modifying Clips for Great Slow Motion Shots

There's a fantastic method of creating great-looking slow motion shots—shoot at a higher frame rate! In film, this was easy; it was called *overcranking*. You'd run the camera faster and play back *slower*, and get a great-looking slow motion shot at the cost of processing the extra film.

There's a way to re-create this film technique using Adobe Premiere Pro. But don't confuse this with changing the speed of a clip or using some of the advanced optical flow processing in Adobe After Effects.

This technique is possible with two requirements:

▶ You need to shoot at 60 fps (or 50 for your PAL fans). You really need to shoot significantly more frames per second.

▶ You need to edit your sequence with *a slower* frame rate—23.98 or 30 (or 25 for those using PAL—yes, I'm waving at you).

This likely means you'll shoot at 720p60 because it has the highest frame rate possible. Yes, there are cameras that shoot higher frame rates. But 720p60 is the fastest *broadcast standard*.

Normally, if you drop a higher frame rate clip into a sequence at a different frame rate, Adobe Premiere Pro will automatically conform the footage (dropping frames) so it seems to play back normally.

The method described here is to select the clip and then choose Clip > Modify> Interpret Footage.

When the Modify Clip dialog (**Figure 2.36**) appears, in the Frame Rate section, select "Assume this frame rate" and type in the frame rate of the sequence (usually 23.98).

Figure 2.36 This shot *says* it's 30 fps, but I know that it's really 720p60 (because I shot it!).

By doing so, Adobe Premiere Pro will then reinterpret the footage, slowing it down and conforming it so that one frame of the clip matches where the frames are on the Timeline. Audio will be slowed down as well, meaning you'll probably want to throw it out.

The result is gorgeous slow motion *before* you do any retiming.

Stereo vs. Mono Audio

There seems to be some confusion about clips that have two waveforms—two audio recordings. In some cases they're two elements and in other cases they're *one*.

If the clip has two discrete audio channels (such as using A1 for an external microphone and A2 for the camera microphone), this clip should be considered as having two *mono* tracks.

If a clip has two *mixed* audio channels (such as music or even an interview recorded with a stereo microphone), it should considered as a having a *single stereo track*.

Take a look at **Figure 2.37**. Which is correct?

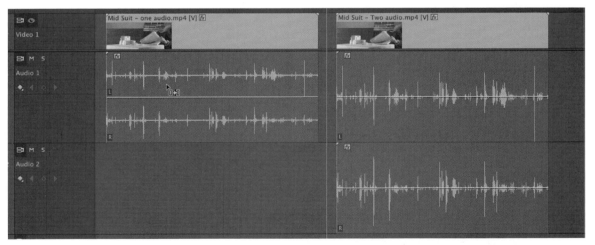

Figure 2.37 Depending on how the audio was recorded, a shot could be either of these two examples. Either way may have been correct: on the left, a stereo recording (with a stereo microphone); on the right, two separate microphones.

To complicate things, Adobe Premiere Pro interprets the clip on import based on what the file says about itself. Often, its description can be wrong. The clip could be mono when it should be stereo or vice versa.

When you encounter these situations where the audio is incorrect, it's useful to know how to fix these problems quickly.

Adjusting two tracks to be a mono pair

When Adobe Premiere Pro has interpreted a clip as a stereo clip, but you want it to instead be a pair of mono clips, follow these steps.

1. Select the clip in the Project panel.

2. Choose Clip > Modify >Audio Channels (or press Shift+G).

3. Change the Preset drop-down menu to Mono (**Figure 2.38**).

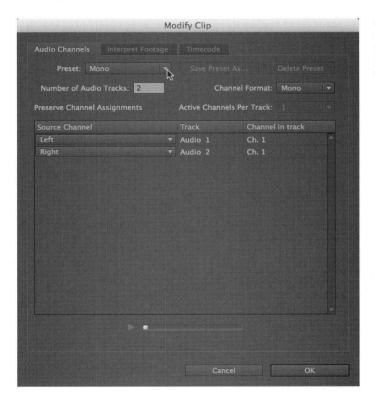

Figure 2.38 The presets (such as Mono) allow quick and easy configurations to be stored. You can always play a specific track at the bottom of the window.

TIP

The modification of audio channels (or any modification for that manner) can be performed on multiple clips simultaneously.

Adjusting two tracks to ignore one completely

You can adjust two tracks to ignore one completely when you know that the camera audio was recorded onto A1 and the microphone was recorded onto A2.

In a perfect world, you'd never see the camera audio, so let's make that happen instead of you having to constantly unlink and delete that track on the Timeline!

1. Select the clip in the Project panel.

2. Choose Clip > Modify >Audio Channels (or press Shift+G).

3. Change the Preset drop-down menu to Mono.

4. Change the number of Audio tracks to 1. This means only *one track* will show up on the Timeline.

5. Change the Source Channel to Right. Left means A1; Right means A2 of the original clip.

6. Save this as a preset (**Figure 2.39**). Call it **Good Audio On A2**. Yes, you should build a second one for those situations where the good channel is on A1 and A2 needs to be ignored.

The clip is never permanently damaged. The information is still there, but Adobe Premiere Pro interprets it differently.

Adjusting a mono pair to be a stereo clip

The opposite case is when you want a clip with two audio tracks to be considered stereo.

1. Select the clip in the Project panel.

2. Choose Clip > Modify >Audio Channels (or press Shift+G).

3. Change the Preset drop-down menu to Stereo.

The only areas where people seem to get confused is that the value of Number of Audio Tracks is 1. It's *one track* on the Timeline, but you can see that the value of Active Channels Per Track is now 2 (**Figure 2.40**).

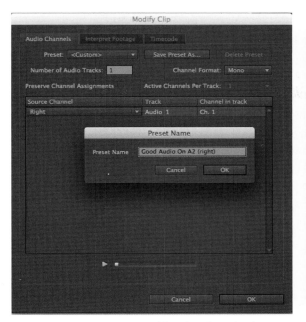

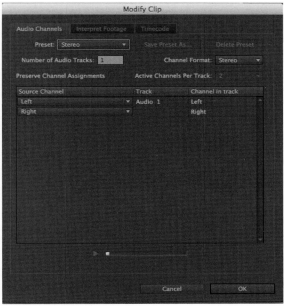

Figure 2.39 Having a preset saved for either channel makes modifying multiple clips a breeze.

Figure 2.40 Setting the preset to stereo means that one track on the Timeline contains two channels.

Dealing with Too Many Dead Audio Tracks

Sometimes you'll receive source footage with more audio channels than you need, and you want to adjust it after importing rather than dealing with all sorts of crazy Timeline patching. XDCam clips are often the culprit of this condition with eight tracks. Let's look at a more extreme example in **Figure 2.41**.

You might receive 16 channels of audio attached to a video clip, but you really only need Source channels 3, 4, 9 and 14, and you want those channels to patch into Timeline Tracks 1, 2, 3, and 4. And, most important, you want Adobe Premiere Pro to ignore the rest as if they didn't exist.

1. Select the clip in the Project panel.

2. Choose Clip > Modify >Audio Channels (or press Shift+G).

3. Change the Preset drop-down menu to Mono.

4. Change the number of Audio tracks to 4. This means only *four tracks* will show up on the Timeline.

5. Change the Source Channels to the arrangement you want. In **Figure 2.42**, I've assigned channels 3, 4, 9, and 14 to 1, 2, 3, and 4.

6. Save this as a preset. Be precise in naming your preset. It's likely that everything that came from that camera on that day of shooting will need these audio adjustments made.

Again, keep in mind that Adobe Premiere Pro doesn't damage these clips. It just interprets them differently. The clips still have all the audio tracks; they're just ignored.

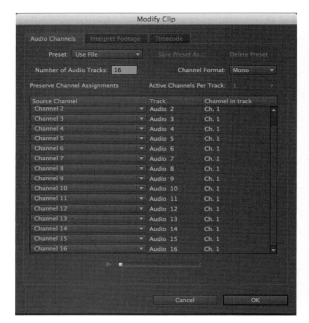

Figure 2.41 Imagine dealing with this on your Timeline and having to delete *multiple* unused audio tracks!

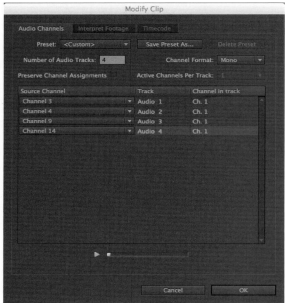

Figure 2.42 Taking a clip that has 16 channels and just displaying the four that are actually used means a greater level of ease for the editor.

Importing a "Generic" Project

Are there elements that you're likely to use in every project—perhaps key pieces of music, an animated intro, or your logo? Rather than importing these elements into every project, it's best to have a "generic" project that contains all of the small pieces that occur. You can then *import* your generic project into your project and instantly get all of those components.

And if you're really clever, you can import it to the project template mentioned earlier in the "Project Setup" section. Then the new project will be set up with the right bins, sequence type, and all of the common media that will help you jumpstart your projects!

Organization

Do you have a sequence named Sequence 1 in your project or a bin named Bin?

Unless you're working in a high-pressure environment where you don't have the time to name files, you're just asking for problems, especially in longer-form projects.

Some editors love the organization step. It gives them a chance to look at their clips, think organically about how they should be organized, and have the opportunity to really get to know the footage. Some editors hate it because it feels like drudgery (especially when the edit is work and not about passion).

But the best editors are great at organization. Editing isn't just about storytelling. It's about being familiar with the footage and being able to find the perfect shot as fast as possible.

If it seems like I'm recommending too much detail, keep in mind that the goal is simple: If you came back to a project after five years, could you figure out what was going on? If you had some life emergency and couldn't continue working on it, could someone else figure it out?

Being organized *now* means that if the client comes back a year from now and asks for a small change, you don't have to rebuild the project from scratch.

TIP

As with the OS (Mac or Windows), you can search for an element if you know part of its name. For whatever reason, the Search box at the top of the project window gets forgotten by editors.

Common Bins for Every Project

There are common bins that you'll need in nearly any sort of project (although they may be a little different for narrative film/TV). The following list of bins covers most needs. You don't have to use all of them, but you should examine the basis behind each to see if you might want to start implementing them:

▶ **Main Sequence(s).** Although this is somewhat obvious, you want to make it easy to find. Prepend the name with either 01 or ** to *force* it to be at the top of the list.

▶ **Old Sequences.** Twice a day, every day, duplicate the sequences you're working on—in the morning just as you start and in the afternoon when you come back from lunch. Add to the end of the sequence the date and terms morn or afternoon. Think of this strategy as a giant undo.

▶ **Outputs.** Every time you output for any reason, duplicate your sequence and rename it with the date, the client, watermark information (if needed), and, if possible, the type of compression (h.264 for iPad) used. If a client calls, you can bring up a sequence that mirrors the file they're looking at.

▶ **Raw Footage.** Mirror your camera cards bin by bin as you import. This way you'll know exactly *what* clip came from what card. If you end up looking for footage from a particular location or time, this will be an easy way to find it.

▶ **Selects.** When you're watching footage and you say, "I have to use this shot," put a copy in this bin. It's my go-to bin when I have a client in the room and need to replace something. I know it's full of good material.

▶ **VO/Narration.** I like to separate these elements from music. Optionally, you can create a bin called Audio for this bin to live in. It's possible to have two of these bins—one for temp and one for final.

▶ **Music.** By separating all your music into its own bin, it's organized and easy to find, but also gives you the ability to quickly adjust the gain lower so you don't blow out your speakers. Again, it's possible to have two of these bins—one for temp and one for final.

- **Interviews.** Place all of your interviews together. Optionally, break them down further by person.

- **Dual Sound.** If you work with dual sound, you'll want raw bins that contain the original import of camera clips plus audio along with a "Merged" bin.

- **Nests.** If you build nests (sequences inside of sequences), it's very useful to place these in their own bin.

- **Adobe Photoshop Files/Graphics.** Use this bin to find that graphic quickly.

- **Titles.** Why make titles hard to find? Go further and create a Lower Third bin and an Opening/Closing credits bin.

- **Adjustment Layers/Color Mattes/Transparent Video.** You don't want any of these elements sitting in a project at the top level. Some editors call this bin Synthetics.

- **Linked Adobe After Effects Compositions.** As with Adobe Photoshop files, if you need to open one of these compositions independently, it's painful to find a specific item but far easier when you keep them in their own set of bins.

- **Other Projects.** Use this bin if you find you're bringing in other projects (such as the generic project or other projects that you need material from).

Sequence Naming

To this day I still see outputs called Sequence 1. You waste time every time you have to rename Sequence 1.

For your main sequence, change it to the name of the project and add relevant details (Main vs. Promo vs. Trailer) to the name. The more you mirror the final name of the output you give your client, the less typing and retyping you'll have to do later.

Add the word *scratch* to any sequence you decide to "play with" or experiment with. Perhaps add a bin for your scratch projects.

CLOSE-UP

Common Bins Used in Television

Most of the common bins mentioned are used in documentary and corporate style productions. Here is a list of common bins used by editors who work in Episodic TV.

The numbered bins actually contain 2–15 or more bins and start with a number to keep them in order.

- Cut 1 bin contains the cut that ends up going to air.
- VFX & Titles bin contains the Visual Effects (VFX) and titles that are created.

1. **Cuts Main.** Cuts are seen, notes are given by each group—Directors, the Network and Show Runners. This is a series of bins that need to be created just to keep all of that straight!

2. **Scenes.** This bin has multiple bins, and each bin contains a sequence for each scene of the show. When all of the scenes are cut, the sequences are then assembled into the sequence that live in Cuts Main bin.

3. **Yet To Be Cut.** This bin contains a bin per scene that includes the footage for that scene that has yet to be cut. As sequences are cut, they are moved into the Scenes bins.

4. **Elements.** This bin contains bins for graphics, purchased stock footage, special effects, voice-overs, the main title, and existing stock footage.

5. **Music and SFX.** This bin contains bins of music and bins for elements like laugh tracks and Foley sound effects (SFX).

6. **Dailies.** For each scene, all the raw footage is placed in a bin per scene.

7. **Outputs.** Each sequence is duplicated and put in a bin of Outputs.

8. **Assist.** Each editor keeps a bin of favorite shots and materials for a possible gag reel.

Clip Naming

The old school of thought is to be specific when naming your clips. Add metadata where it helps to supplement your footage. If each shot is a take, it's best to either add that information to the name of the shot *or* add that information to the Description or Comment column.

Don't be afraid of changing the name of the clip because you fear it will in some way affect your ability to relink. Adobe Premiere Pro maintains a field called Media File Path, *even* if the clip is offline.

The newer school of thought is that because you're dealing with more footage than ever and it's file-based with strange names, you should use bins to organize your footage in a general way and visually find the clips you want.

Subclips

On long clips, it's very common to break them into smaller pieces using subclips. Some common uses of subclips include:

▶ Dividing interviews into just the interviewee's responses

▶ Separating different takes in an actor's performance

▶ Breaking continuous camera movements into individual elements

▶ Splitting long B-roll shots into smaller clips so it's easier to avoid using the same shot multiple times in a project

▶ Identifying best takes and then hiding the original clips in a bin labeled Do Not Use.

Making a subclip (**Figure 2.43**) is as simple as marking an In and Out point on a clip and choosing Clip > Make Subclip.

One footnote about subclips is that most of the time the default option of Restrict Trims To Subclip Boundaries is a great default choice. For example, if you break an interview into subclips, odds are you'll want to make the limit of that subclip "hard" to prevent trimming beyond the sound bite. Of course, there are times when you'll need to break this rule. By selecting the original subclip in the project window, you can choose Edit Subclip (**Figure 2.44**).

Figure 2.43 Don't just use the default name of Subclip001. Write out what the subclip shows!

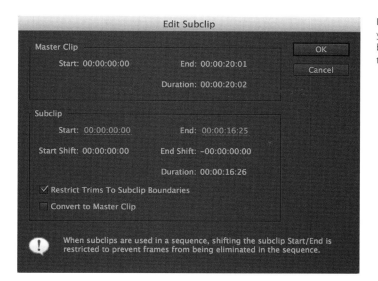

Figure 2.44 Most of the time when you need to adjust a subclip, it can be done by adjusting the end or start time to make it a little longer.

I'm all in favor of keeping those boundaries if you need to modify a clip. And if you need to shift the edges of the clip, just add a little bit at the start and end (instead of deselecting Restrict Trims To Subclip Boundaries).

Adjusting the Bin Views

So much time is spent in the bin view finding and viewing clips that I'm stunned that more editors don't use these keyboard commands:

▶ Shift + \ will switch between Thumbnail view and List view. Command+Page Up/Down (Ctrl+Page Up/Down) will also switch between the two.

▶ Shift + [and Shift +] will cycle between the smallest and largest sizes in both Thumbnail and List views. I like these keys because they sit next to the Page Up/Down keys.

▶ In Thumbnail view you can use JKL, the spacebar, and I/O to play and set marks on a clip (there's a great editorial technique about this in the "Using a Bin as a Source Monitor" section in Chapter 3).

▶ In List view, making clips larger means little unless you turn on thumbnails in the List view (via the Panel menu). Many clips will be black (or show a slate) because the thumbnail (poster frame) shows the first frame of the clip.

▶ You can set the poster frame in a few ways. In Thumbnail view, click a clip and use JKL to find the frame you want. Then press Command+P (Ctrl+P). Or load a clip into the Source Monitor, find a good frame, and use the same keyboard command. Or go to the Panel menu and choose Show Preview area. The Preview area has a button for the thumbnail. I like this method least because it takes up visual real estate at the top of the project.

Remember that the more you use the keyboard, the faster and easier it is to find and evaluate clips that you may want to use!

Maximizing List Views with Metadata

The more footage you have, the more important it will be for you to add information about the shots. If you have only 20 clips, you can pretty much keep all of them in your head. But if you have 100 clips (or more), you'll have to rely on other methods.

Adobe Premiere Pro has a ridiculous amount of metadata for your footage. For some List views you might want to see the duration of your clips; in other cases you might want to see a description or a comment if you thought the shot was good.

Customizing and saving a Metadata view

Let's customize and save a view. This is fairly straightforward.

1. While in a bin, go to the Panel menu and choose Metadata Display.

2. Roll open Premiere Pro Project Metadata (**Figure 2.45**). This metadata is saved with the project and is optimized for video needs. You could add other types of metadata (for example, EXIF information that is optimized for print), but they're optimized for other uses.

3. Click the Premiere Pro Project Metadata check box twice. The first time activates all the fields; the second time deactivates them to quickly choose the fields you want.

4. Add the Video In Point, Video Out Point, Video Duration, and Media Duration. This will quickly let you see all sorts of information about the length of shots.

5. Click the Save Settings button and give the view a descriptive name, like **In-Out+ Duration**.

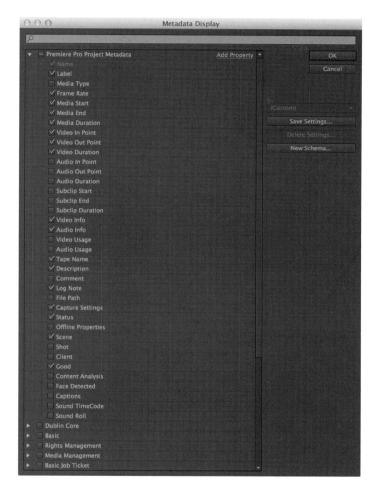

Figure 2.45 By giving you "too many" choices for metadata, Adobe makes it possible to keep pace with nearly everyone's needs.

Some Metadata views you should save

Hopefully you can see the benefit of having some prebuilt, saved Metadata Display settings.

One oversight is the lack of a keyboard command to quickly switch between different Metadata views. I map the Metadata display to Ctrl+Shift+I. Mnemonically, this is about Information, hence the letter I; many of the other variants of the "I" key are bound to In/Out points.

Here are several views that you should build:

▶ A view of the In-Out Duration mentioned previously

▶ A view that has everything that the Premiere Pro Project Metadata supports

▶ A view of Descriptors, which would contain the following fields: Label, Description, Comment, Scene, Good, Shot

▶ An Offline view. Add the fields Status and Offline Properties. The Offline Properties will show you specifically what parts of a clip are offline—video and/or audio.

Suite Relations

Adobe has created powerful interoperability between the different applications in Adobe Creative Cloud. Although there are numerous references to where and how the other applications work throughout this book (and in other books), I really didn't see any real reference for what files are created where or how to configure the cache files. Therefore, I felt it would be valuable to offer you some best practices.

Common Threads Among All Apps

There are some commonalities for utilizing any of the other tools in Adobe Creative Cloud. They involve file naming, media, and caches.

File naming

It's crucial to give descriptive names to any and every file that you create. This is probably the greatest secret to maintaining your sanity, whether you're the sole person working on a project or you end up handing off portions to other specialists. Providing meaningful names goes for clip and bin names as well, but also for Adobe After Effects projects, Adobe Photoshop files, and so on.

Media (in general)

I cannot stress enough the corralling and controlling of every element and asset that you'll handle prior to using Adobe Premiere Pro (or other Adobe tools).

As mentioned earlier a Common Media folder can help you keep everything organized.

Caches

As mentioned at the beginning of this chapter, Adobe uses a series of common Media Caches. There are two directories: Media Cache (which is the database) and Media Cache files (which are the individual files). These two folders contain *conforming caches* along with the database that optimizes playback of some codecs. What makes them common is that these caches are shared by a number of applications the Creative Cloud suite.

What's important is that you configure all the applications to point to the same Common Media Cache folder. And because cache files increase quickly and (by default) are stored on your system drive, I suggest moving them to a fast, nonsystem drive.

Be sure to use the convention of _Adobe Caches at the root of a fast drive to set all caches.

Adobe Prelude

The primary function of Adobe Prelude is to copy file-based media and optionally back up and/or transcode. It has additional capabilities to mark footage and build simple sequences. I consider the copying and backing up of media vital to the health and sanity of all my projects.

Project

An Adobe Prelude project will be created, so I recommend placing it in the project's Common Media 03_Project Files folder. Adobe Prelude Project files use the extension of PLPROJ (PreLude PROJect).

Project cache

Found in the General category of the Preferences is an Adobe Prelude Project cache. The Project cache speeds up the opening of an Adobe Prelude project. You can realistically leave this setting alone (even though the default is to place these files on your internal hard drive).

You may want to experiment with turning it off entirely. If you're working on smaller projects or not going to return to a past Prelude project, you might consider turning this setting off.

Common Media Cache folder

Point the Media Cache Location and the Media Cache folder Location (**Figure 2.46**) to the _Adobe Caches folder.

Figure 2.46 The Media Cache preferences in Adobe Prelude.

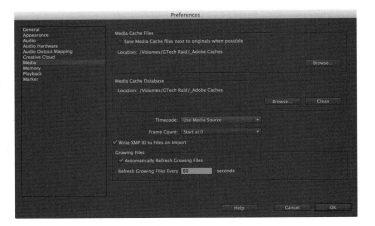

Media

Media will be created based on the destinations chosen in the Ingest panel. The default is a folder based on the current date and time, and should be targeted to your Common Media folder 01_Original footage folder (**Figure 2.47**).

These copies will not be a "set" format for media (such as QuickTime or AVI). Rather, copied media matches the original media format type. QuickTime files will remain QuickTime files. Video in a card format and MXF container will be copied into a folder structure that mirrors the original media.

Transcoded media may be in *any* format that you choose to transcode to.

It's best to leave the transfer settings in the Ingest dialog at the default, adding date and time information.

Additionally, the default of verification is crucial to make sure media is copied correctly.

To send the links of the media to Adobe Premiere Pro, right-click on the clips/bins and choose Send to Premiere Pro.

Figure 2.47 The Ingest dialog in Adobe Prelude allows you to target more than one destination. Here, the footage will be copied twice, once to the Common Media 01_Original footage folder and a second time to another drive as a backup.

Adobe After Effects

It's likely that you already use Adobe After Effects. Its primary function is to build motion graphic animations and composite multiple images. Of course, I do it a disservice to describe it as simply as this.

After Effects utilizes Dynamic Linking—a process where you can replace footage on the Adobe Premiere Pro Timeline with a composition built in After Effects. When you make changes in After Effects, the Adobe Premiere Pro Timeline gets updated.

Just like Adobe Premiere Pro can have a project that can contain multiple sequences, Adobe After Effects can have a project that can contain multiple compositions.

Project

A project will be created each time you use any of the three Dynamic Link features:

▶ Selecting Timeline clips and choosing to replace them with an After Effects composition

▶ Creating a new After Effects composition

▶ Importing an After Effects composition

The projects should be placed in the 03_Project Files in the Common Media folder. Projects will be saved with an extension of AEP (After Effects Project).

I'd strongly suggest duplicating your sequence *prior* to sending materials to Adobe After Effects. You can think of it as a powerful undo. If you really want flexibility, copy the footage to a higher track and send *that* to Adobe After Effects. This will put the Linked Adobe After Effects composition *above* the clips that were used!

Composition naming

When you send over footage from Adobe Premiere Pro to Adobe After Effects, it gets replaced by a composition with the following naming protocol: *Adobe Premiere Pro Project name + Linked Comp #/ Adobe After Effects project name*.aep.

Remember that Adobe Premiere Pro knows where the Adobe After Effects project is *and* which comp you used. It's a good idea to rename this file now in the project and drag it from the project window to the Timeline, destroying the file that was initially sent but now has a better name than "Construction doc Comp 02/ AE project.aep" in your project window and on your Timeline.

Disk Cache

The Disk Cache (**Figure 2.48**) is unique to Adobe After Effects. Each layer in an Adobe After Effects composition is cached individually. Later, when rendering or being referenced by Adobe Premiere Pro, these caches speed up the dynamic display and playback.

The Disk cache is *persistent*. It survives quitting. It will empty oldest elements first.

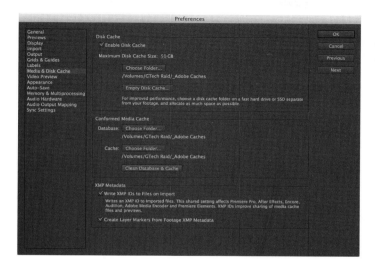

Figure 2.48 Adobe After Effects can utilize the same conforming cache that Adobe Premiere Pro uses, but it also has its own unique Disk Cache.

This must be done on a regular basis. Remember that as with all caches, they're merely time-savers. If you accidentally delete an important cache, it will rebuild itself.

Additionally, it's crucial that you move this specific cache to your fastest drive. Although I advocate moving all of your caches to fast drives, this is the most important application to perform this behavior in the suite.

Because it caches each layer individually (**Figure 2.49**), fast access is crucial. These caches do build up quickly, so having saving them in their default location could easily grow out of control. Fortunately, Adobe After Effects has a default limit of 50 GB.

Figure 2.49 Although Adobe After Effects has a RAM cache for layers (in green), it also has a persistent disk cache in blue. To see this on your system, hold down the Command (Ctrl) key and turn on Show Cache indicators in the Timeline panel menu. Displaying these indicators *does* impact performance.

If you point the Adobe After Effects Disk Cache to the same folder as the rest of your caches, Adobe After Effects will automatically create a folder called "Adobe" and a folder called "After Effects" for you.

Common Media Cache folder (Conformed Media Cache)

Adobe After Effects calls the Common Media Caches folder the Conformed Media Cache.

Point the Media Cache files and the Media Cache folder to the _Adobe Cache folder.

Imported media

Any non–Adobe Premiere Pro media that you import to Adobe After Effects *should* be copied to the project Common Media folder prior to importing. As a result, you'll ensure that media unique to Adobe After Effects is handled with the rest of your project.

Consider rendering for performance

A great performance technique to guarantee real-time playback is to render out of After Effects in a postproduction codec (Avid DNxHD, Apple ProRes, or the Animation codec) and *manually* bring that into Adobe Premiere Pro's Timeline (**Figure 2.50**), putting it above the sources and linked After Effects composition.

Figure 2.50 Here in Adobe Premiere Pro, tracks V1–3 are the sources that were sent to V4's linked After Effects project. The composition was rendered there, imported back into Adobe Premiere Pro, and placed on V5.

A render like this should be labeled with the *same name* as the composition along with the word "Render." This Quick-Time movie file should be then laid above the After Effects composition it represents on the Timeline.

If you dedicate a track for these renders, it's possible to generate the highest quality output by *toggling* the track off prior to output. By doing so, all those render files from Adobe After Effects will be ignored, forcing Adobe Premiere Pro to dynamically link and re-render at the final codec/resolution.

Adobe Media Encoder

Adobe Media Encoder is the engine for all compression throughout the Adobe Creative Cloud suite.

Common Media Cache folder

Point the Media Cache files Location and the Media Cache folder Location to the same _Adobe Cache file as the rest of the suite (**Figure 2.51**).

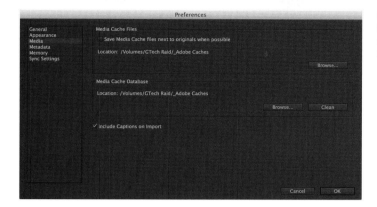

Figure 2.51 If all the Adobe products are targeted to the same cache files, once a clip is seen by one application it won't need to be cached again.

Outputs/media

Adobe Media Encoder is the major method of output from Adobe Premiere Pro. Two best practices come to mind:

▶ **Choosing a naming convention.** This is vital to knowing what the file does and who it is for.

In Chapter 7 I cover duplication of sequences and re-naming directly for the purpose of output, meaning the filename automatically has the correct name.

▶ **Targeting your Common Media 08_Exported files folder.** Whether it's QuickTime, OP1 MXF, MP4, or Flash files, targeting the outputs to the Common Media folder means easy location.

Adobe Photoshop

Adobe Photoshop serves a number of uses for the video editor: It's a powerful title tool or a tool for the sizing, fixing, and repairing of still images.

A lesser-known capability of Photoshop is its ability to load individual video clips. This provides the benefit of being able to draw directly on frames or use filters that are Photoshop specific and not available to the rest of the tools.

TIP

When using Photoshop as a tool to work directly on video, make sure you set the layout of your windows that includes a Timeline. Choose Windows > Workspace > Motion.

Performance cache

In Photoshop's Preferences is a category called Performance (**Figure 2.52**), which is essentially a disk cache. Target the Scratch Disks to your fastest media drives.

If your fastest external drive is USB 2 or FireWire, the internal drive is a better choice.

Figure 2.52 Photoshop's cache files are invisible.

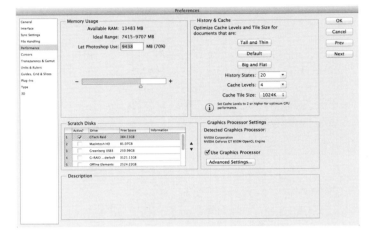

Documents

Photoshop documents have the extension of PSD (PhotoShop Document). PSD files can be used directly in Adobe Premiere Pro. The biggest common mistake that editors tend to make is to have the document in a CMYK color space.

To change the color space to RGB, choose the Image > Mode > RGB Color.

Document setup

Documents can be started in Adobe Premiere Pro via the File menu. Choose File > New > Photoshop File to access a dialog where you can specify the dimensions of the Photoshop file. The dimensions default to the active sequence. I recommend placing the file created into the Common Media 04_Graphic Sources folder.

The import of Adobe Photoshop documents are preset to be a merged file (**Figure 2.53**). Some people who choose to use Photoshop as a titler will create multiple titles in a single file, each on its own separate layer. If this describes your workflow, you'll have to import documents manually instead.

Best practices

When you're creating documents in Photoshop for import, use the prebuilt presets for Film & Video. You'll likely want to use either HDTV 1080p for 1920 x 1080 or HDV/HDTV 720p for 1280 x 720 projects (**Figure 2.54**).

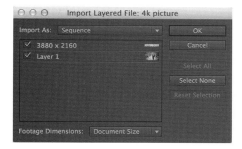

Figure 2.53 When importing a layered Photoshop file into Adobe Premiere Pro, you'll likely want to switch the default (merged) option to a sequence.

Figure 2.54 Photoshop lets you create a file with any dimensions you like. There are presets for Film & Video, which are especially valuable for titles.

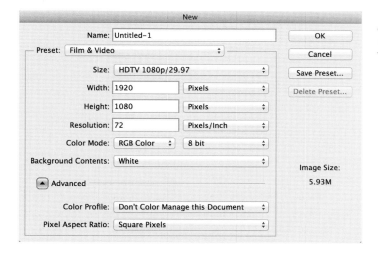

There are times where nonstandard HD sizes are warranted, such as if you intend to pan and scan around an image or construct a title that's larger than the format you're working in.

In an ideal environment, with unlimited time, every photograph that will get loaded into Adobe Premiere Pro will travel to Photoshop for cleanup activities that can (and should) be automated, like applying Auto Tone. Advanced users may want to consider taking multiple steps and making them a Photoshop action to permit automation.

TIP

Adobe Bridge has an amazing ability to batch process a series of elements, such as a folder full of scanned pictures. Select the pictures in Adobe Bridge, and then choose Tools > Photoshop > Image Processor to access a dialog that permits the automated processing of images. Run an action (such as Auto Tone), convert formats from JPEG to TIFF, or perform a resize on a batch of images.

When documents are imported into Adobe Premiere Pro (which should be placed in the project's Common Media folder prior to importing), a dialog offers a choice between four ways of handling layered documents:

- **Merge All Layers.** Results in a single file where all the layers have been merged into a single flattened file.
- **Merged Layers.** Identical to Merge All Layers except it's possible to choose which layers will (or won't) be merged.
- **Individual Layers.** A bin is created and each layer is imported (via a dialog) as individual elements.
- **Sequence.** Identical to Individual Layers except that a sequence is created.

For 95 percent of cases I'd probably recommend the last choice, Sequence. Because each layer is imported, any individual layer can be used and animated. If necessary, using the sequence as a source item (a nest) will permit all of the layers to be treated as a single object.

Adobe Audition

Adobe Audition is a powerful audio mixing environment that focuses on sound design. Two interactions occur with Adobe Premiere Pro: sending individual clips, usually used for audio repair, and sending entire sequences, usually used as a full audio mixing environment.

Disk Cache

Disk Cache is slightly different from other applications' cache adjustments. Although you should reconfigure the Primary Temp cache (**Figure 2.55**) to the _Adobe Cache folder, you need to nest the Primary Temp Disk Cache in its own unique folder. I suggest calling it **Adobe Audition Cache**.

The Secondary Temp location can be left blank. It exists in case your Primary Temp location becomes full.

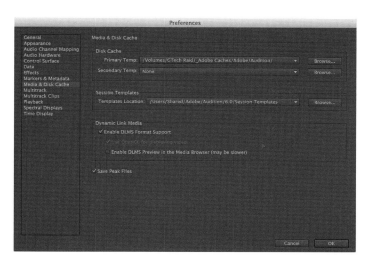

Figure 2.55 Adobe Audition's cache files are likely to be audio-only, small temp files.

Clip

You send a single clip over to Adobe Audition to adjust that one clip by following these steps.

1. Right-click on the clip and choose Edit Clip in Adobe Audition. Or choose Edit > Edit in Adobe Audition > Clip.

   Adobe Audition opens and your clip is loaded, ready for you to make changes.

2. Click Save and the clip is updated in Adobe Premiere Pro.

Now comes the messy part. In the project, in the same bin as the original footage, a new WAV clip appears with the original clip's name plus extracted audio.

The audio portion of a clip is replaced in Adobe Premiere Pro by this extracted audio and linked to the video if there was any. This is easy enough to fix: Just add a bin of extracted audio (if you want, you may want to leave it there, next to the clip it came from).

More worrisome is that the WAV file was created where the project is on your computer. If you move it, you'll have to relink it. And yes, I think you should move it into a different folder in the Common Media folder.

Entire sequences

Another way to work is to use Audition as a full-featured Digital Audio Workstation (DAW).

To send the sequence over to Adobe Audition, follow these steps.

1. Activate the Timeline window.

2. Choose Edit > Edit in Adobe Audition > Sequence.

   The dialog in **Figure 2.56** appears.

Figure 2.56 In addition to the defaults, you'll likely want to select Export Preview Video to watch while you work in Audition.

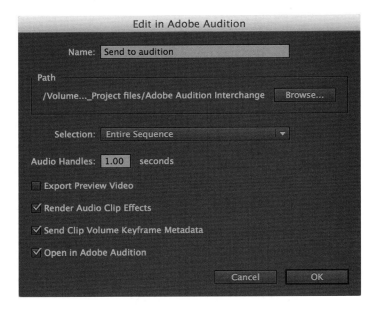

Adobe Premiere Pro wants to (by default) place the Audition project where your Adobe Premiere Pro project is located (03_Project Files in the Common Media folder) in a folder called Adobe Audition Interchange. Within that folder will be the XML that Audition needs to re-create your sequence, a copy of all the audio from every track plus the handle length (default of one second), and a small mixed-down video in standard definition to act as a visual reference while working in Audition.

Back to Adobe Premiere Pro

When you send the material back to Adobe Premiere Pro, you won't get every clip on every track. Classically in DAWs, you create a stereo "bounce" that you export and then import back in your video editor of choice. You can do this in Audition, but there's a better way to work. Choose Multi-track > Export to Adobe Premiere Pro. A dialog that looks like **Figure 2.57** appears.

Put the project (the new XML file) in the Common Media 03_Project Files folder. Make sure you add the words "Final Mix Return" to indicate that this XML file is coming *back* from Audition.

TIP

Before you send anything back to Adobe Premiere Pro, make sure you duplicate the original sequence you sent over, open it, and add the name "audio mix." When Audition sends the audio back, it'll want to create tracks in your sequence. Having a separate sequence means you can look at your work before and after it went to Audition.

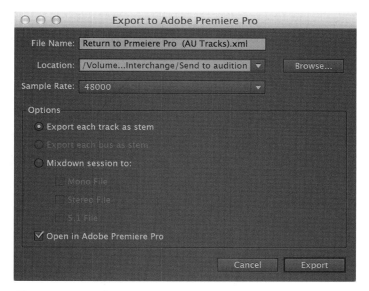

Figure 2.57 By exporting each track as a stem, you'll have some ability to adjust the mix if necessary back in Adobe Premiere Pro.

There are two choices for the actual audio:

▶ **A mixdown of the final format.** This is likely to be a Stereo or 5.1 file.

▶ **Export each track as a stem.** You'll get one "stem" per track, which allows you the option of a last-second adjustment in Adobe Premiere Pro before final output.

Typically, when a project comes back from Audition (or any other DAW), the original tracks are muted and you listen to the final mix instead.

Adobe SpeedGrade

Adobe SpeedGrade is the dedicated color correction environment that exists beyond the color correction filters in Adobe Premiere Pro.

Choosing to include it in your workflow creates very few extra files (compared to the other tools in Adobe Creative Cloud). Adobe SpeedGrade just ends up feeling like a very special "effect" that's external to Adobe Premiere Pro.

LUTs and Looks

Some projects use custom look-up tables (LUTs) to help visually represent the media from the camera. These files will have the extensions of either .ilut or .cube (depending on if they're a one-dimensional LUT or a three-dimensional LUT). If these are created outside of Adobe Speed-Grade, it's best to add them to a dedicated folder in the project Common Media folder.

Lumetri Looks are automatically added as effects on the return trip from SpeedGrade to every clip. If you create any additional Look preset files (.look), they should also be added to a dedicated folder in the project Common Media folder.

Media Setup Summary

Table 2.2 (facing page) provides a summary of what should be created and where for your system setup.

Speech and Script Technologies

Adobe Premiere Pro has a speech recognition engine (in Adobe Media Encoder) that produces adequate results with a clean professional speaker. But even 98 percent recognition means that every minute you'll have something that you need to adjust.

On the other hand, when paired with a transcript or script, via Adobe Story, Adobe Premiere Pro has a whole new capability—the technique of editing directly from text.

Adobe Story (**Figure 2.58**) is really two applications in one.

TABLE 2.2 System Setup

Type	Location
Caches	Target caches to _Adobe Caches on the root of a fast drive. Two folders—Media Caches (database files) and Media Cache files (cache files)—will automatically be created. Delete (and force rebuilding) on a regular basis.
Previews	Target to _Adobe Previews. A folder will be created per project. Delete when finished with the project.
Project file	Placed in 03_Project Files in the Common Media folder.
Backup project files	Manually performed twice a day to a Cloud-based backup.
Camera media	Placed in the Common Media 01_Original Footage folder. Make sure you have a working backup on an external device, such as another hard drive, or better yet an LTO tape.

Figure 2.58 Adobe Story's interface. On the left side are projects; in the center are scripts.

If you're working on narrative fiction or AV scripts, you'll benefit from the fast, efficient writing and editing tools. No regular word processor can compete for speed and flow when it comes to script writing with Story.

As you move into preproduction and production, you'll find that Story offers a range of project management tools, including the creation of production reports based on your script, schedules that can be updated as your script changes, and the ability to generate useful production documents like call sheets or shooting scripts. If you haven't taken the time to explore Adobe Story, I encourage you to do so. You have access to the Plus version as part of Adobe Creative Cloud.

Fast Scriptwriting

Plenty of books and training courses are available on how to write a script well (good luck with that!).

There are also excellent training courses on how to use the advanced features available in Adobe Story. More as encouragement to explore than as a set of full instructions, here are some of the valuable script-writing features in Adobe Story:

▶ Story is cloud-based and provides flexible collaboration tools (**Figure 2.59**). Share your creative work with anyone (whether or not they have a paid subscription to Creative Cloud). You can share individual documents or whole projects (click the Share button).

▶ The Project view (**Figure 2.60**) provides a home for multiple document types, not just scripts. This makes a shared project a great place to store key documents and information associated with a creative project.

▶ Script writing can be tedious, in part because layout and text formatting (**Figure 2.61**) must generally match carefully prescribed standards. Story knows what each type of text is (Character name, Scene Heading, Dialogue, etc.) and automates the writing process. When you press Enter to move to the next line, Story presumes you'll want a different type of text.

Figure 2.59 Adobe Story offers powerful collaboration roles.

Figure 2.60
The Project view helps keep everything organized with all sorts of useful preproduction documentation.

Figure 2.61
By supporting the standard industry formatting, scripts from Adobe Story look professional.

▶ Once Adobe Story knows what each part of your script is, production reports and schedules can be automatically generated. Just click the Create button in the Project view (**Figure 2.62**).

Figure 2.62 Call sheets, projects schedules, and more are a click away.

These features and more make Story an excellent starting place for production. If you're working on reality/actuality television—an unscripted format—you may not get as much out of the application as a fiction/narrative filmmaker.

But one feature stands out, especially for interviews: support for the speech to text workflow in Adobe Premiere Pro.

Speech to Text

As you should already know, Adobe Premiere Pro can analyze clip audio and convert dialogue into typed words displayed in the Metadata panel. Simply right-click on a clip in the Project panel, choose Analyze, select some straightforward options, and the Adobe Media Encoder will perform the analysis.

Once the analysis is complete, you can select words in the Metadata panel and the clip playhead will jump to that moment in time. You can then edit based on the text rather than having to listen to the words—amazing!

The problem is that the analysis is often wrong, and quite a few words won't match the original dialogue. It's impossible for the system to recognize every word perfectly, so it makes a best guess (in fact, every word it identifies is the product of different levels of probability).

So how can you improve the results? Use Adobe Story.

If you have interviews professionally transcribed (which costs far less than it used to), you can then use that transcription text as a reference for the speech to text analysis. The result will be a perfect word for word, exactly as spoken, with no errors (at least as long as the transcription is accurate).

This material is available for download. Please see "A note about downloadable content" in the Introduction of this book.

PROJECTS AUTHORING

Figure 2.63 Each project can have multiple scripts.

Setting up in Adobe Story

To understand the Story workflow, download the Maxim_Intro.mov clip and the Maxim_Intro.stdoc script file, and then follow these steps.

We'll use the integrated Adobe Story panel right inside Adobe Premiere Pro. There are other ways to do this, so consider taking the time to research the options before you decide which workflow is best for you.

1. To access Adobe Story, go to story.adobe.com (not www.adobe.com). Log in using your Adobe ID, and click the Projects button (**Figure 2.63**) at the top of the screen.

2. Choose Projects > New Project, give the new project a name, and click Create.

3. Click Import, browse to the file Maxim_Intro.stdoc and click Open. Although Story is cloud-based, you can save documents to your desktop like any other application and import or export final draft files among others.

4. Switch over to Adobe Premiere Pro. Create a new project and import the file Maxim_Intro.mov. The file is included as a ZIP file because the text that is added during this workflow is stored in the media file, not the Adobe Premiere Pro project. If you want to try the workflow again, unzip another copy of the file.

5. Choose Window > Adobe Story. Log in using your Adobe ID, and you should find the Maxim_Intro script waiting for you. Double-click on it to open it.

This is a very simple script with just one piece of dialogue. If you've recorded an interview and you want to include the questions as well as the answers, be sure to put the speaker's name in where appropriate.

Here's the wonderful shortcut: To the left of the Adobe Story panel is a scene navigator. Actually, there's only one scene in this script (**Figure 2.64**) so it's a list with just one item.

Figure 2.64 Each scene automatically appears in the navigation list.

Scene No	Scene	Duration
1	EXT. VILLA – DAY	00:00:30

Drag that scene listing from the Adobe Story panel onto the Maxim_Intro.mov clip (in Icon view) in the Project panel.

When you do so, very little will appear to happen, but if you look in the Metadata panel, you'll notice that the Speech Analysis heading now mentions an Embedded Adobe Story Script. You have just associated the dialogue from that scene with the clip in the bin using a simple drag-and-drop workflow. How amazing is that!?

All that remains is to click the Analyze button (**Figure 2.65**) at the bottom of the Metadata panel and click OK.

In the Analyze content dialog, you should not need to change any of the settings unless you're working in a language other than US English. If there are multiple speakers, consider selecting the Identify Speakers option. Adobe Premiere Pro will show the speaker names as they appear in the script.

Figure 2.65 Always set this speech analysis to high quality.

Using the Metadata panel to edit

Story's simple workflow might just save you hours of preparation time in post. Once the analysis is complete, the words are highlighted as they are spoken in the Metadata panel, making it easy to locate content. This works in reverse too: Click on a word and the playhead moves to it.

You can even use the Quick Search box at the top of the Metadata panel to locate words. Now that paper edit is more useful than ever. In fact, you could even copy and paste words from the typed transcription into the Quick Search box to locate them.

But best of all, at the bottom of the Metadata panel (**Figure 2.66**) you have the ability to play, mark, and insert/overwrite into the sequence via the buttons or keys.

Figure 2.66 The ability to mark and cut directly from the Metadata panel is a setup process that makes editing significantly easier.

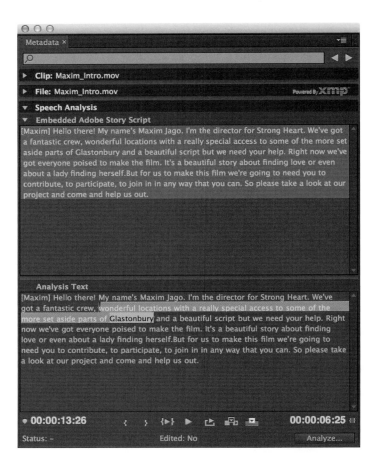

3

Editing Techniques

Author: Christine Steele, with Maxim Jago

You have the courage of your convictions. When you're editing you have to make thousands of decisions every day and if you dither over them all the time, you'll never get anything done.

—Anne V. Coates

Editing Techniques

Crafting a compelling story from images is a process that demands more than just perseverance. Deft hand-and-eye coordination helps, but making art from a folder full of camera files requires learning and continually practicing essential editing skills.

Studio professionals need to perform editing functions in the Timeline as fast as they can think about the changes they want to make. In this chapter you'll learn some tricks-of-the-trade that can help you achieve professional-level speed. Adobe Premiere Pro is designed for the quick and easy joining of visual and audio elements, and it allows you to reorder and refine story ideas—in real time—if you know how to use important editing features and understand when and how to apply specific tools.

Maybe you're already familiar with drag-and-drop editing, and can perform insert and overwrite edits. If so, great! It never hurts to review the basics, so I'll start by covering common methods for assembling a cut. Arranging windows, customizing the Timeline, and incorporating keyboard shortcuts makes working in a sequence easier and more enjoyable, but it's trimming that makes a story flow. Choosing the trimming technique that best fits your needs in the moment is the most important step toward increasing speed and precision.

This chapter focuses on practical steps to improve your overall performance while editing in Adobe Premiere Pro, and it shines light on some familiar tools that often don't get nearly enough use. I'll share a few tips that make editing any sequence more fun. Sometimes the most advanced editing tools seem simple to use once practiced in context, so I'll guide you through some steps to enhance your overall skill set. Finally, you'll move into more refined methods of finessing a cut, using Trim tool shortcuts, and using real-time playback.

An experienced artist is always learning and layering new ideas on top of standard practices. To turn creative insights into tangible forms of expression, editors must keep their primary skills sharp while making adjustments to their editing style when new tools arrive to improve workflow. Dede Allen once said, "Intellect and taste count, but I cut with my feelings." The goal of this chapter is to get you to a skill level that allows you to cut from your feelings without having to think too much about which tool to use or how to use it. Let's get started by implementing basic editing protocol, and then ramp up to professional practices. Patience will turn the use of a few new techniques into habits, and the result will be fast cutting with minimal hassle.

This chapter's project files are available for download. Please see "A note about downloadable content" in the Introduction of this book.

Editing Essentials

You're reading a *Studio Techniques* book, so you probably know how to edit clips into a Timeline. Even if you understand the basics, there are practical methods you can incorporate into your everyday work to improve efficiency and speed while editing. I meet quite a few people who work in professional studios, and many are not making the most of their editing tools. It's easy to get stuck in old patterns, so shake things up and make some new habits!

Workspace Setup

Before you begin editing, familiarize yourself with some of the Workspace presets located on the Window menu. Start with an Adobe Premiere Pro Workspace preset, customize panel groupings, and then save these window arrangements to suit your changing needs throughout the editing process.

Workspace layout presets

For general creative editing, I start by choosing the Editing (CS5.5) Workspace from the Window menu, and then further customize it to fit my own style. The reason I begin with this layout is that it fits my preference regarding the arrangement of the Project and Media Browser panels when I begin a project. When I open this workspace, these two important panels are instantly separated into different tab pane groupings, one on top of the other. I like the Project panel to stay in the upper left, and I want the Media Browser to remain beneath the Project panel.

I dock open bin tabs next to the Project tab, directly above the Media Browser, so I can view and hoverscrub through footage in the Media Browser, and then quickly drag folders and clips directly into my project bins. Once I begin editing in a sequence, I drag the panel boundaries to make the Project and Media Browser panels narrow and maximize the Timeline, Source, and Program panels.

I further customize my workspace by placing the Audio Meter directly underneath my Timeline, so it occupies only a thin horizontal space but is easily visible while I'm playing a sequence. I drag my toolbar to the upper-left corner or delete it altogether in favor of using keyboard shortcuts (**Figure 3.1**).

I recommend trying some of the Adobe Premiere Pro preset workspace arrangements, just to discover panels, features, and layouts that you might not otherwise stumble upon. Choose Window > Workspace, and quickly try these useful layouts:

▶ **Add Metadata and Sync Scripts.** Open the Metalogging Workspace. Whether you're editing a scripted feature, a TV show, or a documentary with transcribed interviews, the Metadata panel is great for syncing scripts to clips. I use this workspace to quickly add descriptions, notes, and scene information to large batches of clips. It's invaluable for documentary work. When combined with script syncing, the Metadata panel helps me locate the exact lines of dialogue I need while editing.

▶ **Apply Effects.** Choosing the Effects Workspace instantly places the Effects panel just to the left of the Effects Control panel, making it easier to add and tweak effects.

Figure 3.1 Example of a single-monitor workspace layout modified from the standard Editing (CS5.5) Workspace. The transport controls and Info panel are closed, the preview area is visible, and tools and meters are relocated to maximize Timeline width.

▶ **Mix Audio.** Open the Audio Workspace, and both the Clip and Track Mixers are ready to use, allowing you to quickly adjust the mix for individual clips or for an entire audio track.

▶ **Color for Broadcast.** The Color Correction Workspace will open a Reference Monitor loaded with video scopes.

Once you're familiar with workspace panel options and layouts, you can access the Window menu, open individual panels that meet your needs, and drag to dock them into appropriate panel groupings.

Customizing and docking panel tabs

Use panel fly-out menus to customize additional, panel-specific features. For example, you can turn on the Preview Area and Thumbnails from the fly-out menu located in the upper-right corner of the Project panel (**Figure 3.2**). The preview area now appears at the top of the Project

Figure 3.2 Use the fly-out/panel menus located at the top right of each panel to activate additional context-specific features.

panel, so you can view clip icons and properties at a glance. Thumbnails appear next to the clip names when the Project panel is set to List view. Use the Source and Program fly-out menus to hide or reveal transport control buttons, markers, and safe margin overlays.

Making decisions about which panels to close or dock with other panels means experimenting to find out what works best for you. I Option-double-click (Alt-double-click) on bins of video footage to dock them right next to the Project panel, and then set the bins to display in Icon view. I prefer the Project panel to display in List view. This setup allows me to quickly switch between the Project tab and the Bin tabs, so I can browse the same group of clips in List view with metadata in the Project tab, and then quickly switch views by clicking the bin tab, where I can visually scrub shots and mark the clips. This is especially useful when working with bins filled with lots of visual imagery, like B-roll footage.

I don't need redundant information provided by both the Info panel and the preview area, so I close the Info panel. You might prefer to close the preview area to save space, in which case the Info panel is useful.

I dock the Marker and History panels in the lower-right pane group next to the Media Browser, because I often use these panels to view marker information and to undo edit steps while I'm working in the Timeline.

From the Source and Program panel fly-out menus, I often choose to close the transport controls, because I rely heavily on keyboard shortcuts.

These choices are mainly a matter of personal editing style, but you might find that your preferences change as a project progresses and new, job-specific panel groupings become helpful.

Saving Workspace presets

The Workspace menu allows you to save and retrieve New Workspace Presets, which are automatically assigned unique keyboard shortcuts.

I often work with two monitors, so I dock most of my bins in Icon view on the left monitor, and then set up my Source, Program, and Timeline panels on the right monitor. Take the time to customize your editing interface the way you like it, and then name and save a preset for your workspace.

I save different Workspace presets for both my laptop and desktop edit sessions, and for single and dual monitor setups. I also save presets for creative story editing, audio, and finishing work. I'll occasionally bounce over to the standard Adobe Premiere Pro Workspace presets to quickly access a needed panel, and then press a keyboard shortcut to return to my favorite arrangement. The workspace you choose is all about personal style and project-specific editing needs (**Figure 3.3**).

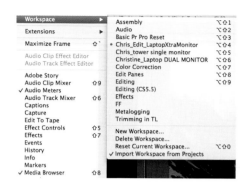

Figure 3.3 Choose Workspace from the Window menu to reset, delete, or create a new workspace. Note that keyboard shortcuts are assigned to your saved, custom workspaces.

Focus on the Timeline

There are specific Timeline options that every editor should know how to customize. Take the time to familiarize yourself with often needed display settings, and master the features that will allow you to easily navigate the Timeline. When you're down to the wire and need to deliver a cut, you won't be hunting around for track displays and cursing the mouse.

The following sections describe a few helpful options that I can't work without.

Scrolling and zooming in the Timeline

No editor or assistant can work efficiently in the Timeline without these shortcuts:

- ▶ **Zoom in and out at the Timeline playhead location.** Select the Timeline and press the keyboard shortcuts for zoom in (+) and zoom out (-).

- ▶ **Scale the sequence to fit all clips within the Timeline length.** Press the backslash (\) key.

- ▶ **Scroll tracks.** If you use a scroll wheel, placing the mouse pointer over the center of the Timeline video or audio tracks allows you to vertically or horizontally scroll tracks. Set this option in the General category of the Preferences panel. When editing with many layers of video or audio tracks, vertical scrolling is necessary.

▶ **Snap to playhead.** While you have the General tab open in the Preferences panel, select the check box next to Snap Playhead in Timeline when Snap is Enabled. This allows clip edges to snap to the playhead when you're dragging to move shots around in the Timeline, or snap the playhead to a cut point while viewing visual guides that indicate the playhead and cut point are lined up.

▶ **Scroll to expand or minimize Timeline track height.** Place the mouse pointer over the empty gray area just to the right of the track targets, and then use the scroll wheel to increase or decrease the size of individual tracks. Hold down the Shift key to increase or decrease all track heights while scrolling.

▶ **Expand or minimize all Timeline tracks.** Press Shift++ and Shift+- to expand or minimize all audio and video tracks at once.

Timeline display settings

While editing, there will be times when you want to quickly expand specific Timeline tracks, view audio waveforms, and access video and audio keyframes too. I find that setting up display preferences is especially important before refining the cut or adjusting audio levels. Timeline preferences can be set and saved for different tasks, so you can quickly switch to a new Timeline display when your edit needs change.

Consider customizing your Timeline display settings as soon as you begin a project. While training a new assistant editor, I noticed he was struggling while editing in the Timeline. He was thrilled when I showed him the Timeline Display Settings button, which I call "the little wrench" (**Figure 3.4**), because he was able to customize his displays to make his work a lot easier. Little things can make a big difference when you're performing repetitive tasks. Here are few settings you can configure to make working with the Timeline more enjoyable:

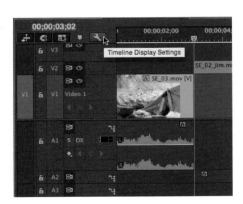

Figure 3.4 Turn on visual aids, such as audio waveforms, video thumbnails, and markers using the Timeline Display Settings button.

▶ Name and save a couple of your preferred track height displays—the ones you use most often.

▶ Configure video and audio track headers to serve your project needs.

▶ Activate visual aids, such as through-edit marks. Through-edit marks are new to the Adobe Premiere Pro CC release. Now when you razor blade a clip, a through-edit mark shows you that those two sections were once one clip.

▶ Toggle audio waveform and keyframe displays on and off.

One of the most helpful Timeline Display Settings button options is the ability to create and save custom presets for my track heights. When editing a dialogue scene, for example, I rely heavily on expanding the video thumbnails in V1 and the audio waveforms in tracks A1 and A2, so I can zoom in and fine-tune the audio that is typically linked to the primary video clips. This track viewing preference allows me to recognize which actor is speaking at a glance and visually identify exactly where the dialogue is located in the Timeline.

To set this up, I use the scroll wheel to expand the height of Tracks V1, A1, and A2 so they're large enough for me to see thumbnail images and waveforms; then I use the Timeline Display Settings menu to save a display preset (**Figure 3.5**).

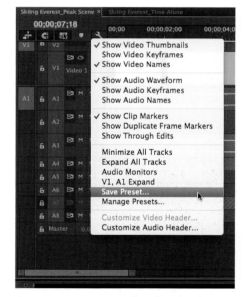

Figure 3.5 Save presets with preferred track heights for common editing tasks, and they'll appear in the Timeline Display Settings menu.

To save your own track height preferences, follow these steps.

1. Make sure Show Audio Waveform and Show Video Thumbnails are selected in the Timeline Display Settings menu.

2. Use the mouse scroll wheel or drag the dividing line between tracks to open the audio tracks so they are tall enough in height to reveal waveforms.

3. Scroll or drag to set the height of individual video tracks to your liking.

4. From the Timeline Display Settings (the wrench icon), name and save your own custom preset for track heights.

5. When you return to the Timeline Display Settings, your new preset will appear in the list.

It's also useful to configure your track headers to accommodate specific editing tasks at the touch of a button.

These features are "at a glance" items. By that I mean that I can see whether they are active or off. For example, I add Mute and Solo buttons to my audio track headers because I constantly solo lines of dialogue or mute music tracks while I'm working. I like this feature because I can glance to the left and see which audio tracks are active or silenced. I keep Toggle Track Output (the little eyeball) in all video track headers for the same reason.

You can customize individual tracks by right-clicking in the empty gray area next to track targets and choosing Customize or Rename. For example, when I want to keep certain types of clips on specific tracks, I name individual tracks VFX for visual effects, GRFX for titles, DX for dialogue, SFX for sound effects, MX for music, VO for voice-over narration, and so on. Typically, only my VO narration track header will contain the R button that enables recording.

From the Timeline Display Settings, you can quickly customize all video and audio track headers at once by following these steps.

1. Click the little wrench and choose Customize Audio Header.

2. Drag and drop to place icons for Mute, Solo, and Record into an audio track header.

3. Drag and drop to place Add-Remove Keyframe or drag the mini Audio Track Meters into the track header area to find out if it's helpful for you to have these visual references in this area of the Timeline.

4. To remove an item from the track header, click and drag it out of the header area.

I always recommend activating the display indicators for Duplicate Frames, Clip Markers, and Through-Edit Marks. Just click the Timeline Display Settings button and make sure these items are selected. You can turn any of these visual indicators on and off as needed, but I typically leave Markers and Through-Edits visible at all times. I like visual indicators to appear when I've added a cut, even if I haven't removed any frames. If I've added a marker, I want to see it!

From the Timeline Display Settings menu you can also activate keyframe displays. This allows you to adjust volume keyframes for individual clips in the track (great for dialogue) or for the entire track (great for adjusting music and voice-over narration). Adjusting track keyframes allows you to replace audio while maintaining previously set volume adjustments. I keep the Show Keyframes button in all audio track headers. I use Clip and Track Keyframes when adjusting audio levels, which allows me to swiftly switch between the two types of keyframes (**Figure 3.6**).

Timeline fly-out (panel) menu

The Timeline fly-out (panel) menu offers even more options for Timeline management. Some of these features are covered in other chapters, but here are a few essentials items that I use when I begin an edit session:

▶ **Change the start time of your sequence.** I set this option at the start of every edit. Professional editors need access to this feature to ensure that time is allowed for slate information, black, and bars and tone at the head of programs. The program typically starts at hour one, whereas the sequence may begin at 00:58:30:00 or 00:59:45:00, for example.

▶ **Alter the look of Timeline waveform displays.** Rectified audio waveforms are easier to work with when audio volume is low and waveforms are consequently small. This view is also helpful when working with Timeline tracks set to smaller heights when there are many tracks that you need to view simultaneously.

▶ **Set up Multi-Camera Audio.** In some multi-cam workflows, audio needs to be independent; in others, it needs to follow the video. This toggle switches between the two capabilities.

▶ **Turn on Show Audio Time Units.** When you want to edit at the subframe levels, select Show Audio Time Units. When you need to zoom in all the way down to the audio sample size, this feature enables you to make a cut at a subframe location, allowing you to add keyframes and remove those annoying clicks and pesky coughs that always seem to occur between frames.

Figure 3.6 When Show Audio Keyframes is selected on the Timeline Display Settings menu, the Show Keyframes button next to audio track headers can display either Track or Clip Keyframes level lines.

Speeding Up Basic Assembly

You can do three things to increase productivity while editing:

▶ Use keyboard shortcuts

▶ Master three-point editing

▶ Mind the tracks

Rock the cut with keyboard shortcuts

A colleague recently said to me, "When you asked if I was using the keyboard, I said yes, but I didn't know you meant using the keyboard like *this*!"

You should rarely look down at the keyboard while performing basic editing operations, like playing footage, marking In and Out points, or putting clips into the Timeline with insert or overwrite. It takes time to perfect, but if you map your keyboard correctly, you'll rarely look down at the keys while assembling the cut. Keep your eyes on the prize—the footage!

You may already be using the JKL keys to play through footage, but perfect this trick and layer on additional keyboard moves to increase your speed while performing the most common editing tasks. The following simple practices will train your muscle memory in preparation for dynamic trimming:

▶ **Use key commands, not buttons.** Always use the JKL keys to play, rewind, and pause rather than clicking buttons with the mouse or pressing the spacebar. Using keyboard shortcuts is the fastest way to navigate through hours of footage and helps prevent carpel tunnel syndrome.

Place three fingers on the "home keys" (JKL) and you'll be able to keep your eyes on the content at all times while playing through clips and sequences. This method is similar to touch-typing (without looking down at the keyboard) and is far faster than hunt-and-peck typing.

▶ **Use the keyboard as a work surface, not as a typing tool.** Consciously place the keyboard so it's easy to reach and comfortable for you. To encourage key command use and reduce hand and arm fatigue, the keyboard should be positioned so your fingers land on the JKL keys when in a neutral position, so the wrist is in alignment with the elbow.

I slide my keyboard to the left so the arrow keys point to the center of my body. You may need to push the keyboard even farther to the left so the number pad is centered in front of your torso. I also angle the keyboard slightly, so the number pad is a little farther from my body than the Esc key. I park my ring finger at the bump on the J key to find "home" position on the keyboard. The keyboard should not be centered in front of your torso like a typewriter! If the JKL keys are in front of your torso, your wrist will be forced to work at an angle. Move the keyboard into a comfortable position and learn to use it "by feel," without looking at it.

▶ **Drive the keyboard with one hand.** Keeping one hand on the keyboard and the other hand on the mouse allows you to work more efficiently with both tools.

▶ **Speed through footage by pressing J and L multiple times.** The fastest way to preview footage is to use the keyboard shortcuts for fast forward and rewind. Press J repeatedly to rewind and press L repeatedly to fast-forward through clips. Press JJ or LL to achieve double speed, or press these keys multiple times to play even faster. You'll eventually be able to hear exactly what is playing at double speed. It's actually a bit freaky.

▶ **Scrub clips.** Hold down both K and L or K and J to scrub footage in the Source and Timeline panels. Turn the option Play Audio While Scrubbing on and off in the Audio category of the Preferences pane (**Figure 3.7** on the next page).

▶ **Move one frame at a time.** Practice moving the playhead back and forth across a cut point in the Timeline in single-frame increments by holding K down while tapping J and L. I call this *rocking the cut.*

▶ **Mark clips on the fly.** While playing footage, always press I and O to mark In and Out points rather than mouse click on the buttons.

▶ **Quickly add shots to a sequence.** Use the comma and period keys to insert and overwrite shots into the Timeline. Insert and overwrite edits are covered in more detail later in this chapter.

Figure 3.7 Audio scrubbing is controlled in Adobe Premiere Pro Preferences.

Learn Adobe Premiere Pro default keyboard shortcuts

Many shortcuts are ready to use, so try them out! Don't miss out on some of the great shortcuts that have been pre-mapped by Adobe.

Here are a few of the default keyboard shortcuts I use constantly while editing:

▶ **Zoom to sequence.** A helpful default keyboard shortcut I use all day long is the backslash (\) key. It zooms the display of clips in the sequence to fit the Timeline panel.

▶ **Zoom in sequence.** To zoom in and out on the clips inside a sequence, press the + and − keys (without modifiers). I use these keys constantly while working in the Timeline. Try remapping these keys to the G and H keys if you find you're looking down at the keyboard to locate + and - too often.

▶ **Maximize frame under cursor.** Pressing the accent (`) key enlarges any panel the mouse is hovering over so it fills the screen. I use this most often to enlarge a bin of clips that are in Icon view or to get a quick view of all Timeline tracks.

▶ **Toggle full screen.** Press Command+` (Ctrl+`) to view the Program panel at the full screen size.

▶ **Restore frame size.** The accent (`) key commands are like light switches. Press them again to return the panel to normal size.

Modify existing keyboard shortcuts

If a pre-mapped keyboard command isn't working for you, change it. I remap keyboard shortcuts mainly so I don't have to look down at the keyboard while I'm working. Place the shortcuts for features you use every few seconds within easy reach of the JKL keys.

Recently, while I was working with the San Francisco 49ers media team, I noticed that some of the guys couldn't use my favorite personalized keyboard shortcuts because their hands were *twice the size* of mine! A few of them could reach the arrow keys with the thumb of their left hand while ring, middle, and index fingers were parked in the "home position" (JKL). That's not an option for me. My thumb rests naturally near the Command and Option (Alt) keys, but the thumb of someone with larger hands can rest on the Ctrl key and might easily stretch to reach the arrows. To move the playhead between cut points in a sequence, which I do all day, I map keyboard shortcuts to the semicolon and apostrophe keys. I move the default lift and extract keyboard shortcuts up a level to the bracket keys, which are located just to the right of the P key.

Mapping the keyboard is very personal, and your choices should accommodate your editing style and physical comfort. The physical size and position of your hand will dictate some mapping options. It makes a huge difference in speed when you get it right.

Saving and using keyboard shortcuts helps me stay in the flow of the creative process. When I'm deeply engaged in editing, I don't want to lose my hold on a fleeting idea because I have to go hunting through a list in a fly-out menu. A simple solution for increasing speed while editing is to set up your keyboard so everything you need is within easy reach. Then practice pressing those keys without looking at the keyboard.

Here are some guidelines when you choose keys to remap:

▶ **Increase speed.** Any shortcut you use all day should be in reach of your "home" hand position on the keyboard. I use the G and H keys to hold some of my favorite editing options (such as sequence zoom in and zoom out) because those keys are right under my pinky finger. Take time to modify the keyboard to suit your needs. It's the simplest thing you can do to fly through the more tedious tasks of the trade.

▶ **Modify pre-mapped shortcuts.** Shift+2 and Shift+3, which toggle focus between the Timeline and Source panels, can be remapped to the 2 and 3 keys (without the modifier) if you're not currently using those commands for multi-cam editing.

▶ **Reclaim unused keys.** Consider remapping infrequently used keyboard shortcuts, like the capture keys (F5 and F6). It's rare to capture from tape-based sources these days, so set these keys to more commonly used commands.

Create custom shortcuts

Add familiar shortcuts from other editing applications, and enhance your own personal editing style by creating custom shortcuts for often-used buttons and items in menus you frequently visit.

If you use a feature more than five times during an edit session, consider creating a shortcut, and then test it while you're editing to see if it speeds up your workflow. Here are the specific steps if you've never done this before.

1. **Open the Keyboard Shortcuts panel.** Choose Premiere Pro > Keyboard Shortcuts (Mac) or Edit > Keyboard Shortcuts (Windows).

2. **Select the Adobe Premiere Pro default keyboard layout.** From the pop-up menu, begin with the Default Layout or choose [Custom].

3. **Twirl the disclosure triangles.** Click the disclosure triangles to view available menu options and panel features.

4. **Map a keyboard shortcut.** Click the Edit button, and then press the desired shortcut keys on your keyboard.

5. **Do not press Return (Enter).** Continue to customize your keyboard layout before you press Return (Enter) or click the OK button.

6. **Click OK.** When you've added all the custom keyboard shortcuts you want, close the Keyboard Shortcuts panel by clicking OK.

Here are a few tips for mapping keys:

▶ **Map features you use repeatedly.** Because I often use markers, I was constantly right-clicking on the markers to add comments, so I created a keyboard shortcut for the Edit Marker panel. Now I can press M to add a marker, and then immediately press Ctrl+M to add information and designate a duration for the marker. The added text appears right on the marker "tail" after the duration has been set (**Figure 3.8**).

Figure 3.8 Create a keyboard shortcut for features you use repeatedly during an edit session, such as Edit Marker.

▶ **Map features that save time.** While you're currently adding and testing new keyboard shortcuts, make a shortcut that opens the Keyboard Shortcuts panel! Type the word **keyboard** into the search field and add your own command for quick access to this panel so you don't have to repeatedly mouse up to the main menu. I use Ctrl+K.

▶ **Learn the default keyboard shortcuts.** Learn the built-in features that Adobe Premiere Pro offers by opening the Keyboard Shortcuts panel, twirling the disclosure triangles, and simply looking at the list of available items.

Save keyboard layout presets

If you engage in different roles, such as creative editing and finishing work, you may need to save a few different keyboard presets. Consider saving a keyboard layout for creative editing, another for audio work, a third for finishing and effects work, and one for multi-cam editing (**Figure 3.9**):

Figure 3.9 Keyboard layout presets can be saved and synced via the Creative Cloud.

▶ **Save your custom keyboard layout.** Open the Keyboard Shortcuts panel. If you've customized keys without saving them, the pop-up menu will be set to [Custom]. Further customize as needed, click Save As, name the set, and then click OK.

▶ **Create additional sets.** Select Custom from the Keyboard Layout Presets pop-up menu, edit or add commands as needed, and then name and save the new set.

▶ **Add to an existing set.** Rather than creating a new set, select an existing preset from the pop-up menu, add or edit some keyboard commands, and then rename the updated set using the same name so it replaces the previously saved layout.

Saving a keyboard preset allows you to quickly adjust your work surface to meet your needs for speed in any given situation. I regularly update my customized keyboard shortcuts, and alter them for specific projects as needed, so I can fly through an edit with ease.

Keyboard presets (along with other saved presets) are saved inside your Adobe Profile folder. You can move the presets to other systems manually, but don't forget that syncing your settings is a fantastic advantage of the Creative Cloud (see Chapter 1).

Three-point Editing

You may love drag-and-drop editing, but the most precise way to add footage to a sequence is to use a standard three-point edit. It's fast and accurate. If you're already seasoned at three-point editing, you may want to move on to the next section.

If you regularly drag and drop footage into the Timeline, cut with the Razor tool, and constantly move groups of clips around inside the Timeline to make room for more shots, I guarantee your workflow will speed up if you master three-point editing using the overwrite and insert keyboard shortcuts to add clips to an existing sequence:

▶ **Overwrite.** An overwrite edit replaces frames in the sequence with new frames from the source clip.

▶ **Insert.** An insert edit adds a clip to your sequence and shifts the existing material to the right (later in the sequence) to make room for the inserted media.

Three-point editing allows you to define the segment of a clip you want to put at a specific place in the sequence or to define a specific range in the sequence that you want to fill with a clip.

Inserts

When you set two of the three points—an In and an Out—in the source clip, and then set either an In or an Out point in the sequence to define the third point, most likely you'll perform an insert edit. The playhead location is assumed to be an In point if you don't set an In or an Out mark in the sequence.

Typically, when adding media of a set duration into a sequence at a specific point in time, I use a three-point insert edit. For example, in the sequence named **Skiing Everest_Time Alone_Insert**, I've placed the playhead at 28:10 to define the point where I want to add a sound bite. In the Source panel I've set an In and Out point for the clip called **SE_03** to bracket the segment where the narrator says, "When you're climbing, you're not talking to your buddies." I press Option+K (Alt+K) to play from In to Out in the Source panel to check my selection, and then press the comma key to insert the footage into the sequence at the Timeline playhead (**Figure 3.10**, facing page).

Overwrites

There may be times when you'll want to define a duration in the sequence and fill it with footage. In this case, two points are set in the Timeline, and one point is marked in the source clip—either an In or an Out point. This is a common technique used for placing B-roll visuals on top of audio bites that are already in the sequence. When this type of three-point selection is set up, you'll typically perform overwrite edits.

Figure 3.10 When In and Out points define a duration for a clip in the Source panel, you're set up to perform a three-point edit into the sequence. This is the common setup for performing an insert edit.

In the **Skiing Everest_Time Alone_Overwrite** sequence, I've defined a range in the Timeline for a clip I want to write over with another shot of B-roll. The narrator is talking about time spent alone, so I've selected a shot of him climbing alone from clip SE_04 and marked an In point in the Source panel. To mark and accurately fill a desired duration in the sequence, I set an In and Out point in the Timeline by clicking to select the clip at 31:07 in the sequence and then pressing the forward slash (/) key to mark the clip I want to write over. Having defined all three edit points, I then press the period (.) key to perform an overwrite edit. Note that I chose a B-roll clip that did not contain audio. The new video clip now perfectly fills the space where the previous clip had been (**Figure 3.11**).

Figure 3.11 Set In and Out points to define a duration in the sequence, and then place an In or Out point in the source clip and press the period (.) key to perform an overwrite edit. This type of edit is often used to place visuals at very specific points in time to complement sequence audio.

Mind the Tracks

Source patching lets you designate which sequence tracks will be affected by insert and overwrite edits. Track targeting also effects many Timeline operations. You may already be familiar with these functions, but if not they are covered later in this chapter and in others. Here are the primary features that depend on track awareness:

- ▶ Insert and Overwrite
- ▶ Add Edit
- ▶ Extract and Lift
- ▶ Copy, Paste, and Paste Insert
- ▶ Move Playhead to Next and Previous Edit

Source patching for insert and overwrite edits

A big advantage of three-point editing is the ability to be precise. You can specify whether to use only the video or audio from a source clip, or both video and audio, and to control exactly which channels of an audio or video source will be edited into specific tracks in the Timeline. Clicking and dragging the Source Patching buttons so they line up with specific video and audio track targets in the Timeline—and making sure they are highlighted in light gray—ensures that source tracks end up right where you want them.

Some of the techniques that require patching include:

Figure 3.12 Toggle Source buttons for video and audio and place them in line with specific Timeline track targets before performing an insert or an overwrite edit.

▶ **Edit source video and audio into Timeline tracks V1 and A1.** This is the most common Timeline configuration for inserting and overwriting clips that contain picture with synced sound, such as dialogue scenes and interviews.

Click to highlight the V1 and A1 Source buttons. "Patch," or align, the Source buttons with the corresponding V1 and A1 Timeline track targets (these do not need to be highlighted). Mark an In point in the sequence, or use the playhead location as the In point, and then press insert (,) or overwrite (.) (**Figure 3.12**).

▶ **Edit a sound bite from the source video onto the A2 track in the Timeline.** Sometimes I want to use a sound bite from a clip but don't need the picture. This is especially common while editing promos, trailers, and commercials where fast-paced cutting makes synced dialogue less important than placing the most exciting visuals above sparse but powerful sound bites.

To edit the audio track only from a source clip into the sequence, first select an In to Out range in the Source panel. For the Skiing Everest scene called **Time Alone**, I marked In and Out points around a sound bite from clip SE_03 that says, "We had great weather…we were psyched." Click in the Timeline source patching area next to the A2 track to highlight and place the A1 Source button next the A2 Timeline track target. Make sure the Video Source buttons are dark (not highlighted), and then press overwrite (.) (**Figure 3.13**).

Figure 3.13 To insert or overwrite only the audio from a source clip into the sequence, toggle Audio Source buttons on and line them up next to specific Timeline audio track targets. Make sure Video Source buttons are dark (not selected).

In this documentary about skiing Mount Everest, I want to build a "radio cut"(sketch out the story in sound bites) and later choose B-roll imagery. I typically "checkerboard" the tracks when working with audio that isn't in sync with the picture. In other words, I place sound that isn't dependent on sync onto a lower audio track, such as A2, so it stands out from the audio that is in sync with the picture on V1. After a few more edits, the audio on A1 and A2 will take on a checkerboard pattern in the Timeline. To see exactly what I mean, investigate the **Skiing Everest_Time Alone** sequence in the included project where audio on track A1 is linked and in sync with the picture on V1, and audio on track A2 is not synced or linked to the picture tracks and can be easily slid around (**Figure 3.14**).

Figure 3.14 Place audio that is not synced to the picture on a separate audio track, so it can be easily moved around. This helps preserve sync on other tracks and makes it visually clear which sound bites are in sync and linked to the picture.

▶ **Edit video without audio into the Timeline.** To place the video portion of a clip into the Timeline without its synced audio, patch the V1 Source button to a specific Timeline track target by clicking in the empty Source button area where you want the source video to end up. Make sure the Audio Source buttons are dark (not highlighted), and then press overwrite (.)

In the **Skiing Everest_Time Alone** sequence, I edited a video-only portion of clip SE_02 onto V2, so I could slide it around and check placement over different sound bites. Later, I changed my mind and performed an overwrite edit to try out another image from the clip called SE_03 above the sound bite I'd chosen to use in this scene. Feel free to try this out using the provided project and sequences (**Figure 3.15**).

Figure 3.15 To insert or overwrite the source video without sound onto specific sequence tracks, click to toggle on the V1 Source button and line it up next to a specific Timeline video track target. Make sure the Audio Source buttons are dark (not selected).

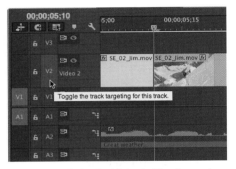

Figure 3.16 Click to highlight the Timeline track where you want to add a splice. Leave other track targets dark.

Track targeting

In addition to source patching, mind the track targets to make the best use of Adobe Premiere Pro's editing tools and keyboard commands. These essential features depend on track targeting:

▶ **Add Edit.** Using the Add Edit command to make cuts across multiple tracks is faster and more precise than using the Razor tool. Clips under the playhead will be spliced only for targeted tracks when you press the keyboard shortcut for Add Edit (Command+K [Ctrl+K]).

In the **Skiing Everest_Time Alone** sequence, toggle (highlight) the Track Targeting button for V2, but leave other audio and video tracks dark (not highlighted) (**Figure 3.16**).

Now place the Timeline playhead at 25:21 in the sequence and press Command+K (Ctrl+K) to place a cut on the video track and isolate the onscreen lip-synced interview. The video portion of the clip will be spliced, but the audio portion of the clip will remain whole, making it easy to replace the B-roll portion above the sound bite while preserving the on-camera interview segment.

▶ **Cut, Copy, and Paste.** Pasting clips is a quick way to rearrange clips in the Timeline or to move segments from one sequence to another. Toggling the Timeline track targets allows you to paste audio or video into specific Timeline tracks with intent when using Cut, Copy, and Paste commands.

Select and cut (Command+X [Ctrl+X]) or copy (Command+C [Ctrl+C]) a clip or group of clips in the Timeline. Toggle (highlight) the track targets for specific video and/or audio tracks and then paste (Command+V [Ctrl+V]) to overwrite clips at the playhead location.

▶ **Go To commands.** Track targets affect the Go to Next Edit and Go to Previous Edit buttons and keyboard shortcuts (Up and Down arrow keys). Targeting all tracks results in the playhead stopping at cut points on every track.

Back-timing

Sometimes the completion of an action is more important when building a scene than seeing where the action begins. For example, you might want the viewer to see an actor exit the frame or watch a ball connect with a bat in close-up just before cutting to the wide shot.

It's not uncommon to set an Out point for the source clip to specify where a clip should end, and then allow Adobe Premiere Pro to "back-time" the clip to fill a duration in the sequence. When you perform this type of three-point edit, the frame under the Out point in the source clip will be placed exactly where the Out point is set inside the sequence. The clip is edited into the Timeline for the duration defined by the third point—most often, the In point in the sequence.

Check out the example sequence I've set up for you called **Skiing Everest_Peak Scene_Backtiming.** I've marked In and Out points in the sequence around a clip I'd like to write over to set a duration that I'll fill using another shot. I want to use clip SE_01 where there is a close-up of the skier in red. After loading SE_01 into the Source panel, I mark an Out point where the skier is closest to the viewer and largest in the frame. I want the Out point I've selected in this source clip to replace the frame under the Out point in my sequence. After I press overwrite (.) the viewer will see a wide shot of a skier in red completing a left turn that began in the close-up. The Out point of the action is more important to me than where the shot begins, because I want it to match-cut with the next shot in the sequence. Allowing the Out point to be dominant in this case helps me create the feeling of continuous action across the cut, which was my intent. I'll play around this area in the sequence after completing the edit to make sure the close-up shot of the skier in red contained enough footage to fill the Timeline duration I selected (**Figure 3.17** on the next page).

Generally, when an Out point is set in the source clip and two points are set in the Timeline, you'll want to perform this special type of overwrite edit, where the source clip's Out point is timed to the Out Point in the Timeline.

TIP

Press the Shift key while targeting Timeline Track buttons or Source Patch buttons to quickly select and deselect all video or audio sources or tracks. Keyboard shortcuts for Toggling All Source and Video Tracks can be found by typing Toggle All in the search field in the Keyboard Shortcuts panel.

TIP

Put the playhead over a clip inside the Timeline and press the X key to quickly mark an In to Out range around that specific clip. The In/Out Duration field in the Program panel will update with the selected clip's duration. This is another feature that follows track targets! Deselect the V1 track target to perform Mark Clip on Targeted V2 Track.

Figure 3.17 When backtiming a three-point edit, the frame under the Out point in the source clip will be added to the Timeline at the location of the sequence Out point, and footage from the source clip will be "back-timed" to fill the sequence In-to-Out duration.

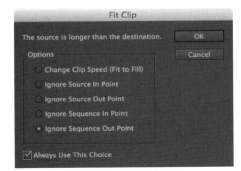

Figure 3.18 The Fit Clip panel offers five options for resolving an edit range mismatch. Fit Clip panel options can be customized to "stick" to your preference.

Four-point editing

When four points are defined by marking In and Out points in both the Source panel and in the Timeline sequence, you'll need to make a decision about how Adobe Premiere Pro should resolve the four-point edit. After setting four points and pressing insert or overwrite, the Fit Clip panel opens and offers you the option to ignore one of the points or change the speed of the clip when performing the edit (**Figure 3.18**).

Here are the variations of the Fit Clip panel:

▶ **Change Clip Speed.** In and Out points for the source clip are preserved, and the clip's speed is adjusted to fill the duration set by the sequence In and Out points.

- ▶ **Ignore Source In Point.** The frame marked with an Out point in the source clip is placed at the Out point mark in the Timeline. The duration is determined by the sequence In and Out points. This only works when the source clip is longer than the range set in the sequence.

- ▶ **Ignore Source Out Point.** The Out point in the source clip is ignored. Duration is determined by the sequence's In and Out points, and the frame marked by the In point in the source clip is placed at the In point mark in the Timeline. The source clip must be longer than the range set in the sequence.

- ▶ **Ignore Sequence In Point.** This choice will ignore the sequence In point and perform a standard three-point edit. Duration is defined by the source clip points. If the clip is shorter than the duration defined, you might need to clean up unwanted video in the sequence.

- ▶ **Ignore Sequence Out Point.** The sequence Out point is ignored, and a standard three-point edit is placed in the sequence with duration defined by the source clip In and Out points.

When I accidentally make a fourth point and simply intended to add a clip to the Timeline using a standard three-point edit, I typically choose to ignore the Out point in the sequence and perform an insert edit. When my intention is to fill a set duration in the Timeline with a specific piece of footage, such as B-roll that illustrates a great sound bite, I commonly choose to ignore the Out point in the source clip. However, when the Out frame in the source clip defines action for a match-cut—pertinent action is happening at the end of the shot and I want it to continue in the incoming shot—I'll choose to ignore the source In point and press overwrite to back-time the shot.

Fit to Fill

Performing a Fit to Fill is the main reason I set four points! I don't mind the Fit Clip dialog opening when I set four edit points, because I typically only set four edit points when I intend to change a clip's speed. Often, I need all of the action that takes place in a shot, and I need to fit that action into a very specific duration in the sequence. In this case, I usually set In and Out points in the Timeline that define a section of dialogue, bracket a music cue, or support an audio sound bite.

Test this feature in your own work. Set In and Out marks in both a sequence and a source clip, and then press insert or overwrite with the very clear idea that you're going to force the source clip to speed up or slow down to fill an intentionally defined range in the sequence.

Here are some nuances of the Fit to Fill choice:

▶ **Be deliberate in your actions.** Learn how the different Fit Clip options work so you can choose what best suits your needs. Use four-point editing to place a speed-varied clip into a specific duration in the Timeline.

▶ **Set Preferences.** It's great that Adobe Premiere Pro offers so many four-point editing options, but because every second counts when a deadline is looming, you might want to deactivate this pop-up dialog. Set Fit Clip to perform one specific task every time you insert or overwrite with four points chosen by clicking the radio button next to the option you prefer in the Fit Clip panel. Then select Always Use This Choice. The Fit Clip panel will no longer open when you perform four-point edits.

▶ **Or Reset Preferences.** If you've adjusted the Fit Clip dialog to perform one specific function—for example, you've selected Change Clip Speed and then selected Always Use This Choice—you might later find you want to choose another option and the Fit Clip panel no longer opens. Go to the Adobe Premiere Pro Preferences panel and in the General category select "Fit clip dialogue opens for edit range mismatches." The Fit Clip dialog will become active again (**Figure 3.19**).

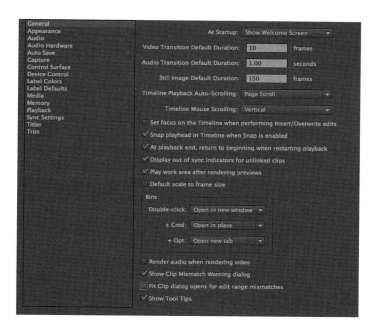

Figure 3.19 The Fit Clip dialog can be deactivated and reactivated in the Adobe Premiere Pro Preferences panel.

Automate to Sequence

Automate to Sequence is a great feature you can use in Adobe Premiere Pro to quickly rough out an idea. It allows you to edit multiple shots into a sequence simultaneously. You could just drag and drop multiple clips to a sequence, but you won't have quite as much control over specific source audio and video tracks if you're using the drag-and-drop method. Automate to Sequence performs an insert or overwrite using multiple clips, so you can place selected video and audio into the Timeline deliberately and with precise results.

I use this feature while storyboard editing to rough out a quick assembly. It's great when you want to grab interview sound bites and assemble them in order or insert several B-roll clips at once into the Timeline. It's the fastest way to edit a montage with dissolves, and you can use it to place clips precisely at numbered markers in the Timeline.

Using a bin as a Source Monitor

The fastest way I've found to rough out an assembly is to treat a bin of clips like it's a multiple-Source Monitor. Set In to Out marks for clips in the bin, and then use Automate to Sequence to edit several shots into the Timeline all at once. This is the main reason I use Automate to Sequence!

You usually have an idea about the order you'd like to see certain clips play in a sequence. It's time-consuming to load a single clip into the Source Monitor, mark In and Out points, edit the clip into the sequence, and then double-click another clip from the project to load it into the Source Monitor, mark In and Out points, edit that clip next to the first, and so on. Instead, open a bin of clips and use it as a multiple-Source Monitor.

Although you could drag and drop several clips into the Timeline all at once, using the Automate to Sequence feature gives you finer control over how clips are edited into the Timeline. Preparing the interface for this process will make rough cutting and B-roll editing fast, easy, and fun. Here's how to set up your workspace:

1. Option-double click (Alt-double-click) on a bin of video clips to open it into a tab (or set Preferences so bins open into a tab when double-clicked to avoid holding down the Option [Alt] key).

2. Drag the bin by its tab and drop it in the center of the Source panel. You don't really need to relocate a bin to the same panel as the Source Monitor, because the bin can be docked anywhere, but try this for now so you'll grow accustomed to a bin behaving like a Source Monitor.

3. Set the bin to display the clips in Icon view by selecting the bin and pressing Command+Page Down (Ctrl+Page Down). Drag the size slider so the images are larger and, if needed, drag the edge of the Source panel so it's large enough to see multiple clips. You'll now have multiple source clips available while editing, and you won't need to double-click to open each clip into the source window for marking—the clips are already open!

4. Play through each of the clips using JKL. Set an In-to-Out range for each clip you want to add to the Timeline (**Figure 3.20**).

Figure 3.20 Dock a bin of clips next to the Source Monitor and set view to Icon mode. When In and Out points are set, a small orange line indicates the marked area of the clip, and the In-to-Out duration is displayed at the lower-right corner of each clip.

Now that you've set up a bin as a multiple-Source Monitor, let's use the Automate to Sequence feature to edit several clips into a sequence. You can use these steps in your own project, or open the project I've included for this chapter and double-click on the **Skiing Everest_Automate** sequence. If you're using the sequence I've prepared, you'll also want to open the bin named SE_Video. I suggest dragging the tab and docking that video bin inside the Source Monitor.

1. Play through the sequence to get familiar with the sound bites.

2. If any clips are selected in the sequence, deselect all by pressing Command+Shift+A (Ctrl+Shift+A).

3. Turn on Snapping (S) and move the playhead to the end of the last video clip in the sequence.

4. Press M to set a marker.

5. While playing through the sequence again, press M to set another marker after the narrator says, "We had great weather…," but just before he says "The North ridge…". Adjust your Timeline tracks so you can see the audio waveforms in the dialogue track while

playing the sequence to help you locate each sound bite when adding markers.

6. Place a third marker where the narrator says, "The way that it is…".

I've already set In and Out points for clips SE_02, SE_03, and SE_04 inside the SE_Video bin.

7. Select the clips *in* the order you want them to appear in the sequence by pressing Command-click (Ctrl-click) to select multiple, noncontiguous clips.

8. Click the Lock icon next to the Timeline tracks you don't want affected by the edit.

9. Click the Automate to Sequence button (**Figure 3.21**).

Figure 3.21 Carefully position the playhead and markers in the Timeline to indicate where you'd like to add clips. With a bin of video clips now functioning as a multi-clip Source Monitor, set In and Out points in multiple clips. Command-click (Ctrl-click) to select clips in the order you want them to appear in the sequence. Click Automate to Sequence.

10. The Automate to Sequence dialog appears, giving you options to insert or overwrite clips in sort or selection order. Explore the options that allow you to ignore audio or video and add transitions and still images (**Figure 3.22**).

11. From the Ordering pop-up menu, choose Selection Order.

12. If you've added markers to your sequence, select At Un-numbered Markers for Placement. If you haven't added markers, choose Sequentially.

13. For Method, select Overwrite Edit.

14. Select Use In/Out Range for stills.

15. Deselect Default Video and Audio Transitions.

16. Select Ignore Audio.

17. Click OK.

Figure 3.22 Clips will overwrite onto the targeted Timeline track at marker locations in selection order, ignoring audio when that option is selected in the Automate to Sequence dialog.

For extra credit, try dragging a few more clips to the top your the bin in the order you'd like to add them to the sequence. Place the playhead at a cut point in between two shots in your sequence and Shift-click to lock all audio tracks. Click the Automate to Sequence button and choose Sort Order from the pop-up menu. Choose Insert Edit from the Method pop-up menu and select Ignore Audio. Click OK. Clips will insert onto the targeted tracks, and audio tracks will not be affected.

Using Automate to Sequence is a great way to quickly get a sequence started. It's also useful for inserting several shots simultaneously into an existing sequence. Automating clips to numbered markers is helpful when you want to over-write B-roll or graphics onto a higher level Timeline video track in time to music or audio narration, especially when you know exactly where each shot should be placed in the sequence. If you use this feature regularly, make a key-board shortcut to open the Automate to Sequence dialog. I use Shift+A (**Figure 3.23**).

NOTES

Be aware that inserting clips, like ripple trimming, always has the potential to throw clips out of sync. Mind the tracks.

Figure 3.23 Create a keyboard shortcut, such as Shift+A, for favorite features like Automate to Sequence.

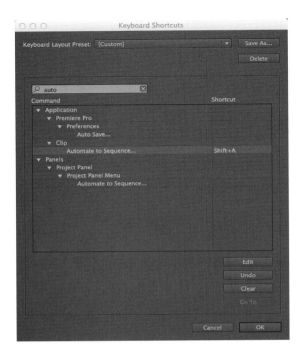

Timeline Finesse

There are several well-known editing functions that are essential to all editors, no matter the story genre. When you choose the right tool for the job, quickly rearranging the order of shots in a sequence becomes easy. Let's look at the best methods for artfully adding, removing, replacing, and rearranging shots in the Timeline.

Match Frame

I use Match Frame dozens of times each day while editing in the Timeline. If you're not already familiar with the feature, place your playhead over a clip in the Timeline and press the F key for Match Frame. The master clip is loaded into the Source Monitor and parked at the same frame as the playhead in the sequence.

Using Match Frame to replace or sync audio

One common reason to use Match Frame is to replace audio channels you didn't originally edit into the sequence along with the picture or to restore audio channels that you deleted and now want.

1. Place the Timeline playhead at the In point of a shot in the sequence (**Figure 3.24**), and then press F to load the master shot into the Source Monitor.

2. Toggle Source Track patching on for audio and off for video.

3. Press period (.) to overwrite the audio track back into the sequence in sync.

TIP

To ignore track targeting when you're working with multiple layered tracks, simply click on the clip you want to Match Frame in the Timeline (it can be either audio or video) before pressing F.

Figure 3.24 Mind the tracks! Put the Timeline playhead on the In point of a sequence clip and press F to perform a Match Frame. To replace Audio only, deselect Video Source Patch buttons and set the Audio Source button to the desired Timeline track target before performing the edit.

Mind the tracks! Track targeting affects Match Frame functionality. When all tracks are targeted, video tracks are dominant over audio tracks and higher-numbered tracks are dominant over lower-numbered tracks. For example, if you Shift-click to highlight all video track targets, and there is layered video on V1 and V2, the V2 master clip will load into the Source panel. Deselect the V2 track target and press F again, and the V1 master clip will load into the Source panel.

Clicking to select a clip under the playhead in the Timeline will give it priority for Match Frame regardless of track target settings. For example, when there is audio under the Timeline playhead that is not linked to video above it and you want to Match Frame on that audio track, click on that specific audio clip to select it before pressing F so the master audio clip will load into the Source Monitor. Clicking the clip is the quickest way to indicate my preference for Match Frame when I want to match anything other than the topmost video track.

Using Match Frame to cut a dialogue scene

My favorite reason for using Match Frame is that it's great for rapidly cutting a dialogue scene between two characters. When a dialogue scene is filmed from two cameras angles (one angle on each character) but is not a multi-camera shoot—in other words, the timing isn't continuous—try this technique.

1. Edit the first line of dialogue from character number one into the sequence. Very likely, this is an over the shoulder (OTS) shot.

2. Edit the first response, either the first line of dialogue or a reaction, from the second character into the sequence as you normally would by performing an overwrite or an insert edit to put the two lines of dialogue together in sequence.

3. Place the Timeline playhead on the *last frame* of character number one's clip, and press F (Match Frame) to quickly reload the clip for the first character back into the Source Monitor.

The source clip is now ready for you to play forward and quickly mark an In-to-Out range in real time for character number one's next line.

4. Press Shift+3 to toggle focus on the Timeline, press the down arrow key to move the playhead into position for the edit, and then press insert (,).

5. Press the up arrow key and then the left arrow key once to put the Timeline playhead on the *last frame* of character number two's clip.

6. Press F. Character number two's master clip is now loaded into the Source panel and ready for you to play forward and mark the next line of dialogue.

7. Continue using Match Frame to quickly build a rough cut of the entire dialogue, alternating between the two actors.

Reveal Master Clip

Another feature I use often is Reveal Clip. Instead of having a selected clip open into the Source Monitor, as it does with the Match Frame command, you can select a clip in the Timeline or Source panel and reveal the master clip for that shot inside the project bin. Simply select a clip in either the Timeline or the Source panel, right-click and choose Reveal in Project. What's really handy is that if your footage is well organized, this command will open the bin full of similar shots, making it quick and easy to replace shots and try out different takes or camera angles in the Timeline (**Figure 3.25**).

Figure 3.25 Right-click on a clip in the Timeline or Source Monitor and choose Reveal in Project to highlight the master clip inside bins in the Project panel.

For extra credit, remember to map keyboard shortcuts for frequently used features! Right-clicking on a clip and hunting through the pop-up menu for Reveal in Project annoyed me because I was looking for this feature several times in an hour. I recommend setting the same keyboard shortcut to access Reveal in Project for *both* the Source and Timeline panels. Then, one keyboard shortcut will open the bin that contains the highlighted clip whether you select the clip inside the Timeline or in the Source panel. Don't forget to save, and type the same name to replace your current keyboard preferences with the newly added shortcuts (**Figure 3.26**).

Figure 3.26 In the Keyboard Shortcuts panel, set the same shortcut for Reveal in Project in both the Timeline and Source panel lists. Click Save, and name and replace the existing keyboard layout with the newly created commands.

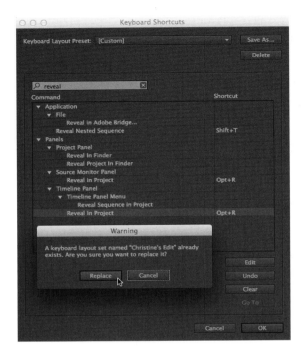

Replace Footage

There will come a time when you'll need to replace a clip, either for the whole project or just for one scene. Whether you've been given updated motion graphics or revised animation, or you simply want to try another take of an actor's performance for a scene inside the sequence, replacing shots is a mainstay of editing. There are several methods for replacing footage inside projects and individual sequences, but I'll focus on the most useful techniques and explain when or why you'd use one instead of another.

Replacing footage in the project

Imagine you have a clip called Logo_001 in the Timeline, which is a temporary graphic that was created for the episode you're working on. You're now on the third version of your cut sequence, and the motion graphics editor sends you the final version of this graphic. The easiest way to replace the temporary version with the new one, throughout multiple sequences (all three versions of your cut), is to use the Replace Footage command in the Project panel.

1. Right-click the footage you want to update inside the Project panel and choose Replace Footage.

2. Navigate to the new file, and select Rename Clip to File Name.

   The new file is now updated "live" inside all sequences too!

Choosing Replace Footage at the project level is my go-to choice for updating in-sequence motion graphics, because the new graphics are immediately ready to be screened inside all sequences. I also use this method to replace older temporary audio files with final narration and music tracks. The Replace Footage command automatically updates the audio files, so I'm confident that the final recordings have been replaced in every sequence.

This feature saves so much time, especially when the placement of clips inside a sequence won't change at all, and the updated versions of the files make the older versions obsolete. In other words, when you don't need to keep the temporary clips inside the project and you want all sequences updated at once, use this method to replace clips. It's fast and easy.

Replacing Shots in the Timeline

When you want to replace a clip inside a specific sequence rather than updating a shot throughout the entire project, there are several great techniques you can use. In the following sections I'll share my favorite and most commonly used methods for replacing individual shots.

Drag-and-drop replace

The quickest way to replace a single clip inside a sequence is by using the Option-drag (Alt-drag) technique.

To play along, open the example sequence called **Skiing Everest_Time Alone_Replace.** From the SE_Video bin, double-click to open clip SE_04 into the Source panel.

Let's replace the second shot in this Sequence with a wide shot of the tents at Camp 1 to give the viewer a sense of place at the beginning of the climbing day. Set an In Point at about 30:20 in the source clip where the text is fully visible.

The trick is to hold down the Option (Alt) key as you drag the replacement clip from the Source panel into the Timeline. Drop the replacement clip right on top of the existing clip in the sequence by releasing the mouse when you see the green plus symbol over the clip you want to replace. Using this method, the In point of the source clip will be used to define the starting point for the edit (**Figure 3.27**).

If you want to use the In point of the original clip (not the In-point from the replacement clip), hold down Shift+Option (Shift+Alt) when you drag. The only time I use this method is when I'm editing with multi-cam footage that was shot with matching timecode.

Figure 3.27 Hold down the Option (Alt) key while dragging a replacement clip from the Project or Source panel. Release the mouse when you see the green plus symbol on top of the Timeline clip you intend to replace.

If you want to use the Out point from the source clip and back-time, you can select the clip you want to replace inside the Timeline and press the forward slash (/) key to mark that clip. Then perform a standard four-point overwrite edit and select Ignore Source In Point from the Fit Clip panel.

Sync Replace with Match Frame

Dragging while holding down the Option (Alt) key is fast and very cool, but performing a Sync Replace is even better than a simple drag-and-drop replace.

A Sync Replace is the most accurate method for performing a replace edit, because it allows you to precisely sync the exact frame you want to replace in the original clip with a specific frame from the replacement clip. This method uses the playhead in both the Source and Timeline panels to achieve frame-accurate results.

Let's sample this feature in action.

1. Open the example sequence called **Skiing Everest_Peak Scene_Sync Replace**.

2. If needed, clear any In and Out marks from both the Timeline and Source panels by pressing Option+X (Ctrl+Shift+X).

3. Put the Timeline playhead at 05;17 where the skier is turning to his right and has just pulled his poles away from the snow—about six to eight frames past where his poles have touched the ice.

4. Load SE_01 into the Source panel. Put the Source panel playhead at 08;23 where the skier in red is also turning to his right—about six to eight frames past where his poles have touched the ice.

5. Now that you've selected matching action frames using the Source and Timeline playheads, right-click on the clip in the sequence and choose Replace With Clip > From Source Monitor, Match Frame to replace the shot in the sequence with the shot in the Source panel (**Figure 3.28**).

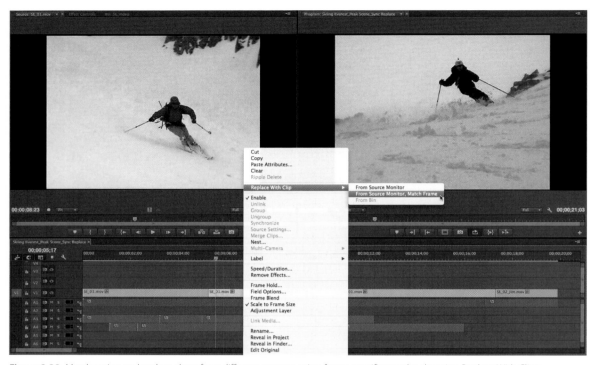

Figure 3.28 Match action and replace shots from different cameras using frame-specific sync by choosing Replace With Clip > From Source Monitor, Match Frame.

TIP

This is so slick: A big advantage of using Replace Edit is that whichever Timeline Replace method you choose, the replaced clip will retain any effects that were applied to the original clip in the sequence. This saves tons of time. Don't overwrite a clip that contains effects—replace it! You can try out several different shot options and effects stay put.

Once you master this technique, you'll use it constantly in your own work. Simply put the playhead over a clip you want to replace inside a sequence at a specific frame of action or even at the start of a specific word or phrase. Open the replacement clip into the Source Monitor and park the playhead over the precise frame of action (or sound bite) that will replace the original frame under the sequence playhead. Right-click on the original clip in the sequence and choose Replace With Clip > From Source Monitor, Match Frame.

This precision style of replacing a clip is super useful when you're trying out multiple takes of action shots, especially while cutting sports sequences, because it allows you to audition different camera angles at critical points in the sequence. I often use this technique for trying out repeated takes of dialogue, and find it most useful when an actor delivers multiple reads at roughly the same speed but with varying emotion and I want to see how each take plays with the surrounding shots.

I highly recommend creating a keyboard shortcut for Re-place Clip with Match Frame. The keyboard shortcut will allow you to quickly test different deliveries of a perfor-mance with the touch of key while maintaining visual sync on the action inside the cut. Place Timeline and Source playheads over desired frames, click to select the sequence clip you want to replace, and press the keyboard shortcut. It's that easy!

Removing Footage from the Timeline

You may be familiar with some of the standard editing fea-tures for quickly removing footage from the Timeline, and if so great! I'm including fundamental techniques because I've trained many people at different companies—editors who've been using editing software for years—and found that they weren't making full use of these simple yet power-ful tools. If you already use the Lift and Extract commands, skip those sections. If you need a bit of review, read on, be-cause these techniques are essential for grasping the more advanced methods of removing footage from the Timeline using keyboard shortcuts.

Lift

A Lift edit removes selected frames from your sequence and leaves a gap in the Timeline to preserve audio sync. The frames removed are determined by setting an In-to-Out range in the Timeline and targeting tracks from which media will be lifted. Remember: Mind the Tracks!

Typically, the Lift command is used when a gap in the se-quence is desired, because you want to fill that gap with B-roll imagery or sound. I often clean up unnecessary audio from sound bites using Lift to leave gaps that will later be filled with room tone or "background air." A big advantage of using Lift is that you can select just a portion of a clip, or portions of multiple clips, by selecting an In-to-Out range in the sequence. You aren't limited to simply deleting or lifting out whole clips. Let's see how it works.

1. In the Timeline, mark In and Out points to set a range for the media to be lifted.

2. Toggle track targets to specify which tracks should be affected by the Lift command.

3. Click the Lift button in the Program Monitor or use the default keyboard shortcut (press ;).

   The media is lifted from selected tracks, leaving a gap in the Timeline.

   Removed frames are copied to the clipboard and can be pasted back into the sequence elsewhere using the Paste (Command+V [Ctrl+V]) or Paste Insert (Command+Shift+V [Ctrl+Shift+V]) commands to overwrite or insert the media to a new location.

Extract

The Extract command is similar to the Lift command except it doesn't leave a gap in the Timeline where media is removed. When you extract footage, clips farther down the Timeline will be shifted to the left (rippled) to fill the gap. The media is removed and the gap is closed in one step. Set In and Out points in the Timeline to specify a range where you want footage removed. The range selected for extraction can include portions of a clip. When you're using Extract:

1. **Check track targets** to select the tracks from which media should be removed.

2. **Click the Sync Lock boxes** next to all Timeline tracks that you want to be shifted when the Extract button is clicked. Gaps will be closed for all sync locked tracks.

3. **Lock tracks** that you don't want rippled (like music tracks).

Sequence runtime is reduced when using Extract. This command is perfect for quickly tightening the cut, whittling down sequences full of interview selects, or trimming out the end of one shot and the beginning of the next shot at the same time.

To quickly see the difference between Lift and Extract, open the example sequence called **Skiing Everest_Lift & Extract**. I've already placed a few interview clips on the A1 track and set markers to indicate portions of clips for lifting an extracting (**Figure 3.29**).

Figure 3.29 Set In-to-Out ranges in the Timeline and use Lift or Extract to remove unwanted portions of clips from the sequence.

1. Mark an In point (I) at the begging of the sequence.

2. Press Shift+M to jump to the first marker.

3. Set an Out point (O).

4. Click the Extract button in the Program Monitor or use the keyboard shortcut for Extract (') to remove the portion of the first clip where the narrator says "The thing is, is…".

   The sound is removed from the first portion of that clip and the gap is closed, so the narrator now begins his line cleaning by saying, "When you're out there on those peaks…" Farther down the Timeline, let's use a Lift edit to remove a portion of a sound bite and leave a gap in the dialogue.

5. Press Shift+M to jump to the second marker in the Timeline.

6. Press I to set an In point.

7. Press the down arrow key to jump the end of that sound bite, and then press O to set an Out point.

8. Click the Lift button in the Program Monitor or use the default keyboard shortcut (;) to remove the sound where the narrator says "Like they say, as you know…"

The unnecessary dialogue is removed, and a gap remains in the sequence.

Delete

Unlike Lift and Extract, which use In and Out points to select a range in the sequence for deletion, the Delete and Ripple Delete commands use the Selection tool to remove *whole clips*. Both Delete and Ripple Delete are used to quickly remove a selected clip or a group of clips from the Timeline. To delete footage, simply select a clip in the Timeline and press Delete. The selected media is removed, leaving a gap in the sequence. Sync is preserved. If you want to delete just a portion of a clip, use the Lift command.

Ripple Delete

Ripple Delete removes footage and closes the gap in one step. Media on all unlocked tracks beyond your selection will be shifted to the left (rippled) to close the gap when you choose Ripple Delete. If you want to prevent an item from moving, lock the track (or turn off Sync Locks).

This method of removing footage is super fast, especially when you want to clean up many pieces of footage at once. I use this feature when editing documentaries, because it's faster to put an entire interview into a sequence and then splice and quickly remove the sections I don't intend to use rather than setting In and Out marks in source clips and overwriting individual sound bites into the Timeline.

Try this: Open the example sequence called **Skiing Everest_Ripple Delete**. I've spliced the track using Command+K (Ctrl+K) to perform an Add Edit and isolated portions of the clips I want to ripple out of the sequence. Alternately, you can use the Razor tool (C) to add edits. I've placed markers that indicate multiple sections of sound bites that can quickly be cleaned up all at once using Ripple Delete. Markers aren't necessary; I simply placed them to make this example clear.

Press Shift and click to select every portion you want to delete from the sequence (**Figure 3.30**). To perform a Ripple Delete, press Shift+Forward Delete (Shift+Delete). All selected portions of clips are removed from the sequence and remaining clips are rippled to close the gaps.

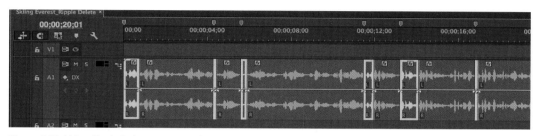

Figure 3.30 Using Ripple Delete to cut up a long interview clip lets you visually delete unwanted portions.

Removing tops and tails

The most advanced method of quickly removing footage from the Timeline involves using keyboard shortcuts to lop off the beginning (top) or ending (tail) portion of a shot. This is one of my favorite Timeline editing tricks. When I want to quickly tighten shots and remove time from the sequence, this technique requires the least amount of clicking with the mouse, and it feels highly intuitive. This is actually a Ripple Trimming technique. Trimming is covered in detail later in this chapter, but because these keyboard shortcuts are used simply to remove unwanted footage from the beginning and end of clips in the Timeline, it makes sense to learn this type of trim now.

Rippling out the top of a clip is similar to marking an In-to-Out range around the beginning portion of a clip and then pressing Extract (') except that it happens in one keystroke! It's often called a "top" trim because you're removing the portion from the top of a clip to the playhead. You don't need to select any cut points. When you press Q, which is the shortcut for Ripple Trim Previous Edit to Playhead, the beginning portion of the clip is removed from the previous cut point to the playhead location.

In the example sequence called **Skiing Everest_Tops & Tails**, let's remove the extra shot at the beginning of the final clip along with the sound bite where the narrator says, "So your mind just wanders wherever it's going to wander to." Performing a Top Trim is the slickest way to remove these frames. This is so slick, you've got to try it.

1. Play the **Skiing Everest_Tops & Tails** sequence in real time.

2. While playing the sequence, press Q after the narrator says, "…it's going to wander to," right after the picture cuts to the image where the clouds are moving through the peak (there is a marker at this location) (**Figure 3.31**).

The top portion of both picture and sound clips are removed, and footage farther down the Timeline ripples to the playhead location to fill the gap.

Figure 3.31 In points of Timeline clips are rippled to the playhead location when you press Q. There is no need to select the edit point or set In and Out points when using the keyboard shortcut for Ripple Trim Previous Edit to Playhead.

Notice in this example sequence that the music track (A7) has been locked. Mind the tracks! When clips are rippled in this way, a splice will be created through all tracks to extract frames. When clips farther down the Timeline are rippled, the entire sequence gets shorter. That fact should alert you to look for potential audio sync issues before performing the edit.

Rippling away the tail is similar to marking an In-to-Out range around the end portion of a clip in the Timeline and then pressing Extract (') except that all steps happen in one keystroke. When you press W, which is the keyboard shortcut for Ripple Trim Next Edit to Playhead, the end or "tail" portion of the clip is removed from the playhead location all the way to the next cut point in the Timeline.

Tail Trimming can feel trickier to master than Top Trimming, especially during real-time playback. It essentially works the same way as Top Trimming but in reverse. To ease the learning curve, begin practicing this technique by parking the playhead in the middle of a clip in the Timeline and then pressing W to get the feel of removing the tail portion of a clip, as described in the following steps.

1. In the **Skiing Everest_Tops & Tails** sequence, park the Timeline playhead at 25;11, just before the narrator says, "We get a lot of time just sitting in the tent reading and relaxing" (**Figure 3.32** on the next page).

2. Press W.

   The tail portion of the clip called SE_03 is extracted, and clips farther down the Timeline are rippled to the playhead to fill the gap where frames were removed.

For extra credit, practice removing footage from the tail portion of clips using the keyboard shortcut (W) while playing the sequence live (in real time).

Adding modifier keys to Q and W will activate different trimming features, which I'll cover in more detail later in this chapter.

Figure 3.32 The tail, or end portion, of clips in the Timeline can be quickly removed by pressing the keyboard shortcut W. It's an amazingly fast way to edit.

Repositioning Timeline Clips

While editing, I often need to move sections of clips around on my Timeline—more than just one or two clips. Frequently, I see editors drag clips into higher tracks to make room on the Timeline. Instead, you can use two great techniques to move clips on the Timeline—Swap Edit and Paste Insert.

Swap Edit

I use the Swap Edit command repeatedly throughout the day when I'm working in the Timeline. By holding a simple modifier key while you drag and drop, you can swap the position of a clip, or several clips, in the sequence with other clips. The repositioned clip will be inserted into a new location. Surrounding clips are rearranged, and gaps are closed or created as needed to preserve sync. Sounds like magic? It seems that way!

This command is similar to both an extract and insert edit in that clips are rippled while being repositioned, or "swapped," in the Timeline. This technique is easier to perform on clips that have not been L or J cut, so if this is new to you, it's best to practice on clips in the Timeline that have straight cuts. In other words, if clips have linked audio and video, practice on shots where the audio portion of the clip cuts at the same time as the video. Try this exercise.

1. Open the provided sequence called **Skiing Everest_ Peak Scene_Swap Edit**.

2. Make sure Snapping (S) is on.

3. Click to select the second video shot.

4. Press and hold Command+Option (Ctrl+Alt) while dragging the second clip to the left, and snap it the very beginning of the sequence.

5. Look for the Swap icon (this is sometimes referred to as the Rearrange icon) (**Figure 3.33**).

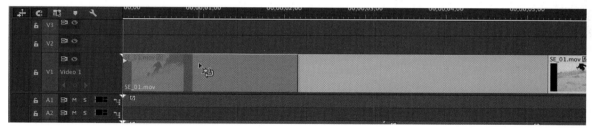

Figure 3.33 Performing a Swap Edit rearranges the order of clips in the Timeline. Turn Snapping on, press and hold Command+Option (Ctrl+Alt), and then drag and drop the clip at the new location. Surrounding clips are rippled to accommodate the repositioned shot.

6. Watch for Snapping symbols and insert arrows as you drag, indicating you have reached the cut point where the first shot is currently located.

7. Release the mouse.

The two shots have swapped position! This worked quite easily in the example because these two video clips are not linked to audio. Don't forget: When linked audio is longer or shorter than the corresponding picture, swapping clips may result in gaps in the Timeline, which preserves audio sync. It's cleaner to swap clips before creating split edits (L and J cuts). I also find it easier to swap clips by dragging to the left, so I'm moving them earlier in the Timeline. Practice this technique on all types of clips so you'll know what to expect when you perform a Swap Edit in different situations.

For extra credit, try swapping the clip that is now at the beginning of the sequence with the second clip in the Timeline. While holding down Command+Option (Ctrl+Alt) you'll need to drag the first clip far to the right to the end of the second clip, and then snap it to the Out point of the second shot in the sequence before releasing the mouse. Next, try selecting several sequential clips and swap them as a unit.

Paste Insert

I briefly mentioned the Paste Insert technique earlier in the chapter, but it's such an efficient method for repositioning groups of clips in the Timeline that I want to reinforce the concept. I'm certain you'll incorporate this into your editing workflow. I use this trick so often that a director I work with called me the other day to ask if I could explain it to his new editor. It you're constantly opening up space in the Timeline by dragging clips farther down the sequence and then repositioning Timeline clips and then closing the gaps, practice this skill.

Master the Paste Insert and you'll rarely need to move clips just to reposition shots. In cases where a Swap Edit just won't work correctly, usually because of audio sync concerns or split edits, try a Paste Insert.

1. Open the sequence called **Skiing Everest_Paste Insert**.

2. Click and drag to select the last two clips of video at the end of the sequence and the corresponding audio (the last sound bite that begins, "You really don't have a lot to think about").

3. Press Command+X (Ctrl+X) to cut those three clips from the sequence.

4. Snap the playhead to the beginning of the clip called SE_04 at the cut point just before the narrator says, "It's hours out there by yourself," at 31;07 in the Timeline.

5. Lock the A7 music track (**Figure 3.34**).

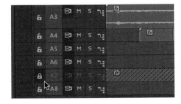

Figure 3.34 Be mindful of audio sync. Before performing a Paste Insert, lock tracks that should not be spliced or moved.

6. Target the V1 track.

7. Press Command+Shift+V (Ctrl+Shift+V) to perform a Paste Insert (**Figure 3.35**).

If you listen to this scene in the sequence after performing the Paste Insert and then press Command+Z (Ctrl+Z) to undo and listen again, you'll hear the difference in shot sequencing and understand how great this technique is for rearranging story ideas in the Timeline. This is my go-to method for repositioning groups of clips when I'm moving toward the fine-cut stage, especially when there are complicated split edits or layered picture and dialogue tracks.

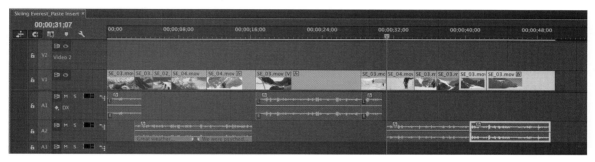

Figure 3.35 After pressing Command+Shift+V, the copied clips will be inserted at the playhead location on dominant targeted tracks. Clips to the right of the playhead will move farther down the Timeline.

When performing a Paste Insert, it's important to remember the following:

▶ **Target Timeline tracks** where you want Audio and video tracks to be pasted as an insert edit.

▶ **Lock Tracks** to prevent accidental adjustments. A splice will be made through all tracks when the playhead is not positioned on a cut point, so lock any music or narration tracks that shouldn't be altered by the insert.

▶ **Clips are rippled** down the Timeline to make room for the insert edit, so keep an eye on audio sync.

For extra credit, open the **Skiing Everest_Peak Scene** sequence. Press Shift while selecting several skiing sound effects and then group them with a matching video clip by pressing Command+G (Ctrl+G). Cut and Paste Insert the group to a new location in the Timeline (**Figure 3.36**).

Figure 3.36 Group unlinked audio and video clips and they will always move, cut, and paste as a single unit.

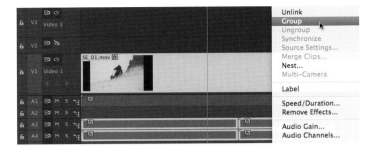

Basic Trimming

Trimming is most useful when it's time to take an assembly edit to a rough cut. Often, this phase of the edit is about trimming to make the story sound right. This process is sometimes called the radio edit. Once the sound bites and fundamental shots are timed to roughly tell the story, more advanced trimming techniques help pace the visual cuts and add tension to the scene.

You may have heard the phrase, "There are three ways to do everything." When it comes to editing, that's true. It's possible to achieve identical results from three different methods of trimming, but one technique may be faster and easier to use in a given situation.

The trimming tools you'll use most often are partly a matter of preference and partly chosen to fit specific needs. You might choose to use the Trim Monitor, while syncing action for a wide shot that cuts to a close-up. The Trim Monitor allows you to view and choose the exact frames on both sides of the cut. A similar trim might be made more rapidly on the Timeline when syncing the visual action isn't a big concern. For example, while working on the radio edit it's often preferable to expand the sequence audio tracks and trim directly in the Timeline while viewing large waveforms to see the space between lines of dialogue.

Learning how all trimming techniques work, and how each trimming tool differs, will help you understand when to choose one method over another when refining a cut sequence. More important, mastering the basic use of these tools will allow you to advance to performing these types of edits using keyboard shortcuts that really speed up the trimming process. The primary trimming tools include:

- ▶ Selection tool
- ▶ Ripple Edit tool
- ▶ Rolling Edit tool
- ▶ Slip tool
- ▶ Slide tool

If you've been using Premiere Pro or another editing application for a while, you might skim this section as a quick review, then move on to the more advanced trimming techniques. If you're yet not making full use of the basic trimming tools, heed the detailed instructions below.

The Selection Tool

I'm sure you're familiar with using the selection tool to click-drag on a cut in the Sequence to adjust the length of clips in the Timeline. This is the trimming at its most basic. Using the Selection tool is safe, because it will never throw clips out-of-sync. It isn't the most elegant method of trimming but, when it's the right tool for the job, it's easy and it works.

Press the Selection Tool keyboard shortcut (V) and place the arrow over a cut point of a clip in a Sequence. When you do, you'll notice that the pointer changes to the Trim Tool. Move the mouse back and forth across the cut, and the Trim Tool arrow will change from left to right, so you can click to create an Incoming or an Outgoing trim.

If you've been performing a trim on both sides of a cut by first trimming to make one clip shorter and then dragging the edge of the next clip to fill the gap, read on!

The Rolling Edit Tool

The problem with using the Selection tool is that when you want to make a clip longer, other clips don't move out of the way. In other words, you can only drag to trim a clip so far with the Selection tool before it bumps up against another shot. You can use the Rolling Edit tool to trim both sides of the cut at the same time (**Figure 3.37**).

Figure 3.37 To access the Rolling Edit tool, select it from the Tools panel, or simply press N.

A Roll is a called a two-sided edit because both points (the In and the Out) on either side of the cut are adjusted simultaneously. The length of one clip adjusts to accommodate the changing length of the other. As one clip gets shorter the other gets longer, provided that there is enough "handle" content available to allow the trim. Handles refer to unused footage surrounding the selected portion of a shot inside the sequence.

When using the Rolling Edit tool in the Timeline, you don't have to worry about throwing tracks out of sync (unless you've locked dialogue tracks that are synced to an unlocked picture).

Rolling an edit point changes the location of the cut inside the sequence. The Rolling Edit tool is often used to create split edits, so that a clip's audio plays for a longer or shorter time than the matching video.

The Ripple Edit Tool

The Ripple Edit tool adds or removes frames while closing gaps (**Figure 3.38**). It's a single-sided trim, which means only one edit point, either the selected In point or the selected Out point, will be changed during the operation.

When you ripple a clip, footage beyond that selected cut point in the sequence will "ripple" (move to the right or left) depending on whether the selected clip is getting longer or shorter. As you trim a clip with the Ripple Edit tool, the entire sequence gets longer or shorter to accommodate the trim.

Figure 3.38 From the Tools panel select the Ripple Edit tool, or press B before selecting a cut point in the Timeline.

The point is this: When you use the Ripple Edit tool, mind the tracks!

Methodology: Using Ripple and Roll in Tandem

The Ripple tool is used to remove unwanted frames from clips in the Timeline, and much like using Extract, it's a quick way to shorten the overall duration of a sequence. It is also used to add and remove frames between two shots to achieve visual sync. For example, when syncing action between two different camera angles of a baseball player swinging a bat, you might use the Ripple tool to add or remove frames and make the action match exactly at the cut point between the medium shot and a close-up.

After using the Ripple tool to add and remove frames, editors frequently use the Roll tool to create split edits, which are known as L or J cuts. Here's an example of how to use both tools to smooth action across a cut:

▶ **Ripple to place the cut anywhere the action is easiest to sync.** Begin by using the Ripple Edit tool (B) to trim the shots on each side of the cut, so you end up putting the cut exactly where the ball hits the bat in both shots or where someone's footstep hits the ground from both camera angles.

▶ **Roll to create a split edit.** Once the visual action is in sync at the cut point, the Roll tool comes into play. Hold down the Option (Alt) key and click to select only the video portion of the clip with the Rolling Edit tool (N). Offset the video cut point so that action begins in the first shot and completes in the second shot.

In summary, sync the shots on action using the Ripple Edit tool, and then switch to the Rolling Edit tool to move the video cut point earlier, so the bat begins to swing in the first shot and then connects with the ball and completes the swing in the second shot.

The technique of beginning action in the first clip and continuing or completing the action in the next clip makes the cuts between shots go unnoticed by viewers, because their eyes are literally "on the ball," not on the cut between shots. By rolling only the video portion of the clip, you also offset the picture cut from the sound cut. This helps smooth the change from one shot to the next, making a more elegant transition between shots that will likely go unnoticed by the audience. Quickly achieving frame accurate, invisible cuts is the point of mastering the Ripple and Roll Edit tools.

Let's practice performing Ripple and Roll Edits in tandem. I'll throw in a few bonus techniques and some review in the process.

TIP

Holding down the Option (Alt) key while selecting a clip or a cut point temporarily unlinks audio from video, allowing you to quickly create a split edit. The resulting edit is often called an L cut or a J cut because, as a result of splitting the edit, the clips in the Timeline now mimic the letter L (when audio continues after picture cuts) or the letter J (when the audio cuts before the picture changes).

1. Open the example sequence called **Skiing Everest_ Trimming**.

2. Look at the track configuration. Synced dialogue has been placed on the A1 track, and narration that is not linked to video clips has been placed on A2. Notice that all audio tracks except A1 are locked. This configuration allows an editor to easily perform ripple trims while keeping linked audio in sync with the picture.

3. While holding down the Shift key, click on the track target for A1. This will turn off all audio track targets, so you can use keyboard shortcuts to jump to cut points only on the video tracks and ignore the audio cuts.

4. Use the up and down arrow keys to place the playhead at the cut point between the first two video clips in the sequence.

5. Zoom into the Timeline using the plus (+) key.

6. Press B to activate the Ripple Edit tool.

7. Click and drag on the left side of the playhead, and drag to ripple the outgoing shot so that it's shorter.

8. Look at the Program Monitor while dragging the Ripple tool. Release the mouse when you visually see the skier in blue dig his skis and poles into the snow, so he is facing perpendicular to the camera with his skis pointing to the left side of the screen. The timecode overlay on the outgoing shot in the Program Monitor should read 04:20. The overlay in the Timeline should indicate that you've shortened the shot (**Figure 3.39**).

9. Click with the Ripple Edit tool on the incoming shot, just to the right of the same cut point, and drag to the left again, lengthening the second shot.

10. Release the mouse when the timecode overlay on the incoming shot in the Program Monitor reads about 06:20. The skier in red should be in roughly the same position as the skier in blue from the previous shot. Snow should be flying off the skis toward the right of the frame in both shots (**Figure 3.40**).

Figure 3.39 It's always helpful to use the visual two-up display in the Program Monitor, as well as timecode overlays, to help position the edit point while making the trim.

Figure 3.40 Moving a trim of the head, or top, of the clip to the left makes the clip longer.

TIP

If you have difficulty trimming a cut to a specific frame because the selected trim keeps snapping to the playhead, you can press S to turn Snapping off, even mid trim while dragging.

11. The cut point is now positioned on matching action in both clips. Play through the edit.

12. Press N to activate the Rolling Edit tool, and select the same cut point as a Roll (red I-bar).

13. Drag to roll the cut point to the right, later in time. Release the mouse when both athletes are in mid turn, with poles and skis released from the snow as though they're floating above the earth (**Figure 3.41**).

14. Play through the edit. The action of the turn is initiated by the first skier and completed by the second. The cut across matching action should feel smooth, not jarring. This works even better using two camera angles of the same skier.

Figure 3.41 A Roll edit (N) affects both sides of the trim.

Trimming in the Program Panel

Trimming in the Program panel provides you with a two-up display (**Figure 3.42**). This is the best way to view images on either side of the cut while trimming. When I want to cut away from a shot on a very specific frame—and I want to make that decision visually—I use the Program panel to perform the trim rather than adjusting the edit by dragging in the Timeline.

To trim in the Program panel, start by activating the two-up display (Trim mode). Using the Selection tool, double-click on a cut in the Timeline (or select the edit and press T) to load the edit into the Program Monitor.

Here are some guidelines about using the Trim mode:

▶ **Roll the edit.** If you want to trim visually while dragging, you can click in between the two images in the Program panel to select the edit point as a roll, and then drag the Rolling Edit tool left or right to move the cut point earlier or later in the Timeline.

▶ **Ripple the edit.** Move the mouse across the cut in the Program Monitor and look for the yellow ripple indicators. Click to select either the incoming or outgoing shot. Drag with the Ripple tool, or use the trim buttons to add or remove frames.

▶ **Perform a single or multi-frame trim.** Use the Trim Forward and Trim Backward buttons to add and remove frames.

Timeline Trimming Tips

Here are some tips to trim smarter directly on the Timeline:

▶ Press Option+left arrow (Alt+left arrow) and Option+right arrow (Alt+right arrow) to trim in single frame increments.

▶ Press Option+Shift+left arrow (Alt+Shift+left arrow) and Option+Shift+right arrow (Alt+Shift+right arrow) for multi-frame trims.

▶ Holding down the Option (Alt) key while clicking with the Selection, Ripple, or Roll tools allows you to select just the video or audio cut point (temporary unlink).

▶ Right-click on a cut point with the edit tools to see Trim In and Trim Out options.

▶ Press the keyboard shortcut to toggle Snapping (S) while trimming so cuts snap to the playhead or move freely as needed.

▶ When trimming, mind the Timeline tracks targets, because targeting affects cut point selection while navigating with the up and down arrow keys (Go to Next Edit and Go to Previous Edit shortcuts).

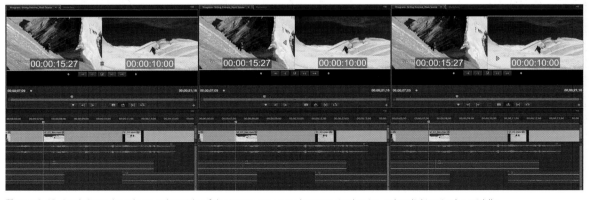

Figure 3.42 By clicking directly on either side of the image, you can choose a ripple trim, or by clicking in the middle, you can choose a roll trim.

Trim Tool Guide

It's useful to have a cheat sheet of the trim tool possibilities and colors:

▶ A Red Bracket is a basic trim, which behaves like a Lift edit (leaves a gap).

▶ A Yellow Bracket performs a Ripple Edit, which adds or removes frames and makes the sequence longer or shorter.

▶ When a trim bracket is open to the left, the Out point of the outgoing clip is trimmed. If the bracket is open to the right, the In point of the incoming clip is trimmed.

▶ The Red I-bar is a Rolling edit, which adjusts only the two clips on either side of the selected cut. Trimming with the Roll tool moves the cut point a bit earlier or later but does not change the length of the sequence.

▶ As you drag a cut point with any of the Trim tools, you'll see a yellow timecode indicator showing how many frames have been trimmed (forward or backward).

▶ Shots trimmed in the Timeline update dynamically in the Program Monitor.

▶ **Loop playback.** Pressing the spacebar will loop playback in the Program panel and keep Trim Mode active.

▶ **Improve functionality.** Use the JKL keys while trimming in the Program Monitor.

▶ **Use keyboard shortcuts.** Press Option+left arrow (Alt+left arrow) and Option+right arrow (Alt+right arrow) to perform "live" trimming during looped playback. Keep an eye on the Timeline as it dynamically updates.

We'll look at more advanced keyboard shortcuts that you can use in conjunction with Program Monitor trimming in the "Advanced Trimming" section later in this chapter.

Extend Edit

Extend Edit is one of the easiest and most useful features to use while trimming. I couldn't work without it! Select a cut in the Timeline with the Rolling Edit tool, and then simply press E to "extend" that cut to the playhead location. Of course, this feature requires you to have enough handle frames available to allow the trim to function.

1. Open the example sequence you previously used called **Skiing Everest_Tops & Tails**.

2. Press N to select the second video cut point as a rolling edit.

3. Zoom into the Timeline (+) if needed.

4. Play backward (J) and then forward (L), and press pause (K) to stop the playhead after the narrator says "The North Ridge."

5. Press E to move the cut to the playhead location.

6. Move the next edit point by pressing the down arrow key; then Extend the third shot in the sequence so it covers the line, "The way that it is more often than not...."

This is so easy and effective that I thought about sharing this information earlier. But here is the coolest part: This trick also works when the cut is selected as a Ripple Edit! It works with the basic Trim tool (selection arrow) too. If the cut point is selected as a ripple incoming or a ripple outgoing (yellow brackets), mind your tracks for sync.

For extra credit, the Extend Edit can be employed to quickly create L and J cuts (split edits). Option-click (Alt-click) on a video cut point when selecting with a Trim tool, which will temporarily unlink the audio, to trim only the video edit point.

The Slip Tool

When you like the duration and location of a clip in the Timeline sequence but want to use a different portion of the shot's content, use the Slip tool to simultaneously change both the In and Out points for the shot. You won't be repositioning the clip in time; rather, you'll be slipping the clip's content by selecting a new In and Out frame for the shot that's being slipped. Performing a Slip edit in the Timeline is so much easier than reloading the master clip into the Source Monitor to choose a new segment of the shot.

To fully grasp how fast and easy it is to slip a shot, try this exercise.

1. Open the example sequence called **Skiing Everest_ Trimming**.

2. In the Tools panel select the Slip tool (Y).

3. With the Slip tool active, place it over the clip called SE_02 (about 12 seconds into the sequence). This clip contains two shots with lower-third text that reads Mustagh Ata and Everest.

4. Click and drag to the right with the Slip tool. In the Program Monitor you'll see the new In and Out frames for the clip displayed and updating as you perform the slip (**Figure 3.43** on the next page).

5. When you see the Mustagh Ata shot displaying frames without text for both the In point (left image in a two-up display) and Out point (right image in a two-up display), release the mouse.

6. Play through the edit to ensure that the Mustagh Ata text fades up and out on the shot. Adjust the trim as needed.

Figure 3.43 Activate the Slip tool (Y) to readjust the In and Out points of a clip in the Timeline. Use the two-up display in the Program Monitor to help you perform the trim.

The Slide Tool

Let's say you have a great shot in your sequence but you'd like to cut to it just a bit earlier so that it times up better with the music cue. This is a perfect moment to use the Slide tool.

When you like the content and duration of a clip in the Timeline but want to reposition that clip to a new location that's just a bit earlier or bit later in the sequence, use the Slide tool. When you click and drag on a clip in the Timeline with the Slide tool, the Out frame of the clip to the left and the In frame of the clip to the right update.

Using the Slide tool does not result in a change to the duration of your sequence, because the clips on either side of the shot you're sliding are adjusted to accommodate the clip you're moving.

Let's slide a clip to fit with a line of narration.

1. Open the example sequence called **Skiing Everest_ Trimming**.

2. In the Tools panel select the Slide tool (U).

3. Play the clip called SE_01 (about 11 seconds into the sequence), and stop the playhead just after the narrator says, "…accomplishing a goal" and before he says, "It's like nothing else."

4. Make sure Snapping is on (S).

5. With the Slide tool active, click and drag the clip so the Out point snaps to the playhead and release the mouse.

6. In the Program Monitor you'll see new In and Out frames updating for the clips on either side of the shot you're sliding. The mini-frames above the two-up display show you the In and Out points of the clip you're sliding (**Figure 3.44**).

Figure 3.44 Activate the Slide tool (Y) to reposition a clip in the Timeline. Use the two-up display in the Program Monitor to help you make the trim.

7. Play through the edit to ensure that the shot ends after the narrator says, "...goal" and that both the outgoing and incoming shots on either side had enough handle to accommodate the trim.

Maintaining Sync

While editing, it's extremely important to manage Linked Selection in the Timeline, maintain sync while trimming, and fix clips that have lost sync in a sequence. There are several features in Adobe Premiere Pro that help preserve audio and picture sync. Let's review a few of them next.

Linked Selection

When the Linked Selection button is active (dark), all clips in the Timeline with linked video and audio can be selected, moved, and trimmed as a unit. Turn off Linked Selection and all clips in the Timeline will behave as though they are unlinked.

I typically work with Linked Selection active, but when editing movie trailers or promos it's helpful to deactivate this feature. During this style of editing, I'm more interested in using compelling imagery over narration like, "In a world... full of renegade cops who don't play by the rules...one man will be tested." Because I'm not working with a lot of synced dialogue while making a promo, I prefer to turn off Linked Selection so I can quickly place short, dramatic sound bites under the most intriguing action shots (**Figure 3.45**).

Figure 3.45 Linking can be turned on/off quickly with this switch. Just be careful!

Temporarily unlink audio and video

Because I use temporary unlink feature more often than any other method of unlinking, I'll walk you through using this feature.

Open the example sequence called **Skiing Everest_ Trimming**. The last clip in the Timeline is Jim speaking about climbers. Let's clean up his audio by trimming off the beginning portion where he says, "Like they say, as you know...."

With the audio waveform visible on the A1 track, it's easy to see exactly where Jim begins his next line, "Climbers have short memories." Place the playhead just before Jim says the word "Climbers." Press V for the Selection tool and drag to trim the audio portion of the clip. Because Linked Selection is active, the linked picture is trimmed too, leaving a gap on the video track. Whoops. Undo. I want to see Jim onscreen at the end of the scene. I don't want to permanently unlink Jim's audio from his picture because I intend to Ripple Trim other clips in this sequence, and I want Jim's onscreen clip to maintain sync!

Do the following to trim Jim's linked audio clip: Press the Option (Alt) key while dragging the edge of the sound clip to trim out the unwanted audio. The picture track will be ignored. After you release the mouse to complete the trim, the clip will behave as a typical linked clip, so it will maintain the split edit (L or J cut) and stay in sync when other clips are trimmed (**Figure 3.46**).

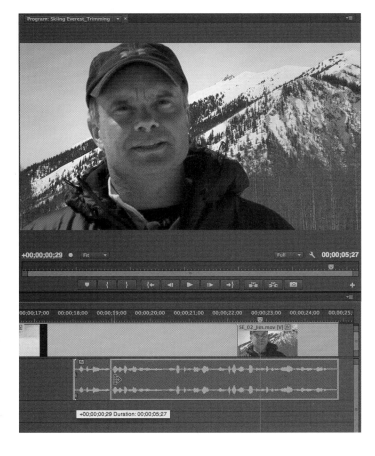

Figure 3.46 Press Option (Alt) to temporarily unlink when trimming the edge of the audio clip to avoid trimming the linked picture and creating a gap on the video track.

This temporary unlink feature is also handy to delete unwanted tracks from linked clips. Use this technique to clean up the Timeline when you've unintentionally brought in audio tracks that you don't need. If you wanted only A1 and A2, but A3 and A4 are still linked to the picture because you didn't modify the clip before editing it into the Timeline, hold down Option (Alt) when you select the unneeded audio and press Delete.

Unlink and relink individual clips

In some cases, you'll want to unlink video from audio for an individual clip in the sequence and leave it permanently unlinked. When I use audio from a clip—let's say it's sound from an on-camera interview—and I've spliced it to remove a long "um..uh," and I intend to cover the pause and the cut with B-roll footage, I'll use this method to permanently unlink that sound bite from the picture of the speaker who will appear in sync later in the program.

You can select the clip and either choose Clip > Unlink or right-click on the clip and choose Unlink. To relink clips that are unlinked, Shift-click to select both audio and video portions, and then choose Clip > Link or right-click on the clip and choose Link.

The best way to quickly Link and Unlink individual clips is to use keyboard shortcuts. Try this exercise.

1. Open the **Skiing Everest_Trimming** sequence.

2. Put the playhead at the beginning of Jim's on camera video clip.

3. Press Command+K (Ctrl+K) to add an edit through the linked audio track.

4. Click to select the video portion of Jim's clip.

   Darn it! The portion of the clip that should stay linked to Jim—where he is on-camera speaking—was unlinked as a result of adding a splice, but the earlier portion of the clip that is hidden by B-roll is still linked to the picture. This situation will happen often, I promise (**Figure 3.47**).

Figure 3.47 Press Command+L (Ctrl+L) to link or unlink picture and sound for selected clips.

5. Select Jim's video clip and press Command+L (Ctrl+L) to unlink it from the audio that's under B-roll.

6. To preserve lip-sync, hold down Shift to select both the picture and audio clips at the end, where Jim is on-camera, and press Command+L (Ctrl+L) to relink that portion.

Group clips

As I mentioned earlier in this chapter, clips that were never linked can be selected and grouped together. Let's dive in and get familiar with how this works.

1. Return to the **Skiing Everest_Trimming** sequence in Adobe Premiere Pro.

2. Unlock the A4 track that contains natural skiing sound effects, which were recorded on location.

3. Select the third video clip in the sequence, the shot with the skier in black wearing a white helmet. Beneath this shot is a sound effect that is in sync with the action.

4. Press Shift to select the sound effect on V4 below the video clip.

5. Press Command+G (Ctrl+G), or right-click on either the selected video or audio clip and choose Group (**Figure 3.48**).

Figure 3.48 Grouped clips behave as a single items for operations such as Move, Copy, Paste, Paste Insert, or Swap Edit.

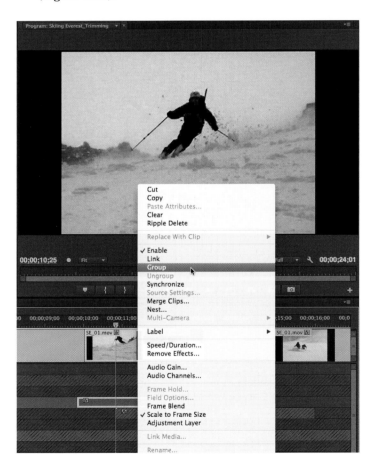

6. Lock track A4 and notice that the video portion of this grouped clip will behave as an independent clip again if you try to Slip, Slide, move, or perform any other edit function when you select it, because the audio is locked down.

Grouped clips will behave as if they are ungrouped if the Linked Selection button is not active for the Timeline.

Once grouped, these clips will move, copy, and trim as though linked, even though they originated from separate source footage. The real advantage of grouping is that you can link not only several synced sound effect clips to a single video clip, but you can group multiple video and audio clips together, and then Cut and Paste Insert, reposition, and quickly Swap Edit the grouped clips using keyboard commands. It allows you to keep an entire scene, or a portion of a scene, together and behaving as a single, grouped clip. It's an invaluable technique for taking a portion of a scene that is working well, including video, several layers of dialogue, background sound, and graphics, and moving the entire scene to a new location in the film.

For extra credit, return to the **Skiing Everest_Trimming** sequence. Zoom (+) into the first three video clips at the beginning of the sequence. Reposition, Slip, or, Slide the matching sound effects on A4, so they sync with picture. View audio waveforms if needed. Group the first three video clips with the four sound clips beneath them. Click to select the group, and move, or Cut and Paste Insert the group of clips to a new location, or into a new sequence.

Grouping isn't necessary simply to keep separate sound effects in sync while trimming other clips in the sequence. There is no need to group clips if you don't plan to move them as a single unit. Sync Lock will help you maintain sync while inserting shots and trimming without grouping clips.

Sync Lock

Sync Lock help keep all tracks in sync while trimming. This feature is helpful for maintaining audio sync when inserting footage or performing Ripple Trims and Ripple Deletes, whether or not you're targeting to insert source media onto those tracks.

If a Timeline track does not have a Source Track Patch connected and activated but has Sync Lock enabled, an insert edit will affect that track. Media on tracks that have Sync Lock enabled will ripple when the insert is performed, and in some cases empty track background will be inserted on the track for the duration that matches the inserted source clip.

In other words, if you have Sync Lock on, gaps may appear to preserve sync.

To clarify this concept, let's experiment with Sync Lock in the **Skiing Everest_Trimming** sequence.

1. Hold down the Shift key and click on an audio track lock icon to unlock all audio tracks.

2. Make sure Sync Lock is enabled for all audio tracks by Shift-clicking on the Sync Lock icon for one of the audio tracks until all are active (no slash mark through the sync icons).

3. Press B to activate the Ripple Edit tool.

4. Drag with the Ripple Edit tool on the incoming edge of the second video shot in the sequence to make it longer.

   A gap appears in the sound effects tracks, A4 and A5, to preserve sync (**Figure 3.49**).

5. Press Command+Z (Ctrl+Z) to undo.

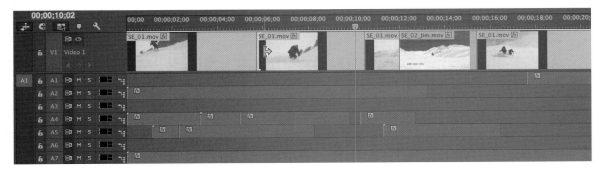

Figure 3.49 When Sync Lock is active for a track, clips will ripple or a gap may be inserted, to preserve sync while performing insert edits, Ripple Deletes, and Ripple Trims.

6. Drag with the Ripple Edit tool on the incoming edge of the second video shot in the sequence to make it shorter. You won't able to trim the video shorter because with Sync Lock active the clip is blocked by the clip on A4. The Timeline overlay indicates that the natural sound effect track is blocking the trim.

7. Click to deactivate the Sync Lock icons next to tracks A4 and A5.

8. Drag with the Ripple Edit tool on the incoming edge of the second video shot in the sequence to make it shorter. With Sync Lock deactivated for the sound effects tracks, frames can be removed from the video clip to make it shorter (**Figure 3.50**).

   Notice that the audio linked to Jim's onscreen interview (the last shot in the sequence) has maintained sync during the trim.

9. Click to deactivate Sync Lock on A1.

10. Again, drag with the Ripple Edit tool on the incoming edge of the second video shot in the sequence, toward the left, to make the shot longer again.

    Out of sync markers may appear for linked clips, like Jim's onscreen interview, when Sync Lock is deactivated.

11. Press Command+Z (Ctrl+Z) to undo.

Figure 3.50 With Sync Lock off on A4 and A5, the video clip can be rippled and the trim is not limited by the preservation of sync. In most cases, Sync Lock should remain enabled for primary video and dialogue tracks.

TIP

It's faster to lock all tracks and then selectively unlock an individual track you want to use, or vice versa, rather than clicking on each lock icon individually. To lock all video or audio tracks at once, Shift-click on a Sync or Track Lock icon in the Timeline panel, and then click once on the individual track you want to unlock.

When Sync Lock is active for corresponding linked tracks, clips on those tracks will all shift when a Ripple Trim is performed and sync will be preserved. Turn off Sync Lock for linked audio tracks, and those tracks will stay put when you perform the Ripple Trim. I recommend leaving Sync Lock active for all linked dialogue tracks to preserve sync when insert and ripple edits are performed anywhere in the Timeline.

Repairing Sync Issues

When a clip goes out of sync, a sync flag appears on the upper-left corner of the clip. Right-click on a clip's audio or video sync flag, and you'll be presented with two options—Move into Sync and Slip into Sync:

▶ **Move clips into sync.** If you choose Move into Sync, Adobe Premiere Pro just moves the out of sync portion back into sync with the other part of the clip. The video or audio (depending on which sync flag you right-clicked) is repositioned in the Timeline to achieve sync.

▶ **Slip clips into sync.** If you choose Slip into Sync, Adobe Premiere Pro slips the out of sync audio or video back into sync. Slipping the clip won't change the location of the out of sync clip in the Timeline. The clip will remain where it is in the sequence, and Adobe Premiere Pro will slip the part of the clip you selected back into sync. This is a great way to create a split edit! If you intentionally want the audio to lead the viewer into the upcoming picture shot, move the sound portion of the clip so it begins before the video, and then slip it back into sync with the picture (**Figure 3.51**).

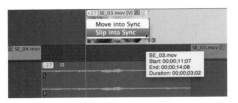

Figure 3.51 Right-click on the out of sync indicators to select an option for repairing sync. Selecting Slip into Sync in this situation will preserve the J cut configuration of the split edit while slipping the picture back into sync.

And when sync really goes wrong, use Match Frame and Replace. It's possible to use a Match Frame and then perform a Replace edit to bring audio and picture back into sync in the Timeline.

Advanced Timeline Editing

Once you've mastered basic trimming techniques in the Timeline and regularly use keyboard shortcuts, accelerate your process by adding a few advanced trimming methods to your daily workflow.

Replacing and reordering shots in the Timeline is critical, but when it comes time to join ideas and match cuts so they work invisibly to tell a story, you'll want to master the more advanced Timeline trimming features. Trimming really is the heart of editing, so let's get you up to speed with the most elegant techniques for finessing the cut.

Extend Edit Live

Using Extend Edit (E) with Real-Time Playback is an amazing method of trimming a cut point directly in the Timeline when visual frame accuracy is less important than speed. I especially like trimming while watching the sequence in real time, because it allows me to "feel" where the cut should occur while the program is in play.

Let's take your skills up a notch.

1. Instead of using the Trim tools to select the cut point, press T, the keyboard shortcut for trim. The edit point nearest to the playhead will be selected as a rolling edit (red I-bar). The clips on each side of the selected edit point will be loaded into the two-up display in the Program Monitor.

2. Toggle through Trim types by pressing Command+T (Ctrl+T). Incoming and Outgoing shots are selected and update in the Program monitor as you toggle.

3. Turn on Looping by pressing Command+L (Ctrl+L) (**Figure 3.52**).

4. Press Shift+K to Play Around the current edit (**Figure 3.53**).

5. With playback looping live, press E to make the trim.

6. Let looping continue to play and watch the cut.

7. Press E again as playback continues to refine the trim as needed.

Modified Tops and Tails

Using modifier keys to perform top and tail trims during real-time playback is a great way to rapidly cut the sequence down to the final running time while pacing the timing of cuts to match music and dialogue cues. If you

Figure 3.52 Click the plus symbol at the bottom right in the Program panel to add the Loop button to your transport controls. Or press Command+L (Ctrl+L) to toggle Looping on.

Figure 3.53 Click the Play Around button in the Program panel, or press Shift+K to play the edit.

need to review top and tail trims, jump back a bit earlier in this chapter. I'm revisiting the tops and tails technique in the advanced trimming section to encourage your practice of real-time trimming.

The most elegant way to perform a top or tail trim is to become so proficient at understanding it's operation in the Timeline that you can perform the trim during real-time playback. You'll be trimming clips faster than you can think *I want to trim off this bit here.*

There is no need to select the edit as a ripple or a roll! There is no need to mark an In or Out point and use Lift or Extract! There is no need to press a keyboard shortcut to toggle the trim type! The start or end (In or Out point) of a clip in the sequence works with the location of the playhead to designate the frames that will be trimmed from the sequence. The keyboard shortcut you press determines the trim type. It's so easy!

Let's practice this technique with real-time playback.

1. Open the example sequence called **Skiing Everest_ Advanced Trimming**.

2. Select the clip called SE_02 Jim and press the forward slash (/) key to mark the clip. This is not necessary to perform the trim; I'm just lending you training wheels to help you develop real-time trimming chops.

3. Lock all audio tracks except A1 (the track linked to the onscreen interview).

4. With Looping active, press Option+K (Alt+K) to play the clip from In to Out points.

   This clip contains two shots. The goal is to make the trim after the Mustagh Ata text fades but just before the Everest shot begins.

5. When the clip changes from the Mustagh Ata shot to the Everest shot, press W to ripple away the tail portion of the clip (**Figure 3.54**).

6. Press Command+Z (Ctrl+Z) to Undo the previous trim.

00;00;13;16 ● Fit ▾   Full ▾

SE_01.mov 𝑓𝑥   SE_02_Jim.mov 𝑓𝑥   SE_01.mov 𝑓𝑥

Figure 3.54 Press W when the playhead reaches the frame where the Mustagh Ata text has faded. Because playback is looping, watch the shot once or twice for accuracy before performing the trim.

TIP

During playback, when the playhead reaches the middle of a clip in the Timeline, simply press Q and the first half of the clip will be extracted from the sequence. If you press W, the second half of the clip will be extracted from the sequence. Add the Shift key to perform a Rolling Extend Edit, or hold down Option (Alt) to perform a Lift edit (**Figure 3.55**).

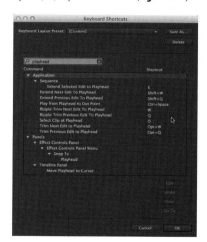

Figure 3.55 Review the needed keys for real-time trimming by entering "playhead" into the Keyboard Shortcuts panel's search field.

7. While playback continues to loop, repeat the trim but add the Option (Alt) modifier key when you press W to perform a Lift edit.

8. With playback looping, press Command+Z (Ctrl+Z) to Undo.

9. Repeat this trim again, but add the Shift modifier key when you press W to perform a Rolling Edit. Allow playback to continue looping, so you can evaluate the result of the trim.

10. While playback continues to loop, press Command+Z (Ctrl+Z) to Undo.

WARNING

Performing edits while looping real-time playback could prove hazardous if easily annoyed humans are nearby. Use headphones if the situation requires consideration.

Let's take this trick to 11! Now that you've got the hang of trimming tops and tails in real time, prepare to perform a one-two punch. In **Skiing Everest_Advanced Trimming** try the following exercise.

1. Press Option+K (Alt+K) to loop playback of the clip from In to Out points.

2. Place your fingers on the Q and W keys. Watch and listen to the clip once or twice.

3. With playback looping, press W to trim out the Everest shot and then quickly press Q to trim the top half of the next shot, after the Shisha Pangma text appears (**Figure 3.56**).

Figure 3.56 Press Q to perform a top trim when the playhead reaches the frame where the Shisha Pangma text is fully visible. Because playback is looping, watch the shot once or twice for accuracy before performing the trim.

Dynamic Trimming

If you want to be a superhero of the editing world, learn how to trim dynamically. After you get the hang of this trimming method, you'll wonder why you haven't always been trimming in real time while looping playback in the Timeline.

Dramatically increase your speed while trimming by following these simple rules:

▶ **Always press T** instead of clicking cut points with the Selection arrow or the Ripple or Roll tools to select the edit points as a trim.

▶ **Always press Command+T (Ctrl+T)** to toggle the trim type.

▶ **Always use the up and down arrow keys** (or your preferred keyboard shortcuts for Go to Next and Go to Previous Edit Point) to move the trim selection to another cut point.

▶ **Mind track targeting** to control where the playhead stops when using Go to Next and Previous Edit shortcuts.

Practice dynamic trimming in the sequence called **Skiing Everest_Advanced Trimming**. Some of the following steps should feel like review but will help you build on your existing skills while adding new techniques.

1. Put your Timeline playhead at the first video cut in the sequence.

2. Make sure nothing is selected in the Timeline by pressing Command+Shift+A (Ctrl+Shift+A).

3. Press T to select the first cut point and automatically open the shots on either side of the selected cut into the Program panel.

4. Press Command+T (Ctrl+T) to toggle the Trim mode to a Ripple Outgoing (yellow bracket facing left).

5. Before you trim, always glance over at your Timeline track targets. Linked and selected video and audio tracks will trim together. Selected audio tracks containing unlinked audio may prevent certain types of trims.

6. Put your fingers in the home position (three fingers on JKL keys).

7. Press J to play in reverse until the skier is up at the top of the hill, and then without stopping playback press L to play forward.

8. Watch the Program Monitor and press K to make the trim when the image of the skier in blue matches the action of the skier in red and the narrator begins to say, "…and moving around" (**Figure 3.57**).

The cut should now be somewhere between 04:12 and 04:20 in the Timeline.

Figure 3.57 While in Trim mode, press JKL to play and trim in real time. Watch the Program Monitor and press K to ripple the trim to the playhead location in real time when the action matches on both sides of the cut.

If you want to try again, there's no need to undo. The cut should remain selected as a Ripple Trim. If you've lost the two-up display in the Program Monitor, press T again and press Command+T (Ctrl+T) to toggle the cut back to a Ripple Outgoing selection. Press J and K, and the trim updates. Press L and K, and the trim updates again, in real time. Watch the two-up display and practice this until you achieve the best cut between the shots.

Work those home keys! Now try this trick.

1. Press T to select the first video cut point.

2. Press Command+T (Ctrl+T) to toggle the trim type to Ripple Incoming.

3. Watch the two-up display in the Program Monitor.

4. Fine-tune this edit by holding down the K key while tapping J or L to move one frame at time. When you release K, the trim is complete.

5. Further refine the edit by pressing and holding the K and L keys together to scrub the footage in slow motion. When you release the keys, the trim is made.

6. Use the Go to Next Edit Point (down arrow) and Go to Previous Edit Point (up arrow) shortcuts to jump the playhead to the next edit point.

   Cut points will stay selected in Trim mode, so you can continue to quickly adjust additional edit points.

Trimming dynamically (so the K key makes the trim instantly) is one of the best ways to make edit changes because it's quick and allows you to watch the edit points update in the Program and Timeline panels as you trim. You can adjust the edits while playing based on where the cut change feels right visually.

Consider practicing this technique with the audio tracks deselected at first (Shift-click on one of the audio track targets to deselect all), and toggle the video track cut point so it's selected as a roll (red I bar). Rolling only the video track cut points is a great way to get good at this technique without breaking sync in your audio tracks. As you get more comfortable with this method of trimming, select linked audio tracks to Ripple Trim dynamically with picture with sound.

If dynamic trimming is new to you, it may take time to get used to the feel of the K key enacting the trim. If you don't like this method, choose another that suits you! Try all methods of trimming, and work to develop speed using the technique that best fits your style.

Live Trimming on the Timeline

What I call "trimming live" is similar to, but slightly different from, pressing the K key to enact a trim (dynamic trimming).

The Play Around keyboard shortcut, Shift+K, is imperative for reviewing all trims, but it's especially helpful when using Extend Edit and Ripple Trimming during live trimming in the Timeline. To trim "live," follow these steps.

1. **Make Looping active.** Press Command+L (Ctrl+L) to turn Looping on.

2. **Activate Trim mode.** Press T to select and open the cut point into the Program panel.

3. **Select trim type.** Toggle the trim type by pressing Command+T (Ctrl+T).

4. **Play Around the edit.** Press Shift+K to Play Around. The playhead will back up and play through the edit point.

5. **Trim live in the Timeline while playback is looping.** Press Option+right arrow (Alt+right arrow) and Option+left arrow (Alt+left arrow) to trim the selected cut point in single frame increments while playback is active and looping in the Program Monitor. The cut location will update in the Timeline. Add the Shift key to the preceding shortcuts to trim in multiframe increments.

6. **Use the best trimming shortcuts ever invented.** While looping playback around the edit (Shift+K) press the Q and W keys to ripple and the E key to roll the edit.

Dynamic and live trimming tips

Once you get a handle on the concept of how live trimming works, you can make a number of little adjustments to improve the "feel" of trimming dynamically:

▶ **Make live trimming even better.** Remap the keyboard shortcuts for Trim Backward and Trim Forward Many. Place them in easy reach of the home keys (JKL) (**Figure 3.58**).

▶ **Customize Preroll and Postroll duration for the Play Around edit command.** When you use the Play Around keyboard shortcut with the playhead positioned on or near an edit point, the playhead will back up a few seconds, play through the cut, and stop a few seconds after the original playhead position. You can customize how far back and how far forward the playhead moves by adjusting Preroll and Postroll settings in the General category of the Preferences panel.

▶ **Customize Large Trim Offset.** Set Large Trim Offset as a multiple of the sequence timebase. For example, when you're working in a sequence with a 24 fps timebase, you might choose a multi-trim frame size of 4 or 6. When you're working at 25 or 30 fps, you might prefer a 5 frame offset (**Figure 3.59**).

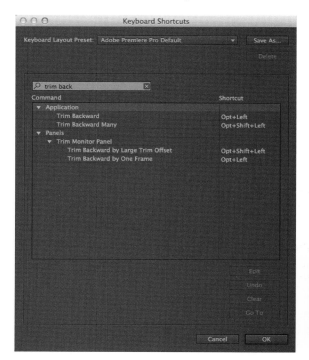

Figure 3.58 Consider remapping the Trim Backward keyboard shortcuts to make live trimming even faster.

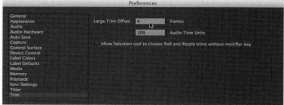

Figure 3.59 Set your preference for multiframe trims in the Large Trim Offset box located in the Trim category of the Preferences panel.

▶ **Toggle Snapping while trimming live.** Snapping (S) can be toggled on and off anytime, even when you're dragging a clip or dynamically trimming a cut point.

Asymmetrical Trimming

When finessing a sequence, I always take time to smooth the cut points between shots by creating split edits, so the picture and sound cut at different times. By splitting the edit, audio can "lead the cut," in which case the audience hears a sound and then sees the pictures that syncs with the sound a moment later. This feels very natural, because people tend to hear a sound and then quickly turn to look at what made the sound. In other cases, the picture will cut while the audience continues to hear the sound from a previous clip. For example, an actor is speaking and the picture cuts to a reaction shot of another actor while the first character is still speaking. Straight cuts tend to look and sound a bit harsh. In most cases, split edits feels much smoother. In a moment I'll show you an advanced technique for creating split edits that I use at some point during every project.

Asymmetrical trimming is another way of creating split edits, which are also referred to as an L cuts or J cuts. A basic split edit doesn't require any special, asymmetrical trimming techniques. Creating a simple L cut is easy when you're trimming only the video or audio portion of one clip, but things can get a bit tricky when you want to select and edit multiple edit points simultaneously.

Selecting cut points across multiple edits, on different tracks, allows me to accomplish two things in one quick step. I can offset the timing for the change in picture and sound while extending or shortening a shot. It takes a bit of practice, but once you know what to expect when performing these types of trims, you'll use them all over the place.

In the sequence called **Skiing Everest_Time Alone**, I want to add frames to the close-up shot of the climber to see and hear him breathing heavily as he hauls his ski gear up the mountain. I want the image and sound of the climber's struggle to lead the viewer into the next line of dialogue where he says, "I think the hardest thing about climbing is...." At the same time I extend this shot, I also want to extend the audio from the preceding clip underneath this one to smooth the cut by overlapping the audio tracks. In other words, I want to add frames to two shots at the same time *and* soften the cut with a split edit. Here's how to accomplish this type of trim.

1. Play Around the cut point between the fifth and sixth shot in the Timeline, around 16 seconds into the sequence.

2. Select the cut with the Ripple tool (B) at the start of the close-up shot on the climbing gear when the climber says, "I think the hardest thing to explain...."

3. Be sure to select the cut as a Ripple In trim (yellow bracket facing right). Toggle the trim by pressing Command+T (Ctrl+T) if needed.

4. If the Linked Selection button is active for the Timeline, the linked audio track is also selected as an Incoming Ripple Trim. If audio and picture are not linked, or if Linked Selection is off, Shift-click the audio cut point to add it to the selection as an Incoming Ripple to preserve sync.

5. Press the Shift key, move the mouse to the left, and click to select the previous clip's audio track as an Outgoing Ripple Trim (**Figure 3.60**).

6. Drag the Ripple tool to the right to add about one second to the shot (**Figure 3.61**).

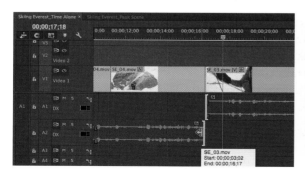

Figure 3.60 Use the Shift key to select multiple cut points asymmetrically. While the edit point on V1 and A1 are selected as a Ripple Incoming trim, press Shift and click to add the audio on A2 as a Ripple Outgoing trim.

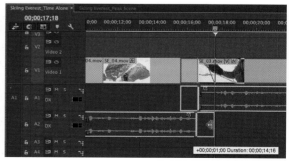

Figure 3.61 As you drag to the right, a yellow rectangular overlay will show a plus sign to indicate the number of frames or seconds you're adding to the trim.

7. Release the mouse when you see that you've added a second to both the outgoing audio track and the incoming video and audio tracks.

The resulting asymmetrical trim creates an L cut while adding one second of content—in opposite directions—to multiple shots at the same time (**Figure 3.62**).

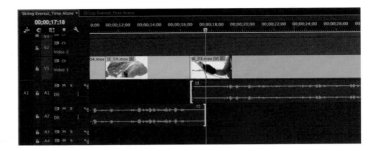

Figure 3.62 The asymmetrical trim adds frames to the close-up shot of the climber and creates an L cut to soften the edit.

Another great reason to select cut points across multiple cuts is to adjust edits in a way that keeps all tracks in sync without leaving gaps in the audio tracks by pulling sound from an audio clip on another track to fill the gap.

In the sequence called **Skiing Everest_Peak Scene**, I've taken the time to place and sync "nat sound" (natural sound effects of skiing that were recorded on location). I want to ripple the video, maintain sync with previously placed sound effects while I add frames to the Mustagh Ata shot, and extend those natural sound effects to fill in the gaps. If I ripple only the video clip, Adobe Premiere Pro will leave a gap in the sequence to preserve audio sync (**Figure 3.63**).

Instead, I'll asymmetrically select the video cut as a Ripple Incoming, and then Shift-click to select the synced natural sounds on Audio Track 3 as a Ripple Incoming too, which will pull out more of the matching natural sound effects to fill the gap. Because I'm selecting cut points, I'll move the Ripple tool to the left and Shift-click to select the sound effects on Audio Track 4 as a Ripple Outgoing Trim (**Figure 3.64**).

Now, when I drag to the left with the Ripple tool over the video cut to lengthen the shot, the audio from A3 will fill the gap, and audio on Track 4 will overlap the above cut and smooth the edit.

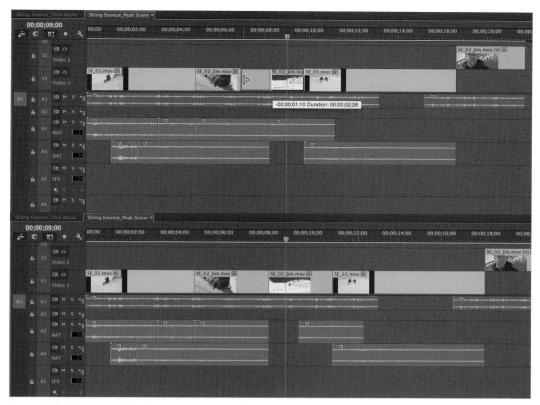

Figure 3.63 Rippling only the video results in a gap in the sequence on sound effects tracks. Where Sync Lock is active, inserting black video gaps keeps sound in sync with the trimmed picture.

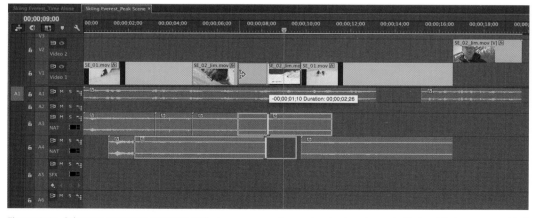

Figure 3.64 Selecting cut points asymmetrically preserves sync for previously placed sound effects while frames are added to the picture and fills the gaps with overlapping sound to smooth the edit.

If I had dragged to the left rather than to the right over the A4 track, which was selected as a Ripple Outgoing Trim, I would have ended up shortening the video clip (and the sequence) instead of adding frames to the shot. Try this on your own so you know what to expect.

Selecting multiple edit points across many tracks allows you to asymmetrically adjust the cuts in complex sequences while maintaining sync. Remember to use the Shift key with any Trim tool to select edit points across multiple tracks, and then drag or use keyboard trimming shortcuts to trim several shots in unison.

Marquee-drag to Group-Select cuts

Another quick way to maintain sync while trimming is to Group-Select the edit points across multiple tracks. Try this exercise.

1. Park the playhead at the cut point between the shots you want to adjust.

2. Hold down the Command (Ctrl) key while dragging a marquee around all cut points. The resulting asymmetrical selection will automatically favor sync.

   The cuts open into the two-up display in the Program panel, ready for trimming.

3. Press Command+T (Ctrl+T) to toggle the trim type.

Next I'll walk you through an example of how to use marquee-drag for asymmetrical selection. Open **Skiing Everest_Peak Scene**.

I want to remove frames from the final B-roll shot, just before Jim says, "the stuff you don't like you forget real quick." If I select the clip of the two skiers as a Ripple Outgoing to shorten that shot, it could throw Jim's audio out of sync. Instead, I'll hold down Command (Ctrl) and drag a marquee around all cut points (**Figure 3.65**).

Now I'll press Command+T (Ctrl+T) to toggle to Ripple Outgoing (yellow brackets facing left) and drag to the left to remove frames. When I release the edit, the B-roll shot is shorter and lip sync is preserved in the interview.

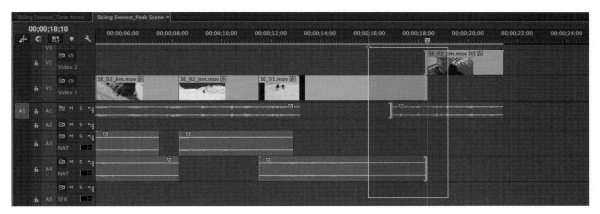

Figure 3.65 Hold down the Command (Ctrl) key and drag a marquee around multiple edits.

If I'd also wanted to have the skiing sound effects under the cut as I trimmed, I could have dragged a marquee to select all cuts but then pressed Command+Shift (Ctrl+Shift) to reselect the empty track area to the right of the clip on A4 as an Incoming trim (yellow bracket facing right). As I click and drag with this asymmetrical arrangement, the audio clip on A4 will not be trimmed shorter as I remove frames from the clips above (**Figure 3.66**).

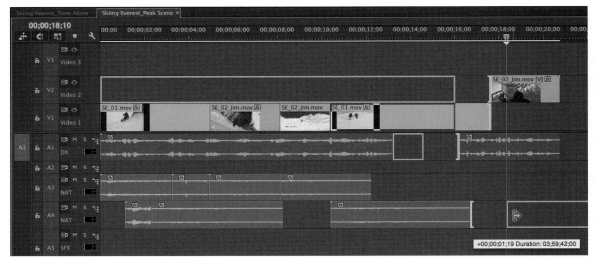

Figure 3.66 After dragging a marquee around multiple edits, press Command+Shift (Ctrl+Shift) to select the empty track area on A4 as an Outgoing Ripple to keep the audio clip on A4 from getting shorter.

TIP

If you have a full-size keyboard, you can use the numeric keypad for frame-specific moves and trims. Select a clip in the Timeline with the Selection tool, and then Slip, Slide, or select a cut point with a Trim tool like Ripple or Roll. Press the plus (+) or the minus (-) key and then enter a number, like 12, to indicate how many frames you want to trim or move or trim to the left or right. Press Return (Enter) to reposition or trim the clip. To move or trim in one-second increments, press plus or minus, and then type a number, followed by a period (for example -1 followed by a period). Then press Return (Enter) to trim or move a whole second to the left. This is the only time when 99 is greater than 100: When you select a clip and type +99, the clip will move 99 frames to the right, but if you type +100, periods are automatically entered and the clip is moved only one second to the right.

Use asymmetrical trimming when you want to trim the picture but have several tracks of audio beneath and need to preserve the sync work you've already done. In the case of very complex edits, this is the best way to achieve the trim you want and maintain sync.

CLOSE-UP

Tail Trim Jim

In the example from **Skiing Everest_Peak Scene,** I could have chosen an easier trimming method to obtain similar results. The shot of the skiers isn't linked to Jim's audio, so I can choose a trim method that will maintain sync while I'm shortening the shot. I'll perform a tail trim on the outgoing B-roll just before Jim delivers his line. Because Jim's clip is already a split edit in the shape of a J cut (the audio begins before his video plays), this method will only maintain sync on Jim if I position the playhead on a frame *before* Jim's audio begins.

1. Place the playhead before Jim's audio begins. Press W, the keyboard shortcut for Ripple Trim Next Edit to Playhead.

   The B-roll shot is now shorter, and Jim's onscreen footage remains in sync.

2. Press Option (Alt) and use the Selection tool to trim the beginning of Jim's line to the left.

   This method was a good choice in this instance, because I was willing to shorten the B-roll shot quite a bit to a frame before Jim's audio began. Had I wanted to trim the B-roll shot to a very specific frame that was beyond where Jim's audio began, this method would not preserve sync.

   To perform this trim with frame-accurate precision *and* preserve sync, I could put the playhead on the cut point between the B-roll and Jim's picture, and then press Ripple (B) or Roll (N) and marquee-drag to select all edit points. I could then watch the two-up display in the Program panel while pressing the keyboard shortcuts for Trim Backward or Trim Forward, or add the Shift key for Trim Backward or Trim Forward Many and watch the frames update until I found the perfect cut point between the B-roll and Jim.

   For a faster, more elegant trim, I'd marquee-drag to select the cut points, click on one of the clip edges with the Selection tool, and toggle by pressing Command+T (Ctrl+T) to select the edit type; then I'd dynamically trim in real time using the JKL keys. With Looping on, I can press Shift+K to Play Around the cut, and while keeping my eyes on the Program panel, press K to make the trim when it feels right. It takes time to get used to playing backwards and forwards with J and L, and then pressing K to enact the trim.

   Practice all these different trimming techniques to learn which method makes sense to use in different situations. It's partly a matter of editing style, but most of the time I choose the option that provides fast results. When it comes to editing, there are many means to achieve the same ends. Some techniques require fewer clicks, whereas others just feel easier to accomplish.

Advanced Workflows

There are so many advanced workflow topics that I want to include in this section, but I'll stick to two less intuitive workflow-oriented editing techniques that every studio editor should know.

Scale to Frame Size

Adobe Premiere Pro allows you to mix footage frame sizes and frame rates. There is no need to transcode, compress, or make proxy files for "offline" editing and then reconnect full-size footage for the "online" edit or finishing work. Editing can be completed at the native resolution of the footage and later be transcoded or compressed during output. In addition, Adobe Premiere Pro can take 4k footage, and when it's dropped into a 1080p sequence, it downsamples the high-resolution media and effectively plays it back at the lower-resolution settings. This is an amazing feature and has revolutionized studio workflows.

When Default Scale to Frame Size is selected, imported elements are set to fit sequence dimensions, downsampling video and stills to the size of the sequence. You can edit using the downsampled footage, and when you want to create camera moves or recompose a shot, instantly scale the frame size back to the original dimensions. The image will appear "zoomed in," and you can then scale and move the image around to create camera moves or recompose a shot using the full resolution of the original file.

It's important to have a clear understanding of how this process works and what will happen when a clip of any size is downsampled to match the sequence settings:

▶ **Default Scale to Frame Size affects images upon import into the project.** If you have footage already saved in your project, changing this preference will only affect images you import after the setting has been altered. If you want all images scaled to match sequence settings, select Default Scale to Frame Size in the General category of the Preferences panel *before importing*, or you'll need to reimport a folder of clips after changing the setting.

▶ **When Default Scale to Frame Size is not selected,** imported elements are left alone and not downsampled (**Figure 3.67**).

Figure 3.67 Images that have not been Scaled to Frame Size may appear zoomed in.

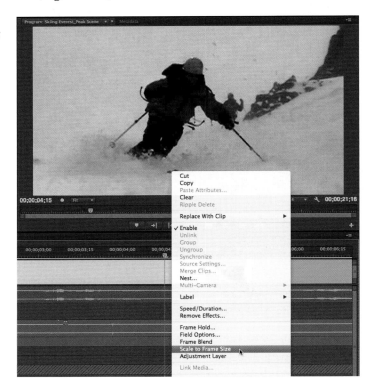

▶ **When Default Scale to Frame Size is selected,** pictures may appear with letterboxing or pillar-boxing (black areas around the image) when image and sequence dimensions don't match (**Figure 3.68**).

▶ **Default Scale to Frame Size options can be changed** for clips already inside a Timeline. Right-click on a clip in the sequence (or on a group of selected clips) and choose Scale to Frame Size.

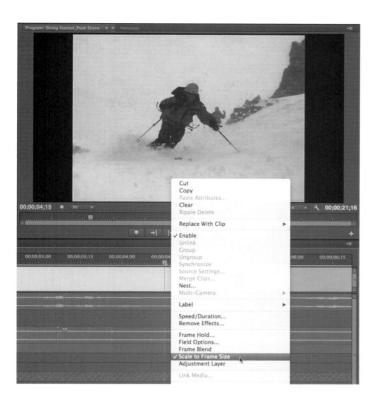

Figure 3.68 Images may appear letterboxed when Scaled to Frame Size.

▶ **When Scale to Frame Size is selected, images are downsampled.** If you try to zoom into a downsampled image beyond 100%, the image quality will be degraded.

▶ **To zoom or recompose a shot,** make sure Scale to Frame Size is not selected for the clip you're altering, so you have access to the full resolution of the image.

▶ **Remember that using Scale to Frame size works best** with video or stills that are larger than the sequence dimensions, because it results in better quality images. With Scale to Frame Size selected, images that are smaller than the sequence dimensions will be scaled up, and the resulting image could look soft. You can recompose the shot and animate keyframes to create camera moves without degrading image quality by keeping Scale settings below 100%.

Combining Scenes: Sequence into Sequence

Similar to nesting, but more well-organized and far less problematic, editing one sequence into another allows you to focus on scene building and then later combine those scenes with control over Source and Timeline track patching.

Often, I'll create three separate sequences for Act One, Act Two, and Act Three of a narrative film. At any time I can quickly edit these three sequences together to get an overall feeling of assembly length for the entire program.

Here are some general suggestions for using techniques as sources:

▶ **Separate sections, scenes, or acts.** Simplify complex or long-form editing by editing in several sequences; then later combine those sequences into one final Timeline without the hassle of nested elements.

▶ **Load a sequence into the Source panel and edit it like it's a clip.** Right-click the sequence icon in the Project panel and choose Open in the Source Monitor, or click and drag the sequence into the Source panel. Select segments of the source sequence for insert or overwrite into the Timeline by setting In and Out points in the Source panel for editing into the Timeline.

▶ **Target specific tracks.** Patch Source buttons to Timeline targets for total control over where video and audio tracks from the source sequence end up in the Timeline sequence.

To activate the toggle to edit clips from a sequence (rather than treating a source sequence as a nest) in the Timeline, click the Nests or Individual Clips button to make source targets active for the source sequence (**Figure 3.69**).

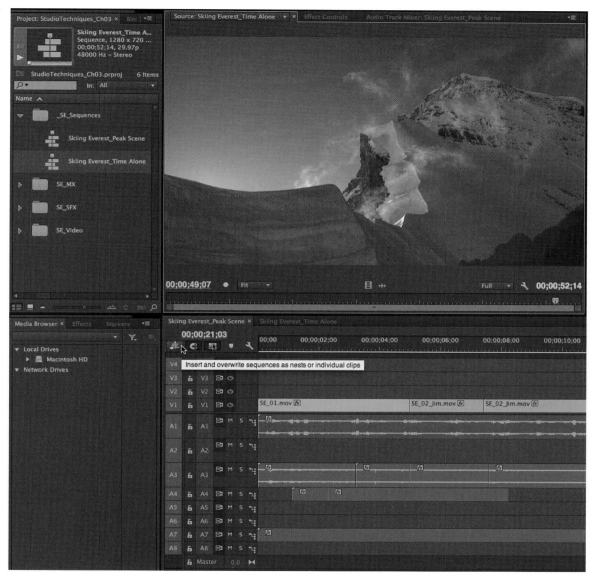

Figure 3.69 Drag a sequence into the Source panel and click the Insert and Overwrite Sequences as Nests or Individual Clips button in the Timeline to make source targets active for patching into Timeline targets.

TIP

Do your research! It's well worth finding out the format and codec of each camera on the shoot ahead of production. The more information you have before you arrive on location, the better prepared you'll be.

CLOSE-UP

Fixing It in Post

There are some issues that Adobe Premiere Pro can't fix automatically—like color matching shots, choosing angles, and timing cuts. That's your job. Adobe SpeedGrade can open Adobe Premiere Pro projects for quick color matching. The adjustments are stored as a LUT (color look-up table) file, which is assigned to clips in Adobe Premiere Pro via the Lumetri effect. Use this smart and fast workflow to quickly color match angles for multi-camera edits.

Multi-camera Editing

With the cost of high-quality camera equipment falling and considering the obvious creative benefits of shooting Multi-Camera, having access to effective tools to deal with multi-angle, multi-format media is perhaps more important than ever.

It's common to work with owner-operators who bring "a camera" to the shoot. That is, for lower-budget productions you may not have much control over the camera equipment you'll use. The good news is that I haven't seen a bad picture from a professional camera for some years. But calibration and codecs can vary enormously depending on the hardware and the preferences of your operator.

Fortunately, Adobe Premiere Pro has powerful multi-format editing features that remove many of the challenges you'll face when working with multiple cameras. Briefly, you can leave aside worries about mixed format editing, because Adobe Premiere Pro will conform everything on the Timeline to your sequence settings automatically. Of course, this makes careful selection of sequence settings (**Figure 3.70**) particularly important when you're working with mixed formats.

Figure 3.70 Adobe Premiere Pro makes multi-camera editing easy.

The Multi-Camera Workflow

You may have performed a multi-camera edit before. To summarize, here's the workflow in Adobe Premiere Pro.

1. **Acquire your media.** Be sure to record sync marks. A clapper board is perfect. Get enough visual variation to avoid apparent jump-cuts when editing, and decide on timings to change storage cards to ensure that only one camera at a time stops recording.

2. **Organize your media.** Merge external audio with video clips if needed, add metadata if required, and rename clips to avoid confusion.

3. **Prepare the multi-camera sequence.** Automatically create a sequence with each camera angle synchronized and on separate tracks. Nest this sequence (edit it into another sequence as a clip). You'll be performing your multi-camera edit on the nested version.

4. **Perform the multi-camera edit.** You can do this while playing your camera angles in the Multi-Camera Program Monitor view or cut by cut directly on the Timeline.

5. **Adjust the multi-camera edit.** Change the timing or contents of your cuts.

Let's deal with each of these steps in turn to discover good habits for creative excellence.

Acquire Your Media

Some of the best postproduction results come from preparation during preproduction. Plan your shoot carefully to ensure that you arrive at the edit suite with all the information you need and rushes that are easy to sync and work with.

Tips for multi-camera shooting

With file-based cameras, the historical tape length limits are no longer a challenge. However, just about every other challenge remains. Here are a few:

▶ **Avoid stops and starts.** Avoid stopping and starting recordings, because every time a camera is paused it will have to be re-synced with the other camera angles in post. This is time-consuming and adds to the risk of making mistakes. Anything you can do to simplify the process in post is a good idea!

▶ **Get sync marks.** Even if you're not forced to pause during the action, try to get a sync mark at the beginning and end of your recordings, just in case. It's a small time cost on-set that will make you very happy if you need it.

▶ **Use a clapper/slate.** Clapper boards are *great* for recording sync marks. Information on the board is genuinely useful to the editor (don't bother with shot logs; if you can read it on the board, you can be confident you have the right clip). The audio and visual clap of the clapper board presents an easy-to-find mark for all cameras.

▶ **Change Timeline views.** Adobe Premiere Pro allows you to view Audio Time Units rather than frames, both in the monitors and on the Timeline. If you switch your Source Monitor to audio waveform display (**Figure 3.71**) and turn on audio time units (both in the Panel Settings menu), you'll find it quick and easy to sync source audio and video clips without the playhead jumping between frames that are just slightly out from the clap.

Adobe Premiere Pro will place the mark on one frame or another, but it's a little more precise to use audio time units (**Figure 3.72**). Try it and see.

Use sync timecode

If you're shooting in a studio or on a larger budget on location, you may have external sync timecode. This gives every camera the same timecode, so sync in post is extremely easy. In practice, it doesn't save that many hours and the cost of cameras and equipment that support this feature can be relatively high, but if you have the opportunity to use this option, go for it. When you want to sync audio and video, or multiple camera angles, Adobe Premiere Pro can use the timecode (**Figure 3.73**).

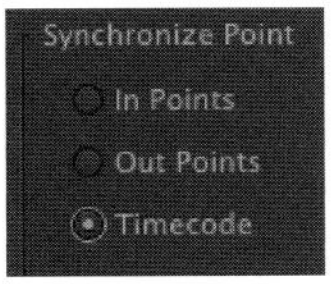

Figure 3.71 If you switch to Audio Time Units, you can zoom in to a single audio sample.

Figure 3.72 It's often easier to find the audio mark by looking at the waveform.

Figure 3.73 Using timecode to sync is usually the fastest option. If you've got it, use it!

Without external sync timecode, be sure to get at least a clapper board clap or some other kind of sync mark at the beginning of your recording. It doesn't matter all that much what you use as a sync mark as long as you have one. Many wedding videographers use a flash gun because it's unnoticed at a wedding but provides a clear visual mark.

It also isn't all that important where your sync mark is. I once edited the World Judo Championship using media from multiple TV stations. I often found there was just one moment every camera caught—when the losing competitor's head hit the floor!

Record sync marks

Adobe Premiere Pro needs just one sync mark somewhere on the clip. For some events, it's not possible to record that mark before or during the recording, so it has to come at the end. In this case, be clear with all camera operators that they must not stop recording until the sync mark has been recorded. This can be as simple as everyone coming together and pointing their cameras at an assistant who claps his hands a couple of times (twice in case an operator forgets to focus or turn his mic up).

Try to get a visual *and* auditory sync mark to give you more options in the edit. Also, be sure to record audio on *every* camera, not just the one getting a clean mix from a sound desk. However poor the on-camera audio is, the editor will thank you for it because it makes it so much easier to locate content.

If there's simply no way to record a sync mark, don't worry. I've synced using speech or even action where someone is reaching for a cup or opening a door. You can use just about any event that is on every camera, but note one important detail: Every camera *must* capture the same event, or you'll have no visual references to set your sync mark.

When you get into post, sync marks for all camera angles have to be from the same moment. It's a challenge to sync different parts of different clips (although it can be done—see the section "Manually creating a multi-camera sequence").

Use camera logs

As much as possible, record useful information about each camera angle. Much of this information won't be needed, but every now and then just one camera catches an important piece of action and in among the mix it might easily be missed. Make rough notes about these kinds of events—such as someone tripping or a particularly lucky composition when people happen to come together in the right way—and bring them to the edit.

Decide early on which camera is which number. You should be doing this anyway, but if all the names and notes match, it will make the edit easier.

Make a note of each camera model, format, and codec. Although it's simpler if you have matching cameras and settings, it's not as important as it once was thanks to the mixed format editing facilities in Adobe Premiere Pro. Still, the more information known about the production, the easier your job will be when you perform the editorial work, especially if you weren't involved with the production. Unexpected issues with content from one camera or you need to choose a rendering codec for a mixed format Timeline can complicate the editorial process unnecessarily.

Record overlap

While shooting multi-camera, try to minimize any occasions where more than one camera is missing the action. It's impossible to avoid ill-timed events like suddenly discovering the battery is about to run out or that someone forgot to change the storage card before recording, or to have to move the camera during recording because an obstacle appears.

Agree on a signal for camera operators to use if recording has to be paused. While one camera is changing cards or batteries, the other cameras can go easy on the movement, tend toward shooting wide, and generally aim for "safe" footage rather than exciting (but potentially unusable) footage. Once the camera in question is up and running again, everyone can resume looking for creative excellence.

It's important to agree on a pause signal in advance. I've worked on shoots where an operator tries to signal something like he has to change a storage card and the other operators all nod in agreement, thinking they're being told by the operator that he's getting great shots or some other equally misunderstood communication that could have been avoided.

Shoot wide

A book on postproduction techniques is not the place to give advice on production aesthetics. But if you're shooting a one-off event, consider shooting a little wider than you would usually.

Although closer angles are often more engaging, there's nothing quite as *disengaging* as missing the action. If you shoot a little wider, it's easier to catch unexpected movements or adjust to include action that enters the shot. You usually can scale up the shot a little if needed (about 20–30%), providing a tighter shot than the original wide shot.

If you can, have one camera on full wide catching the entire event. Your editor may never use this angle, but he'll be extremely grateful if he needs it to cover a gap in the action the main cameras failed to capture. This camera doesn't need an operator; it just needs to start and finish with the other cameras, *and* have a shared sync mark.

Of course, this is not always possible—I know of a production in the UK that sometimes shoots with 60 cameras spread over a large area. The important thing is finding a way to sync.

Organize Your Media

Consider creating a bin for each multi-camera shoot to make it easier to identify the media you intend to include. It's all too easy to miss a camera angle among the other shots in a production, and grouping media in a bin (**Figure 3.74**) helps you stay in control.

If you're working with raw media, such as RED R3D files, consider making source setting adjustments before you do anything else. The results will show in the Source Monitor,

Figure 3.74 Get organized at the start, and you'll find it easier to stay organized later.

Figure 3.75 Clip renaming should be early on your list of steps to prepare for editing.

on the Timeline, and in the Multi-Camera display. Leveling out strong color differences will help you focus on the action when performing your multi-camera edit.

It can't hurt to rename your source clips Cam 1, Cam 2 (or C1, C2), and so on (**Figure 3.75**). It will make it easier to locate the content later and you can view the clip names overlaid on the angles as you perform your edit. You'll also find it easier to stay organized in the Project panel.

Prepare for the Multi-Camera Edit

Before you perform your multi-camera edit, consider adjusting your workspace. You may want to shrink your Source Monitor and expand your Program Monitor, and save this as a workspace for multi-camera that suits your display setup.

You'll need to provide Adobe Premiere Pro with one of the following sync point marks on every clip. All clips must have the same kind of mark, and of course, every mark must be in sync with every other mark:

▶ In point or Out point marks

▶ Synchronized timecode

▶ A clip marker

▶ Sync audio recorded on all clips

Once you've set the sync points, you're ready to create a multi-camera sequence.

Automatically creating a multi-camera sequence

Creating a multi-camera sequence is super easy. If you want to try this, use the **Multi-Camera.prproj** sequence and associated clips in the Multi-Camera_Media folder.

In the Project panel, select the clips you want to combine into a multi-camera sequence, right-click on any one, and choose Create Multi-Camera Source Sequence (**Figure 3.76**).

The dialog that appears includes important options that tell Adobe Premiere Pro how to synchronize your source clips and which audio you want to use. When you click OK, Adobe Premiere Pro will create a sequence that is

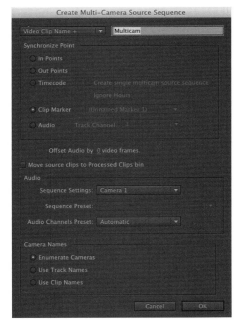

Figure 3.76 Choose a few simple options and you're ready to produce a multi-camera edit.

synchronized and ready to nest, with the Multi-Camera mode already enabled. Let's look at a few of the options:

- **Name.** The box at the top of the dialog simply names the newly created sequence.

- **Synchronize Point.** The Synchronize Point options are used to tell Adobe Premiere Pro what is in sync. If you can, you'll use the Timecode option. I wouldn't particularly recommend using In Points or Out Points because these will trim the clips. Instead, add a marker (M) at the sync point on each clip.

- **Synchronize Point Audio option.** If you have source audio on all of the clips, the Audio option will automatically sync your clips (this makes it well worth shooting sync audio on every camera). Depending on your original audio, this option might not work. If this is the case, just revert to adding a marker manually to each clip.

- **Create single multi-cam source sequence.** If you have a group of clips from one time period and another group from another, Adobe Premiere Pro will normally put them in separate multi-camera sequences. If you select this option, they'll all be included in one long sequence instead. This is perfect if you have camera operators stopping and starting at different times. Be warned: You are likely to have gaps in that sequence (which is fine as long as you know to expect it).

- **Audio.** The Audio options relate to the sequence you are about to create. Remember that this will be a sequence just like any other, with conforming settings. The visual settings (image size, frame rate, and so on) will come from the clips, but you must tell Adobe Premiere Pro which audio mastering option you want to use.

- **Camera Names.** The Camera Names options set the on-screen overlay information you'll see during the multi-camera edit and the angles you'll see in the right-click menu when choosing a multi-camera angle. Making the names visible makes it worth prenaming your clips in the bin.

Stay in control: Remember that when you're manually building a multi-cam sequence, each track should have clips from just one camera each. Don't mix and match angles on the same track or you risk getting lost during the edit.

Figure 3.77 A synced multi-camera sequence is a quick click away.

Things you need to know about creating multi-camera sequences

Here are a few things to keep in mind:

▶ The Adobe Premiere Pro multi-camera workflow is made possible by combining a number of standard features, including nesting a sequence, a particular Program Monitor view, and even regular trimming. If you've been using Adobe Premiere Pro for a while, none of these will be new to you.

▶ When you select multiple clips in the Project panel, right-click, and choose Create Multi-Camera Source Sequence (**Figure 3.77**), Adobe Premiere Pro gives you options to combine them in a new sequence (ready to be placed in a different sequence for editing) specially configured for multi-camera editing:

  ▶ Each clip will be placed on its own track, and the sequence will have a unique icon to indicate that the Multi-Camera option is already enabled.

  ▶ If you have a single long clip from each camera, building the multi-camera sequence in the Project panel saves a few clicks and offers automatic syncing.

Adobe Premiere Pro displays the results of special effects while performing a multi-camera cut during playback. This might have an impact on playback performance, so consider working with effects after you have applied the cut if you can. You can always open the nested multi-camera sequence later and apply effects to a camera angle (clip) as a whole. You'll see the result update in each instance of the nest automatically, as you would expect with any nested sequence. If you work with nested effects this way, it's quick and easy to temporarily disable effects on clips (by using the Effect Controls panel), improving performance while performing your multi-camera cut.

Manually creating a multi-camera sequence

If you have multiple clips from each camera and each one needs to be placed in sync at different times, it's best to build the nested sequence the manual way, clip by clip.

Place each camera angle clip on a separate track, stacked one above the other and synchronized. You can sync manually: Just display the waveforms and move each clip until the clapper board clap is lined up, or use the same automatic syncing options that you find in the Project panel. Select each stack of clips that should be in sync, right-click, and choose Synchronize (**Figure 3.78**).

If you want to add sync markers, it's usually easier to do so in the Source Monitor before adding them to the Timeline. Once clips are on the Timeline, you can add markers by double-clicking on each clip to open it in the Source Monitor and adding it there. You'll be opening the instance of the clip that appears on the Timeline, and the marker will appear on the segment you selected.

If you have lots of media to sync, consider using PluralEyes by Red Giant. The workflow is simple and fast, and automatically syncs all the clips on your Timeline based on in-camera audio.

Then all you need to do is nest that sequence in another, right-click on it in the Timeline, and choose Multi-Camera > Enable (**Figure 3.79**).

Creating sync in a sequence you have created manually requires exactly the same marks, timecode, or audio as you'd need if you were syncing in the Project panel. The marker can be anywhere in the clips, as long as it is on a frame that truly is meant to be in sync (**Figure 3.80**, next page). This will be the reference for Adobe Premiere Pro.

TIP

Map shortcut keys when you need them: Unless you're using Adobe Premiere Pro's automatic audio sync or external sync timecode, consider mapping the Source Monitor audio waveform display to a keyboard shortcut. This is quicker to switch the view than using the Settings menu.

Figure 3.78 Synching on the Timeline is the same as in the Project panel.

Figure 3.79 You can turn Multi-Camera mode off and on for clip segments.

Broken Sync

If you can't find a single sync point that is shared by all cameras, don't lose hope. As long as you can find some part of your clips that overlap, you can calculate different sync points and work out the timecode differences to set a common sync point.

Consider this example: Camera 1 and Camera 2 have a common sync point at 00:00:05:00. Camera 3 doesn't have an identifiable sync point at 00:00:05:00, but it *does* have an easily visual sync point shared with just Camera 2 (but not Camera 1) at 00:00:10:00.

Find that second sync point, and then use the numerical keypad to jump back by the difference in time from the first sync point on Camera 2 and the second sync point on Camera 2. In this example, let's say it's a five second difference. Mark a sync point on Camera 3 five seconds back from the current synced frame (using an unnumbered marker).

You now have three clips with perfectly synced markers, even though you couldn't originally find a shared mark.

This example has simple timecode to illustrate the point; yours is likely to be more complex, but the calculation is the same: Work out the difference and subtract.

Figure 3.80 You'll save a lot of time in post if you record sync marks on location.

Perform the Multi-camera Edit

Once you've nested your multi-camera sequence you are ready to perform a cut during playback. If you've used the option to create a multi-camera sequence in the Project panel automatically, the Multi-Camera > Enable option will already be on. If you haven't, right-click on the nested sequence now and you're ready to go.

Once a sequence is marked as a multi-camera source, double-clicking on it *no longer* opens the nested sequence in the Timeline. Instead, it'll open in the Source Monitor (**Figure 3.81**).

Figure 3.81 The Source Monitor allows you to choose camera angles too.

Selecting one or other angle in the Source Monitor will update the selected angle in the current Timeline. Be warned! This is easy to do by accident, and you'll be changing your sequence.

If you ever want to change the current angle without right-clicking, you can do so by opening the clip in the Source Monitor. Keyboard shortcuts are available for this as well, provided you've enabled the correct Timeline track (to tell Adobe Premiere Pro which content you're working on): Pressing Command+1 (Ctrl+1) adds a cut at the playhead and switches to Camera 1, pressing Command+2 (Ctrl+2) adds a cut at the playhead and switches to Camera 2, and so on.

You can override opening multi-camera sequences in the Source Monitor by holding down Command (Ctrl) when you double-click on the nested sequence. Doing so will open the sequence in a separate Timeline panel, as normal.

Set the Program Monitor to the Multi-Camera display mode (**Figure 3.82**) and turn on Overlays if you want to see your camera angles displayed on the images. You can configure this in the Overlay settings (both options are on the Program Monitor Settings menu).

Now all you need to do is start playing the video and click on the angle you want. But you won't be clicking, will you? The number keys along the top of your keyboard can be used to select camera angles, and you should definitely use them. It's faster than clicking and allows you to focus your attention on your content.

Adjust the Multi-Camera Edit

When your multi-camera cut is complete, you're free to change the timing of your cuts as you would with any other clip on the Timeline. You can trim, extract, copy, and paste—whatever you like. There is nothing strange about a multi-camera enabled nested sequence in terms of editing. It's just a nested sequence.

You can also select all of the multi-camera sequence segments, right-click on them, and choose Multi-Camera > Flatten to replace the nested sequence with its selected

Figure 3.82 Be sure you have the correct track enabled (turn on the track header), or you won't see the contents of your nested sequence.

Choosing Cameras

Before you start the actual multi-camera edit, you may want to change the order the cameras appear in the Multi-Camera display. This is possible thanks to the Edit Cameras option in the Program Monitor Settings menu.

Select the check boxes to enable or disable cameras, and drag and drop up or down the list to change the order.

Choose some semblance of order by placing similar shots together, if possible. If you're working with footage from a musical performance, you may want to have your isolated shots before your wider shots. If you're working with performance footage, perhaps line up your lead actors.

clips. Use this option with care: There's little benefit in terms of playback performance, and you will lose the option to open the nested sequence and apply effects to whole camera angles. This may be exactly what you want to do, but think it through before you take this one-way step.

Switching Video with Matching Audio

You'll notice there are options for audio handling when setting up your multi-camera sequence. Adobe Premiere Pro needs to know if you want to take the audio that comes with each camera angle as you cut or stick with one particular source audio. There is, of course, no right or wrong here. You'll need to make a choice based on your media. If you are working with cameras that are very far apart, where it would be natural to cut to the different audio, go for it. If, instead, you have a clean feed on just one camera, you'll want to stick with that.

It's not unheard of to have a completely separate audio recording that you add to the master sequence, ignoring the original in-camera audio completely.

4

Professional Audio

Author: Luisa Winters

...the visuals and the audio have to be of a certain quality before I start to get excited about the thing.

—Hans Zimmer

Professional Audio

This chapter's project files are available for download. Please see "A note about downloadable content" in the Introduction of this book.

In video and film, it's been said that audio is the most important thing to get right, and I agree with that statement. In fact, in the old days of silent movies, the movie theater would hire a professional musician to improvise and live perform a score while the movie was playing. Even then, moviemakers and theater owners understood the power of audio when viewing a feature film. Audio has the power to change how you feel about a character, the power to affect your mood, and definitely the power to change a mere adventure into an epic story.

However, I find that most people in my classes lack basic audio knowledge and the know-how to create a good, solid audio mix of their work. In many cases, even good and experienced editors have never seen an audio engineer at work, and have no idea about how to start. So, they'll experiment with different volume levels and effects, trying to get a good mix and balanced audio. But without basic knowledge of what to do, they usually fail.

Most people perceive video as being of lower quality if the audio is low quality, which means that you can improve your production quality by improving your audio quality.

Although this book is about postproduction, keep in mind that maintaining good quality audio in the production process will be invaluable in the postproduction stage. "Fixing audio in post" is unrealistic and will rarely yield good results.

This chapter will help you start to generate great audio in your program. Because you don't always get to work with perfect audio, this chapter also features a section on how to fix common audio problems using Adobe Premiere Pro and Adobe Audition CC. From setting up your working environment to adjusting levels to adding effects, you'll work with audio just like the pros do.

Listening Environment

The importance of your listening environment cannot be overstated. Two tools will determine how you treat your audio: your *ears* and the *equipment* that gets the sounds to them.

Your Ears

Some people are born with natural abilities that make their perception of audio and therefore their processing tasks very easy for them; others are not. Just like any other skill, you can train your ears to detect the nuances of audio. You can also train your ears to know what to do to adjust your audio to get the desired results. Perceiving good audio does not happen overnight; sometimes it takes years of training. I recommend constantly comparing your work to the original recording (unprocessed) and to recordings that you know are good and that you like. Start training your ears to hear what you've been missing!

Equipment and Your Audio Setup

Having sounds get to your ears in the most accurate way possible is essential to the successful mixing and mastering of your program. Needless to say, you should work in a quiet room. But besides quiet, you can use certain equipment and do many things to improve the way you listen to your audio in your editing space. Some of them are costly (a pair of quality monitor speakers will set you back a few dollars), and some don't cost a penny:

- ▶ **Quality of speakers.** Get the best speakers you can afford. A wide variety of models and sizes (and prices) are available. Educate yourself as to what the best models and sizes are for your room and your work (speaker manufacturer websites are an excellent source of information). Your speakers don't have to necessarily be huge and or extremely expensive. They just need to have a decent response to the signal that is being fed to them. If possible, try to use speakers in two different sizes: larger ones (not necessarily big; mine are bookshelf size) and smaller ones so you can compare what your program will sound like on two different systems. Make sure that the same output from your system feeds both pairs.

TIP

During production you need to get the strongest audio signal possible without it being too loud. You also need the noise in the environment to be as negligible as possible. This ratio of desired audio versus noise is known as signal-to-noise ratio. The idea is to have a strong "good" signal and a weak noise level. One of the techniques that you should use is to decrease the distance between the source of audio (instrument, voice, etc.) and the microphone, thereby decreasing the levels of noise. (Microphone placement and recording techniques are beyond the scope of this book.)

NOTES

When used in reference to sound, "brightness" indicates the amount of high frequency content. Bright sounds contain more high frequencies, and dark sounds more low frequencies. In music it also refers to the speed of the beat and the key signature used in composing.

On the other hand, "muddy" is a demeaning term for sounds that have a lot of low-to-mid frequency content in them. These sounds lack clarity, because it is hard to distinguish different instruments and voices.

Figure 4.1 Position your speakers so you're in the "sweet spot," preferably in the center of the room away from corners.

▶ **Wall material.** Various materials will have distinct sound absorption properties. One side of the room may be brighter than the other, and your mix will suffer. If is not that difficult and not very costly, make sure all of your walls use the same type of absorption material (foam, curtains, Sheetrock, etc.).

▶ **Position the speakers.** Assuming you have decent speakers, follow these guidelines for the best positioning:

    ▶ **Try to place yourself in the middle of the speakers.** They should be at the same distance on the left and on the right (the "sweet spot") (**Figure 4.1**). If they are small, bookshelf-type speakers, position them between three and four feet from your head. The size and position of the speaker is referred to as a *near-field monitor*, because they are near the listener and therefore are minimizing the room's influence on the audio waveforms.

    ▶ **Ensure that some space is between the speaker and the wall.** This will prevent the wall reflection from distorting how the audio gets to you.

    ▶ **Avoid placing speakers in the corners of the room.** All of your walls reflect sound waves, so your ears will receive audio that is not quite accurate if your speakers are in the corners of the room. Some extra reverb or distortion may be added, which will cause you to overcompensate and deliver a faulty mix or implementation of effects.

▶ **Speaker height.** Consult the manufacturer for the correct speaker height. But sometimes all you need to do is place the speakers at ear level. You may need to purchase a pair of short pedestals from a local pro-audio distributor to achieve optimal elevation.

▶ **Listen to good recordings.** After you've placed your speakers correctly, listen to tracks that you know well and know are mastered correctly. Try to match the genre of the tracks. For example, if you are mixing audio for a commercial, listen to a commercial that you like and compare your mix with the commercial. You can then judge how the speakers sound. Pay close attention to the evenness of the audio, and make sure that the audio is balanced in the left and right channels. Make adjustments to the speakers if needed.

▶ **Speaker volume.** Play tone through the speakers and adjust the volume until the level is comfortable, as if someone is speaking normally to you in the room (do this for both sets of speakers, if it applies). You can find tone by choosing File > New > Bars and Tone or File > New > HD Bars and Tone. Thereafter, do not adjust the level of the speakers (or of your computer's audio). If you alter the speakers' volume, you'll throw off your sense of level and never be sure about the levels of your program.

▶ **Headphones.** Sometimes, you'll need to keep your sound volume to a minimum, forcing you to wear headphones. Headphones have both good and bad qualities to them.

If you combine a set of high-quality, professional headphones with a clean amplification system, you can get the most accurate and uncolored sound content. You won't need to consider room acoustics or other problems because when you rotate your head, the headphones will rotate with you, which means that no matter what you will always be in the "sweet spot."

There are also negative aspects to wearing headphones:

▶ **Your ears get tired more easily.** Most earphones are uncomfortable, and you tend to raise the audio level.

► **Frequency response varies.** The frequency response of the headphones can be quite different from that of loudspeakers, so you will get a false sense of what the mix sounds like. You might overcompensate with various forms of sound treatment like EQ, reverberation, and so on.

► **Waveform refers to waves.** Sound moves in waves. Lower tones, particularly deeper/bass tones, have a wave that can be as long as six feet, making them difficult to truly represent in headphones.

Adobe Premiere Pro's Workspace

As you know, you can change Adobe Premiere Pro's workspace to suit your needs. I usually change the workspace when working with audio because doing so places the panels that I use the most in a place that I can easily find. Changing workspaces is easy, and Adobe Premiere Pro ships with predesigned workspaces that are very convenient. The one I use for audio editing is the Audio workspace. To access this workspace, choose Window > Workspace > Audio (**Figure 4.2**).

Figure 4.2 Adobe Premiere Pro lets you change your workspace to suit your audio needs.

Gain and Levels

Both gain and levels refer to the loudness of the audio. However, **gain** is the input level of the clips and **volume** is the output. In recording audio, gain is the first control that the microphone signal goes through in a mixer while levels are adjusted after that.

In Adobe Premiere Pro, we adjust the gain before doing anything else to the clip, and then individually adjust the different levels of the clips so they match throughout the program (**Figure 4.3** and **Figure 4.4**).

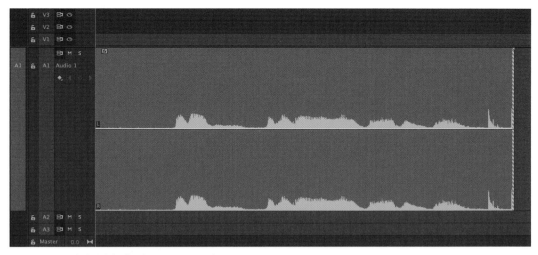

Figure 4.3 Audio levels before being processed.

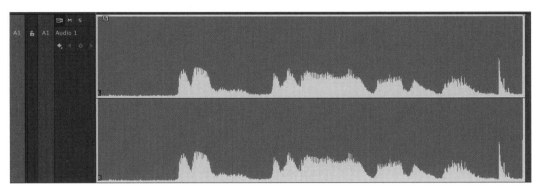

Figure 4.4 Audio levels after being normalized to -12dB.

Why should we worry about the loudness of the clips matching? Because it is important to establish audio continuity in your work. You should not have a portion of your program be disproportionally louder than the rest; it will cause confusion to the viewer and your message will not be as clear to them. Most viewers (listeners) will expect some kind of evenness of the audio levels in the program. Of course, there are exceptions. Sometimes audio levels are used to produce an emotional response.

Unless there is a really good reason for not doing so, our audio levels should be even throughout our program.

TIP

Keep an eye on the Peak Amplitude measurement at the bottom of the Audio Gain window. It displays the peak amplitude in a clip before gain has been applied. If the Peak Amplitude value is -12dB, theoretically you can add 12dB of gain. However, this will give you a peak value that is way too loud. Use this value as a guide, not as a setting suggestion (a good reference level for broadcast is -12dB with a dynamic range [DR] of 6dB).

Adjusting Gain in the Project Panel

Before you add clips to the Timeline, you should start doing some pre-mixing. This is easy to do, and it will save you time. Most of the audio that you will get in your project will come in at a level that is not ideal. Music, for example, usually comes in too loud, so it will definitely save you time if these elements are already at a better level before you add the clip to the Timeline.

What I do is select all of my foreground audio (voice-over or dialogue) and adjust the gain of all of these clips at the same time, and then select the background audio (music and Foleys) and do the same. To adjust this gain, I select the clips first and then press G to open a dialog that I use to adjust my clips. I usually set background audio elements to an average of -22dB (or so) and foreground elements to an average of -12dB with nothing peaking above -6dB.

The process is as follows.

1. Select multiple clips from the Project panel.

2. Choose Clip > Audio Options > Audio Gain. In the Audio Gain panel that appears, adjust the gain of multiple clips using one of these four methods:

   ▶ Set Gain to

   ▶ Adjust Gain by

   ▶ Normalize Max Peak to

   ▶ Normalize All Peaks to

Set Gain to

The Set Gain to adjustment affects the net amount of gain by which you are adjusting the clip. You can increase or decrease gain by as much as 96dB.

Adjust Gain by

The Adjust Gain by option is similar to the Set Gain to option, but it allows you to add or decrease the net gain amount by incremental amounts. As you enter amounts, the Set Gain to amount automatically adjusts. Set Gain to is absolute, but Adjust Gain by is incremental, meaning that if you adjust it twice by 2dB, you will get an increment of 4dB.

Normalize Max Peak to

When you apply the Normalize Max Peak to a single clip, the highest peak in the clip is normalized to peak at the decibel level you enter, effectively increasing or decreasing the gain of the entire clip. When you apply this option to a group of selected clips, all clips are normalized by the same amount of gain so that the highest peak across all the selected clips peaks at the decibel level you enter. In essence, this option will treat all the clips as if they were just one clip, and the level of the loudest clip will be used to normalize all three of them. The level of all three will be adjusted by the same amount regardless of how soft one of the clips may be.

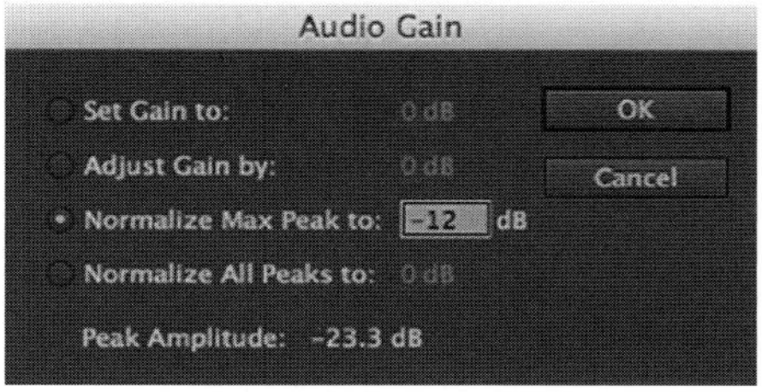

Normalize All Peaks to

When multiple clips are selected, the Normalize All Peaks to gain option normalizes the peak of each clip to the decibel value you enter. Each clip will receive its own setting (**Figure 4.5** and **Figure 4.6**).

Figure 4.5 Normalize Max Peak to treats all of the clip's volumes as if they were just one clip. Adobe Premiere Pro will not take into consideration that they are separate clips and will adjust all of them by the same value.

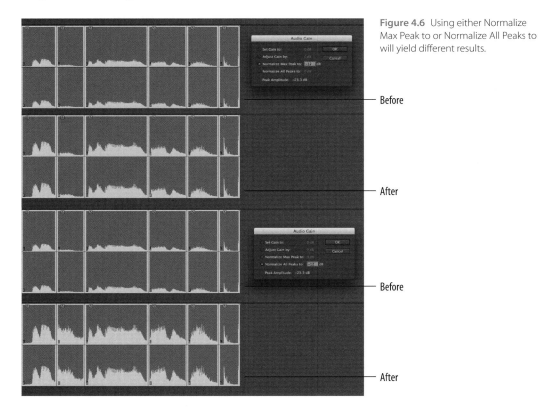

Before

After

Before

After

Figure 4.6 Using either Normalize Max Peak to or Normalize All Peaks to will yield different results.

Useful Audio Terms

Here are some definitions of terms you'll use often:

▶ **Decibels (dBs).** Units used to measure the intensity of sound: 0dB is near silence; 10dB is 10 times as loud; 20dB is 100 times as loud; 30dB is 1000 times as loud; and so on.

▶ **Audio normalizing.** Is the process of changing the overall volume of an audio clip so that you reach (and don't pass) a target level. I usually normalize spoken audio to -6dB and background music to -18dB.

▶ **Peak amplitude.** Is the maximum absolute value of the signal. This is the loudest that it will be.

▶ **LUFS (Loudness Units relative to digital Full Scale).** The European Broadcast Union (EBU) uses the term LUFS. These are absolute units used to measure audio levels. The loudness target level could be -23 LUFS. In conjunction with this they use Loudness Units (LU). LUs are used to show relative level changes (-23 LUFS is 2 LUs lower than -21 LUFS). One unit of LUFS equals one decibel.

▶ **Dynamic range (DR).** Is the difference between the loudest and the quietest part of your audio, and is measured in decibels. Depending on which genre of audio you're working with, you'll need to have a wider or narrower DR, so keep this in mind. Classical music, for example, will have a much wider DR than Pop or Rock.

Figure 4.7 You also access the Audio Gain panel by choosing Clip > Audio Options > Audio Gain (or press G).

Normalization in action

To see and hear the difference between different normalization methods, open Chapter04_Audio.prproj, and then open the sequence named **Normalize**. This sequence contains three groups of clips. The first group has no processing, the second group uses Normalize Max Peak to, and the third group uses Normalize All Peaks to. The voiceover (VO) track was normalized to -12dB, the music track to -18dB, and all other audio to -22dB. The difference is not huge, but you can definitely hear it.

Experiment with this sequence by following these steps.

1. Select one of the clips in the Timeline (sequence **Normalize**).

2. Press G or choose Clip > Audio Options > Audio Gain (**Figure 4.7**).

3. Choose any of the options in the dialog and listen to the clip.

4. Choose Edit > Undo or press Command+Z (Ctrl+Z).

5. Apply a different normalization choice and listen to the clip again.

6. Repeat steps 4 and 5 until it becomes apparent what the different options do.

Adjusting Gain on the Timeline

Adjusting gain on the Timeline is as simple as right-clicking on the audio clip and choosing Audio Gain to launch the Audio Gain panel (or press G). You'll be presented with the same four choices described earlier. You can also choose Clip > Audio Options > Audio Gain as described earlier.

Timeline Interface

Making Timeline adjustments doesn't add functionality that isn't available elsewhere in Adobe Premiere Pro. But putting additional meters and buttons directly on the Timeline makes it easier to tweak and monitor audio settings at any stage in the editing and mixing process. In this section I'll discuss expanding the tracks, adding buttons to the track header, and keyframing.

Expand Audio Track

The first helpful customization when you're working with audio is the ability to expand the audio track to show the audio waveforms. You need a visual representation of the peaks and valleys of your audio clips, and displaying the waveforms is the easiest way to accomplish that.

New in Adobe Premiere Pro CC is the ability to save this expanded view as a preset. This preset is especially useful when you're adding keyframes, searching for the start or end of dialogue, or finding unwanted sounds that were recorded. To save the waveform view as a preset, simply click the wrench icon at the top of your Timeline and choose Save Preset (**Figure 4.8**).

Give the preset a name you'll remember, and you're done! To recall your preset, choose it from the same menu.

You can adjust the height of a track by placing your mouse in the track header and in between the different tracks. When your mouse cursor changes shape to a double-headed arrow with two lines through it, click and drag to adjust the height of the track.

Figure 4.8 You can now save the Timeline track height view as a preset.

CLOSE-UP

Why You May Not Want to Normalize

I've used the Normalize Gain option successfully, but in general I find that short bursts of very loud audio affect the normalization level, resulting in audio that is too low.

A better way to normalize audio levels is to use a compressor, such as the Adobe Premiere Pro CC Multiband Compressor effect, which I discuss later in this chapter.

If, on the other hand, you want to normalize clip(s) that have loud unwanted sounds, you can always cut right before and right after the unwanted sound. The unwanted sound will not affect the normalization of the clip, and it will not affect the gain of the "normal" volume section of the clip.

TIP

You can also adjust the size of the audio track by hovering your mouse pointer over the track button area and using the scroll wheel on your mouse to increase or decrease the size of the track. Additionally, you can change the height of all tracks (video or audio) by adding the Shift key as a modifier.

TIP

The disclosure triangle below the Show Keyframes button means that additional settings are available. Clicking the Show Keyframes button disclosure triangle allows you to select between track keyframes and clip keyframes. I discuss both in the next section.

Figure 4.9 The audio track header view in the Timeline.

Figure 4.10 You can show either clip or track keyframes in the Timeline.

Audio Track Buttons

Adobe Premiere Pro CC includes by default some common audio track buttons, such as Mute, Solo, Toggle Sync, Keyframe, and more (**Figure 4.9**). These buttons are used in the editing process to help you better perform your edit. If you need to keyframe the volume level of a particular clip, it might be better to listen to just that track; so soloing that clip makes sense. By the same token, if you need to see track keyframes instead of clip keyframes, you would select the appropriate setting using these buttons:

▶ The **Mute** button mutes the corresponding audio track and is useful when you want to isolate audio between tracks during playback. This button is used when you need to stop listening to a particular audio track momentarily so that it will not distract you.

▶ The **Solo** button mutes all other tracks during playback. You can solo multiple audio tracks, which effectively mutes all tracks with the exception of those soloed. This is particularly useful when you have many audio tracks but at the moment you only need to listen to a few.

▶ The **Show Keyframes** button toggles the display of keyframes in the audio waveform on the track. If you have used track keyframes in your work, you will need to see them at some point. This button enables you to change the display of the Timeline to show you the track keyframes instead of the clip keyframes. To display the clip keyframes again, just select the option from the same button (**Figure 4.10**).

▶ The **Previous Keyframe** and **Next Keyframe** buttons navigate between existing keyframes on the audio track. These buttons are particularly important when you need to navigate between keyframes to adjust their settings. It is easy to miss the time position of the keyframe if you drag the playhead, making any adjustments you make create a new keyframe. Therefore, it is better to use these buttons to navigate when you need to adjust an existing keyframe.

- The **Add/Remove Keyframe** button adds or removes keyframes (depending on the position of your playhead). If the playhead is on a keyframe, clicking here will delete it. If the playhead is not directly on a keyframe, clicking here will add a new keyframe at that point in the Timeline.

- The audio **Toggle Sync Lock** determines which tracks will be affected when you perform an insert, ripple, or trim edit. Imagine you have several clips in several different tracks in your Timeline and you need to perform a ripple edit. Only the clips in the track that contain the edited clip will be affected. However, if the Sync Lock button is enabled in all of the tracks, any edit you perform in any of the tracks will make the clips in the other tracks adjust their time position to allow for the edit.

- The audio **Track Lock** button goes a step further and locks the audio track completely, which prevents any change, accidental or intended. In essence, the Track Lock button "saves you from you." Using this button will prevent you from accidentally making changes to a track.

Additional Audio Track Buttons

In addition to the default audio track controls mentioned in the previous section, Adobe Premiere Pro CC offers several additional buttons that you can add to the audio tracks. To add (or delete) any of these buttons, right-click on the track button area and choose Customize, or click the Timeline Display Settings button and choose Customize Audio Header. You can then drag and drop additional buttons to the track button area, or you can reset the layout by clicking the Reset Layout button in the Button Editor panel (**Figure 4.11**).

These buttons are the Track Meter, Left/Right Balance, Track Volume, and Enable Track for Recording. To me, the ability to control some settings directly in the Timeline is both exciting and time-saving.

Figure 4.11 The Button Editor lets you drag and drop additional buttons to the track header area.

Tip: The numeric value for ∞ is -100.

The most important track buttons that you might want to add are

▶ The **Track Meter** button adds audio meters to the corresponding audio track. This is useful when you're working with multiple audio tracks and you want to see the audio levels from individual audio tracks without switching to the Audio Clip Mixer panel.

▶ The **Left/Right Balance** button adds a left/right pan dial.

▶ The **Track Volume** control allows you to increase the track volume level by +6dB or decrease it to ∞ (infinity). The reason this is referred to as infinity is because dB (decibels) are a ratio. As stated earlier in this chapter, 0dB is near silence; 10dB is 10 times as loud; 20dB is 100 times as loud; 30dB is 1000 times as loud; and so on. You can click and drag left to decrease or drag right to increase the volume level, or simply enter a numeric value.

▶ The **Enable Track for Recording** button lets you record audio directly to the corresponding audio track.

Keyframes

Clicking the Show Keyframes button will let you choose between showing Clip Keyframes and Track Keyframes. Showing Clip Keyframes displays keyframes that are clip based, so if you move the clip, the keyframes follow the clip because they belong with the clip. These keyframes are the same keyframes that you would add in the Effect Controls panel. I discuss clip keyframes later in the chapter.

Track Keyframes

Track keyframes are added to the track and not the clip. Imagine you are editing your program and you need to add background music. You are not sure which track of music you want to add to your program. You add one clip to the track, and you add clip keyframes to the volume of that clip so that the music becomes softer when the voice-over starts. After listening to the edit several times, you decide that you no longer want to use that music clip, but instead you want to use a different clip. You delete the clip in the Timeline and add the new clip. However, the keyframes that you added to the original clip have disappeared when you deleted the clip.

Now imagine that instead of clip keyframes you added track keyframes to the original edit. Instead of the keyframes disappearing when you delete the clip, they will stay with the track and apply to any clip you add to that track at that point in time. Now you can add as many different music clips to that track and the keyframes will apply.

Keyframes in action

To get a better understanding of how keyframes work, follow these steps.

1. Open the project Chapter04_Audio.prproj, and then open the sequence named **Keyframes**.

   You will see two different tracks, one showing clip keyframes and the other showing track keyframes.

2. Move the clip with the clip keyframes, and then do the same with the clip in the other track. The clip with the keyframes maintains them, but the other clip does not because the keyframes belong to the track. If you find that you cannot move the clip that is in the track with the keyframes, temporarily show clip keyframes, move the clip, and then switch back to the track keyframes view.

Working with Separate Audio Tracks

Imagine you recorded an interview with your video camera and have different microphones going to different audio sources. It would be difficult for you to edit these clips separately if they show up together in the Timeline as a stereo clip, so you may want to separate both of these channels. To separate these channels into distinct (but linked) clips, choose Preferences > Audio and change the Default Audio Tracks options to fit your needs (**Figure 4.12**). In the previous scenario, you need the clips to come in as mono clips when importing that footage so you can edit each of the channels separately from the other one. Each channel of recorded audio will appear in its own track. Although having each channel in its own track is not always necessary, it is very useful when needed.

One Track per Person?

Consider a documentary: There may be a narrator, some interviews (both male and female), background music, and some sound effects and natural (nat) sound. A professional audio engineer using an audio editing tool like Adobe Audition might give each audio its own track so adjustments can be easily made because each type of audio is isolated. However, in Adobe Premiere Pro, using so many tracks will be difficult unless you have a very tall monitor.

Instead, I recommend that you place similar type clips together in a track. For example, add the narrator to a track, female voices to another track, male voices to a yet a different track, music to a fourth track, and sound effects to yet another track. You will still have the opportunity to apply track-level effects but will keep the number of tracks used to a minimum.

Figure 4.12 Check your Audio Preference settings to ensure that each audio channel appears in the Timeline as a separate track.

Track naming

It is always a best practice to name your tracks. As a result, it will be easier to distinguish your audio when you're working in the Mixer or even in the Timeline. You can easily name your track by right-clicking in the track header and choosing Rename. You can also rename the track using the Audio Track Mixer.

Mixing Sound

You have adjusted the gain of your clips and they are starting to sound OK. However, you're not done; you need to do more to your clips. Maybe some parts of your clips are still a little too loud, or maybe some of the different sounds on the different tracks are competing with each other. You need to make sure that this is not an issue, so you need to start mixing sound. To help you with this task, use the Audio meters (VU Meters).

VU Meters

A VU meter lets you see how loud (and soft) your audio is. You need to constantly monitor how loud your audio is not only to maintain uniformity, but also to make sure that your audio does not clip: If the audio is so loud that the media cannot reproduce it, you'll end up with a clip lacking in dynamics, or a "square" instead of a wavy waveform, and the result will be distorted audio, which of course is highly undesirable (**Figure 4.13**).

Figure 4.13 Waveforms with square or "flat" areas at the top usually mean clipping/distortion has occurred.

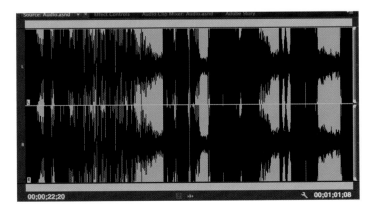

Clipping

To better understand how clipping negatively affects your audio, follow these steps.

1. Open the project Chapter04_Audio.prproj, and then open the sequence named **Clipping**. The sequence contains two different clips.

2. Listen to the first clip; it hasn't been processed.

3. Listen to the second clip; it's been processed through gain.

In the second clip you'll notice that there are less dynamics and that the audio goes into the red in the VU meter. The sound is also harsher and distorted in this second clip.

Dynamic range

All audio material has a DR. DR is the difference between the loudest and the softest part of your audio, and is measured in decibels. Depending on which genre of audio you're working with, you'll need to have a wider or narrower DR, so keep this is mind. As mentioned earlier, Classical music, for example, will have a much wider DR than Pop or Rock.

To see this DR, you need to use the VU Audio meters.

1. Open Chapter04_Audio.prproj, and then open the sequence named **Dynamic Range**. The sequence contains two different clips.

2. Listen to the first clip and then the second clip. As they play, look at the Audio meters. The first clip has a DR of -28dB to -6dB. The second clip (through compression, described later in this chapter) has a DR of -16dB to -12dB.

Adobe Premiere Pro's VU meter (**Figure 4.14** on the next page) defaults to a 60dB range, displaying dynamic peaks, and shows color gradients that correspond to the audio levels. A gradient that progresses from green to yellow to orange to red indicates low audio levels, normal audio levels, and peaking audio levels.

Figure 4.14 Audio VU meters provide a clear view of your audio peaks and your DR.

You can customize the audio track meter by right-clicking and choosing one of the available options. Some of the options will be grayed out, depending on the type of audio master that you are using. Some of them are available only to 5.1 surround masters, or adaptive tracks. I prefer showing static peaks and valleys, and not showing the color gradients. This lets me see with more detail what my levels are and what my DR is. I use this information to help me set my levels (**Figure 4.15**). These options are

▶ **Show Valleys.** Displays an indicator on the audio track meter that corresponds to the lowest audio amplitude in the portion of the clip that you play back. This is effectively the noise floor. You should know what the noise floor is because it will help you determine the DR.

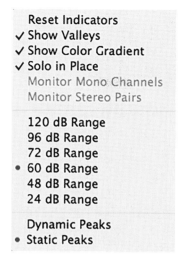

Figure 4.15 Right-click on the VU meter and customize its display by choosing from these options.

Figure 4.16 You could change which channels you are listening to by choosing one of these options.

▶ **Show Color Gradient.** Indicates track meter levels in a gradual gradient rather than hard color changes, although in such a small meter the difference is very subtle. Showing the color gradient is a little softer on the eyes, and it is fine if you don't need to be very precise with the levels. I usually leave these off. However, I've met several editors who prefer to see the color gradients here.

▶ **Solo in Place.** Allows you to solo one or more channels without changing their speaker assignment (available for Source Monitor and Timeline panels). You may want to use this option if you need to temporarily listen to just one or some of the channels. When you select this option, you'll see solo buttons at the bottom of the VU meters, one per channel (**Figure 4.16**).

▶ **Monitor Mono Channels.** Allows you to listen to one specific channel out of both of your stereo monitoring speakers regardless of its assignment (available for adaptive clips and multichannel masters). You may want to use this option if you need to temporarily listen to just one of the channels. When you select this option, you will also see solo buttons at the bottom of the

CLOSE-UP

Audio VU Meter Target

Setting and monitoring audio levels in your program requires more than just making sure the audio is not too loud so it doesn't distort Audio target levels differ depending on how you will deliver the final product. The Loudness Radar effect (discussed later in this chapter) will help you tremendously to achieve target levels. Here are two common targets:

▶ **Broadcast.** Traditionally, many broadcasters have maintained strict audio level requirements of -10dBFS for peak audio with average audio levels at -20dBFS. But some broadcasters are allowing editors to "work hot" and submit video with audio that has non-broadcast peaks of -3 or -6dBFS. Always check with your broadcaster because its requirements will vary.

▶ **Non-broadcast.** Similar to how online video delivery doesn't have a hard 100 IRE limit, online audio delivery doesn't have a set peak limit. Therefore, I recommend limiting audio peaks to somewhere around -6dBFS and have average audio levels around -12dBFS.

VU meters, one per channel. However, you will be able to solo only one of the channels at a time.

▶ **Monitor Stereo Pairs (default option).** Allows you to monitor some of the channels from the left and right speakers (available for multichannel masters).

▶ **120–24 dB Ranges.** Allows you to change the decibel range from six options that range from 24dB to 120dB. You may want to change this range depending on how precise you need to be with your audio levels. Obviously, if you select the 120dB range, you will be able to more accurately see your level values than if you selected the 20dB range.

▶ **Dynamic Peaks.** Allows you to see the max peak of the audio change depending on the part of the clips you are listening to. Levels are constantly refreshed every three seconds.

▶ **Static Peaks.** Displays the loudest peak until the indicator is reset (by clicking on the meter) or playback is restarted.

▶ **Reset Indicators.** Resets your indicators.

Level Adjustment in the Timeline

By default Adobe Premiere Pro is set up to show clip keyframes, which, as discussed earlier, also means that audio adjustments you make on the Timeline affect individual clips (not the entire track).

You can adjust the volume level of an individual clip by hovering your pointer over the volume band until it changes to a volume band pointer (**Figure 4.17**). Then drag the volume band up to increase the volume by up to 6dB or down to lower the volume to -∞. This adjustment affects the volume for the entire clip that is selected (if it doesn't have any existing keyframes). But often you'll want to make changes to the volume of a clip over time; you can do this by adding keyframes. This can be useful to fade in and out audio clips or to adjust for loud or soft sections in an individual clip.

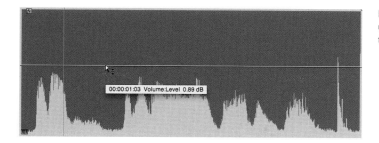

Figure 4.17 You can change the volume levels of your clips by dragging the volume band up or down.

You can add clip keyframes either in the Timeline or by using the Effect Controls panel. If you're working in the Timeline, you can add, select, move, and remove keyframes using the Pen tool.

1. Select the Pen tool (press P) from the toolbar (**Figure 4.18**).

2. Play the Timeline and determine the points in time at which you need the audio to become softer or louder. Then click on the band to add the keyframe.

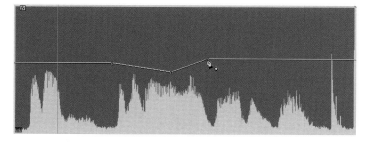

Figure 4.18 You can balance the audio levels over time by adding keyframes in the Timeline.

3. Using the Selection tool, drag individual keyframes or sections between keyframes up or down to increase the clip volume at that point in time.

4. Play back the audio clip, and look at the peaks and valleys of the audio in the VU meter.

5. In some cases you'll need the same keyframes in more than one place or in more than one clip. You could have more than one track or music or dialogue that requires the same changes in volume. You could copy these keyframes and then paste them as needed, either to the same clip in a different point in time or to a different clip.

Other ways of adding keyframes

Here are a few other ways you can use to add keyframes to the Timeline:

▶ Use the Selection tool instead of the Pen tool by holding down the Command (Ctrl) key and clicking on the points at which you want to add a keyframe along the clip's volume band (also known as the *rubber band*).

▶ Use the Add/Remove Keyframe button.

▶ Adjust the audio volume of a nonselected clip by using the [and] keys . If the playhead is on a keyframe, you will adjust that keyframe only. If the playhead is not on a keyframe, you will adjust the span between keyframes

▶ Quickly reset keyframes by clicking on clip(s) and choosing Clip > Remove Effects.

Keyframes in action

To get a practical understanding of how to use keyframes, follow these steps.

1. Open the project Chapter04_Audio.prproj, and then open the sequence named **Begin Keyframes**.

2. Play the sequence. You will hear that the music fades as the voice starts.

3. If necessary, expand the track; then notice that some keyframes were added.

4. Play the sequence again and listen to the audio levels as the playhead goes through the sections with keyframes.

5. Add other keyframes to make the audio get louder and softer over time.

Track Keyframes

Track keyframes are identical to clip keyframes except they are applied to the track, not to the clip. So, if you were to move, remove, or change a clip in the Timeline, these keyframes would remain unaffected and would apply to any clip placed in the track where the keyframes are located. I'll discuss track keyframes further in the "Track Mixer" section later in this chapter.

Crossfades

Crossfades are the gradual lessening of the audio volume in one clip at the same time as the gradual increase of the volume of a different audio clip. They are used in two different ways: to fade in between two clips and to fade up from silence. It is common to fade a clip up from silence at the beginning and fade down to silence at the end because not doing so may cause the sound of those clips to "pop" in and out (there might be loud ambient sound or a loud first sound in the clip). This means that you would need to fade in and out every audio clip in your entire program.

To avoid manually keyframing these clips, you usually use crossfades. An audio crossfade is a transition, a lot like a video crossfade, that is used instead of manually keyframing the clips to fade them up from or down to silence.

Open the project Chapter04_Audio.prproj, and then open the sequence named **Crossfades**. Play the sequence. You'll notice that there are crossfades added to the first clip in the Timeline and that it fades in at the beginning and out at the end.

If both clips are adjacent in the same track, you can easily add a crossfade by adding a transition: Adobe Premiere Pro creates the overlap from handle media, and a single transition will suffice for the edit point. You can see an example of a crossfade on the next set of clips in the **Crossfade** sequence. Notice how the crossfades affect the audio. If the clips are in two different tracks, you can still use the audio transition, but you need to ensure that the clips overlap by the amount of time that you want the crossfade to last. Of course, you can also use keyframes to accomplish the crossfade. You can see an example of crossfades that exist between clips in different tracks in the next set of clips in the **Crossfade** sequence.

For multiple clips

To add crossfades to multiple clips at the same time, adjust the default transition duration for the audio crossfade first and then use the transition. You can change this value by choosing Preferences > General and changing the Audio

Figure 4.19 You can adjust the default duration of the audio transition by accessing the General preferences and changing the time duration.

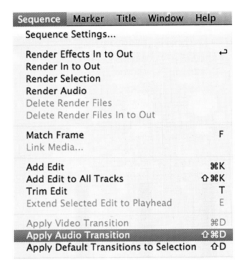

Figure 4.20 You can apply audio transitions to your selected clips by choosing Sequence > Apply Audio Transition.

Transition Default Duration (**Figure 4.19**). Because I prefer a fast crossfade, I usually set this value to between 0.10 and 0.17 seconds, which in NTSC will give me a duration of three to five frames.

Then select the clips you want to affect and choose Sequence > Apply Audio Transition (**Figure 4.20**).

When you're doing crossfades, avoid these two mistakes:

▶ If you made your cuts a little too close, the audio might fade out too soon.

▶ If you do a crossfade in between two clips, you may be adding unwanted sounds, because Adobe Premiere Pro will add enough frames to the edit to create the crossfade.

Exponential Fade, Constant Power, Constant Gain

As you may already know, there is more than one type of crossfade. The difference is in the rate of change of the levels during the transition. You should use Exponential Fade when coming up from silence and Constant Power when using a crossfade in between two different clips. The different types of crossfades are

▶ **Constant Gain.** Changes the audio at a constant rate. This is not very natural, which is why it is not used much (**Figure 4.21**).

▶ **Constant Power.** Creates a slow fade that gradually changes to a faster rate of change when fading out. When fading in, the opposite occurs: Constant Power increases the rate of the audio and then as the fade progresses the rate of change slows down. This causes the levels to not "lose power" during the transition, which is what would have happened if you had used Exponential Fade (**Figure 4.22**).

▶ **Exponential Fade.** Uses a logarithmic curve to fade up and down. It is very similar to the Constant Power fade but is more gradual. This is more natural to your ears because this is how you naturally perceive sound (**Figure 4.23**).

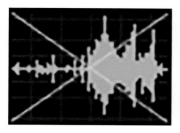

Figure 4.21 Constant Gain changes the audio at a constant rate.

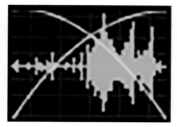

Figure 4.22 Constant Power changes gradually and then speeds up the rate of change.

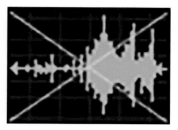

Figure 4.23 Exponential Fade uses a logarithmic curve to fade up and down. The fade is slower at the beginning but gets faster in the middle of the duration of the transition.

Noise Floor/Room Tone

All rooms have a "sound," or "room tone," that is generated by lights, furniture, and even the people in it. No place is totally silent (unless you're in a vacuum). You should record at least 20 seconds (at the very minimum) of this room tone (make sure you record it during production). Mixing it with your clips on a separate track will help you create the illusion of evenness.

Panning

Panning places the signal anywhere between hard left and hard right in a stereo recording (or in any of the channels of a 5.1 surround panning). It is used to give the perception of depth and space (**Figure 4.24**). In other words, panning will give listeners a better illusion that they were present during the events presented in your program.

For example, if you see a car moving from left to right, the sound should move from left to right following the car. Panning accomplishes that through animating (keyframing) the panning so that the sound goes from one channel to the other gradually, just like the sound of the car would travel from one side to the other in real life.

You can adjust panning on a global basis, or you can animate it (as just explained in the preceding moving car example). Most of the time I'll set panning to about 30 percent into a channel (rarely any more than that). I won't

TIP

No room tone? Find the longest amount of silence in a spoken track for a minimum of one second. Place this little audio piece into its own sequence and then reverse it. You now have at least two seconds of room tone and don't have to play games with crossfades to make it work. Build 30–40 seconds and you can add it to your clips as needed.

Figure 4.24 Adjusting the pan of a stereo clip adjusts both channels. However, adjusting a mono clip's pan adjusts independently by clip or track.

go all the way to 100 percent unless the sound is coming from offscreen.

In my experience, the following is usually true:

▶ True stereo recordings (most commercially available music) will not need any panning modification.

▶ Voice-overs will almost always be right in the center.

▶ Interviews can pan (a little) to the left and right to correspond with the speaker's positioning on the screen.

▶ SFX will also correspond to whatever on the screen is producing the sound.

Mixers and Submixes

Mixing audio on the Timeline alone can be restrictive, especially when you're trying to mix down several different clips and audio on multiple tracks. For more advanced audio mixing controls, Adobe Premiere Pro CC offers two different audio mixers that you can use to speed up and increase your control over the audio mixing levels.

These mixers are the Audio Clip Mixer and the Audio Track Mixer. You use the Audio Clip Mixer when you need to change the levels of individual clips on a clip-by-clip basis. You use the Audio Track Mixer when you need to change the levels of audio on a track basis, when you don't need the changes to travel with the clips in case you need to replace the clips with different ones. Track and clip keyframes were discussed earlier in this chapter.

Clip Mixer

The Audio Clip Mixer is a new feature in Adobe Premiere Pro CC that allows you to view and adjust audio on a clip-by-clip basis. You can access this new window by choosing Window > Audio Clip Mixer or by pressing Shift+9.

Using the Audio Clip Mixer (**Figure 4.25**) lets you monitor and adjust individual clips on the go, even if they are in the Timeline. If you play your program in the Timeline and use the Audio Clip Mixer to adjust levels during the playback, the Clip Mixer will affect the clips as you hear the audio being played from the Timeline. You'll be able to

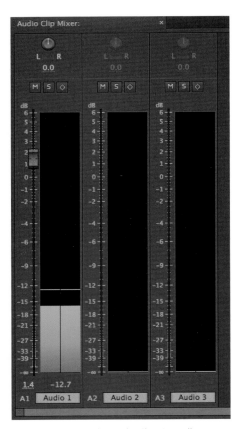

Figure 4.25 Using the Audio Clip Mixer allows you to add clip keyframes in real time as you listen to the clip being played in the Timeline.

perform changes on the fly. Any changes you make to the volume of the clip using this tool will be reflected in the Timeline volume line (rubber band). When you're using the Clip Mixer, note that only the clip is affected, not the track (the Track Mixer affects the track level).

As you move the playhead along, tracks that contain audio clips will become available to control; the controls for those tracks that don't contain audio clips will be grayed out.

To better understand how the Audio Clip Mixer works, follow these steps.

1. Move the playhead to the spot in the Timeline where you want to start your changes.

2. In the Audio Clip Mixer panel select the keyframe icon for the tracks that you want to affect. Remember that although this selection is on a track-by-track basis, the adjustments made are applied to clips, not tracks.

3. Mute any tracks you don't want to hear or solo a single track if you need to.

4. Start playback, move the volume level up and down, and pan left and right as desired.

   When you stop playback, keyframes will be added.

5. Adjust the keyframes if needed, or even record a second pass.

6. Play back and enjoy your work!

Audio Clip Mixer practice

To better understand how the Audio Clip Mixer works, follow these steps.

1. Open the project Chapter04_Audio.prproj, and then open the sequence named **Clip Keyframes**.

2. Open the Audio Clip Mixer panel and click the Write Keyframes icon.

3. Play the Timeline, and as it plays, adjust the Volume fader.

   Notice that when you're done, keyframes are on your clip (if you do not see them, make sure Clip Keyframes is selected in the audio track header).

TIP

When you stop recording keyframes in the Audio Clip Mixer panel, Adobe Premiere Pro creates a final keyframe at the point in time where you stopped. This keyframe is often an abrupt change from the next-to-last keyframe, so I recommend deleting it. Simply select that keyframe and then press the Delete key.

Figure 4.26 The Audio Track Mixer makes changes to the audio tracks through keyframes or through changes to the whole track's level.

Figure 4.27 The automation modes in the Audio Track Mixer panel create keyframes on the go as you listen to the audio in the Timeline.

Track Mixer

The Audio Track Mixer has Volume and Pan controls, and it will add keyframes, but instead of making changes to a clip it makes changes to the audio tracks. I usually use these track keyframes in conjunction with clip keyframes. If I'm editing a segment with a voice-over preceded by music, I'll add track keyframes to fade the music at the appropriate time, and if needed, add clip keyframes to further adjust the level of the music.

To open this tool, choose Window > Audio Track Mixer (**Figure 4.26**).

Several automation modes help you create the keyframes that will affect your track (**Figure 4.27**):

▶ **Off.** This setting, as you may have guessed, ignores existing keyframes. Even though you can still make changes to the track, these changes will not be recorded. Off is simply, *off*.

▶ **Read.** After you've created some keyframes, change the automation mode to Read to hear how they sound. Read mode will read any changes that you've already performed on the clip. If a clip has no keyframes and you adjust a track, the changes will affect the entire track. Once you stop adjusting, the fader will return to its former value. The speed of the return is determined by the Automatch Time option (Preferences > Audio > Automatch Time).

▶ **Write.** This automation mode lets you record any changes to volume or pan that you make to the track (as long as the Automation Mode is not set to Safe During Write). When you adjust the levels using this automation mode, new keyframes will be added, overwriting existing ones. You could also preserve a track property while recording the mix by right-clicking an effect or send and choosing Safe During Write from the menu.

▶ **Latch.** Similar to Write, but Latch changes don't start recording until you begin adjusting the property. So, if you are set to Latch and you play the track, nothing will be altered until you actively start adjusting.

▶ **Touch.** Same as Write, but when you stop adjusting a property, the fader will continue following existing keyframes, or return to the original value of the clip if there are no keyframes present. The speed of the return is determined by the Automatch Time option (Preferences > Audio > Automatch Time).

To better understand how the Audio Track Mixer works, follow these steps.

1. Move the playhead to the spot in the Timeline where you want to start your changes.

2. In the Audio Track Mixer panel select the desired automation mode.

3. Mute any tracks you don't want to hear or solo a single track if needed.

4. Start playback, move the volume level fader up and down, and pan left and right as desired.

5. When you stop playback, keyframes will be added. If you do not see these keyframes, click the Show Keyframes button in the track header and choose Track Keyframes.

6. Adjust the keyframes if needed, or even record a second pass.

7. Play back and enjoy your work!

If you feel you are adding too many keyframes, check and adjust the value in Preferences > Audio > Minimum Time Interval Thinning; larger values will reduce the number of keyframes. If you create keyframes that make changes that last one second, this option will create only the necessary keyframes at the beginning and at the end of the change. Otherwise, Adobe Premiere Pro may create other keyframes in the middle of these.

To make this process easier, rename your audio tracks from the default of Audio 1, Audio 2, and so on to reflect the type of clips you'll be placing on the track, such as male voice, female voice, nat sound, music, effects, and the like. You can rename your audio tracks in the Audio Track

Mixer or in the Timeline. To see an example of renaming tracks, open the project Chapter04_Audio.prproj, and then open the sequence named **Mix**. Notice the names of the tracks in the Audio Track Mixer.

Audio Track Mixer practice

To better understand how the Audio Track Mixer works, follow these steps.

1. Open the project Chapter04_Audio.prproj, and then open the sequence named **Track Keyframes**.

2. Open the Audio Track Mixer panel and select the Write automation mode.

3. Play the Timeline, and as it plays, adjust the Volume fader or the Pan control.

   Notice that when you're done, keyframes are added to your track (if you don't see them, make sure you have Track Keyframes selected in the audio track header).

4. Test the different automation modes and experience their differences. Remember to adjust the Automatch Time value in the Audio Preferences if you need to do so.

Submixes

In audio a submix is a grouping of tracks that are processed together to add some common effects. In Adobe Premiere Pro you use a submix mainly to avoid having to add the same effects over and over to many clips, and to be able to adjust levels of several tracks at the same time.

A submix is akin to a nested sequence, where you can add effects to the nested sequence instead of adding many different effects to many different clips (**Figure 4.28**). Consider a submix an intermediary track between the original tracks and the master track. The source for this intermediary track is other audio tracks, so you cannot add clips directly to this submix track; however, you can add as many tracks to a submix as you need.

A send takes the audio signal from a track and "sends" it somewhere else before it goes to the master track. This is what you use to route audio tracks through submixes.

Figure 4.28 Submixes let you adjust several tracks at the same time.

To create a submix, you can use the Send Assignment menu on the Track Mixer, or you can right-click on the audio track button area in the Timeline and choose Add a Submix Audio Track. Then, in the Audio Track Mixer panel, select the Sends drop-down from the track(s) you want to send to the Submix track and choose Submix.

In the Audio Track Mixer panel you can adjust the fader and/or add any effects you desire to the submix.

Submixes practice

To better understand how submixes work, follow these steps.

1. Open the project Chapter04_Audio.prproj, and then open the sequence named **Submix**.

2. Open the Audio Track Mixer panel, which contains two submixes: one called SFX submix the other called VO Submix. The different tracks are being routed to different submixes except for the music track, which goes directly to the master. Some effects are already applied.

3. Test different settings and experiment with different effects to hear how they affect your sound.

Audio FX

Even after you've mixed your audio, it still might not sound right. Some clips may have unwanted noise or still be too loud or too soft. Effects are the solution to these problems, although some clips cannot be completely fixed. This section discusses some of the most commonly used audio effects.

Using Your Master Track

Although it is generally not recommended, you could use your master track in lieu of a submix. All of your tracks will be added to the master track anyway, so why not use it to your advantage?

You could use your master track to add effects and even to adjust volume. In a pinch, you could also use it to do a quick but effective last-minute adjustment to your program.

Pre-fader or Post-fader?

Sends can be applied pre-fader or post-fader (**Figure 4.29**). If you choose pre-fader, the send ignores the fader control track, which means that it will ignore any level changes applied to the track. If you choose post-fader, the send level is based on the fader control (and still has its own level of adjustment too). So, if your fader is set to −4dB, a post-fader send will begin at −4dB, but a pre-fader send will be at 0dB regardless of the fader level.

Most of the time you will want a post-fader send, because it seems natural that if you adjust the track's volume, the signal that is sent to the submix would be adjusted in turn. However, sometimes you want the signal that is being sent to the submix to remain unchanged no matter what happens to the fader of the track. A good example of using a pre-fader send is to keep a reverb effect consistent regardless of the track fader level. To change the post-fader default of the send, right-click on the send's name in the Track Send Assignment menu (in the Audio Track Mixer) and choose Pre-Fader.

Figure 4.29 Pre-faders and post-faders will ignore or follow the fader in the Audio Track Mixer before going to the submix.

The Multiband Compressor is powered by iZotope and is the same compressor found in Adobe Audition.

Multiband Compressor

A compressor is the tool that can help raise or attenuate the relative level of the clip and gives your audio punch and strength (**Figure 4.30**). You may want to use a compressor when you need your audio levels not to go any louder than a certain value or to remain between a certain range of values. When editing for broadcast (usually commercials), I usually run all of my audio through a compressor/limiter on the master track, which helps me remain within the broadcast audio levels.

You should think about audio levels in two different ways: One is the absolute level—the level that the meter displays—and the other one is the subjective level, which is how loud you perceive the volume.

Figure 4.30 A compressor is one of the most commonly used tools; it lets you control the DR of voices and/or instruments.

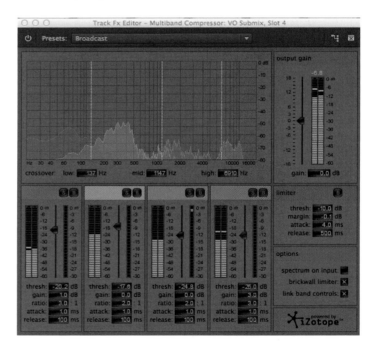

Can you recall a certain bathroom tissue commercial where people were whispering? This gave the perceived level of being quiet. In reality the audio levels were just as loud as when the announcer was plugging that particular brand. What the meter displays and what you perceive are sometimes different.

Adobe Premiere Pro's Multiband Compressor effect separates the audio into different frequencies (or bands) and processes them separately; what this means is that you could affect some frequencies in one way and other frequencies in a different way. Based on frequencies, you could affect some instruments and not others. This could be useful if you are editing a music video and need to master the audio as well, for example, maybe the bass is too soft or too loud. Using this effect you could affect only the frequency in which the bass sound exists.

Here are some controls in the Multiband Compressor that you should know:

- **Threshold.** Threshold is the minimum level that will make the compressor start working. Depending on the ratio (described next), the compressor will "kick in" when your audio levels reach the threshold you set on this effect. The threshold is commonly set in decibels; a lower threshold (e.g., -60dB) means more of the clip will be compressed.

- **Ratio.** The amount of gain reduction is determined by the ratio: A ratio of 3:1 means that if the input level is 3dB over the threshold, the output signal level will be 1dB over the threshold. In this case, the gain (level) is reduced by 2dB. For example:

  - Threshold = −10dB

  - Input = −7dB (3dB above the threshold)

  - Output = −9dB (1dB above the threshold)

  Try to keep the ratio at no more than 3:1 to maintain a gentle-sounding effect. If the ratio goes above 3:1, the audio might sound unnatural.

TIP

Do not overcompress your audio. Hypercompressed programs do not sound natural. Too much compression robs the mix of vivacity. In fact, they are tiresome and dull. Also, keep in mind that MP3s have difficulties encoding hypercompressed material. You can tell when audio has been over compressed not just by the sound but by how the waveforms look when you see them in the Timeline. Hardly any waves are displayed; they are all flat!

CLOSE-UP

Using a Limiter

Within the Fx Editor of the Multiband Compressor effect is a Limiter section. Imagine, if you will, that most of your audio levels are fairly even and that you have short (in duration) waves that get pretty loud. This is the perfect scenario in which to use a limiter. The limiter affects only those short duration bursts without affecting the overall level of audio. If you control these peaks, you can raise the entire level of the program without fear of distortion.

A *brick wall limiter* ensures that the levels will not exceed a certain indicated level.

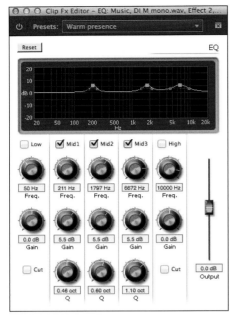

Figure 4.31 An EQ helps balance the frequencies throughout your program.

▶ **Attack.** Attack is the time that it takes to reach maximum level of compression. Attack will affect drums if the release is too fast, which will result in unnatural level changes.

▶ **Release.** Release is the time that it takes for the audio level to return to normal (no compression). You should have slow release times to minimize the unnatural level changes (pumping).

If your clip has a wide DR, you'll notice the compression more because it will click more often and for a less amount of time.

EQ

An equalizer (EQ) is an effect that will let you balance different frequencies throughout your program (**Figure 4.31**). You will be able to select a specific frequency (or range of frequencies) and adjust their levels to increase or decrease their volume.

For example, if you are working with a music clip in which you can hardly hear bass, you could add the EQ effect and increase the volume of the bass only, making it more present in the mix.

To better accomplish this task, you can train your ears to recognize a well-balanced audio program by playing good audio through your system. Play audio that is similar to the program that you are mixing. If you are mixing a high-impact commercial, listen to something comparable. It's best if the sample audio is the same genre as the program you're working on.

As you become more familiar with the EQ tool and your ears begin to detect audio nuances, your changes will be very small. You will have changes in many places, but these changes will be minimal—for example, 2dB or 3dB at the very most.

When you want to use the EQ effect because you need to do more than make small adjustments, reconsider your microphone placement and your audio recording techniques.

A Little About the Sound Spectrum and EQs

An equalizer allows you to lower or raise any individual frequency in the sound spectrum and it's helpful to have a general understanding of the "map" of frequencies.

Human hearing ranges from about 20 Hertz (Hz) (very low tones) to approximately 20,000 Hz (very high whistles).

Low bass sounds (think hums and rumbles) register at about 50–60 Hz. Men's voices register in the 600–800 Hz range, whereas women and children's voices tend to be a little higher (800–1200 Hz for women and 1000–1400 Hz for children). Voices may be higher or lower (harmonics, certain parts of speech) but these ranges are generally where the strength of the voice exists.

Above 3,000 Hz (or 3 KHz), you'll find higher pitched sounds. Above that, we begin to get into the ranges of whistles. The sibilant "S" sound that some people make registers at around 5 KHz. A *DeEsser* is a specialized EQ that lowers sound in that range.

Classically, an EQ designed for speed lowers the section below 100 Hz (taking out rumbles in a room), boosts the area around 700 Hz just a couple of DB (for a male's speech to come through clearly), and lowers the spectrum higher that 3 KHz (removing high whines).

A great technique is to reverse this for non-speech sections (such as music) during moments where both music and speech occur. Since the speech EQ increases the speech ranges and the music EQ lowers those same exact ranges, they tend not to be perceived as competing as much during playback.

Feathering is a commonly used technique where instead of increasing one frequency you increase a number of adjacent frequencies to produce a smoother curve.

When you're working with the EQ, do not alter the volume of your speakers (seriously, don't touch this volume at all). If you do, you might overcompensate and the EQ will not be accurate.

Constantly compare the processed audio with the original version. Also, compare your clips with each other. Using the EQ is one of the ways to achieve audio continuity in your program.

To use the EQ effect, follow these steps.

1. Add the EQ effect to the clip (or the track).

2. Launch the clip Fx Editor by clicking the Edit button in the Effect Controls panel. To launch the Track Mixer, double-click the Fx slot where the EQ is located.

TIP

Double-check your levels. An EQ effect can increase the volume of specific frequencies, and it is common that in the process of EQing your audio clip or track you increase (or decrease) the overall level. This can easily be adjusted using the Output Gain slider in the Fx Editor.

3. Choose from several presets that are available. Once you become familiar with this tool, you can even create your own. Sometimes it's easier to start from a preset and then adjust it rather than starting from scratch.

4. Select the appropriate check boxes in the Fx Editor. To make adjustments, you can either use the knobs or simply click and drag the control points. Notice that the control points are "connected," which means that the resulting feathering effect will sound more natural.

5. Adjust the Q control, which controls the smoothness of the curves that "connect" the control points. You can either adjust these control points by using the knob or by clicking and dragging the handles directly on the control points.

6. Adjust the overall gain by using the Output Gain slider to the right of the knobs.

EQ practice

To better understand how the EQ works, follow these steps.

1. Open the project Chapter04_Audio.prproj, and then open the sequence named **EQ**. The sequence contains two different groups of clips in the Timeline in two different tracks. The first one is unprocessed; the second clip has the EQ effect added to the track

2. Listen to both clips.

3. Open the Audio Track Mixer.

4. Open the Fx Editor for the EQ applied to the second track (by double-clicking on it).

5. Note how the frequencies were modified (Warm Presence preset), and try making some changes of your own

   Start training your ears to distinguish between the sound qualities of the different changes.

Loudness Radar

The Loudness Radar effect (**Figure 4.32**) is a tool that lets you read the loudness of your program over time. If the audio will be used in a program destined for broadcast, you are probably aware that you'll need to comply with loudness standards. If you don't, the broadcast house may adjust your audio levels or it might simply reject your program. You could also use this effect to compare the levels of the different clips of your program; that is, how much louder than the music is the voice-over track?

The Loudness Radar displays audio levels in two rings: The outer ring shows current audio levels, and the inner ring shows the audio levels over time (a useful history of loudness). At the bottom of the Loudness Radar screen you can also see loudness range values and the overall program loudness.

The yellow area is the loudest level (don't exceed this level). The blue level is too low (below the noise floor), so you want your audio to stay between the green and the yellow levels.

You can change the loudness standards, and see where your program falls within the different standards. These Loudness Standard presets are in the settings of the effect, and you can choose between BS.1770-3 and Leq(K). These standards are presets that change the values in the Settings tab. Here are some of those settings:

Figure 4.32 The Loudness Radar effect is new in Adobe Premiere Pro CC. It lets you ensure that your program is compliant with broadcast standards.

- ▶ **Radar Speed.** You can change this value to an appropriate time (the length of the program) to display the history of the program's loudness.

- ▶ **Radar Resolution.** This is the space increment of the inner circles.

- ▶ **Momentary Range.** This sets the loudness for the momentary range. It offers two different choices: EBU +9 is meant for normal broadcast, and EBU +18 is meant for film, drama, and a wide range of music.

- ▶ **Low Level Below.** With this setting you can set the shift between the green and blue colors on the momentary loudness ring. This could be set to indicate that the level may be below the noise floor level.

TIP

You can also apply the Loudness Radar effect to individual tracks in the Audio Track Mixer. This is useful when you want to monitor the levels of music on one track and dialogue on another to ensure that the music is quieter than the dialogue.

▶ **Overall Audio Units.** This sets the loudness units to be displayed on the radar. Choose between units for the International Telecommunications Union (ITU) and the European Broadcast Union (EBU).

▶ **Loudness Standard.** This sets the loudness standard. Choose between BS.1770-3 and the Leq(K) loudness standard.

▶ **Peak Indicator.** This sets the value at which the peak indicator will be activated. The red peak indicator lights up if you exceed the indicated level.

The Loudness Radar applied to just one clip isn't that useful when you have multiple audio clips and multiple audio tracks.

This effect is best used in the master audio track. You can either nest your Timeline into a new sequence or add the effect directly to the master track in the Audio Track Mixer.

Loudness Radar practice

To better understand the Loudness Radar effect, follow these steps.

1. Open the project Chapter04_Audio.prproj, and then open the sequence named **Loudness Radar**.

2. In the Audio Track Mixer, open the Fx Editor for the Loudness Radar applied to the master track.

3. Mark In and Out points, and then click the "Loop playback" icon. This will place your playback in a repeat mode that will only stop when you manually pause the playback.

4. Start playing your Timeline.

5. As it plays, note how the effect works by changing the levels of the track (not the master), and notice how the radar display changes.

6. Increase levels so you can see the peak warning.

DeHummer

A DeHummer is an effect that will help you get rid of an unwanted frequency that is usually caused by power lines from lights and electronics. I'm sure you have heard a loud hum that seems to come from everywhere and almost totally ruins the good audio you want to retain. Hum in your audio is never good, and quite frankly, should have been caught during the recording process. However, sometimes you don't have a say in which audio you get and who recorded it, so you might end up with audio with hum (**Figure 4.33**).

More often than not, audio hum comes from improperly electrically grounded audio equipment or induction (audio lines next to power lines). The frequency of your ground hum will match your electrical power—60Hz in North America and 50Hz in Europe.

To use the DeHummer effect, follow these steps.

1. Add the DeHummer effect to the affected clip in your Timeline.

2. In the Effect Controls panel locate the DeHummer effect, and click Edit to launch the Clip Fx Editor for the DeHummer effect.

3. Select one of the available presets, which is a good place to start.

4. Adjust the following parameters until the hum is gone:

   ▶ **Frequency.** Specifies the frequency you target.

   ▶ **Q.** Specifies the width of the frequency band. A frequency band is a small section of the spectrum of frequencies.

   ▶ **Gain.** Specifies the amount by which to decrease the band.

   ▶ **Number of Harmonics.** Adjust this value to determine the number of harmonic frequencies to filter. In addition to the common 50Hz and 60Hz electrical hum, you can also experience hum at the multiples of the base frequency (100, 200, 400 or 120, 240, 480Hz, etc.).

For example, if you choose 60Hz as the Frequency value and choose 4# as the Filter value, the DeHummer filters the 60Hz frequency along with three harmonic frequencies (120Hz, 240Hz, and 480Hz). A total of four frequencies are filtered, hence the value of 4#.

Avoid Hum While Recording

If you're experiencing hum while recording, try these tactics:

▶ Power your camera with a battery instead of an AC adapter.

▶ Place your audio and video cables at least one foot apart, or (if you can) at right angles to each other.

▶ Use balanced audio cables.

▶ Shut off fluorescent lights that can sometimes cause hum.

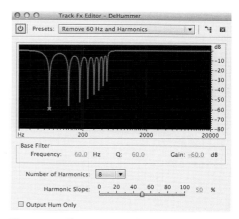

Figure 4.33 The DeHummer helps remove unwanted specific frequencies from the audio—more specifically 50Hz and 60Hz hum.

The frequency of hum isn't exactly at 50Hz or 60Hz because electrical frequency can vary. Adjust the base frequency +/- 5Hz to see if that makes a difference. The more precise your base frequency and the smaller your Q value, the less damage you do to the good audio. Use only the necessary number of harmonics.

TIP

To better pinpoint your base hum frequency, find a spot in your clip where there is no good audio and mark In and Out points. Loop this playback. Add the DeHummer effect and change the settings to a narrow notch (Q). Raise the gain as far as it goes and gradually change the frequency value. Once it gets awful, you have identified the base frequency to eliminate. Change the harmonics to a number that will work with your clip and then lower the gain, fixing the hum.

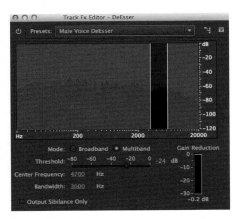

Figure 4.34 A DeEsser removes unwanted sibilance from your audio.

5. Preview changes to your audio, select the Output Hum Only check box, and resume playback. If you hear too much of your good audio, adjust your settings.

DeHummer practice

To better understand how the DeHummer works, follow these steps.

1. Open the project Chapter04_Audio.prproj, and then open the sequence named **Hum**.

2. In the Audio Track Mixer, open the Fx Editor for the DeHummer applied to the master track.

3. Mark In and Out points, click the "Loop playback" icon, and start playing your Timeline.

4. As it plays, alter the values of the effect (not the master), and note the changes. To hear it work, choose the preset "Remove 60Hz and Harmonics."

DeEsser

A DeEsser is an effect used to reduce the amount of sibilance ("sss") in a clip. Some recordings can sound as though someone is scraping fingernails on a blackboard (**Figure 4.34**). This is the undesirable effect that a huge sibilance sound has on me. Sibilance is a short burst of high frequency sound where the "esses" are emphasized. In some voices the "esses" are very prominent. This is usually caused by a combination of voice quality, pattern of speech, and poor microphone placement.

Most DeEssers have two main controls: Threshold and Frequency, which are used to compress only a very narrow band of frequencies—anywhere between 3K and 10K to eliminate sibilance. Sibilance usually exists somewhere between 4Khz to 10Khz depending on the voice and the recording.

Apply the DeEsser to your clip and use one of the handy presets. If the preset is not quite right, you can adjust some of its settings. However, if you don't want to use a preset, raise the Threshold control until the sibilance is gone but you can still hear the esses. Next, adjust the Frequency range until you find the exact setting that will fix the issue. Then go back to the Threshold again and adjust it until it sounds natural.

DeEsser practice

To better understand how the DeEsser works, follow these steps.

1. Open the project Chapter04_Audio.prproj, and then open the sequence named **DeEsser**.

2. In the Audio Track Mixer, open the Fx Editor for the DeEsser applied to the master track.

3. Mark In and Out points, and click the "Loop playback" icon.

4. Start playing your Timeline, and as it plays, experiment with the values of the effect (not the master) and note the changes.

5. Bypass the effect so you can get a clear idea of the before and after sound.

TIP

You can use a DeEsser for more than just voice. You can control some of the frequencies produced by cymbals and snares, and even guitars!

Reverb

A reverb effect is a room simulator; it imitates the characteristics of a place and adds the necessary changes to the audio to give the audience the illusion that the sound is coming from a room of a particular size and acoustical properties (**Figure 4.35**).

Arguably, reverb is one of the most commonly used effects. Actually, it is one of the most commonly *misused* effects. Therefore, you should use reverb to affect the acoustical continuity of your program—in other words, to put different sources of audio in the *same room*.

To use reverb in a clip, follow these steps.

1. Add the Reverb effect to the clip (available for 5.1, stereo, or mono clips).

2. Open the Fx Editor.

3. Choose the presets that will most closely resemble the environment you want to duplicate:

   ▶ **Pre Delay.** Specifies how long the sound will take to go from the originator of the sound to the virtual reflecting wall and back to the origin again.

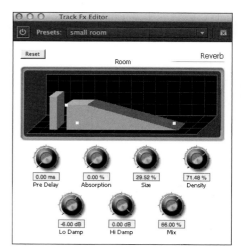

Figure 4.35 A reverb is a room simulator that will help give your clips continuity.

> ▶ **Absorption.** Specifies how much of the sound will be absorbed by the material in the room.

> ▶ **Size.** Specifies the size of the room (as a percentage).

> ▶ **Density.** Specifies the number of reflections in an ambient space and is related to the size. High-density values create rich-sounding reverbs.

> ▶ **Lo Damp.** Specifies the amount of attenuation for low frequencies to preserve clarity.

> ▶ **Hi Damp.** Specifies the amount of dampening of high frequencies.

> ▶ **Mix.** Controls the amount of reverb.

Reverb practice

To better understand how the Reverb effect works, follow these steps.

1. Open the project Chapter04_Audio.prproj, and then open the sequence named **Reverb**.

2. In the Audio Track Mixer, open the Fx Editor for the Reverb applied to the VO track.

3. Play your Timeline, and as it plays, bypass the effect so you can get a clear idea of the before and after sound.

4. Experiment with the presets and the settings to start training your ears to hear what reverb does for your audio.

Adobe Audition

Adobe Premiere Pro CC is powerful in that it can mix, adjust, and even clean up your audio, but it can't replace a professional, audio, postproduction, digital audio workstation (DAW) like Adobe Audition (**Figure 4.36**). Sometimes you'll need to mix and fix your audio in a professional audio environment. I'll demonstrate two of my favorite solutions in Adobe Audition: removing noise and fixing clipped audio.

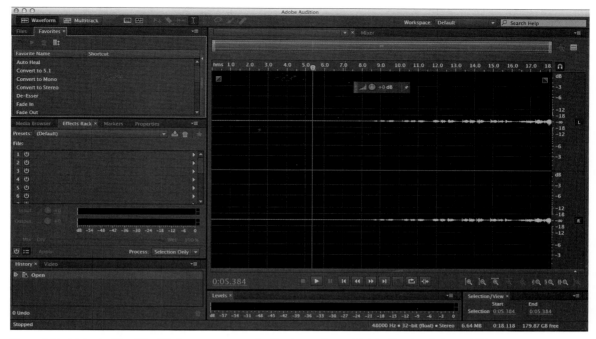

Figure 4.36 Adobe Audition CC will help you process audio clips that are beyond Adobe Premiere Pro's capabilities.

Removing Noise

Noise doesn't always fit in a tidy frequency range notch, and it can be quicker, more effective, and much easier to fix your audio noise problem in Adobe Audition by using its effective, two-step, noise removal tool.

The process is to send a clip to Adobe Audition, select an area of the noise alone (without foreground audio) for Adobe Audition to "memorize," and then select the entire clip to help it eliminate noise from the clip. What happens during this process is that Adobe Audition will generate the necessary signal to eliminate the noise and only the noise. To accomplish this task, follow these steps.

1. Right-click on the clip you want to send to Adobe Audition, and choose Edit Clip in Adobe Audition (**Figure 4.37**). This command renders your clip and replaces your audio with a dynamically linked audio clip, and launches Adobe Audition with this clip open.

Figure 4.37 Choose Edit Clip in Adobe Audition to repair noise in your clip.

Adobe Premiere Pro will not send the original audio to Adobe Audition in order to preserve the original audio untouched, because any changes you make in Audition will permanently change this audio clip.

2. Using the Audition Time Select tool (T), select a portion of the waveform that contains the noise but no dialogue.

3. Right-click on the selected area, and choose Capture Noise Print (**Figure 4.38**). Alternatively, you can press Shift+P. Then deselect your selection on the audio waveform so that the next step will apply to the entire waveform, not just the sample audio selection.

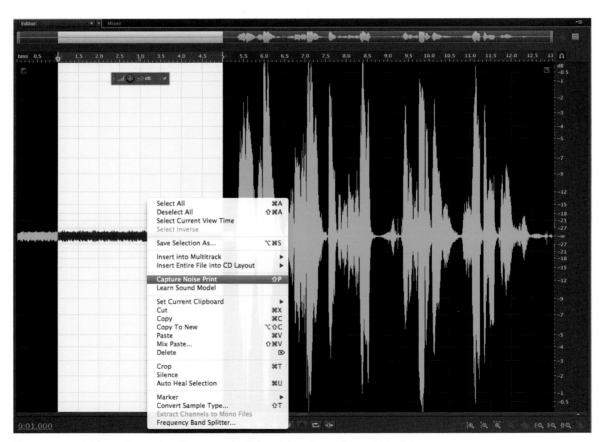

Figure 4.38 In Adobe Audition, select the noise, right-click, and then choose Capture Noise Print.

4. In the Effects menu, choose Noise Removal/Restoration, and then select Noise Reduction (process) (**Figure 4.39**) to launch the Noise Reduction Effect panel. You can also access this panel by pressing Command+Shift+P (Ctrl+Shift+P).

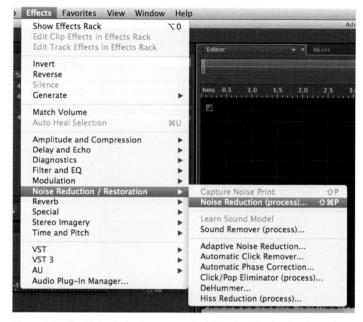

Figure 4.39 The Noise Reduction process in Adobe Audition is effective and easy to use. The best part is that you can send a copy of your audio clip directly to Adobe Audition from within Adobe Premiere Pro.

5. Play your clip by clicking the play icon. Toggle the Effect Power State on and off as well as the Output Noise Only option while playing back the clip to further refine the noise reduction settings.

6. Click the Apply button. Adobe Audition likely does a pretty good job of removing the unwanted noise floor automatically, but you can make further adjustments by using a noise gate or an EQ.

7. Save your changes by pressing Command+S (Ctrl+S), and return to Adobe Premiere Pro. Your audio file will update with the fixed audio.

Using Adobe Audition to remove background noise

To get a better understanding of how the noise removal process in Adobe Audition works, follow these steps.

1. Open the project Chapter04_Audio.prproj, and then open the sequence named **Audition Noise**.

2. On the Timeline, right-click the clip and choose Edit Clip in Adobe Audition.

3. Once in Audition, select a part of the clip that contains only the background noise and nothing else (click and drag to select). You can even zoom in if you desire (press +). This selects the background noise for that clip.

4. Choose Effects > Noise Reduction / Restoration > Capture Noise Print (or press Shift+P).

5. Click OK in the dialog that opens

6. Click anywhere in the wave to deselect.

7. Apply the effect by choosing Effects > Noise Reduction / Restoration > Noise Reduction (process).

8. When the panel opens, play the clip and move the sliders until the room noise disappears. I used the values of 92% for Noise Reduction and Reduce by 46dB.

9. While the clip plays, bypass the effect so you can get a good idea of the before and after (toggle the effect off and on again) sound.

10. When you're happy with the settings, click Apply and save your clip.

11. Go back to Adobe Premiere Pro; your clip is waiting for you there!

Fix Clipped Audio

As mentioned earlier, it's best to record your audio properly to begin with than have to fix it in postproduction. However, sometimes you have no choice but to work with what you have. If you do need to fix a clip that is clipped, you can fix it somewhat using Adobe Audition CC.

1. Right-click the clip you want to send to Adobe Audition, and choose Edit Clip in Adobe Audition. This

command renders and replaces your audio with a dynamically linked audio clip, and launches Adobe Audition with this clip open.

2. In Audition, choose Window > Amplitude Statistics (**Figure 4.40**).

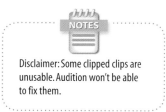

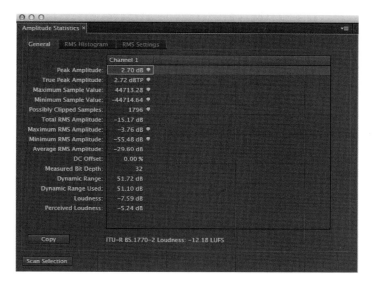

Figure 4.40 The Amplitude Statistics panel in Adobe Audition calculates statistics from an entire file or selection.

3. Click the Scan button, and look at the Possibly Clipped Samples property to get a good idea of how much clipping is in your clip. Using this value will let you set the correct preset when using the effect. (You will be able to determine if the clip is heavily or lightly clipped.)

4. Choose Effects > Diagnostics > DeClipper (process) to open a new panel (**Figure 4.41** on the next page).

5. Choose the preset that best represents the amount of clipping in the clip. Experiment with different presets if you're not sure.

6. Click the Scan button.

7. Click Repair All.

8. Save your changes by pressing Command+S (Ctrl+S), and return to Adobe Premiere Pro. Your dynamically linked audio file will update with the fixed audio.

Figure 4.41 The DeClipper effect repairs clipped waveforms.

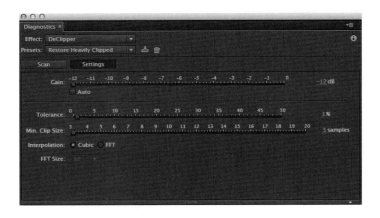

Using Adobe Audition to restore clipped audio

To get a better understanding of how to restore clipped audio, follow these steps.

1. Open the project Chapter04_Audio.prproj, and then open the sequence named **Audition DeClipper**.

2. On the Timeline, right-click the clip and choose Edit Clip in Adobe Audition.

3. In Audition, choose Window > Amplitude Statistics to display the statistics and determine how much clipping is in the audio. This panel is for diagnostics only.

4. Click the Scan button.

5. Choose Effects > Diagnostics > DeClipper (process).

6. When the panel opens, choose Restore Heavily Clipped and click the Scan button to identify which parts of the clips need to be fixed. A list of the problem areas appears at the bottom of the panel.

7. Click Repair All and the effect will start working.

8. Look at the waveforms when it is done. Much better, right?

9. Experiment with the settings; repeat the process over and over to get a good idea of how the effect works and what the settings do (you can use undo to reverse your changes).

10. When you're happy with the settings, save your clip and return to Adobe Premiere Pro.

5

Advanced Compositing
and Effects

Author: Tim Kolb

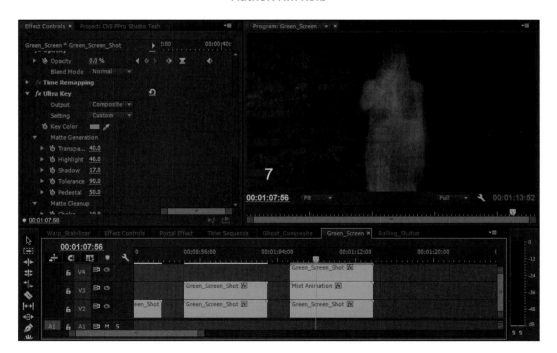

Special effects are just a tool, a means of telling a story. People have a tendency to confuse them as an end to themselves.

—George Lucas

Advanced Compositing and Effects

Video editing is about refinement. Images and sound are acquired to document an event or to illustrate a story outlined by a script, but the final message is changed and enhanced substantially by the choices made in the edit room.

Decisions on what images and sound are cut away, and the order and emphasis of what is included are important, but what is done to further enhance or change that material through additional processing in postproduction has significant influence as well.

Adobe Premiere Pro is a capable editing system, but it has more video effects capacity than even many experienced users realize.

In this chapter, we'll investigate how Adobe Premiere Pro processes effects and I'll demonstrate several advanced techniques by examining and then combining various effects in ways that will ideally help you expand how you think about Adobe Premiere Pro as a postproduction tool.

Adobe Premiere Pro Effects Processing

When you open the Effects panel (Window > Effects or Shift+7) to examine the inventory of effects and transitions, you'll notice that some effects have one or more symbols to the right of their name. There are three designations that represent very specific and important aspects of how each effect operates: GPU acceleration, 32 bit float color precision, and YUV color.

Using the sort buttons at the top of the Effects panel, you can view only the effects with the chosen designation or a combination of designations. Selecting YUV hides all effects that do not operate in YUV color (**Figure 5.1**).

GPU Acceleration

By employing a GPU with at least 1 GB of RAM, GPU-enabled effects are rendered much faster than they would be if they were processed by the CPU alone. In the Project Settings on the General tab, select Mercury Playback Engine GPU Acceleration to enable GPU processing for GPU-enabled effects.

32 Bit Float Color Precision

Some video effects in Adobe Premiere Pro process at 32 color bits per channel as opposed to the 8 bits per channel standard in most video formats. Choosing these effects enables video effects rendering that doesn't compromise the quality of high bit-depth video formats, such as v210, ProRes, or 10 bit DNxHD.

To enable preview rendering with 32 bit float color precision when using these effects, select the Maximum Bit-Depth option in the Settings tab (and choose an appropriate preview format for working in color precision deeper than 8 bits) in the Sequence Settings dialog. To process your sequence effects at maximum depth when you export your final project, there is an additional check box for the Maximum Bit Depth option in the Export dialog.

Figure 5.1 Use the sort buttons at the top of the Effects panel to hide any effects without that designation.

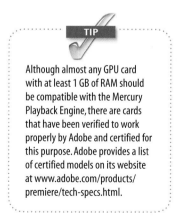

TIP

Although almost any GPU card with at least 1 GB of RAM should be compatible with the Mercury Playback Engine, there are cards that have been verified to work properly by Adobe and certified for this purpose. Adobe provides a list of certified models on its website at www.adobe.com/products/premiere/tech-specs.html.

TIP

If you want to apply fixed effect adjustments like Position or Scale and have them render in an order you set prior to the processing of one or more standard effects, use the standard effect named Transform instead of Motion and the effect named Alpha Adjust to make Opacity changes.

YUV Color

Some effects in Adobe Premiere Pro process in YUV color. Typically, computers work in RGB color—one channel each of red, green, and blue. Each primary channel stores information for that component color, and the full palette is created by combining the channels. Video recording technology usually works a bit differently than the standard computer-based RGB color system. Many video formats use a system in which one grayscale channel is stored as a complete black and white image with all the luma detail in one channel, and two additional channels store hue and saturation information, referred to as Y'UV in notation associated with standard definition, analog video.

In current industry terminology, the "black and white" channel is designated as Y. The other two channels are designated as Pb and Pr in analog systems and Cb and Cr in digital terms, spelled out as YPbPr or YCbCr to represent this system in many applications or on modern video equipment.

Fixed and Standard Effects

The two basic types of effects in Adobe Premiere Pro are fixed effects and standard effects. Fixed effects are those that are on a clip automatically when it's placed on a sequence. For example, Motion, Scale, Opacity, and Time Remapping (and Volume for clips containing audio) are applied to every clip (**Figure 5.2**).

Figure 5.2 The Effect Controls panel displays fixed video and audio effects.

Standard effects are those that need to be applied manually, including most third-party effects plug-ins you might have installed.

Standard effects are rendered in the order they're listed in the Effect Controls panel (which you can change by dragging each effect up or down in the list), but the fixed effects are always rendered last (**Figure 5.3**).

Animating Effects

Many effects need to be applied with settings that change over time. The keyframing system in Adobe Premiere Pro is designed to interpolate effect properties between points in time. Although the mechanism of keyframing is not difficult to learn, advancing toward animating effects to create complex visual sequences or more important, solving a complicated visual problem, has more to do with your thought process. We'll examine keyframing as a component of several visual effect scenarios moving forward in this chapter.

Keyframes in the Effect Controls Panel

The majority of the effects available in Adobe Premiere Pro have adjustable parameters that control the various aspects of the effect. When a clip on an edit sequence is selected, the settings associated with that clip and its fixed and standard effects are accessible in the Effect Controls panel.

To follow along, in the Chapter 5 project, open the sequence named **Effect Controls**. Slide the playhead left to the beginning of the Timeline and click on the clip named Conversation. Once the clip is selected, the clip's effects properties will be visible in the Effect Controls panel. When you play through the clip, you'll notice that the playhead moves through the Effect Controls panel synchronously with the sequence.

In the Effect Controls panel, you'll see an empty square to the left of the Motion properties. Select this square to enable the Motion properties (the letters fx will appear in the box to confirm this) (**Figure 5.4** on the next page).

When you play the clip on the Timeline with Motion properties enabled, the shot now gradually zooms to the man's face, which could indicate that whatever his reaction is to the conversation is significant to the story.

Figure 5.3 Standard video effects subdirectories are listed in the Video Effects category on the Effects panel.

TIP

If the Effect Controls panel is not visible, you can access it from the Window menu or by pressing Shift+5.

Figure 5.4 The Effects toggle button to the left of Motion.

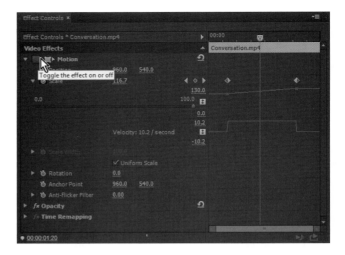

This movement is animated with the clip's Motion-Scale properties (click the disclosure triangle to the left of the Motion check box if Scale and Position values are hidden). The change happens between the two keyframes visible in the Timeline in the Effect Controls panel. Animation of the Scale property is enabled by the stopwatch button to the immediate left.

By using the Go To Next/Previous Keyframe buttons, you can move between the first keyframe (where the clip's Scale value is 100% of original size) and the second keyframe (set at 120%). When you're on a keyframe, you can select the Scale value and type a new value (or click and drag over the value to alter it). You can also select and drag keyframes to change their position in time.

The Add/Remove Keyframe button adds or removes a keyframe at the playhead's position (**Figure 5.5**). You can also automatically add a keyframe by positioning the playhead at a point where one doesn't exist and changing the property's value.

Figure 5.5 The Add/Remove Keyframe button in the Effect Controls panel with the Previous Keyframe button pointing to the left and the Next Keyframe button to the right.

Keyframes like those currently on the Effect Controls Timeline are linear. If you click the disclosure triangle next to the Scale property, you'll see the graph of the animation. Linear keyframes create a steady interpolation between the two keyframes. By right-clicking on a keyframe, you'll see that other choices are available (**Figure 5.6**). Change the first keyframe to Ease Out and the second keyframe to Ease In. Notice the change in the graph and the change in the move when you play the clip now. Using the Ease In/Out and Bezier keyframe interpolation settings makes animated moves and effects look less "mechanical," and in this case, the camera zoom starts to look a bit more natural.

TIP

Dragging the playhead to a keyframe in the Effect Controls panel to change its settings can be a temptation, but using the Previous/Next Keyframe arrows is still the best method to move to a keyframe and make a change. Depending on your eye and dragging the playhead alone can create unintended keyframes that exist so close to an adjacent keyframe that they are impossible to see without being extremely zoomed in.

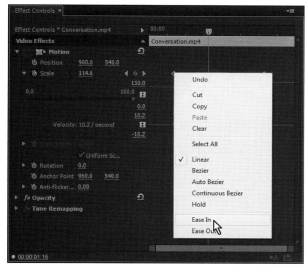

Figure 5.6 Right-click on a keyframe to reveal the interpolation options.

Keyframes in the Sequence

There will be times when you'll want to position keyframes for properties on one clip by seeing the relationship to something in another clip in your sequence. Because the Effect Controls panel only shows one clip at a time, these type of adjustments can be more intuitively done directly on the sequence. All changes made to keyframes update in both the sequence and the Effect Controls panel regardless of where you make the change.

To make keyframes visible on the sequence, click the Timeline Display Settings icon (it looks like a wrench) below the timecode display in the upper-left corner of the Sequence panel, and enable Show Video Keyframes (**Figure 5.7**).

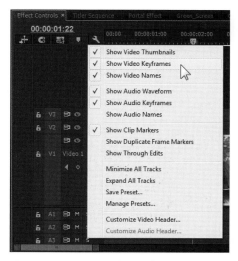

Figure 5.7 Turning on Video Keyframes in a sequence permits easy visualization and timing of keyframes compared to other elements on the Timeline.

The clip will only show one set of keyframes in the sequence at a time, so if you have multiple animated effects on a single clip, you can change which effect's keyframes you're viewing by right-clicking on the clip, choosing Show Clip Keyframes, and then choosing the effect from the submenu (**Figure 5.8**). For the Conversation clip, choosing Motion > Scale will show the Scale keyframes.

Figure 5.8 Only a single parameter's keyframes can be seen on the Timeline at a time.

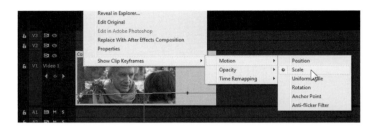

You can adjust the keyframes visible on the clip in the sequence by simply dragging them left or right to change their position in time and up or down to change their values. The keyframe interpolation can also be changed by right-clicking on the keyframe and choosing from the menu, similar to how it would be done in the Effect Controls panel.

The keyframe interpolation can be altered with visible "handles" when using one of the Bezier interpolation properties, changing the angle and length of the handle (**Figure 5.9**).

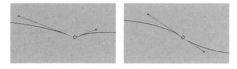

Figure 5.9 Two clip keyframes from an edit sequence showing Bezier "handles" in blue. On the left is a Bezier keyframe where the incoming and outgoing handles can be adjusted individually. On the right is a Continuous Bezier keyframe where the angle is adjustable but constant through the keyframe.

One Effect, Multiple Approaches

When looking at effects and effect design, I felt it was advantageous to show various builds and techniques. This way you can see how the same media could be used from different approaches.

In the **Portal Effect** sequence, you'll see a series of clip segments that I'll use to illustrate a number of effects concepts in Adobe Premiere Pro. Each group has a number in the bottom left of the frame to differentiate the groups. As we move forward we'll examine several ways to approach an effect within Adobe Premiere Pro, as well as methods for combining techniques that build on each other to create the final example.

Find the clip **Apprentice Enters** in the Portal Effect bin in the Project panel, and double-click it to open it in the Source panel (**Figure 5.10**).

When you view the source clip in its entirety, you can see that the younger man enters screen left foreground and walks to his position next to the older man. Working within the **Portal Effect** sequence (which you can also find in the Portal Effect bin) we'll enhance his entrance significantly.

Using Transition as Effect

At times, simply creating a cut with the right transition will get the job done. A transition like a dissolve is typically used to imply a change of time or place in a narrative project, but in this case we can use one to make the young man suddenly appear in the scene as opposed to his long physical approach in the original shot. The older man on the bench affords us this opportunity by staying relatively still.

When you play the first group of clips (with the number 1 visible in the lower left of the screen), you can see that I've made a rather simple edit (**Figure 5.11**). By cutting out the approach segment of the shot and using a cross dissolve, I've made the younger man appear in the shot. It looks a little more interesting than just watching him walk in, but it isn't terribly mystical.

Animating an Effect

We can add an animated effect to the transition and add some interest. In the second group of clips (labeled 2) I've added a Lens Flare effect and used keyframes to animate its settings (we examined keyframes in the previous "Animating Effects" section).

When you play through effect number 2, you'll see the Lens Flare effect. (If your system is having difficulty playing the effect back, you may want to preview render the segment.)

Click on the second clip in the sequence to view the clip's properties in the Effect Controls panel. You'll see the Lens

Figure 5.10 The Apprentice Enters clip in the Portal Effect bin.

Figure 5.11 Portal Effect group 1 uses a transition and an edit to change the entry method of the young actor.

Flare effect applied, and the Flare Brightness property is animated. In this case the flare comes into view with the second clip, but it might be more convincing if it moved a bit with the appearing character.

Clicking the Next Keyframe or Previous Keyframe button next to the Flare Brightness property will position the playhead on the first keyframe. Enabling animation for the Flare Center property by clicking on the stopwatch (**Figure 5.12**) will automatically create a Flare Center keyframe for the same position.

Figure 5.12 Portal Effect group 2 shows a Lens Flare effect added to the second clip with settings visible in the Effect Controls panel.

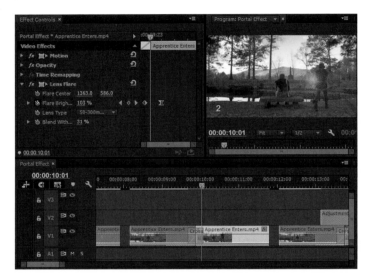

Positioning the playhead over the last keyframe for the Flare Brightness property and changing the horizontal position of the Flare Center value from 1363 to something around 1505 will make the flare move with the actor.

Now it looks like the young man is entering from somewhere a bit magical, or at least someplace well lit.

Using an Adjustment Layer

Adjustment layers in Adobe Premiere Pro work similarly (although not identically) to Adobe After Effects or Adobe Photoshop. Using adjustment layers is an easy way to apply one effect across a group of clips over time, as well as affect all the video layers below the adjustment layer. Imagine having a simple color correction that needs to be applied to 30 edited clips. Copying the settings from the first and pasting to the other 29 may not be too daunting, but what if you need to make a change in the settings? It's much quicker to make one change to the effect on the adjustment clip than on 30 individual clips with the same effect applied 30 times.

An adjustment layer can host an effect, such as color correction or in example number 3, a lens flare, and apply it to all the layers that are visible below the adjustment layer (**Figure 5.13**).

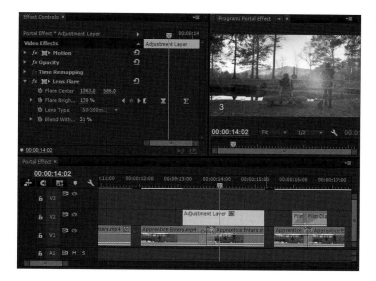

Figure 5.13 Portal Effect group 3 moves the lens flare to an adjustment layer, making the effect more flexible because it is not restricted to the second clip by the video transition.

In effect number 2, the lens flare is applied to the second clip and is only visible when the second clip is visible, which happens through the transition. In this case, moving the Lens Flare effect to the adjustment layer, you can start animating the effect prior to the transition, gradually building the lens flare to indicate something is coming.

When you click on the adjustment layer, the effect and its keyframes will be displayed in the Effect Controls panel. You can once again animate the Flare Center if you desire. You may also want to explore the other Lens Type options.

Adjustment layers are very useful for testing effects work like color correction. In cases where I have clients in the room and they want me to try out a color correction change, I turn off the original correction and add an adjustment layer to test the new color correction without altering my original settings should I need to return to them. I've also used several adjustment layers with different color correction options for clients to evaluate, simply enabling and disabling video tracks containing the various treatments as needed.

The Blend With Original property controls how much of the original image you see along with the effect. In this case it isn't set to animate, but by clicking the stopwatch you could add keyframes for this property through the course of the effect if necessary.

Using Track Mattes

Any time you want to restrict visual content to a certain area onscreen you have to generate a matte to define the area. Adobe Premiere Pro has garbage mattes that can be useful for some purposes, but when you're looking for a sophisticated shape and softer edges, the best approach is to create a track matte.

Most track mattes are grayscale images that define transparent areas (black) and opaque areas (white) for the source video, with the gray shades in between representing proportional transparency. You can make a track matte in a number of ways. Any paint program can be used to make a still matte. For the example we're using, we'll use the drawing tools in Adobe Premiere Pro's Title Designer (**Figure 5.14**).

Figure 5.14 Portal Effect group 4a shows the blur obscuring the transition by layering the second clip in the sequence on V2.

When you view the clips in number 4a and number 4b, you'll notice that two effects are set up: The first effect blurs the entire screen in an attempt to create a sort of visual distortion aesthetic as the young man appears. But with the entire screen blurred we can't tell if he's a powerful magician or just got off the school bus because the entire screen is blurry.

Using a track matte we can confine the effect to the screen position where the actor is appearing (**Figure 5.15**).

Figure 5.15 Portal Effect group 4b makes a more convincing effect by restricting the blur to the area where the actor enters the screen using a track matte effect on the clip on V2 confined by the matte we placed on V3.

In the second effect in group 4, if you double-click on the portal matte clip on V3, you'll notice that it doesn't pop up in the Source panel. Instead, it opens the Title Designer interface. The Title Designer is an excellent tool you can use to create quick mattes using the drawing tools, and the bonus is that you can draw the matte while looking at the video underneath. You'll be creating some interesting effects with the Title Designer later in the chapter. For the moment, close the Title Designer dialog.

Back in the sequence you can see that V2 has the same shot, and it's synchronized to the second shot in the sequence. If you select either clip on V2 in group number 4a or number 4b, you'll see that they have an identical Gaussian Blur effects applied. The difference is that the second clip has a Track Matte Key in the Effect Controls panel, and its Matte setting is targeted at Video 3 and the portal matte.

In this case, we'd choose Composite Using > Matte Luma because the matte document is black and white. You could also choose to use the alpha channel on the matte

CLOSE-UP

Standard Effect Rendering Order

To see the effect of altering the order of standard effects, position the Timeline playhead at the transition point where the blur is most evident in group number 4b. With the clip on V2 selected, drag the Track Matte Key effect below the Gaussian Blur effect in the Effect Controls panel. In the original arrangement, the blur was applied after the matte, blurring the entire matted image and blending it into the shot. When the Track Matte Key is applied after the blur, the matte becomes very sharp and obvious because it is being applied after the blur.

document as the matte definition if you're using a document with an alpha channel as your matte. When the actor appears in the second effect, he almost looks as if he's moving through some relatively defined time/space distortion (work with me here) because the blurred clip has been confined to just the area where the actor enters the scene by the portal matte.

Using Opacity Blend Modes

Opacity Blend modes may be one of the most underutilized compositing features in Adobe Premiere Pro. Once you find them under the Opacity heading in the Effect Controls panel, it's easy to become a frequent user.

We'll use Opacity Blend modes in several of our effects approaches in this chapter and go through a detailed listing of the available modes and how they are designed to work later in the chapter.

Moving to the clips in group number 5, you can see that the Track Matte Key is still defining the area of the effect, but now the portal area is bright white, making the young apprentice appear to be arriving through the portal from someplace—foggy? This is the result of adding a Luma Curve Standard effect (**Figure 5.16**) and making a change in the Opacity Blend Mode for the matted clip on V2.

Figure 5.16 Portal Effect group number 5 adds a Luma Curve effect to the video clip on V2.

You can view the Luma Curve settings if they're hidden by clicking the disclosure triangle to the left of the effect name. Click the fx box to the left of the effect name to turn the effect on and off to see the difference.

In the Opacity Fixed effect, the Blend Mode has been changed from Normal to Linear Dodge (Add). You can choose from a selection of Blend modes very similar to those in After Effects or Photoshop. The right Blend mode can make a significant contribution to an effect. For an alternative, try the Pin Light Blend mode, or for a significant change, try the Exclusion or Subtract options (more information on Blend modes later).

Scaling Height/Width Independently

Under the Motion fixed effect, the Scale property can be used proportionately, or you can choose to scale clip height and width independently. It doesn't seem complex or sexy, but when we apply some basic scaling animation to our matte to make our portal a bit more "elastic," we contribute another aspect to the effect that doesn't necessarily appear basic.

The effect setup in clip group number 6 has the same effects as those in group number 5 with one addition: The portal now scales up and down as the actor crosses the threshold from points unknown into the scene. To change from the "one-size-fits-all" portal of the effects in number 4 and number 5 to the elastic rift in time and space in group number 6, some specific scaling has been applied to the portal matte clip.

When you click on the portal matte clip, you'll see that Scale keyframes are applied in the Effect Controls panel, but by deselecting the Uniform Scale option, Scale Height and Scale Width become separate properties that can be animated independently (**Figure 5.17** on the next page). The keyframes are currently placed to create the height expansion before the width expansion in the opening of the portal, and close in reverse order. As with all keyframes, they can be moved and the interpolation can be changed, so you may want to experiment to make the effect your own.

Figure 5.17 Portal Effect group number 6 animates scale height and width independently.

Putting It All Together: The Portal Effect

We've examined transitions; adjustment layers; standard effects like lens flares, blurs, and curves; track mattes; and Opacity Blend modes. It becomes obvious as you layer these approaches together that the strengths of any one of these features pales in comparison to the capabilities of building on combinations.

Group number 7 combines all the effects we've worked with thus far. Every effect from group number 6 is included. Plus, the Lens Flare effect was brought back from group number 2 (**Figure 5.18**), which animates in from the top of the frame on an adjustment layer, landing on the portal. The flare not only scales up and opens, but also moves horizontally to follow the actor during the transition. This complex Portal Effect utilizes just four video layers to bring the young actor from a dimension or a time far away, thus allowing him to just drop his stuff anywhere he pleases.

Saving Effect Presets

When you have a set of parameters set up for an effect or group of effects on a clip, you can select and save that effect or combination of effects as a preset for use at a later time.

After pressing Command (Ctrl) to select each effect in the Effect Controls panel that you want to include, right-click and choose Save Preset (**Figure 5.19**).

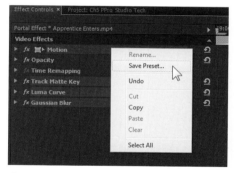

Figure 5.19 After selecting the Motion, Track Matte Key, Luma Curve, and Gaussian Blur effects, right-click to bring up the menu to save the preset.

The next dialog will prompt you to name the preset and specify how it should be applied over time. With effects that have keyframes that animate the beginning of a clip, choosing to Anchor to In Point will ensure your animation maintains its length and relationship to the In point of the clip.

Keyframed presets saved to Scale adjust the keyframe distance to the relative length of the clip. A ten frame entrance animation on the In point of a one second clip saved as a preset that "scales," would become 600 frames long on a one-minute clip—quite an entrance.

Scale is ideal if the effect is a static color correction or something that doesn't change. But for almost any effect animated over time, you'll want to choose to anchor to the In or Out point.

When the preset is saved, you'll find it in the Presets folder in the Effects panel.

The Warp Stabilizer

The Warp Stabilizer is one of the most talked about features in Adobe Premiere Pro, which meant it was important to write about, given how much it gets used. This effect is extremely effective at making handheld or walking shots steady.

One component of the Warp Stabilizer that was very popular was the Rolling Shutter correction, which compensated for the tendency of certain CMOS camera sensors that scanned an image top to bottom to show skewed horizontal movement or sheared vertical edges if something moved horizontally through the frame faster than the image was scanned.

Although the Rolling Shutter component of the Warp Stabilizer is still in place, it's also available as its own effect if you don't need stabilization.

The Warp Stabilizer sequence in the Chapter 5 project contains one shot (**Figure 5.20**). If you play it back, you'll notice how the videographer did an amazing job of shooting steadily while running up the stairs. When you select the clip and realize that the Warp Stabilizer is applied in the Effect Controls panel, you might want to turn it off to see what the original shot looked like. And this application was just with the default settings.

Figure 5.20 The Warp Stabilizer sequence.

Warp Stabilizer Settings

Using the disclosure triangles to open all the properties in the Warp Stabilizer's settings in the Effect Controls panel reveals the control the user has over the process. These settings can be adjusted to alter the result, but they also affect the processing time; thus, understanding them can be very helpful.

Under Stabilization, choosing Smooth Motion is a good default, because you rarely want to (or even could) lock them down as if they were a static camera, so Smooth Motion is frequently used. No Motion is typically achievable if the camera only moves slightly of course. But for the most part the No Motion result works best if the target object or person is in the frame 100 percent of the time.

The Smoothness property applies to the Smooth Motion Result setting and is fairly straightforward. As you increase this number, you can expect to increase the processing time for the effect as well as more aggressive zooming, and using 50% as the default setting produces impressive results in most cases.

The Method parameter is often left at Subspace Warp; however, this specific method requires the most sophisticated set of calculations. Four methods are available. If one method can't maintain enough tracking points, the mechanism will drop down a level to try to simplify the stabilization. The four stabilization methods include:

▶ **Position.** Computed based strictly on X-Y axis movement in the frame. By far it's the simplest and fastest analyze method.

▶ **Position, Scale, Rotation.** Adds frame scaling and rotation to X-Y tracking. This option is still quick but is more sophisticated than Position alone. It is often appropriate for long handheld shots where the videographer loses track of the horizon.

▶ **Perspective.** Basically works as a corner-pinning method. It's not as resource intensive as Subspace Warp but can cause unwanted keystoning if the footage is really active.

▶ **Subspace Warp.** The heavy lifter of the group. It takes the image and literally warps it in different parts of the frame to create a steady image. It is very effective on most footage but can introduce some Jell-O-like artifacts in certain circumstances.

Under Borders you'll see the Framing controls. How you treat the edges during stabilization is as important as how you stop the shaking. The Framing controls include:

▶ **Stabilize Only.** No reframing will occur, just the stabilization. This method is very fast but assumes you'll be doing a frame-crop somewhere else. It could be useful for a quick pass to send on to visual effects editors who might crop it later.

▶ **Stabilize, Crop.** Will also not zoom or scale the frame. But this option will create straight edges inside of the frame around the stabilized image.

▶ **Stabilize, Crop, Auto Scale.** The most frequently employed method. It steadies the shot and scales it up to refill the frame based on the maximum scale settings you specify under Auto Scale.

▶ **Stabilize, Synthesize edges.** Has the computer looking at previous and upcoming frames within a range you specify in the Synthesis Range Input property for content to insert in the areas where stabilization is creating visible edges. I suppose if you're on a greenscreen background or something extremely constant it might work acceptably, but even if you use the Synthesis Edge Feather aggressively, having a computer decide what is supposed to be just outside the edge of a moving video frame probably isn't anyone's first choice.

The Borders section essentially directs how the effect should handle the edges of a clip. After all, if you're moving the clip around to stabilize it (opposite of the shake), you may have to scale up the clip to hide the now visible edges.

You can define the Maximum Scale as well as define an area around the frame edges you don't feel would be visible (and would be therefore left unfilled by Auto Scale if necessary) by specifying a percentage of Action-safe Margin.

And when the effect is not working (or you want to really fine-tune the effect), you can use the Advanced set of parameters:

▶ **Detailed Analysis.** I turn on Detailed Analysis probably more often than I should. It does help in cases where the footage is problematic and may require extra tracking points. Each new tracking point creates more data that is stored with the Adobe Premiere Pro project. If you have a two-hour documentary that is all handheld footage, you'll start creating a *very large* project file.

▶ **Rolling Shutter Ripple.** Automatic Reduction is usually adequate for most tasks, but if there are some really obvious issues, you may want to try Enhanced Reduction. Often, some Rolling Shutter artifacts may be made more obvious once a shot is stabilized, and this process is optimized to deal with that situation.

▶ **Crop Less <-> Smooth More.** This slider determines the balance you want between maintaining as much image as possible versus how smooth you want the motion to be.

To see the stand-alone Rolling Shutter Repair effect applied to some footage at a race track, you can view the **Rolling Shutter** sequence and disable the effect during the rapid pan to see the difference in the overall skew of the image (**Figure 5.21**).

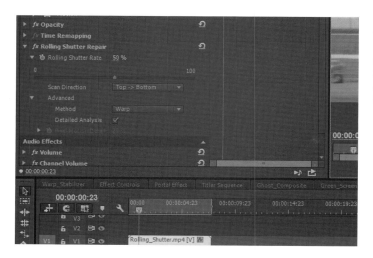

Figure 5.21 Disabling and enabling the Rolling Shutter Repair effect in the Effect Controls panel will reveal how much image skew exists during the rapid pan at the beginning of the shot and how little there is after the pan in the later part of the shot.

Rolling Shutter Repair

The stand-alone Rolling Shutter Repair effect has a few more controls than the process that is part of the Warp Stabilizer. Here are some tips for adjusting the parameters:

▶ **Rolling Shutter Rate.** The Rolling Shutter Rate defines the percentage of "when" the shutter closes. If you have a skewed edge in the shot, you should be able to see it shift as you adjust this property. Most camera shutters will be around 50% or just slightly more than that. Cell phone cameras are wild cards, so don't rule out trying a higher value if you're working with phone video.

▶ **Scan Direction.** Scan Direction of the sensor is always top to bottom, but because you can hold a phone or similar handheld device at almost any angle, you have the option to change the direction.

▶ **Advanced.** The two methods listed here have a different approach to limiting the rolling shutters. The Warp method tries to point track and warp the image. Optionally, you can select Detailed Analysis to increase the tracking data density. The other option is the Pixel Motion method, which tackles the problem with optical-flow vector computation—a morph-like correction. This uses the Pixel Motion Detail setting to determine the density of the information tracked to attempt to repair the shot.

Using the Title Designer

To Adobe Premiere Pro users, the Title Designer's capabilities are thought to be well-known. Basic and even moderately sophisticated titles are deceptively easy to create, but the true versatility of this tool is frequently overlooked.

We'll explore this versatility by looking at examples of styles, adjusting of the fine points of type, and using the Title Designer to perform some advanced effects.

Opening the Titler Sequence

In the Chapter 5 Adobe Premiere Pro Project panel you'll see a bin labeled Title Designer. Inside that bin you'll find the **Titler Sequence**. Double-click to open that sequence, or bring it to the front (**Figure 5.22**).

Figure 5.22 The Typestyle 1 title features metallic styles.

304

Most users understand that you can create custom type-styles in the Title Designer, but they don't have the time to explore all the tool's capabilities. I've assembled a small set of custom typestyles to help you unlock the possibilities.

The first clips on the Timeline are two titles over black video with large, colorful characters. Each of these characters represents a different custom typestyle created with Adobe Premiere Pro's Title Designer. Large, single character examples allow the type to be large, making the details clear. These styles are contained in a custom typestyle library I created and included in the Chapter 5 media.

Load the Custom Style Library

The Custom Style Library is a function of the Title Designer that makes saving and recalling different libraries of styles effortless.

Move the playhead past the two typestyle clips on the Timeline to a point where only the black video fills the screen. Double-click on Typestyle 1 on the Timeline to open the Title Designer interface.

Below the canvas you'll see the default Title Style Library displayed with thumbnails. After clicking on the panel menu icon at the top right of the Title Styles panel, you'll see the options to Reset, Append, Save, or Replace the Style Library among the menu options (**Figure 5.23**).

You can add a Style Library to the existing styles by choosing Append Style Library, or you can replace it completely. You can reset the Style Library at anytime to return to the original Style Library.

After choosing to Append or Replace the Style Library, browse to where you've stored the Chapter 5 media, and select the StudioTech_TypeStyles Library to load the new Style Library (**Figure 5.24**).

Examples of Metallic Styles

The metallic type styles in group number 1 were created inside the Title Designer with the tools you see in the interface. By clicking on each letter with the Selection tool, the settings on the Title Properties tab on the right change.

NOTES

If the characters on your system look different than the illustration, it's possible that your computer system's font library is slightly different than the computer the styles were built on. The edge and color characteristics should be the same. You can use the style with a different font and save the new font/color/edge combination by choosing New Style in the Title Style panel menu.

Figure 5.23 Right-click on the Title Styles panel menu and choose Replace Style Library.

Figure 5.24 The StudioTech_TypeStyles Library.

Each typestyle has specific parameters that combine the fill, stroke, and shadow properties to create a certain look.

Hover over the swatches in the Title Styles panel to see the names of each style pop up as a tool tip. For example, the R character has the Rust Double Edge style applied. In the Title Properties panel, you may have to click the disclosure triangles to see the settings for the Fill properties and the Inner and Outer Strokes. Find the Inner Stroke size property, which currently displays a value of 10 (**Figure 5.25**).

You can change this property like any property in any other Adobe application by dragging left and right across it, or by simply clicking on it and keying in a new property. By changing this property to 65 (**Figure 5.26**), the Inner Stroke will completely fill the face of the character, making it appear concave—almost the reverse of a lowercase "k" on the right side of the frame. Changing the Outer Stroke size to 25 creates a heavy outer edge that gives the character an engraved metal appearance.

Notice that the Lit property is enabled for each stroke. Try deselecting the check box for this property for each stroke and notice the change. Using the Lit property along with its Light Angle setting adds a convincing feeling of depth. You can click back and forth between the k and the R to see how the difference in lighting angle affects the perception of whether the character is convex or concave.

Figure 5.25 Each letter is a separate type object, and clicking to select a letter shows the Title Properties in the panel to the right.

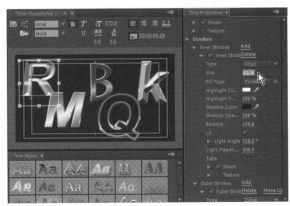

Figure 5.26 Raising the Inner Stroke Size value to 65 changes the look of the R character.

On the orange R character, the Sheen property is selected for each stroke. Deselecting Sheen for the Inner or Outer (or both) Stroke properties removes the metallic appearance. Each character in the Typestyle 1 document has Sheens applied to the Fill (face) or to Strokes, or to both. The metallic look in the characters in Typestyle 1 are the result of different use of color and light properties. For the Q character, the Chrome Thick Trace style has the Fill property set to Eliminate to show through to the background (**Figure 5.27**).

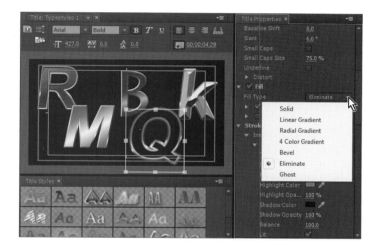

Figure 5.27 Using the Eliminate Fill Type makes the text transparent, showing only the strokes.

To save any changes you've made for later use, choose New Style from the Title Styles panel menu. If you want to return the R character to its original style, simply select it and click on the style from the swatches in the Title Styles panel.

Close the Title Designer dialog.

Examples of More Colorful Styles

Although it may set your teeth on edge, sometimes more colorful styles are needed. Whether it's to be loud, satisfy client demands, or just for fun, these styles show off the flexibility of the Title Designer.

Double-click on the Typestyle 2 from the Timeline. When the Title Designer is open, click the N character in the upper left. If your system doesn't have the Comic Sans font installed, other lightweight (slim, not bold) fonts could illustrate the intent behind the Yellow Neon typestyle. In this typestyle you'll notice that several strokes transition from the "hot" fill color to the more subdued colors in the strokes toward the edge, but the Shadow properties are probably the most significant feature. When you scroll down in the Title Properties tab to the Shadow properties, you'll see that the color is actually quite bright. By thinking a bit "out of the shadow box" a glow effect has been created (**Figure 5.28**).

You can adjust the glow effect by changing the Opacity, Size, and Spread settings until they fit your taste. You can also change the color of the neon by changing the Fill and Stroke colors. If you've made a change you want to keep, make sure the N text object is selected, choose New Style from the Title Styles menu, and save your style for later use.

Click the Q character next (**Figure 5.29**). This typestyle is named Striper, and it gets its candy cane appearance from the Linear Gradient Fill Type. In the list of properties under Fill Type, you'll see the Repeat property, which creates the stripes by repeating the red-to-white gradient seven times. If you change the Repeat property to its maximum value of 20 or reduce it to 3, the look of the style changes considerably.

You can also deselect the Sheen option and see what it adds to the nonmetallic surface.

Figure 5.28 Clicking the N character reveals the unconventional use of the Shadow parameter in the Title Properties.

Figure 5.29 Select the Q character to view and edit the Title Properties.

Note that only an Outer Stroke is enabled, and the two Inner Strokes that are disabled are actually left over from a typestyle that started out as green, obviously not a particularly appetizing addition to the candy cane lettering at this stage.

You can create new custom typestyles by making changes to these or the standard style library styles and saving them as you gradually become comfortable enough to create typestyles from scratch.

Character Spacing, Kerning/Tracking

Kerning adjusts the space between two specific letters, whereas tracking adjusts the space between multiple letters in a word or line.

They're are critical components in creating appealing type graphics. Letters have flow, and the appropriate spacing can help the readability of titles more than most users realize.

Most fonts have some intelligent spacing built in, but that only goes so far. A capital T will appear to be unusually distant from the next lowercase letter because of the space between the T's narrow base and the next letter, whereas replacing the capital T with an A may create the opposite issue, appearing to leave too little space. Being observant of how type is laid out around you and being aware of it in your own projects will raise the production value of your entire program.

Move down the Titler Sequence to example number 3, which reads Candy and has a white matte on the track below it. The typestyle used is Hard Candy 1 from the custom typestyle set (if your system doesn't have the font Lithos Pro, you can substitute a bold or black font). Many typestyles, or even a particular font, may have character spacing inconsistencies. In this case, the typestyle Outer Stroke weight has created a heavy character overlap that detracts from the effect. To revise this, double-click on the Candy title to open it in the Title Designer. Click the text object in the canvas and adjust the Tracking property in the Title Properties tab (**Figure 5.30**).

Figure 5.30 The Candy title open in the Title Designer with the Tracking value changed to 9.

Increasing the Tracking value increases the uniform spacing for the characters in the text object. Kerning serves a similar purpose but works in between specific letters where you need it. To change kerning, click the Type tool, click into the word Candy between any two letters, and adjust the Kerning value to see the adjustment.

Using Gradients in Titles

It's likely you're familiar with gradients. The Title Designer allows you to create and adjust text and other objects that start with one color and finish with another.

Typestyles with gradients often appear to be more attractive aesthetically, and the color treatment of the title can also contribute to a compositing effect.

In group number 4 the text BRIKZ is superimposed over an appropriate background. Double-click on the first BRIKZ text document to open it in the Title Designer. The Fill Type is a Linear Gradient, and the color gradient is displayed below the Fill Type, showing two color swatches and a gradient strip (**Figure 5.31**).

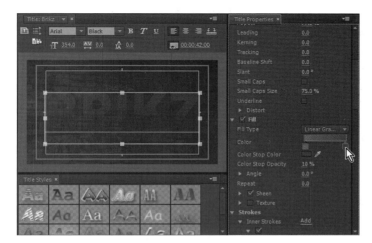

Figure 5.31 The color blocks at the ends of the gradient swatch each have a different Color Stop Opacity value.

Note that the text is partially transparent, and if you click on each color swatch and observe the Color Stop Opacity property (below the swatches), you'll notice that neither color is set to 100%. The difference in the two values is the reason that the text is more transparent at the bottom than the top. If you invert the two values, making the darker shade 44% and the lighter shade 10%, the effect won't change symmetrically because darker and lighter colors blend differently. This text object also has a 50% overall Opacity setting at the top of the Title Properties tab under Transform. If you've made changes but want to return the document to its original state, simply select the text object and click the Earth Blended typestyle swatch.

Titles with Effects and Blends

Titles can also be combined with other effects or Blend modes to complete the effect.

The second BRIKZ clip positioned in group number 5 is composited with the wall in such a way as to almost imply graffiti. Title Designer documents can be used in conjunction with other effects and Blend modes just like any other video or graphic source in Adobe Premiere Pro.

On the second BRIKZ document (from number 5), the Effect Controls panel shows the effects that are applied to the title. Through the use of the Basic 3D effect, the title was moved and angled to appear as if it's attached to the wall on the right. The Divide Blend mode in the Opacity settings was also used to change how it combines with the background, and the overall Opacity was reduced to achieve a bit more blend (**Figure 5.32**).

Figure 5.32 The second BRIKZ title with the Divide Blend mode and the Basic 3D effect applied.

You can run through the selection of Blend modes available to see the results of each; however, note that once you employ a Blend mode other than Normal, the Color Stop Opacity gradient will interact with each differently.

Title Effect Using a Nested Sequence and a Track Matte

A nested sequence in Adobe Premiere Pro acts like a clip when it's placed on another edit Timeline. There are any number of advantages to working with nested sequences—for instance, the ability to work on each scene in a long program separately and nest the edited sequences to one final Timeline for mastering. In group number 6 we'll use a nested sequence to "pre-animate" a still graphic before we composite the nested sequence of the animation into our effect.

In the grouping under number 6, you'll see that the **Titler Sequence** features the text Epic Title. Play through them to see a glint of light animate left to right across the metallic edges of the title (**Figure 5.33**). Many users would like to have animated effects within the Title Designer, but Adobe Premiere Pro's animation capabilities can be used to animate effects for titles like any other video or graphics clip.

Notice the brick wall background on V1 and the Epic Title Base title document on V2. A nested sequence is on V3. If you double-click on **Glare Animation Nested**, you'll open another sequence that shows the title document called Glare animating from left to right with some Position keyframes visible in the Effect Controls panel along with a Gaussian Blue effect applied. This is the moving glare on the text (**Figure 5.34**).

Figure 5.33 The Epic Title traveling glare effect uses a Track Matte Key.

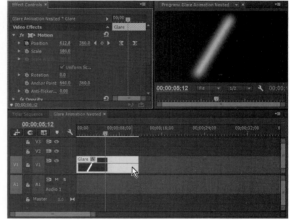

Figure 5.34 The **Glare Animation Nested** sequence is a simple animation of the white graphic from left to right.

Click into the **Titler Sequence** to view the nested sequence. In the Effect Controls panel you'll see that the **Glare Animation Nested** sequence has the Track Matte Key applied.

Similar to the track matte in the Portal Effect earlier in the chapter, the luminance values of the matte determine the matting, and we've targeted that matte on Video Track V4. On V4 the Epic Title Matte restricts the glare to the "metallic" edges of the text. Double-click on the Epic Title Matte to open it in the Title Designer. The title simply consists of white strokes that create the outline of the text; shadows are off and a black background is turned on. This matte title document is a duplicate of the foreground title that I created at the same time by simply saving a version with the face transparent and the outline changed to white with a black background (**Figure 5.35**).

Figure 5.35 The matte is a copy of the main title and uses the Eliminate Fill Type and a black background.

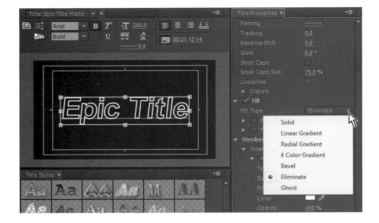

To make the effect even more convincing, enable the Gaussian Blur effect on the Epic Title Matte clip on V4 by selecting the box next to the effect in the Effect Controls panel (**Figure 5.36**).

Figure 5.36 Switch on the Gaussian Blur effect on the Epic Title Matte to view its effect on the light glare.

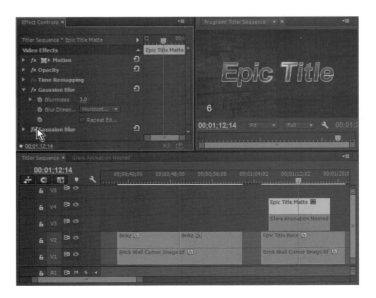

The Glare document in this example consists of a line that was drawn in the Title Designer because it's a quick solution versus opening another art application like Illustrator or Photoshop.

The animated glare must be a nested sequence because the Track Matte effect will link the matte to the key source clip, thus animating the matte from left to right with the glare if we would have simply animated the glare on the master Timeline.

Keying and Compositing

Everyone knows about chroma keying, which is often greenscreen keying where the background color (chroma) is measured and turned into a transparent area in video.

Different chroma keyers use different math to produce this transparency area. Adobe bought Serious Magic for its Ultra Key technology, making the Ultra Key effect one of the best "original equipment" color keyers available. The Ultra Key gets very good results and is easy to use.

In the real world, there aren't many effects that begin and end with a simple chroma key application. But there are many other tools that a compositor could use to contribute to delivering a completed effect, such as mattes and additional Blend modes or effects, such as color correction and so on.

Using Adobe Premiere Pro's Ultra Key

Let's look at an effect that goes beyond a normal color key. You'll recognize many of the concepts I've addressed thus far in the chapter. We'll add a few new tricks and once again allow them to build on each other and employ them along with the Ultra Key to create an ultimate, ghostly effect.

Open the **Green_Screen_Shot** sequence. Using a similar numbering system as in previous exercises, the first clip is the effect group 1. Play the Timeline to see a young girl in a white gown on a greenscreen background reaching toward the screen with an expressionless gesture as if beckoning from the beyond (or perhaps she's just a typical teenager being distant and cryptic). The girl was shot horizontally to maximize image resolution for this vertical shot, so we start with the key source rotated 90 degrees and scaled down to an appropriate size (**Figure 5.37**).

To apply the Ultra Key to this clip, go to the Effects panel, type **Ultra** in the search field, and drag the Ultra Key to the first Green_Screen_Shot clip on V2. After dropping the effect onto the clip, make sure the clip is selected, and in the Effect Controls panel, use the arrow to reveal the settings for the Ultra Key effect.

Use the Key Color eyedropper to choose the clip's green background in the Program Monitor. Keep in mind that the background is not absolutely uniform, so you may want to try using the eyedropper in several places to determine which gives you the best color (**Figure 5.38**).

Figure 5.37 Find the Ultra Key effect in the Effects panel and drag it to the Green_Screen_Shot in group 1.

Figure 5.38 Use the Key Color eyedropper to select the green background.

Figure 5.39 You can choose the Alpha Channel Output setting to evaluate your matte.

Directly under the Ultra Key effect name, you can change the Output to show the alpha or color channel associated with the Key setting instead of the composite (**Figure 5.39**).

The Alpha Channel setting is usually the best mode for making adjustments under the Matte Generation and Matte Cleanup headings to get the cleanest key. For quick, somewhat less nuanced adjustments, using the preset Default, Relaxed, and Aggressive Setting choices can help you avoid some manual adjustments by giving you a good start.

If you're adjusting the key manually, you may want to use the eyedropper in the bottom-right area of the background and raise the Contrast and Mid Point values while watching the alpha channel output to achieve the cleanest black and white areas in the matte (**Figure 5.40**).

Refining the Key Background

The Green_Screen_Shot is probably far from the most challenging key most of you have been faced with in post-production, but some finesse is still called for. As versatile as the Ultra Key is, there are still occasions when having some additional strategies to better prepare key source footage can still be helpful.

Group number 2 shows the green screen shot once again. When you click on it, you can see in the Effect Controls panel that the clip has an RGB Curves effect applied but disabled. RGB curves, and color correction in more comprehensive terms are covered in Chapter 6, but in this case the Secondary Color Correction feature was used in the effect to isolate a correction to the green background (**Figure 5.41**).

Figure 5.40 After choosing a key color, you can use one of the Setting presets as a starting point, and then follow it with fine adjustments.

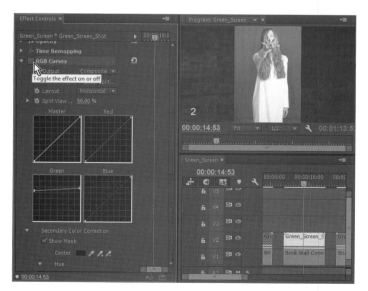

Figure 5.41 Toggle the RGB Curves effect to see the matte.

If you enable the RGB Curves effect in the Effect Controls panel, you'll see the matte that defines the area of operation for the correction. As with the mattes you've worked with thus far, white represents the area of operation and black represents the area protected from the effect.

Scroll down in the Effect Controls panel to the settings just below the graphs and deselect Show Mask to see the correction (**Figure 5.42**). You can switch the RGB Curves effect on and off to see the change. The greenscreen is nearly the same value throughout the image. The curve adjustment evident in the curve on the Green channel shows the adjustment made. Basically, it reduces contrast and thus most of the variation in the green background, but most important, the fabric border that intersects our talent disappears.

Figure 5.42 Deselect the Show Mask option in the RGB Curves effect to shut off the matte and view the change.

Apply the Ultra Key effect to this clip, ensuring that it is listed after the RGB Curves effect in the Effect Controls panel, and see how much easier the clip is to key with almost no fine adjustments needed.

Ultra Key as Matte Generator

There are times when an effect will require a matte beyond a simple greenscreen key. You've already worked with track mattes several times in this chapter, and the Ultra Key can be used to generate a moving matte for a color background key shot like the **Green_Screen_Shot** sequence. In clip group number 3, the Ultra Key is used to generate a matte by simply leaving it set on Alpha Channel Output. By generating a track matte in this way, the movement is an exact match for the clip (**Figure 5.43**).

Ultra Key and Added Effects

As noted earlier, the Ultra Key can be combined with other effects to expand what's possible: We're beginning to move toward a ghost-like final effect.

NOTES

The Green_Screen_Shot sequence group number 4 is another occasion to observe how changing the order of the standard effects in the Effect Controls panel (the Gaussian Blur and the Ultra Key in this case) will create an obvious difference in the combined effect.

In group number 4 the Ultra Key effect was combined with keyframes for Opacity (instead of the Film Dissolves used in the Portal Effect), and a keyframed Gaussian Blur was added as well. The foreground clip is starting to look a little ghostly but still a little mechanical, even with the blurring and transparency (**Figure 5.44**).

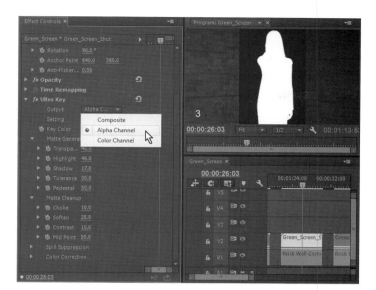

Figure 5.43 The Ultra Key effect can be used to generate a matte by using it with the Alpha Channel setting.

Figure 5.44 In group 4, adding a Gaussian Blur effect and animating its settings makes the keyed young woman look less defined as she fades in and out.

Ultra Key and Blend Modes

If you've read this far in the chapter, you must have known that we'd use Blend modes at some point as we build this effect, right?

Even though a greenscreen key is already a type of Blend mode, you can still combine any standard effect key with various Opacity Blend modes to create more detailed effects. In group number 5, the Screen Opacity Blend Mode was applied and combined with the effect that was constructed in group number 4 (**Figure 5.45**).

Figure 5.45 In clip group number 5, changing the Opacity Blend Mode changes the way the foreground blends with the background.

By using the Screen Blend Mode, the Opacity value at the second keyframe is actually increased, yet maintains or even enhances the appearance of the girl as something of an illusion because the wall behind her seems to be seen through her more prominently, in a way different than just adjusting opacity.

Duplicate the Key Source

An old trick when using transfer modes is to duplicate the clip that's set to one of the Blend modes, like Screen, Overlay, or Multiply. I tend to use layers multiple times to intensify an effect in many compositing jobs. It creates more opportunity to be subtle and to capitalize on the strengths of multiple Opacity Blend modes.

So, in group number 6, the key layer, V2 is duplicated onto track V3, and to intensify the effect further, the V3 clip's Blend mode was switched to Hard Light.

The V2 clip is a very soft, bright, blurry layer because of the added Luma Curve effect and the fact that the Gaussian Blur value was kept rather high. This treatment along with dropping the color saturation to zero in the Ultra

NOTES

Using a double-layered key can be useful in a variety of circumstances, including instances where a challenging key source means choosing between a clean outer edge and some interior areas that may show through. Placing another layer behind the primary layer and adding a slight blur can help fill interior holes and also soften edges to help subdue the feeling of separation between the key source and the background.

Key's post-key color correction properties helps make the girl appear a bit less defined (**Figure 5.46**).

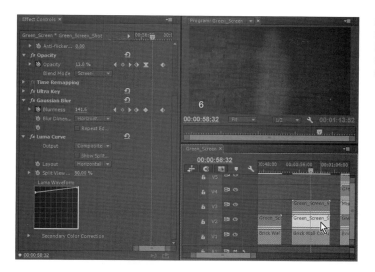

Figure 5.46 Duplicating the **Green_Screen_Shot** on V3 and adding a Luma Curve effect on top of an intensified Gaussian Blur to the clip on V2 adds even more softness to the effect.

Combining Techniques: Keying

In group number 7 the techniques mentioned in the preceding sections are combined. At this point we have a keyed element, which has been duplicated to intensify the ghost effect. Now, we'll add another element—a Mist animation (**Figure 5.47**).

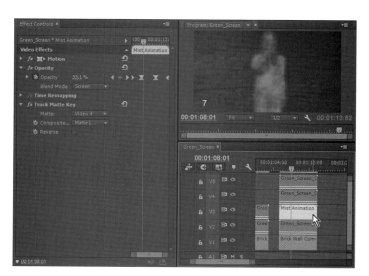

Figure 5.47 In group number 7 the **Mist Animation** nested sequence is inserted on V3 and a matte is inserted on V4, pushing the duplicate **Green_Screen_Shot** clip from V3 in group number 6 to V5 in group number 7.

A simple document was created in Photoshop (mist smoke.tif) and animated with some simple movement on a nested sequence (**Mist Animation**). Double-clicking on the **Mist Animation** clip on V3 will open the sequence and enable you to adjust the animation if you desire (**Figure 5.48**).

Figure 5.48 The **Mist Animation** sequence is a simple Motion animation of a TIF document, also altered with a Luma Curve effect.

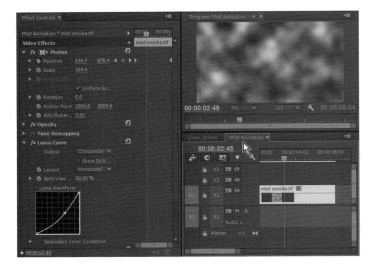

The **Mist Animation** nested sequence is contained in an area defined by the Track Matte effect using the matte created with the Ultra Key from the **Green_Screen_Shot** on V4. By using soft, blurred layers on V2 and V5, and using various Blend modes to complete the illusion, the ghost forms from the smoky vapor and fades back to it after only a glimpse.

Opacity Blend Modes

In this chapter we've worked with Opacity Blend modes. You may be familiar with them if you're experienced with the Blend modes in Photoshop or After Effects. But often, even those of us who use these Blend modes frequently don't necessarily know how each one calculates a result. So, I've compiled a description of each mode and how it is designed to calculate the blend.

TIP

Opacity Blend modes can also be applied by using the standard effect Calculations so you can control their rendering order in relation to other effects.

Adobe has divided them into six categories with borders in the menu, although the groups have no labeling in the menu. They are listed here from top to bottom the way they display in the menu (**Figure 5.49**).

Normal Category

Normal in this case means each layer is treated "normally" with no additional mathematical formula:

▶ **Normal.** The pixels of the source layer are not affected by the pixel values of underlying layers unless Opacity is set to less than 100% The result color is the source color. This mode ignores the underlying color. Normal is the default mode.

▶ **Dissolve.** Each pixel is either completely opaque or completely transparent depending on the opacity setting and the pixel values. This tends to look like old-school pixel dithering to me.

Subtractive Category

Subtractive Blend modes involve measuring the RGB value of the pixel of a clip and subtracting information from it as it blends with an element below itself on the Timeline:

▶ **Darken.** Each color channel will look at the source and the underlying values at each pixel and adopt the darker value of the two.

▶ **Multiply.** The math starts to get a bit more sophisticated as you get into the modes that truly blend instead of simply choosing a pixel value. Multiply takes each source pixel color channel value, multiplies it with the underlying pixel color channel value, and then divides by the maximum value for the color precision you're working in (255 being the maximum for 8-bits per channel material, etc.). You're guaranteed to never produce a brighter value because if either value is full white, the other value is adopted, and if either color is full black, then black is adopted.

▶ **Color Burn.** Each pixel of the source layer is darkened according to the value of the underlying layer color by increasing the contrast. Pure white in the source layer does not change the underlying color.

Figure 5.49 The full list of Opacity Blend modes available in the Effect Controls panel.

In cases where I have footage that is somewhat overexposed or has milky blacks, I duplicate the footage on the video track above and Multiply Blend it on top of itself, using the Opacity value of the top layer to moderate the effect. Although it isn't as versatile as a full color correction pass, it's a quick way to use the actual image to redefine the grayscale "slope."

Although I use Multiply on overexposed or bright shots, I use Screen on underexposed shots in the same way. By duplicating the footage on the video track above and Screening it on top of itself, the grayscale within the footage scales various brightness values proportionately.

▶ **Linear Burn.** Similar to Color Burn, the source pixels are darkened according to the value of the underlying color. Pure white produces no change. I prefer the results I get from Linear Burn because it doesn't "pop" contrast as much as Color Burn.

▶ **Darker Color.** Each pixel adopts the darker of the source color value or the underlying color value. Darker Color operates on the combined pixel color value as opposed to affecting each color channel as in the Darken Blend mode.

Additive Category

Additive Blend modes involve measuring the RGB value of the pixel of a clip and adding information from it as it blends with an element below itself on the Timeline:

▶ **Lighten.** Each pixel color channel chooses between the source and the underlying color channel value, adopting whichever value is lighter (or higher).

▶ **Screen.** Adobe explains that the Screen Blend mode "Multiplies the complements of the channel values, and then takes the complement of the result." Although explaining this mathematical formula in literal terms would put most artists to sleep, Adobe has a more intuitive description to help those of us without a slide rule; "Using the Screen mode is similar to projecting multiple photographic slides simultaneously onto a single screen." As with overlapping two slide projectors, this Blend mode will never produce a darker value.

▶ **Color Dodge.** Each source pixel is lightened by decreasing contrast based on the value of the underlying layer color, except where the source layer color is black, in which case the underlying color will be adopted.

▶ **Linear Dodge (Add).** This Blend mode is rather straightforward. Each source color channel value is "added" to the corresponding color channel values of the underlying color. Because the only results of a Linear Dodge calculation are additive, you will never create a pixel value darker than either original color. This is Screen mode's bully of a big brother.

- **Lighter Color.** Each pixel adopts the lighter of the source color value or the underlying color value. Lighter Color operates on the combined pixel color value as opposed to affecting each color channel as in the Lighten Blend mode.

Complex Category

The complex Blend modes involve measuring the RGB value of the pixel of a clip, and based on more complex math to produce a result, it blends with an element below itself on the Timeline:

- **Overlay.** A combination of Multiply and Screen, it applies both calculations to each color channel of the image, applying a Multiply blend to values less than 50% and Screen blend to values more than 50%. The bright and dark values of an underlying image layer will be preserved.

- **Soft Light.** The results of Soft Light will remind you of a "kinder, gentler" Overlay. The two calculations applied are more of a dodge and burn than a Screen and Multiply. If you've applied Overlay and your reaction was "I love that effect but with a bit more subtlety please," you may want to try Soft Light blend as an alternative.

- **Hard Light.** The Hard Light Blend mode does less "blending" with underlying images than some of the other modes. It multiplies or screens the input color channel values similar to Overlay, but it operates by focusing far more on the original source color values for input. Hard Light may improve on the results achieved with Overlay or Soft Light when the video layer you're blending is disappearing, or at least becoming more transparent than you intend.

- **Vivid Light.** Working a bit like Soft Light mode, it burns or dodges the colors according to whether the underlying color is lighter or darker than 50% gray by increasing or decreasing the contrast. The result can be "contrasty," visually similar to the Hard Light Blend mode except that even very bright areas of the blended layer are more likely to become completely transparent when over very dark colors or black in the underlying clip.

TIP

Because Overlay and Soft Light Blend modes both "stretch" gray scales to add contrast to images, I'll often use one or the other on raw footage shot with a log curve. This footage usually looks milky and low contrast until color corrected because the flattened curve facilitates the storage of more grayscale information. Duplicating the footage over itself and applying Overlay or Soft Light is a way to add contrast to the footage rapidly when you have to edit but may have to leave final color correction for a later time.

▶ **Linear Light.** Similar to Vivid or Soft Light modes, you are applying a burn or dodge calculation to the colors by decreasing or increasing the brightness, depending on the underlying color. If the underlying color is lighter than 50% gray, the layer is lightened because the brightness is increased. If the underlying color is darker than 50% gray, the layer is darkened because the brightness is decreased.

▶ **Pin Light.** This mode is tough to predict without trying it. This is another Blend mode that doesn't so much blend as just replace pixels. If the underlying color is lighter than 50% gray, pixels brighter than the underlying color don't change, but pixels darker than that color get replaced. Pixels lighter than the underlying color are replaced if the underlying color is darker than 50% gray, leaving pixels darker than the underlying color untouched.

▶ **Hard Mix.** Adobe's description of Hard Mix is that it "enhances the contrast of the underlying layer that is visible beneath a mask on the source layer. The mask size determines the contrasted area; the inverted source layer determines the center of the contrasted area." Honestly when I'm trying out Blend modes in After Effects, Photoshop, or Adobe Premiere Pro, I always try this mode and prefer pretty much any other Blend mode in pretty much every situation. Until I find a use for this Blend mode, I'll have to leave you with the official Adobe description.

Difference Category

The difference Blend modes involve measuring the RGB value of the pixel of a clip and the clip beneath it, and displaying how much "difference" there is between the two:

▶ **Difference.** The darker value is subtracted from the lighter input value on each color channel. This effect is more obvious with lighter backgrounds because a white background will invert most colors, but a black background will have almost no effect.

▶ **Exclusion.** Basically, this is Difference mode with less contrast for a more subtle effect.

- **Subtract.** Takes the pixel values of your source file and (oddly enough) subtracts them from the underlying values unless the source color is black, in which case the underlying value is adopted. The calculation for this Blend mode could actually result in values less than 1.0 in a 32-bit per channel sequence (where Max Bit Depth is enabled).

- **Divide.** Not surprisingly, this Blend mode divides the underlying color value by the source color value. This is the opposite of Subtract mode. If the source color is white, the underlying color is adopted. Funky math is possible with this Blend mode as well because it's possible to calculate values greater than 1.0 in 32-bit per channel sequences.

HSL Category

The HSL Blend modes don't use math or difference, but rather substitute hue, saturation, color, or luminance between the blend of two clips:

- **Hue.** The hue value from the source clip is applied to the underlying clip, maintaining the underlying clip's luminosity and saturation levels.

- **Saturation.** The saturation value from the source clip is applied to the underlying clip, maintaining the underlying clip's luminosity and hue values.

- **Color.** The underlying clip maintains its original luminosity value but takes on the hue and saturation values of the source clip.

- **Luminosity.** The underlying clip maintains its hue and saturation while taking on the luminosity of the source clip.

TIP

If you are stickler for detail with footage or a graphic you are trying to position precisely over itself in perfect alignment, using the Difference Blend mode on the top layer will allow you to hit the position exactly because the clip will turn completely black when the difference between the pixels is zero and the clip is perfectly aligned.

Dynamic Link

Dynamic Link provides you with the powerful ability to transfer Adobe After Effects compositions directly into Adobe Premiere Pro. When you change your composition in After Effects and click Save, the results are updated *dynamically* in Adobe Premiere Pro's Timeline.

As versatile as the effects capabilities of Adobe Premiere Pro are, some effects will still require more than a video editing application to complete. Adobe After Effects is designed not only to do complex visual effects and motion graphics work, but also to work very closely with Adobe Premiere Pro through Adobe Dynamic Link.

In the Chapter 5 project is a sequence titled **Ghost Composite**, which you can open from the Dynamic Link bin in the Project panel, or simply bring it to the front if it's already a tab in the Timeline panel (**Figure 5.50**).

Figure 5.50 The unaltered **Ghost Composite** clip is first in the sequence.

The first clip on the Timeline is a compiled clip showing the completed ghost composite. The second clip started as the same media but was changed to a Dynamic Linked After Effects Composition.

Provided you have Adobe After Effects installed on your system, you can right-click on the Ch5 PPro Studio Tech Linked Comp 01 clip and choose Edit Original to open the After Effects project and view the After Effects Composition.

Because After Effects has a 3D camera, it can be used to make the ghost shot seem a bit more spontaneous, as if the videographer was startled and struggling to capture a proper image. The 3D camera imitates a handheld camera and introduces camera movement and focus adjustments in After Effects. Any adjustments you make to the After Effects comp will be reflected in Adobe Premiere Pro, allowing you to render the effect only once (**Figure 5.51**).

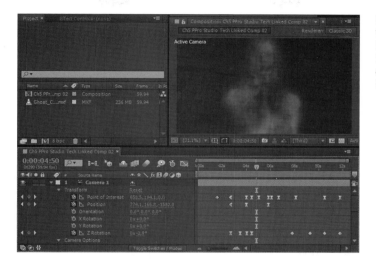

Figure 5.51 Using Dynamic Link, the clip from Adobe Premiere Pro is animated using the 3D camera in After Effects, and the changes are immediately updated in Adobe Premiere Pro.

You can create a new Dynamic Link to an After Effects comp from a clip in a sequence by choosing File > Adobe Dynamic Link or by right-clicking on a clip and choosing Replace with After Effects Composition (**Figure 5.52**).

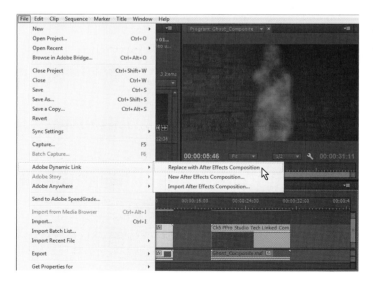

Figure 5.52 With a clip selected on the Timeline, choose Replace with After Effects Composition to open it in After Effects.

After Effects opens, and after you've named the project and specified a location to save it to, an After Effects composition opens with the same settings as the Adobe Premiere Pro sequence you're currently working on.

As much as the result of our longer scenarios was a matter of combining effects and using them together, the goal of this chapter was to create some situations where these techniques are used in some sort of context. The idea was to expand the list of options you have as you use Adobe Premiere Pro in postproduction to solve problems and create value for your clients. Hopefully this chapter held some value for you, even if you're an experienced user.

6

Color Correction

Author: Jeff I. Greenberg

Color is my day-long obsession, joy, and torment.
—Claude Monet

Color Correction

Even if you've managed to practice your best videography techniques with expert lighting and export camera work, there is always some improvement in the finished image via color correction.

Your eyes are these amazing, white-balancing organs that constantly interpret and reinterpret your environment. But the same qualities that make your eyes great for the everyday world limit you in the postproduction suite because your eyes are continually adjusting and adapting to what they're viewing.

For color correction, you need a more consistent way to examine your images, and for this you need to be proficient in using color scopes. Each shot needs to be adjusted and controlled to make sure it doesn't exceed broadcast limits; even today when the final delivery may only be to digital devices, such as an iPad or YouTube, broadcast limitations are still valuable restrictions for finished work.

Getting two shots to match, especially when they're shot under different lighting conditions and exposures can be difficult. It should never be a guessing game. The overall goal is to move *beyond* just getting the picture to "look good." Color correction can also be an expert storytelling technique, intentionally warming up (adding red/orange) for more romantic shots or cooling down (adding some blue) a shot to make it appear more serious.

Defining "looks" of a scene can further communicate location: For example, images of Miami have a warmer look than images of Alaska.

Color correction is a crucial, *necessary* technique that can help any production look more professional.

Corrections and Grades

To prevent confusion, it's important to understand two similar concepts when referencing color correction:

- A *correction* refers to a specific adjustment made on a shot, such as adjusting the Gamma to make a shot appear brighter.
- A *grade* refers to everything done to adjust a shot—quite possibly adding multiple effects to build a finished "look."

You may be reading this chapter and saying, "I already color correct." Yes, but are you using all of your scopes? Do you know how to match shots? If you're not using the Parade scope and if you struggle to match shots, this chapter dives into those topics in depth as well.

Plan Your Time Wisely

Procedurally, color correcting all of your footage will take time, and it's nearly always during the worst time—close to deadlines and delivery.

Professional colorists, with optimum hardware setups and working as fast as they can, will correct 10–20 minutes of finished work a day. If in 10 minutes they can complete about 200 shots, it takes them, *on average*, about a minute a clip. Expect that you'll be slower than this. Make sure you budget and measure how fast you can correct shots to guarantee your delivery schedule. Although you'll become faster after practice, full-time colorists also have the advantage of using some dedicated hardware.

Goals of Color Correction

What are the goals of color correction? Your initial response might be to make the shot look "better." But concepts like better or worse are inaccurate descriptors, even if you recognize that you're happy or not happy with adjustments.

You need your goals to be more concrete and to serve storytelling.

Here are the four goals of color correction in order:

1. Establish the appropriate tonal range.

2. Remove any color casts.

3. Match shots for shot-to-shot consistency.

4. Create a look (if appropriate).

All of these goals, *except* the last one, should be invisible to viewers; well done color correction doesn't call attention to itself.

A Note About the Downloadable Content for This Chapter

The project for Chapter 6 has sequences that are numbered according to the order in which they appear in the chapter. Be sure to open the Marker panel. The markers are numbered to match the figure order in the book. For instructions on downloading the contents for this chapter, please refer to the Introduction of this book.

In 2011, Adobe bought Iridas and quickly added SpeedGrade to the Creative Suite. It's a fantastic dedicated program for color correction (and stereoscopic finishing). Check out Alexis Van Hurkman's book *Adobe SpeedGrade CC: Classroom in a Book* (Adobe Press, 2013) to learn how to use this Adobe tool.

The first two goals, establishing a tonal range and removing any color casts, are about *neutralizing* your image. These two goals are about basic cleanup and establishing a starting point for your images.

When possible, it's ideal to have some communication with a DP or Director about the on-set intentions of the shoot for color correcting. If the intent during shooting included adding a cool filter (blue) to the lens but you weren't aware of that, you'd be fighting the intentional blue cast on the footage.

Matching shots is more about hiding any shooting defects, such as the color temperature of an indoor shot compared to an exterior shot. It's not about matching something like a Pantone color. You can get close, but you can't truly match print items. The reason is that there is a difference between reflected light (print) and emitted light (LCDs and CRTs). Again, if the matching is done well, nobody notices it.

Developing a "look" means adding an artistic impression to the footage. Movies like the *Matrix*, *Minority Report*, and *Se7en* all have stylistic, visual adjustments to communicate concepts like technology, emotion, and danger (**Figure 6.1**). This type of work is typically left until the end of color correction, because a given scene or series of shots should all be similar before a look is added.

Figure 6.1 This same shot with three different looks shows a warm look on the left, a colder look in the middle, and a harder contrast on the right. Each look helps communicate emotion in a scene.

Understanding Light

When discussing color correction, it's crucial to have some understanding of light and the electromagnetic spectrum. What is meant when you hear about the temperature of light and how computers process light? Light behaves differently in video than how it's processed by your eyes!

The human eye is sensitive to only a small portion of the energy emitted from the sun—which is called the *visible spectrum*. It ranges from (ultra) violet on the left through (infra) red on the right (**Figure 6.2**).

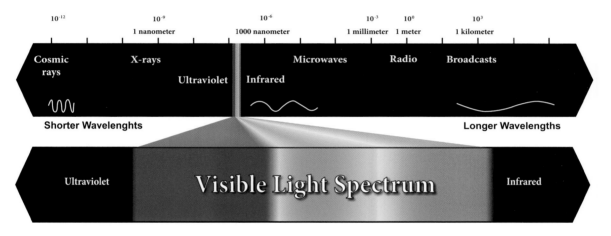

Figure 6.2 The visible spectrum represents the colors people can see.

Color Temperature

The colors on the spectrum are described as ranging from warm (reds and oranges) to cool (blues). Technically speaking, they're also described in absolute degrees (Kelvin units or K). Oddly, the values for warmer colors are actually *lower* than the cooler values. Heating a metal object, like the filament of a lightbulb, starts at red, and as it gets warmer the color changes to blue (**Table 6.1**).

When your clients ask for a warm or cool look (**Figure 6.3**), you need to understand what they're thinking.

TABLE 6.1   Color Temperature

TEMPERATURE	SOURCE
1,850 K	Sunrise/Sunset, Candle flame
3,000 K	Soft white lights (indoor)
4,100 K	Moonlight, xenon lights
5,000 K	CFL lights
6,500 K	Daylight (65k) (overcast)
10,000+K	"Blue" sky

Figure 6.3 Here is an example of a warm look (on the left) and a cooler look (on the right).

RGB or Primary Colors

Computers use three colors to describe a pixel: red, green, and blue. To describe a color space—the range of colors that a computer can display—it is called RGB color space. You may already be familiar with the RGB adjustments from tools like Adobe Photoshop or Adobe After Effects. Every color the computer can display can be described as a percentage of these three colors.

Adding the maximum R, G, and B to a pixel (**Figure 6.4**)—let's call this 100%—yields a white pixel.

The opposite, removing all RGB (0%) yields a black pixel (**Figure 6.5**).

Figure 6.4 The maximum RGB on this Color Picker—255, 255, 255—results in a white pixel.

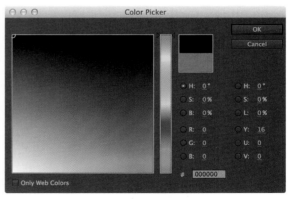

Figure 6.5 RGB at its lowest level results in a black pixel.

Gray *can be* the result of all three sliders at 50%, but it can *also* be any point where all RGB are identical. All RGB at 5% is a very dark gray, and all RGB at 87% is a light gray. The core concept is that when all *three values* are the same (**Figure 6.6**), the color is gray.

Because computers work with these three channels, you should take a moment to look at each channel individually (in the next section "CMY(K) or secondary colors," you'll look at the lack of color in each channel with possibly surprising results).

With green and blue at 0, increasing *just* the red to 255 results in a swatch that is (obviously) red. Similarly, you can do this with *just* the green control and then *just* the blue control (**Figure 6.7**). Although the results may seem obvious, this is an important step in understanding the way computers handle these three color channels.

Figure 6.6 As long as RGB are all the same value, you end up with a gray pixel. In this case, it's 35% gray with a value of 90,90,90.

Figure 6.7 Each channel maximized individually to 255 yields (from left to right) red, green, and then blue.

CLOSE-UP

8 Bits vs. 10 Bits

Why do you see values in RGB of 255? Computers use a Base 2, or binary, system—either a bit is off (0) or on (1). You can describe a pixel in a percentage, which may or may not be a whole number, or as the amount of bits it uses, which is more direct and precise.

Video commonly uses 8 bits, or has up to 8 binary places (for example: 00101010 [based 2], which corresponds to 42 [base 10]) to describe a pixel. That's 256 values. And because the count starts at 0, the range is 0–255.

Some video formats can shoot 10 bits, or up to 10 places ($2 \wedge 10$), to describe a pixel. That would be 1024 values, or 0–1023. The two key concepts to consider are:

▶ Both 8 bit and 10 bit have white and black at the top and bottom of the scale, but in 10 bit there are more steps between white and black.

▶ When possible, it's best to use a camera that shoots in 10 bits because there is more information in the picture, giving you the ability to make smaller, more refined adjustments.

CMY(K) or secondary colors

Something very interesting happens when you perform the *opposite* of increasing a given channel:

▶ If you maximize the Blue and Green channels (at 255) and *reduce Red* to 0, the lack of red results in cyan, making it the opposite of red (**Figure 6.8**).

▶ If you maximize the Red and Blue channels and *reduce Green* to 0, the lack of green results in magenta.

▶ If you maximize the Red and Green channels and *reduce Blue* to 0, the lack of blue results in yellow.

Figure 6.8 When you remove all of the color in one channel, the result is the opposite color. The removal of Red is Cyan (left). The removal of Green is Magenta (middle), and the removal of Blue is Yellow (right).

CMY colors are described as the *secondary* colors to RGB. It's likely you recognize them from your color printer inks. Computers use *emitted* light, but paper uses *reflected* light, which requires a different method to achieve black and white. With a computer, all the colors (RGB) need to be on to get white. But in print, zero information is needed (no ink) to get white. This is the opposite of RGB. Even still, using all three colors in print, CMY only produces a dark brown, so it's necessary to actually use black ink to yield black.

As an aside, when you look at print, which is reflective of light (versus computers, which emit light), it uses the CMYK (Cyan, Magenta, Yellow, and Black) color space to represent color.

RGB + CMY = Color Wheel

If you plot out RGB against CMY, you should see something you're familiar with—a color wheel. The one in **Figure 6.9** has been altered from Adobe Premiere Pro to help you see the labeled colors.

These colors match the layout of the Vectorscope: The scope that allows you to measure the overall color vectors in an image; they also match the layout of the colors in the Three-Way Color Corrector. Once you understand this idea that the Vectorscope and the Three-Way Color Corrector correspond, you'll intuitively know how to compensate for chroma issues.

YCr'Cb' or YUV space

Although computers use RGB and print uses CMYK, video uses Y (luma) and U+V (chroma). A little history will help you understand this space.

Video started out in black and white only, and it was only necessary to record and store the luminance of an image—called *Y* by video engineers.

Later, in the 60s, color was added to the existing signal. It was possible to describe just the color information without the luminance (brightness). This additional information was only a *small amount of* extra information because your eyes don't see color detail as well as luminance details.

In video, the color channels are described as Cr' (color red prime) and Cb' (color blue prime), and the green information is mathematically divided into all three channels.

In an *ideal world* you'd be able to handle all of your video the way it's stored, which would be in YCr'Cb' math rather than converting it to RGB math and back again. There are a number of reasons you can't, many of which have to do with your expected results. You expect the mosaic effect to transform the image in a certain way; YCr'Cb' wouldn't produce results that you'd be happy with.

This conversion of from YCr'Cb' color space to RGB and back can create a small amount of damage to the color information, because multiplication and division are

TIP

When you use a color picker to measure a pixel that's supposed to be neutral (a gray), look at the RGB values. If they're identical, the pixel is neutral. If they're not, adding/removing information from each channel so they agree is a method of neutralizing color casts.

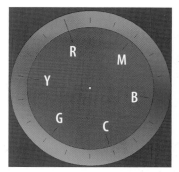

Figure 6.9 RGB and CMY represented as a color wheel.

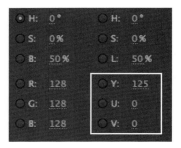

Figure 6.10 The YUV color channels in color pickers in Adobe Premiere Pro.

Figure 6.11 Throw this switch and you'll see only the effects that process in the video's native color space.

occurring, and at some point, some of the information may be discarded (rounded up or down).

For many, YCr'Cb' is a mouthful, so it's acceptable to use the term YUV (technically, it's the analog description) instead of YCr'Cb' (the digital description). Adobe Premiere Pro shows this information in color palettes (**Figure 6.10**).

So, whenever possible when you're adding effects, you want to do little or no damage to your video's color space. Adobe Premiere Pro has a specific filter (switch) for effects that are only calculated using YUV space. **Figure 6.11** shows the YUV Effects icon.

When you use these effects, you'll process the picture in its native color space and *generally* not affect the chroma when you work with luma or vice versa.

What happens to the effects that aren't YUV? They're processed using RGB. Because RGB mixes luminance (black and white) and chrominance (color) together, adjusting the controls may affect both the luma and the chroma.

Now that you have a more thorough understanding of color, the next step is to examine your system setup.

Color Correction Interface Setup

Now that you have some understanding of goals and color space, let's determine what your software needs to do for you. It has to provide tools to analyze the image along with effects that will not damage the color signal.

What tools do you need?

▶ You need tools to process in YUV space to adjust video with as little damage to its information as possible.

▶ You need video scopes, particularly the Waveform, Vectorscope, and RGB Parade, to accurately measure your pictures.

▶ You need to have a layout that permits you to optimize your workflow.

▶ You need to be able to quickly turn off or on your corrections to help your eyes reevaluate the picture.

Adobe Premiere Pro has all of these tools and capabilities. Let's start by looking at the measurement tools, the video scopes.

Video Scopes

You can find the video scopes by clicking the Settings icon (which looks like a wrench) in the lower-right corner of the Program Monitor. Additionally, you can access them in the Program Monitor's panel menu.

Even if you think you're familiar with scopes (**Figure 6.12**), it's probably valuable to review this section. Most people don't have enough experience with the RGB Parade scope, which builds on ideas from the YC Waveform and Vectorscope. The RGB Parade scope provides vital information about color casts and more.

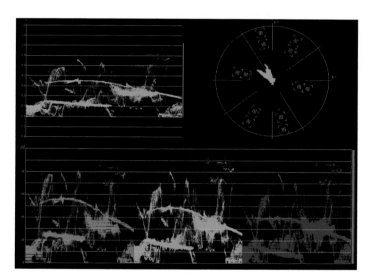

Figure 6.12 A combo view of the most commonly used scopes: the YC Waveform, Vectorscope, and RGB Parade.

YC Waveform

The YC Waveform measures luminance and chrominance left to right across the image. The brighter the pixel, the higher it is in the YC Waveform. The darker the pixel the lower it is in the YC Waveform. The YC Waveform ranges from .3 (it's based on signal voltage), which represents black, through 1.0, which represents white. This gradient

TIP

Once you identify something large or common across a waveform, such as a wall or a sky, it's easier to compare other elements as being brighter or darker on the waveform.

can be found at marker 6.13 in the CH 06 sequences called **1 Waveform**. The YC Waveform looks like the illustration in **Figure 6.13**.

It's generally accepted that the best use of this scope is to solely examine luminance. *Turn off the Chroma setting.*

The brighter or denser the clustering of data means that there are *more pixels* at a given luma value. Look at the sequence **1 Waveform** marker 6.14 (**Figure 6.14**). On the left side of the screen most of the pixels represent a darker area (the wall), which shows a large clustering of energy on the YC Waveform.

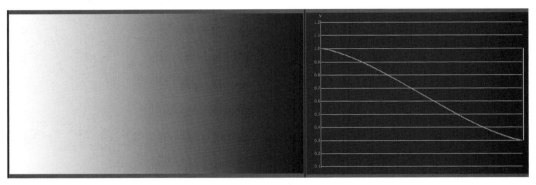

Figure 6.13 Note how the bright pixels on the left side correspond to the traces on the left side of the YC Waveform.

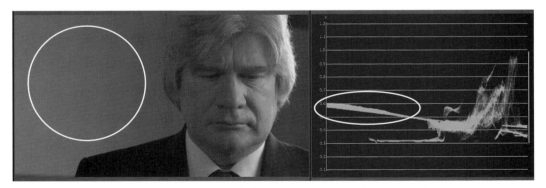

Figure 6.14 Also, notice the man's suit (not circled), which is to the right of the circle and low on the scope.

A common way to examine the YC Waveform is by breaking it down mentally into three regions, the leftmost, rightmost, and center regions. This makes it easier to help identify "landmarks" in your image, particularly elements that are bright or dark and those that are easily identifiable.

TIP

Know where neutral items are on the waveform scope (gray/white).

In **Figure 6.15** (sequence **1 Waveform** marker 6.15), by breaking down the image into sections, it's easier to look at the center section and identify the wall (brightest part, lower on the scope) and the man's jacket (darkest part, higher on the scope).

Figure 6.15 Breaking down images into thirds can be done via cropping but takes too much time.

Vectorscope

The Vectorscope has no measure of left/right/up/down from an image. It merely shows the vectors of color that the entire image has. The more pixels of a similar color yield more *energy* to a given vector. This area is called a *blob*. Generally, the blob should have some coverage over the center (but may not be centered).

When you examine the gradient ramp in **Figure 6.16**, (sequence **2 Vectorscope** marker 6.16), there is no information on the Vectorscope. This should be expected: There is no chroma (color) in the black to white gradient.

Let's look at the color bars in **Figure 6.17** (marker 6.17).

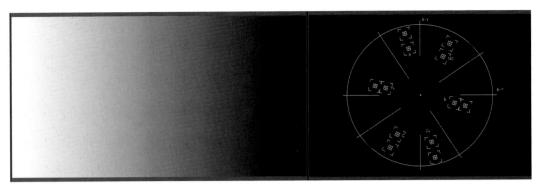

Figure 6.16   Notice the targets RGB and CMY. They're identical to the color wheel.

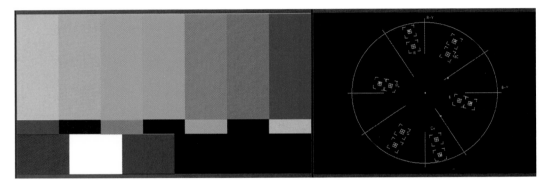

Figure 6.17   Color bars show tiny points on the Vectorscope that correspond with their color.

You now see a dot at each of the RGB and CMY targets. These are at the outer target, which is normally at 100%, the maximum color permitted, but the top of the scope is set at 75%. A general rule is to draw an imaginary shape connecting the dots and keep any color vectors inside of that shape to keep the video broadcast legal.

Now that you've seen a gradient and bars, let's look at what happens when you point your camera at something more interesting—people. Look at the image in **Figure 6.18** (marker 6.18). I've intentionally added saturation to help make the colors more visible on the Vectorscope.

The sugar packet shows a strong yellow color near the yellow target, and the pixels near the red target represent the man's shirt. But the flesh tones are more interesting. The line between yellow and red is unofficially called the *flesh*

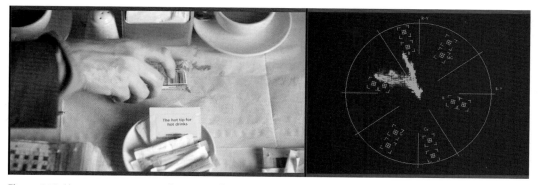

Figure 6.18 Here you see a strong yellow vector (from the sugar packet), a strong red vector (man's shirt), and the man's flesh tones, which fall in between the yellow and red targets.

line by many colorists because flesh tones *generally* should fall on that line. Regardless of heritage or how much melanin is in people's skin, nearly all faces (unless sunburnt) should fall along this line.

RGB Parade

The RGB Parade is very similar to the YC Waveform in that it's a representation of the luminance, but for *each* channel. And in many ways it's probably the *most important scope* because it shows both *luma* and *chroma* information. It ranges from 0% to 100% for each channel.

There are several major signposts that you should look for on an RGB Parade:

▶ **Neutral items.** If you can find a neutral item (sheet of paper or any gray or white object) on a waveform, you can find it in the RGB Parade, and it should be at the same level in each channel. If not, you have a color cast.

In **Figure 6.19**, a neutral item (circled in cyan on the image and Parade) would be the road. Blue is a little higher compared to the other two scopes, which means there's a blue color cast.

▶ **Bright/Darks.** As images become very bright or very dark, the chroma disappears. If you point a camera at a light, it's always white regardless of the color of the light. If you have an element in very dark shadows, you can't identify the color at all. As portions of images approach having black or white values, the RGB elements at the brightest/darkest levels should have similar values.

In Figure 6.19 from sequence **3 RGB Parade** at marker 6.19 you see a magenta area, which is a shadow of the bushes; it should have a little extra green (because it's in the shadow of trees). But notice that on the RGB Parade this region is the same on all three channels, showing that there's no color cast in the shadows.

Also, note the sky (the yellow circles). The sky is a little higher in the Blue channel than the Red or Green channel, but not terribly so, which is part of the reason the sky looks grayish. If this was higher, toward 100 in all three channels, it would be "neutral" and therefore all the colors would be blown out—not something you'd want in the sky.

Figure 6.19 The yellow circles indicate the sky, the cyan circles indicate the road, and the magenta circles indicate the shadows of the trees.

▶ **Flesh tones.** Looking across all three channels, flesh tones should descend from R to G to B (**Figure 6.20**). The way to think about this goes back to the color wheel. If three channels (RGB) are the same, the result is gray. To create a flesh tone (which is an orange) with just these three colors, you need to add red and subtract blue (adding yellow). Correspondingly, the Red channel would be the highest, the Blue channel would be the lowest, and the Green channel would be in between on the RGB Parade.

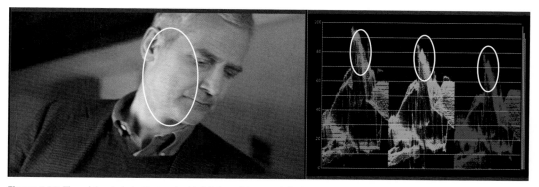

Figure 6.20 The white circle indicates the highlights of the man's flesh tone. They descend properly but may be a little bright, especially in the Red channel.

The RGB Parade scope is probably the most important scope you're not using well.

YCbCr Parade

Although the YCbCr Parade scope shows the true values of the video signal, few people find the feedback from the scope helpful for color correction. It shows what's going on for the signal, but it's difficult to read for qualitative information, such as a color cast.

Combination view

The Combination views are valuable (**Figure 6.21**), but the problem is that they're fairly small, even when they are blown up to full screen.

Because you'll primarily use the YC Waveform, Vectorscope, and RGB Parade, in the next section I'll talk about mapping them to the keyboard.

Customizing Your Setup

You can make some small tweaks to your setup to make color correction go faster. At the end of the day, what's important is that you're able to quickly evaluate and grade images.

Two adjustments should be made: one to your workspace and the other to the keyboard. As always, refine these adjustments beyond the default setups, because it's important to test and explore what works best for your system.

TIP

Press the accent (`) key to go full screen. This shortcut is super valuable when you're looking at software scopes and when you're evaluating images.

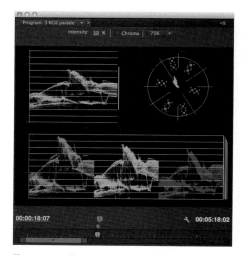

Figure 6.21 There are two combination views: one with the RGB Parade (shown) and one with the YCbCr Parade.

Modify your workspace

Adobe provides a workspace preset for color correction (**Figure 6.22**), and it does a great job (especially if you hide the keyframe area of the effect view to give you more space for color correction).

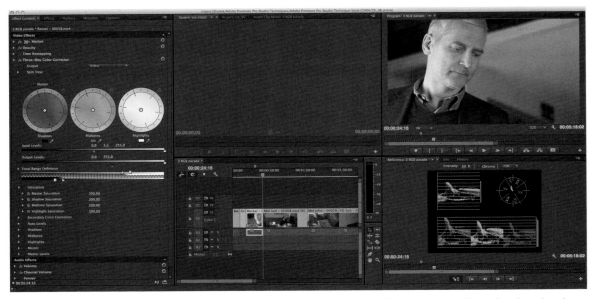

Figure 6.22 The Adobe color correction workspace with scopes open on the Reference Monitor (bottom right), a clip selected on the Timeline, and the Three-Way Color Corrector visible in the Effect Controls panel (left side).

Figure 6.23 Clicking the texture is the key to dragging panels. The mouse cursor is right on the panel texture here.

Depending on your system (you might have two screens or a wide screen), you may want to adjust the workspace for an easier workflow. I'd rather have the scopes in the reference in the *center* than at the bottom and the effects off to the left. This setup makes it a little faster and easier to adjust using the Three-Way Color Corrector and keep your eyes on the image.

Here's how I built my workspace:

1. Choose Window> Workspace > Color Correction to start with the default Color Correction Workspace. If you've customized it, reset it to the original layout.

2. Click and hold the panel texture next to the reference monitor you want to merge with the top-center frame. Make sure you click the texture area to drag (**Figure 6.23**).

3. Drag the reference to the center of the top frame. Be sure to hit the center of the trapezoidal overlay (**Figure 6.24**). By dragging the reference to the center of the trapezoid, it'll merge with the Source Monitor (if you drag to one of the edges, it will subdivide the panel).

Figure 6.24 The key is to target the center of the trapezoid to merge a panel into a frame.

4. Click the Effect Controls on the left pane, and close the keyframe area (**Figure 6.25**). Although you might want to keyframe some color correction effects, it's move valuable to close the panel to have more workspace real estate.

Figure 6.25 No clip is selected, which is why the panel is empty. The cursor is on the switch to remove the keyframe area.

5. Save this workspace by choosing Windows > Workspace > New Workspace. By doing so, you'll be able to recall it quickly in the future.

This workspace is built into the accompanying project for this chapter. It's called *Adjusted Color Correction* and is visible in **Figure 6.26**.

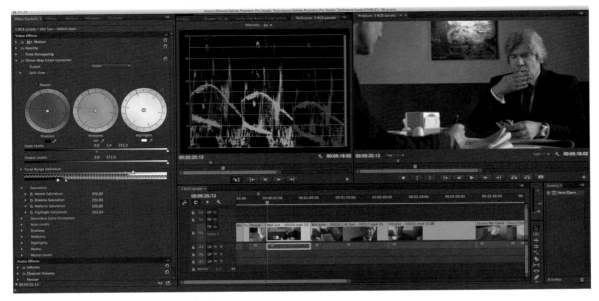

Figure 6.26 My adjusted color correction workspace.

Adapt your keyboard

To quickly toggle between any of the scopes, it's best to add keyboard shortcuts for each of the scopes. In addition, you can add a shortcut to toggle an effect on and off.

My number one rule for shortcuts is that that any mapping on my keyboard *must* make sense. I map the scopes to numbers 1, 2, and 3 because I don't need or use multicam when color correcting. If you do use multicam often, save a separate keyboard shortcut just for color correction.

To remap the keyboard, follow these steps.

1. On a Mac choose Premiere Pro > Keyboard Shortcuts. On Windows choose Edit > Keyboard shortcuts.

   You need to map the Waveform, Vectorscope, RGB Parade, and Composite Video of the Program Monitor. The easiest way to do this is to type part of each word into the search box at the top. When the command appears, double-click the text box to the right.

2. Map Waveform to 1, Vectorscope to 2, the RGB Parade to 3, and Composite Video to 4 to quickly toggle between the three.

Make sure you chose the Program Monitor panel, *not* the Source Monitor panel.

3. Optional: Map "Effect" Enabled to any key you like. I chose the 1 key (which overlaps the Waveform monitor), which is OK because it's a different window.

Now that your setup is customized and accurate, let's explore goals and process.

Process: What to Do First?

Process involves which controls to touch first *and* which shot to choose first. Ideally, you should start with a medium shot or a medium close-up, preferably one that is well shot to begin with and needs little change.

Recall the original goals of color correction: It's the first two that are important here: Establish the appropriate tonal range and remove any color casts. Using your chosen shot, work backwards and forwards in a scene, correcting other shots to match it. This sets up the third rule: Match shots for shot-to-shot consistency.

Optionally, apply a look to the scene, which is the fourth rule (and the least important when you're rushing): Create a look (if appropriate).

Fundamental Color Correction Effects

Approximately 20 different effects are in the Color Correction section of the Effect panel. Although each one has some value, three are the most important:

▶ **Three-Way Color Corrector.** This effect has become the workhorse of color correcting footage. It offers three adjustments for luma and three for chroma, each divided into the ranges of Shadows, Midtones, and Highlights. It's the major method of color correction because it easily maps to control surfaces.

▶ **RGB Curves.** Some colorists prefer curves because they allow for a higher degree of adjustment than the three ranges (Shadows, Midtones, and Highlights). Using RGB Curves is neither worse nor better but rather a different method based on different mathematics.

CLOSE-UP

Real-world Setup

A tough fact about color correction is that *you can't color correct on a computer monitor.* There's no way to calibrate the monitor or trick it to work because it's just not engineered for video color correction.

Colorists adhere to a strict set of rules to compensate for the inconsistencies in vision, and in doing so can replicate their results and look, which helps to standardize their methods.

For professional color correction, here is the equipment you need:

▶ **Lighting.** Your lights need to be at a specific color temperature of 6500 degrees Kelvin. These lights are commonly called D65 lights. Additionally, no exterior lights should be used, particularly sunlight. Blackout curtains can be used as well.

▶ **Paint.** Gray walls are best, especially behind your editorial system. Mine is at 18% gray.

▶ **Broadcast monitor.** Invest in a monitor that is explicitly meant for color correction. Companies like Flanders Scientific or HP's Dreamcolor screens work well.

▶ **Hardware connections.** DVI doesn't cut it for color correction. Hardware output from certain companies, such as AJA, Black Magic Designs, Matrox, or Bluefish, made specifically for Adobe Premiere Pro are needed.

▶ **Hardware scopes.** Although the scopes in Adobe Premiere Pro work, they can't be truly trusted because they don't show the entire raster (every pixel). External scopes are preferred.

Yes, these items will increase the cost of your system, but they enable you to produce professional, replicable results.

▶ **Video Limiter.** Using this effect keeps your final work legal for output, which is crucial, even if it's never meant for broadcast.

Could you use other effects in the panel? Yes, and they do some great things; for example, Leave Color and Tint are stylistic effects. But for the ease and speed of color correction, the three effects in the preceding list will be the key to achieving the goals of color correction.

Another very valuable effect that is new to the Adobe Premiere Pro Creative Cloud release is the *Lumetri effect*. This effect harnesses the engine of Adobe SpeedGrade in Adobe Premiere Pro CC by allowing you to apply Looks (stylizing the footage) from Adobe SpeedGrade directly into Adobe Premiere Pro.

Three-Way Color Corrector

The Three-Way Color Corrector is considered the work-horse effect in color correction because of its ability to quickly balance images.

It can be used in one of two ways:

▶ **Primary correction.** Primary correction uses the three color wheels and the Input and Output levels (**Figure 6.27**) to adjust the overall image.

▶ **Secondary corrections.** When you activate this section of the Three-Way Color Corrector, you limit your adjustments to just part of the image.

Secondary controls can be found under the category called Secondary Color Correction. The controls are a keyer, which uses the same concept as greenscreen effects. It limits the Three-Way Color Corrector to *adjusting only* what falls on the inside or the outside of the keyer. When activated, the entire effect becomes a secondary effect; it's generally used *after* primary correction has been done (with a Three-Way Color Corrector or RGB Curves). In **Figure 6.28**, a key has been done to adjust the actor's face with the mask left on.

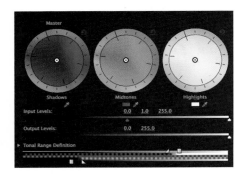

Figure 6.27 The three color wheels and the Input and Output levels.

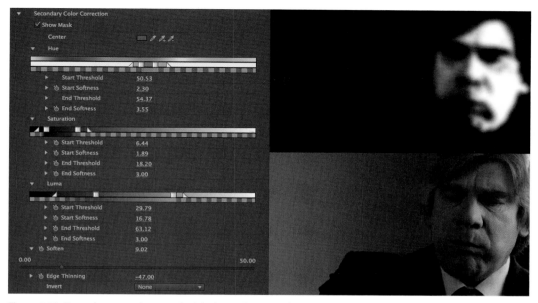

Figure 6.28 Secondary controls are on the left, the mask is top right, and the bottom right is the final image. This is from sequence **4 Effect overview** marker 6.28.

Three ranges

The Three-Way Color Corrector's "three ways" refers to the different ranges that the effect works on: commonly known as the Shadows, the Midtones, and the Highlights.

A check box on the Tonal Range Definition (when opened, **Figure 6.29**) helps you visualize where each of the three wheels work. Select the Show Tonal Range check box to see the three ranges.

A well-exposed shot will have some exposure in all three ranges.

> **TIP**
>
> Many colorists prefer just a little more overlap in the ranges that the default Three-Way Color Corrector provides. Click and drag the triangles to extend their range for a bit more overlap.

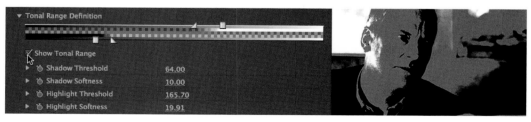

Figure 6.29 With Show Tonal Range selected, it's easy to see where each of the three wheels will work its magic.

Adjusting luma

Typically, you should use three controls on the Input levels (**Figure 6.30**): From left to right they are the Black point, the Gray (gamma) point, and the White point.

Figure 6.30 Instead of dragging the sliders, "scrub" the numbers.

Adjusting the Black point to the right pulls more darker pixels toward black. Adjusting the White point to the left pulls more lighter pixels toward white. And adjusting the Gray point to the left makes an image darker, whereas moving it to the right makes the image brighter.

The general order of operations should be to adjust the Black point, White point, and then Gamma.

Adjusting chroma

To add or remove color, click on one of the three color wheels to add a color you'd like or *opposite* of a color to reduce that color. For example, to reduce green, you'd click opposite of green and into the magentas, as in **Figure 6.31**.

Figure 6.31 Click and drag to add color.

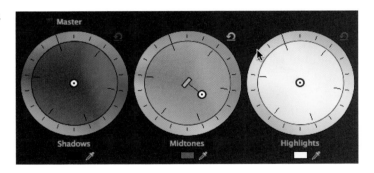

There are three white balance eyedroppers, one at the bottom of each of the three color wheels. Each eyedropper helps to quickly neutralize a color cast in the Shadows, Midtones, or Highlights. The idea is that you use the eyedropper on a part of the image that is neutral (such as a white shirt), and it neutralizes a color cast in that luminance region by adding in the opposite color.

On the rare occasions when you need to magnify the intensity of an adjustment, click and drag on the thin perpendicular line to drag the slider bar (**Figure 6.32**).

Saturation

Under the Saturation category in the Three-Way Color Corrector, you have a choice between the Master Saturation and adjusting the saturation of any of the three ranges. Changes made with the Shadow, Midtone, and Highlight Saturations are often subtle but very powerful, because they can remove (or add) saturation in the corresponding luminance area (the most common is to reduce saturation in shadows). In **Figure 6.33**, from sequence **4 Effect Overview** marker 6.33, I've removed the Saturations for everything but the highlights, leaving the yellow packet to "pop" and be more visible onscreen.

Figure 6.32 Usually, this balance magnitude adjustment doesn't need to be moved.

Saturation	
Master Saturation	100.00
Shadow Saturation	0.00
Midtone Saturation	0.00
Highlight Saturation	200.00

Figure 6.33 Less chroma occurs in shadows and highlights. Being able to reduce these saturation areas selectively is a powerful ability in Adobe Premiere Pro, making it easier to minimize color damage.

RGB Curves

Adobe Photoshop users often prefer to use RGB Curves. Each curve starts with two control points: one at the leftmost bottom, representing the darkest part of the channel, and another point at the rightmost top, the brightest part of the channel.

Dragging them upwards brightens that point; dragging them downwards darkens that point. Just click on the line to add a point, and drag the point from the curve area to remove the point.

The advantage of using RGB Curves lies in being able to manipulate each channel directly versus having to "balance" each range. Many use this capability to build a subtle look, such as in **Figure 6.34**, where I've built a high-contrast S curve on the Master Curve and added a little extra blue into the lower portion (shadows) of the Blue Curve.

The RGB Curves controls allow for adjustments of a Secondary Color Correction but have no saturation controls. If you want saturation controls, you'd have to add another effect (such as the Three-Way Color Corrector) either before or, more likely, after the Curves.

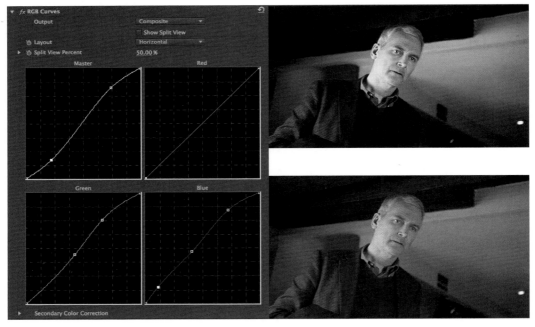

Figure 6.34 The RGB Curves controls permit adding multiple points; generally, fewer is better. The original image is on the bottom. Notice the higher contrast and extra blue in the top image.

Split View

The Split View isn't an effect; it's an option on the Three-Way Color Corrector and the RGB Curves that permits a before and after comparison of the effect.

It's important to be able to compare your corrections with the original image. When you're color correcting, the 90 second rule takes effect: After 90 seconds, your brain begins to compensate for color problems and forgets the original image.

The Split View (**Figure 6.35**) allows for a quick comparison. Between using Split View and toggling the effect on and off, your eyes will "remember" the original image.

Video Limiter

The Video Limiter limits the video levels. The defaults are pretty good (although you should check signal on external scopes). The Limiter can be used on a single clip or on multiple clips via adjustment layers or nesting.

Later in this chapter, I mention a better limiter.

Common Primary Corrections

Now that you've been introduced to the Three-Way Color Corrector, the RGB Curves, and the Video Limiter effects, let's put them to practical use. In this section, you can follow along to meet the first two goals of color correction: to maximize the tonal range and remove any color casts.

Your system may not necessarily match the exact look or output of what you see in this book (or what was done in the project). The sidebar "Real-world Setup" addresses some of these issues.

Most important is that if the image doesn't look good to your eye on a calibrated monitor, it doesn't work!

Use the sequence **5 Common Primary Corrections** to follow along with the examples in this section.

Using the Three-Way Color Corrector

The steps for using the Three-Way Color Corrector are always done in the same order: fix the luminance and then the chrominance. The process looks like this.

1. Fix the luma:

   ▶ Check the Input Black/White levels against the Waveform scope.

   ▶ Adjust the Midpoint/Gamma slider until the image "feels" correctly exposed. You may have to go back and adjust the Black/White levels after this step.

Figure 6.35 This image shows the Split View controls and how they reveal the original part of the image (right) compared to the corrected image (left).

A completely blown out or crushed shot will be very difficult and sometimes impossible to fix. Monitor your images on set to be safe.

2. Fix the chroma:

- ▶ Adjust the midtones by clicking and dragging from the center of the Midtones wheel in the *opposite* direction of any perceived color cast in the Vectorscope.

- ▶ Adjust the Highlights and Shadows color wheels while looking at the RGB Parade.

Fixing luma issues with the Three-Way Color Corrector

Exposure problems are often a by-product of natural lighting. For example, a cloud might have moved and hid the sun or the camera was left in auto-iris mode and through some camera compensation changed the exposure.

The shot at marker 6.36 (**Figure 6.36**) in sequence **5 Common Primary Correction** shows a shot that is fairly dark. Let's assume that this result wasn't the intention of the DP on set.

Reading the Waveform shows shadows at around 0.3 and highlights at 0.9, and most of the shot is below 0.6, meaning that the bulk of the exposure will be dark.

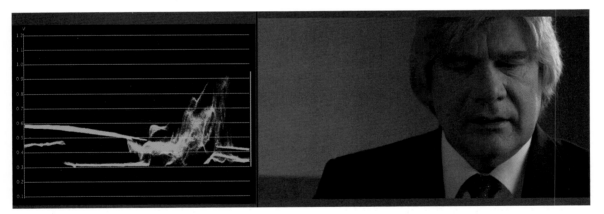

Figure 6.36 With most of the exposure information below .6, this shot is fairly dark.

Additionally, although there is a bright section of the man's hair (right side), most likely, brightest areas shouldn't be set all the way to white but rather about 5% below that. Here are the steps you should take to fix luma issues.

1. **Shadows first.** Because the shadows already fairly dark, the Input Black level probably doesn't need to be changed.

2. **Highlights next.** Adjusting the Input White level to the left brightens the highlights. Only a little adjustment is necessary (236 is what I ended up with), because you don't want the brightest part to be as bright as pointing at a light source.

3. **Midtones/Gammas last.** Adjusting the Midtone slider to 1.3 produces a brighter picture, but it now feels a little washed out. Adjusting the Black level to 5 helps restore some of the contrast.

Feel free to try the preceding technique on the Timeline with the blown out version of this shot at the marker named **Blown out**.

Fixing chroma issues with the Three-Way Color Corrector

Chroma issues may be naturally caused or may be operator error (forgetting to white balance the shot). The order of repair is the *reverse* of luma: You work the midtones first and the highlights and shadows last.

At marker 6.37 is a red shot, as shown in **Figure 6.37**.

Let's look through the scopes. The damage in the Red channel is significant, and looking at the Vectorscope you'll see such strong damage that it may be a struggle to fix the shot.

TIP

A completely blown out shot may be impossible to fix. But sometimes there is data in the blown out area. Reducing the Output White level slider may allow for the recovery of this information.

TIP

When the "blob" in the Vectorscope is weighted heavily away from the center (nearly a single vector), it's usually a sign that you may need to adjust the Saturation controls as well.

Figure 6.37 There's no doubt about the damage in this shot.

The exposure shown in the Waveform monitor is close enough to be OK. The problem with this image is the chroma. Normally, you'd first adjust the luma, but because the image already has good exposure, let's skip it and just deal with the chroma issue.

Looking at the Vectorscope, you need to move *opposite* of the color cast. Because this image has some neutral items (the wall, the newspaper, the man's hair) you can cheat and click those areas.

Move the Midtones wheel toward cyan. Optionally, you can click in the eyedropper and sample the wall (it's a neutral item based on other shots). Then adjust the magnification slider. These adjustments help quite a bit, but the blob has moved about half the distance. (Open the Midtones; the number values I ended up with were Magnitude 41, Gain 100, Angle 47.) That's not enough to repair the image. Let's switch to the RGB Parade and look at the highlight areas and shadows.

The highlights show too much red and green (the man's hair on the right side); some blue/cyan needs to be added to compensate. You can use the eyedropper but not in the brightest spot. Better to use the eyedropper in a spot that's bright but not fully white. (Open the Highlights; the number values I ended up with were Magnitude 46, Gain 71, Angle 29.) But there's still quite a cast in the image.

The Shadows remain, and his jacket (the darkest element on all three scopes) shows too much red. Using the same procedure you did earlier, try to get all three channels closer (like the highlights) at this point, and try to balance the jacket, the neutral item. (Open the Shadows; the number values I ended up with were Magnitude 36, Gain 20, Angle 47.) The image looks much better, but it still has a strong color.

Reducing saturation is the key. Recall an earlier tip in this chapter: When you're struggling with chroma, it's nearly always the shadows that cause problems. Reducing the Shadow Saturation to 50 makes the shot look almost normal. You might also try adjusting the Master Saturation.

The finished effect is on the shot in the sequence that matches **Figure 6.38**.

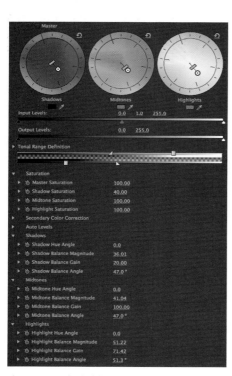

Figure 6.38 The hidden numerical controls are expanded to make the values visible.

Practice with the Three-Way Color Corrector

Let's look at another example of the Three-Way Color Corrector in use. But this time, you'll work from start to finish performing both luma and chroma corrections on the same shot so you can see again the order in which you should use the controls.

Look at the image in **Figure 6.39** at marker 6.39; let's start with luma and then fix the chroma.

Figure 6.39 The waveform of the uncorrected image.

1. Check the Input Black/White levels against the Waveform scope.

   In this step I adjusted the Input Black level by sliding it toward the right a little. I prefer sliding the numbers rather than using the actual arrow. I wanted a slightly more crushed black in the darker areas, so I made more of the image fall toward black. I then adjusted the Input White level.

2. Adjust the Midpoint/Gamma slider until the image "feels" correctly exposed.

   I felt the image was a little too dark (keep in mind the DP or Directors might have wanted that!), so I dragged the middle slider/Gamma to the right, brightening up the image. I set the Input Black level to 15.2 and the Input White level to 235.2. The Gamma slider ended up at 1.4.

By turning on Split View as a comparison (**Figure 6.40**), you can see that the shot is exposed slightly brighter with greater contrast.

Figure 6.40 Using the Split view, you can see the differences between the luma changes on the left and the original image on the right.

Now let's look at chroma.

3. Start with the midtones and focus on the Vectorscope.

The Vectorscope shows some yellow and red energy and quite a bit of energy between the two spots; yellow + red = brown. And when your eyes look at the image (**Figure 6.41**), it has a warm (brown) feel.

To compensate, I added just a little bit of blue in the Midtones color wheel. Then I clicked and dragged just a little toward blue (cooling down the shot.)

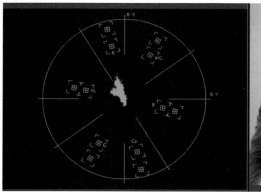

Figure 6.41 The image appears to be warm.

4. Now, let's focus on the Shadows and Highlights chroma wheel while looking at the RGB Parade (**Figure 6.42**).

Generally, any chroma changes in the highlight and shadows are slight, very subtle changes. Looking at the highlights in the image, the brightest spot is the blown out spot on the actor's face.

As the traces approach white (100), there should generally be a loss of color, yet here there is more red than green and blue. I added a little blue in the color wheel to balance that out while being careful not to neutralize the wall.

The shadow areas show no blue (there is almost no blue at the bottom of the RGB Parade), so I added just a little blue in the Shadows color wheel to balance the blue on the RGB Parade to be similar to the red and green shadow areas.

Both of the adjustments I made are very subtle, but by toggling on and off the entire effect (and viewing full screen), you can focus your eyes on the bright and dark areas to see if you can perceive the chroma change.

Figure 6.42 The RGB Parade is the key to spotting color casts. Each of the three circles helps identify a bright/shadow and neutral feature of the image.

CLOSE-UP

How RGB Processing Differs

The Three-Way Color Corrector processes the images based on the way the video is stored, which is in YCr'Cb' space (not RGB). Adding luma (Y) doesn't affect the chroma that's stored in the Cr'Cb'. So adjusting luma doesn't affect chroma and vice versa.

But in RGB processing, adding red, green, and blue makes the image brighter. Because chroma and luma are linked, it's important to work with chroma first and luma second backwards through your scopes compared to how you used them in the Three-Way Color Corrector.

RGB Curves

RGB Curves is exactly the *opposite* of working with the Three-Way Color Corrector. With this effect, you work with the chroma first and then luma.

RGB Curves isn't a better or worse filter than the Three-Way Color Corrector; it's just different. Because it uses different math (see the sidebar "How RGB Processing Differs"), you may have an easier or harder time fixing color problems.

Order of adjustments

When you're using the RGB Curves filter, you'll perform three steps rather than four.

1. Adjust the brightest spots of all three channels to make them similar (as appropriate) while watching the RGB Parade. Repeat this step for the darkest areas.

2. Look at the Vectorscope; add or remove points in the middle of the curves to properly center the blob.

3. If needed, adjust the Master curve to change the luma. Most likely, you'll use a point in the midtones to lighten or darken the image.

Walkthrough of curves

Let's walk through the color correcting steps using RGB Curves the same way you did for the Three-Way Color Corrector.

1. Using the same shot, at marker 6.44, I applied the RGB Curves. Then I checked the top of the RGB Parade and saw that the brightest spot was darker in the Blue channel (about 85%).

   I added a node on the blue RGB curve that's approximately 85% of the way up the slope and pulled it upwards to help the top of the Blue channel. Next, I added a second node at the top of the Red channel to pull it downwards (**Figure 6.43**) to help the Red channel match.

   To adjust the shadows, I then added a node on the bottom of the Blue curve to pull up the Blue channel just a little. The idea is to get some similarity in all three channels (the absence of light/shadow means that all three channels should be similar).

Be aware that the image may not look great. In this case, the image has a cyan/blue cast to it. What was the problem? The midtones.

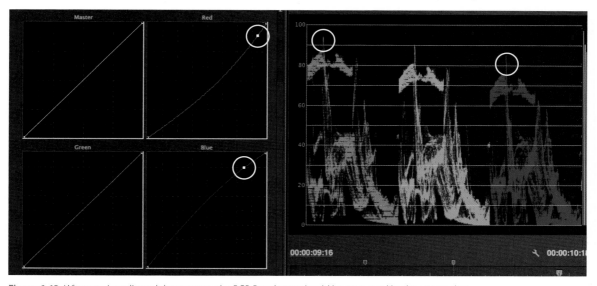

Figure 6.43 When you've adjusted these curves, the RGB Parade top should be even, not like this screen shot.

2. Switch to the Vectorscope.

   Because there is too much cyan/blue, I needed to add red/yellow. And because the problem was in the midtones, I added a point to the Red curve in the middle, pulling it up and adding red. Similarly, I needed to introduce yellow, so I set a midtone dot in the Blue channel and lowered it, adding yellow (**Figure 6.44** on the next page).

3. Now all that was left was to check the exposure on the Waveform and possibly brighten or darken the image here.

   I added a dot in the middle of the Master curve and dragged it upwards to lighten the image. In fact, the Master curve behaves similarly to the way a Gamma correction does in the Three-Way Color Corrector.

You can see the final image in the sequence **5 Common Primary Corrections** at marker 6.44.

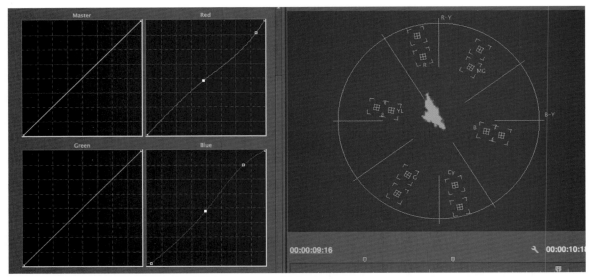

Figure 6.44 With the extra points mid-curve of red and blue, the blob on the Vectorscope looks better (and so does the image).

Fixing a chroma problem with curves

Let's look at the same shot I adjusted the chroma on in the "Practice with the Three-Way Color Corrector" section at marker 6.45. You can see that I've already applied the RGB Curves effect to it. The finished curves are in **Figure 6.45**.

1. Starting with the RGB Parade highlights, the blue highlights were too low and the red highlights were too high. Adjusting the tops of the Blue (1) and Red curves (2) repaired those problems.

2. Next, I repaired the shadows. In the Shadows of the RGB Parade there was too much red, so it needed to be reduced in the Red curve (3).

3. Now to the midtones. The newspaper is a neutral item that exists in the midtones; when I found it on the RGB Parade, it showed too much red. Adding a new point at the halfway mark of the Red curve (4) and reducing it began to repair the problem. At one point, the shot turned green, so I knew I went too far. The Blue channel needed a little assistance, because in the newspaper there wasn't enough blue on the RGB Parade where the newspaper information was, so I lifted the midpoint of the Blue curve (5).

4. I switched to the Vectorscope and saw that there was still quite a red cast. Using just my eyes (and glancing back at the RGB Parade) I saw that it was in the brighter portion of the midtones. So, I added another red node (6) with a second node to limit its effect (7), reducing the reds in the top of the midtones.

5. After checking the Luminance Waveform (and the image), I added some points to produce some slight brightening (8) of the midtones along with restoring some of the black (9) and white points (10) to produce a slightly higher contrast to the image.

The finished version of the shot is on the Timeline. Feel free to turn off the RGB Curves, add your own, and see which method helps you correct the cast faster—the Three-Way Color Corrector or the RGB Curves.

TIP

By adding a point on a curve near where you want to adjust, you minimize how much influence any node has on a curve.

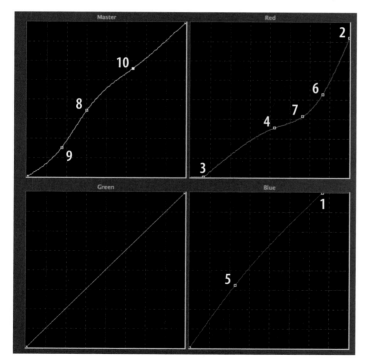

Figure 6.45 Each node added or adjusted corresponds to a number on the image.

Common Secondary Corrections

Do you have a bad sky in your image or a color that is too harsh? What you need is some form of secondary color correction to clean up the image.

A primary color correction affects the entire shot. But a secondary color correction affects only part of the shot, which means the results come from adding an additional second effect (or third, fourth, etc.).

Both the Three-Way Color Corrector and the RGB Curves have a section labeled Secondary Color Correction. In that section are chroma keyer-based corrections. You build a key in the effect to *limit* what part of the shot the effect works on.

Colorists will tell you that there is also a shape-based correction that works on part of the image based on a shape, such as for vignettes or simulating a grad filter. Although Adobe Premiere Pro doesn't have this feature built in, I'll describe a method of creating a shape-based correction.

Key-based Corrections

The Secondary Color Correction section in the Three-Way Color Corrector and the RGB Curves works the same. The corrections allow you to select a "key color," refining that key and limiting the effect to just the sections shown by that key (**Figure 6.46**).

The key is based on three parameters: Hue, Saturation, and Luma (HSL).

The struggle you'll have when using this feature will always be the same—getting a good key. The best technique is to select a color with the eyedropper and then watch to see what parts of the H, S, and L react.

Eyedropper color selection

When you're choosing a color with the eyedropper, try to mentally select an average color, not a dark or light point, but a pixel that most represents the area you want to key.

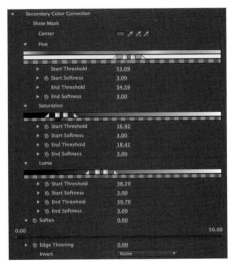

Figure 6.46 The Secondary Color Correction section, along with the Hue, Saturation, and Luma areas, help you "see" what part of an image has been keyed.

Make sure the Hue, Saturation, and Luma areas are open to help identify what the keyer selects. Each section has an area that represents the selection, such as the Saturation range shown in **Figure 6.47**. The two inner squares are the selected region (Start/End Threshold). The two outer triangles (Start/End softens) help the selection gradually include similar nearby regions.

TIP

Holding down the Command (Ctrl) key while using an eyedropper gives you a 5x5 pixel average, which is often much better than the default of single pixels.

Figure 6.47 This is the range for Saturation. Similar controls exist for Hue and Luma.

Select Show Mask

After your initial click on the part of the image you want selected (such as a sky or flesh tone) with the eyedropper, select the Show Mask check box. You'll see a "mask," a black and white representation, of where the Three-Way Color Correct (or RGB Curves) will be limited to. The effect will occur in the white areas, and the black areas will be ignored; gray areas will get a partial amount of the effect.

Use the plus and minus eyedroppers to add or remove from the key. For flesh tones, it's ideal to have a solid selection in the areas of the face (white) and everything else unselected (black).

Refining the selection

To improve the selection, you can manually adjust the selected region (Start/End Threshold) to quickly provide you with feedback when Show Mask is selected.

Here are some additional suggestions to refine your selection:

▶ Luma may require adjustment to either or both the Start/End Threshold. The trick is to look at the image and decide if you're missing dark regions or bright regions.

▶ Saturation usually needs the Start Threshold adjusted (the areas with less saturation).

▶ Hue is probably the least likely adjustment you'll need to make.

▶ If moving an adjustment made no change, return the adjustment to where it started (or click Undo).

Always soften, maybe thin

When you're finished with the correction, always use the Soften control to give the generated mask just a slight blur (a value between 1–5) to help the affected area blend in with the rest of the image.

Adjusting the Thin controls shrinks or expands the mask to help make the adjusted selection a little larger or smaller if needed.

Adjusting a Flesh Tone

Are you happy with the exposure of the image but feel like the flesh tones need a little pop? This is a perfect use for the Secondary section of the Three-Way Color Corrector (or RGB Curves). You can select just those color values.

Because face tones are a mixture of red plus yellow (they lack blue), it may be a little tricky to get a good selection if other elements in the image use similar colors. Rarely are walls painted white. Often, they have a little color in them, and a beige tone is all too common, which can be similar to face tones.

Combining the techniques in the section "Shape-based Corrections," later in this chapter can help you control and limit the secondary to just a region, which is perfect for dealing with a similar unwanted color (e.g., a beige wall would be unwanted when using a secondary on a flesh tone).

In sequence **6 Secondaries** (**Figure 6.48**), on the first shot you can see the results of the effect. It's in Split View to help you see it in print.

A primary correction was built with the first Three-Way Color Corrector and a second Three-Way Color Corrector was added to adjust just the flesh tones. Let's work through the steps.

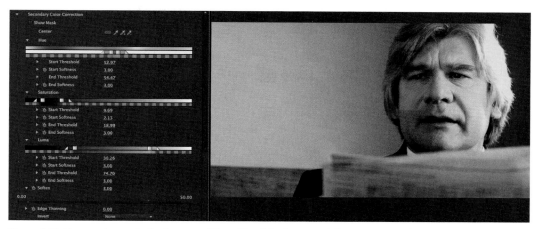

Figure 6.48 Here are the results for the second Three-Way Color Corrector (adjusting only the face) on the clip in Split View to compare with the original shot. Notice that the flesh tones look more saturated and a little brighter.

1. **Make the initial selection.** I made the initial selection by clicking on the left portion of the man's cheek (Figure 6.48) and then selected Show Mask. The mask was missing the darker and brighter parts of his face, so I adjusted the Thresholds rather than use the eyedroppers to add more of a selection.

2. **Adjust Luma Thresholds.** Because I wanted to include the darker and brighter parts of his face, I adjusted the Luma Start and End Thresholds to increase the matte selection. Moving the Luma Start Threshold to the left included more of the left side (darker parts) of the face. Moving the Luma End Threshold included a little more of the right side (brighter parts) of the face.

3. **Adjust Saturation Thresholds.** The right side of his face was still somewhat unselected, because it's the brightest part of the face. And, as you recall from the "RGB Parade" section, as brightness increases, usually less chroma (saturation) exists. Decreasing the Saturation End Threshold helped include the bright areas but also included the bench. In this image it was acceptable to allow the bench selection in order to adjust the face because the adjustment is subtle.

4. **Always Soften.** As always, soften the selection (mask) just a little (in this case, set Soften to 3.0).

Deselect Show Mask and make color adjustments to *just* the flesh tones.

In this example, I added some saturation (Master Saturation at 140) and slightly lifted the Midtone Luma/Gamma to 1.1.

Adjusting a Sky

It's fairly common to need to color correct just the sky in an image, because when exposure is done right in-camera to capture people, the exposure setting can often leave the sky blown out. Even when the exposure is handled well in-camera, some skies just lack color. Not every production can wait for the perfect blue sky!

At marker 6.49 (**Figure 6.49**) you can see the finished version of a sky correction in Split View, comparing the sky in before and after images. The original sky (on the right) is very bright and has nearly no chroma at all, leaving it feeling very stark.

Figure 6.49 Yes, the sky on the right is the "before" image.

A primary correction was built with the first Three-Way Color Corrector and a second Three-Way Color Corrector was added to adjust just the sky. Let's walk through this example.

1. **Make the initial selection.** Skies are usually the brightest element in an image, and in this case, have little information other than being very bright. There was almost no chroma. Making a selection with the eyedropper would have been a mistake; it would have chosen a hue, and with the sky so blown out, I wasn't sure it would

have selected the color blue because there was little to no blue in the sky. So, in this case, instead of using the eyedropper, I wanted the selection to include only the "bright" areas (luma)—but also make sure I kept the hues and all of the saturations— leaving just a question of selecting "bright" (pixels of high luma). Therefore, rather than using the eyedropper, I adjusted just the Luma controls section directly. I skipped making the initial selection and selected Show Mask to see the mask (which was completely white; everything was selected).

2. **Adjust Luma Thresholds.** The entire luma range was selected, from the dark pixels (the Luma Start Threshold) to the bright pixels (the Luma End Threshold). I wanted to select all of the bright pixels, not the darker areas of the image. I then dragged the Luma Start Threshold to the right (to ignore all the darker pixels) until only the sky was selected. I added some start softness (by moving the triangle) to make the selection more graduated.

3. **Adjust Saturation Thresholds.** There was no saturation of color in the sky, so I needed to leave the saturation adjustments alone, because adjusting them would only lessen what was selected. If there was some blue in the sky and white clouds, using the Saturation Thresholds could help because blue clouds have some saturation of color, whereas white clouds do not.

4. **Soften.** As always, I softened the image just a little, using a setting of 2.0.

With a decent selection made, I needed to adjust the second Three-Way Color Corrector to make the sky look like a sky. Because the sky is all highlights, I adjusted the Highlights color wheel and gave the sky a strong blue adjustment, which helped but wasn't convincing.

Looking at the RGB Parade explains why. The red and green "bright" areas are just too bright. Lowering the Output White level *reduced* the brightest part of the image, but because I had added blue on the Highlights wheel, the result is a good, natural-looking sky.

The finished version is on your Timeline at marker 6.49 for you to examine.

Leaving a Single Color

It's a very striking and stylistic choice to leave a single color in an image. At marker 6.50 (**Figure 6.50**) that exact effect has been created and is perfect for calling attention to the sugar packets.

Figure 6.50 Although this image was completely desaturated, it's far more subtle to leave a little color/saturation in the rest of the image.

Adobe includes a prebuilt effect called *Leave Color* that you can use to apply a single color effect. But the advantage of doing it with a Three-Way Color Corrector is that *you take advantage of the full Mercury Engine acceleration* as well as more subtle controls.

The technique is to use a Three-Way Color Corrector's secondary feature, select the color you want to keep, desaturate that area, and at the very end invert the mask, causing the effect to flip-flop and desaturate everything *but* the selected color.

At marker 6.50 a primary correction was built with the first Three-Way Color Corrector, and a second Three-Way Color Corrector was added to adjust the *inversion* of the selected color. Let's walk through the steps.

1. **Make the initial selection.** This time, I relied on using the eyedroppers because the yellow of the image was very distinct. It was quick and easy to use the plus eyedropper to add darker and lighter yellows, because there was no other yellow in the image.

2. **Adjust Luma Thresholds.** By selecting Show Mask, luma was given a broad adjustment, selecting darker yellows and brighter yellows.

3. **Adjust Saturation Thresholds.** What was still missing was some of the less saturated and more saturated yellows. I adjusted the Saturation selections much wider, which really picked up on the details.

4. **Soften.** As always, I softened the selection just a little, using a setting of 2.0.

With a decent selection created, I then needed to open the saturation controls of the Three-Way Color Corrector and lower all four controls: the Master, Shadows, Midtones, and Highlights, desaturating everything.

I then used the Invert switch at the bottom of the effect to *reverse* the key by setting it to Invert Mask (**Figure 6.51**), which desaturated the rest of the image, leaving just the color yellow of the sugar packet.

Figure 6.51 The Invert Mask switch allows adjustments on the "outside" of the secondary correction rather than the inside.

Shape-based Corrections

Shape-based corrections permit a color correction to adjust only part of a shot based on a shape. Adobe Premiere Pro doesn't have shape-based corrections as a direct option, but it does have the capability of building it!

For example, currently, it's trendy to darken the edges of an image to give it a vignette. The reason it's used so often is that it attracts information to "bright" parts of an image and mimics the way your vision falls off to the edges of an image when you focus on something.

Because there isn't a built-in plug-in, I needed to build a stack of a specific recipe. When I use a shape-based corrections technique, I have to copy and paste a video from V1 onto V2, so the same video is on two layers. Then, I need to add a third "top" layer that includes some form of black-and-white shape that I would create to cut the video on V2 onto itself on V1.

This is very much a recipe; if you get the stack right, it works.

At marker 6.52, take a look at the example of a vignette in **Figure 6.52**:

▶ **V3 Shape + Blur.** The top layer needs to be a shape. It can be built anywhere, such as with the Title tool or in Adobe Photoshop. On the Timeline, I built it using the Title tool. It also needs a blur to soften the edges, so I used the Gaussian blur.

▶ **V2 copy of the video + Track Matte.** The middle layer was a brighter version of the color correction done on V1. It needs an additional effect called the *Track Matte Key*. This effect uses the top layer to cut the middle layer over the background. In the Track Matte effect, you must choose V3 in the Matte drop-down menu. This cuts the V2 track, showing only V2 in the white areas from the V3 shape—in this case the circle.

▶ **V1 copy of the video.** The bottom layer is a darker version of the color correction.

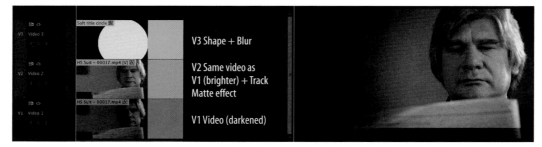

Figure 6.52 This stack of images has been labeled with effects to make understanding it easier.

Building this recipe is solely about getting the recipe right.

Here are some suggestions when you're building shape-based corrections:

▶ Don't set the Gaussian blur on the V3 Shape until the very end of positioning and building the stack. You need to be able to differentiate where the shape is cutting. You know you have the right value when the transition from the foreground to background is seamless.

▶ Your eyes adapt quickly: Toggling the effect on and off seems dramatic, but after your eyes adapt, it looks natural.

▶ You may have to move (keyframe) the shape if there's movement in the frame. One of the advantages of the very soft edge (heavy blur) is that the movement is very subtle.

Practical Shot Matching

Shot matching is a matter of trying to live between your eyes and the scopes (particularly the RGB Parade) while trying to produce a matching *appearance*. Faces and clothes with a specific color are the elements that are immediately noticeable if they don't match shot to shot.

Toggling back and forth between shots quickly (using the up and down arrow keys) is a great way to compare shots. If you need to do this for a frame other than the head frame of a shot, add markers (press M) and toggle using the Go to Next Marker (Shift+M) and Previous Marker (Shift+Command+M [Shift+Ctrl+M]) keys. Another way to work is to place the sequence you're working on in the Source Monitor. The sequence will act as reference with its own separate playhead.

Here are some general guidelines for practical shot matching:

▶ **Match tonal range.** Try to get a similar tonal range between the shots first: the black point, the white point, and most important, the midtone/Gamma. Look for landmarks like where the highlights of flesh tones appear in the Waveform scope.

▶ **Identify vectors and saturation.** Look at the Vectorscope, and compare the saturations, especially.

▶ **Use RGB Parade.** Like color grading, the RGB Parade is the most important scope. Try to find matchable elements in both images.

▶ **Limit your vision I.** Cheat by temporarily surrounding a color you want to match using a Crop effect or a Garbage Matte effect on both images. These methods of cutting an image may help to isolate the image to a single color, and then use the RGB Parade to compare them.

▶ **Limit your vision II.** When you're trying to get two shots from very different moments, it may be worth

TIP

You'll find a free Power Window plug-in at j.mp/PowerWindow. A number of great third-party tools also have a color corrector with shape capabilities built in, such as Colorista II from Red Giant Software.

TIP

Vision Effects makes an inexpensive plug-in that makes shot matching quick.

temporarily moving one shot to V2 and adding a left or right side crop to see both shots simultaneously to compare them in the scopes.

▶ **Eliminate shadow pollution.** Often, when you're struggling to match two shots, the reason is that there's some saturation of color in the shadows. Consider desaturating the shadows.

▶ **Use Secondary Color Correction.** Yes, you can use the Secondary section of a Three-Way Color Corrector or RGB Curves to isolate and fix part of an image that doesn't match, but then you'll just be adjusting a small portion of the total shot. It's part of the arsenal of ways to correct, but don't go to it first.

▶ **Avoid noise.** Watch for noise, particularly in poorly shot (consumer camera) material. In these cases you may have to rely on some type of noise reduction effect.

Adjusting a Pair of Shots to Match

Because so much of shot matching varies based on specific shots, the example I use here, although useful, won't solve your specific issues. But it will give you insight into how you can do shot matching.

On the Timeline in **7 shot matching** at marker 6.53 are two shots (**Figure 6.53**), both of a model walking outside. The first shot looks pretty normal (but shots can always use some primary color correction), but the second shot is very dark (exposure difference) and has some blue coloration, most likely because the light was fading at the end of day!

Figure 6.53 Both shots are before any grading has been done. The shot CU model walking outside (left) is well exposed, but the MS model walking (right) is dark and seems to have lots of blue in it.

A basic correction was done to both shots at **marker 6.54** (**Figure 6.54**). Almost no exposure change was done with the shot CU model walking outside, and a little warmth was added to the midtones. The MS model walking shot had lots of exposure change, brightening the shot. Constant comparison was done with the Waveforms to try to match the luminance of the faces. Saturation was added, which helped visually in getting the overall chroma to match each other, but pushing too much warmth led to the outfit becoming somewhat orange.

A secondary color correction was needed to warm up just the flesh tones (**Figure 6.55**). By adding a second Three-Way Color Corrector and using the keyer for the just face, extra warmth was added in the midtones and the Master Saturation was increased.

If these shots recur on the Timeline, it'd be smart to reuse them, which leads to learning how to save and reuse effects.

Figure 6.54 Base color corrections improved the shots, but the second shot needs just a little more correction in the flesh tones.

Figure 6.55 Adding a secondary color correction gave the flesh tones the extra pop they needed to match the prior shot.

Saving and Reusing Effects

Saving and reusing effects is covered at length in Chapter 5, "Advanced Compositing and Effects," but here are just a couple of quick tips for speeding up your color correction work:

▶ **Copy and paste.** Copy and paste one or several effects via the Paste Attributes command (Option+Command+V [Alt+Ctrl+V]).

▶ **Smart Preset bins.** Create a Preset bin called **Color looks**. All your color corrections should live in that bin. Using the Three-Way Color Corrector to prebuild a look that is already slightly cool or warm can give you a better starting point than just using the default Three-Way Color Corrector.

▶ **Better camera starting points.** Build a correction for the neutral point for each camera. It's faster to start with a neutral point than with the default effect. This is particularly valuable on multicam shoots; once built, you'll have a starting effect where each camera matches each other better.

▶ **Export presets.** Export your presets and keep them organized outside of Adobe Premiere Pro. On the off chance you need to fully reset the software, this export will act as a backup of your customizations. Right-click on the preset/preset bin in the Effects panel to export or import the presets.

▶ **Multiple versions.** If you'll be working with a client, it's a smart idea to build several alternate looks on a shot. Just disable the ones you don't like. Make sure you right-click on the name of the effect and give it a description.

Looks

Once all the basic grading has been done, you need to decide whether or not you want a stylized "look" to a series of shots.

Should the series resemble a warm environment like Miami? How can you visually depict London as different from Chicago? Creating a "look" to represent a location provides a visual method of communicating location to the audience viewing the video. Similarly, warm looks are often called *romantic*. Cooler looks are frequently used for more serious scenes. Technology looks typically have some green in the shadows. Placing one of these looks over an entire scene (rather than just a shot) adds a subtle, consistent visual treatment to a scene.

Some Common Recipes

The following sections describe some common recipes that are either great starting points or finished looks. Where possible they were created with the least amount of effects to try to maximize the Mercury Engine for optimal playback.

Filmic "S curve"

An "S curve" on the Master curve of the RGB Curves produces blown out highlights and crushed shadows, resulting in a higher-contrast "filmic" look.

This S curve looks like **Figure 6.56** at marker 6.56 from the sequence **8 Looks**. Based on the exposure of the shot, it may be necessary to go in and tweak the curve to make it stronger or weaker.

Black and white

Although there is a built-in Black and White effect (in the Image Control category) that is accelerated, the effect is limited because it is generated solely from the luma information.

Often, the black and white information doesn't produce an image with strong contrast. Adobe Photoshop users know this, so instead they use the Black and White adjustment, which permits the output to source from just the Red, Green, or Blue channels rather than the Luma channel.

The Channel Mixer can be set to Monochrome to create a black and white image utilizing only the Red, Green, or Blue channels (or a mixture of two.)

On the Timeline at marker 6.57 are four versions of a shot: one built from the Black and White effect and one built

To discover more on looks, check out Alexis Van Hurkman's book *Color Correction Look Book: Creative Grading Techniques for Film and Video* (Peachpit Press, 2014).

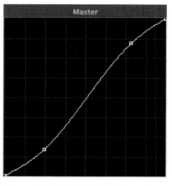

Figure 6.56 The "S" of the S curve is made with two control points.

per channel with the Channel Mixer (**Figure 6.57**). Note that the red controls are the only controls functioning when the Channel Mixer is set to Monochrome. Quickly move from shot to shot to see the difference.

Figure 6.57 Each of the four versions of the black and white shot. From left to right, each of the black and white images was generated from different channels: the Luma, the Red, the Green, and the Blue.

Sepia

Sepia was traditionally a look designed to make photos more durable and add warmth. Most people tend to categorize shots with a sepia effect as "older." Usually, the contrast is fairly high (like the previous S curve adjustment).

To build the shots at marker 6.58 (**Figure 6.58**), I used the Tint effect and took some careful adjustments of the white point to a Hue of 25 degrees (orange, exactly halfway between red and yellow) and a Saturation of 40% (more than that was too strong).

Then the S curve from earlier was added to give it a more contrasty "pop."

Figure 6.58 The results of the Sepia, Bleach Bypass, and Summer looks.

Bleach Bypass

Bleach Bypass refers to the chemical process of developing film. Bypassing the bleaching of the chemicals from the image created an image with more contrast, less saturation, and often some blue in the shadows and midtones.

The next shot on the Timeline after the Sepia shot (Figure 6.58) was built with a Three-Way Color Corrector with an increased contrast in the Input levels, reducing the saturation across the Master, Shadows, Midtones, and Highlights Saturations, and finally adding some blue to the midtones and shadows.

Summer

Building the shot on the Timeline after the Bleach Bypass (Figure 6.58) is a great example of using the RGB Curves instead of the Three-Way Color Corrector, because I wanted to be able to do some subtle changes that the Three-Way Color Corrector couldn't do.

Whereas Bleach Bypass leaves the image washed out, a Summer look in an image of a bright summer day would have some extra green in the midtones (needing a node in the middle of the Green curve of the RGB effect) and some extra orange in the brightest areas (adding some Red in the highlights and reducing blue in the highlights). The advantage of using curves is in the ease of adjusting just part of the highlights and midtones.

A Three-Way Color Corrector was added to boost the Midtones Saturation and reduce the Shadows Saturation to avoid getting too much color in the blacks.

Grad filter

On a camera, a Gradient filter is often used to add a color wash to an image to compensate for imperfect shooting conditions—blue (for bluer skies) or orange (for warm sunlight).

Simulating a Gradient filter required the technique used in the section "Shape-based Corrections." The V3 track had a black to white gradient and was adjusted and rotated to cover the area of the sky. The shot is the second to last on the Timeline. The "orange" version of the shot is on V2 along with a Track Matte Key effect. The normal version of the clip is on V1. The image now looks like the sun is warming up the sky (**Figure 6.59**).

Figure 6.59 Applying the Grad filter and then the Summer+Grad filter looks requires multiple tracks for shape-based secondaries.

Summer + Grad filter

The last shot on the Timeline isn't a new item; it merely reuses the prior Summer effect and the Grad filter. The shot now looks like it was shot in the high point of summer.

Lumetri Looks

NOTES

The only drawback when you're utilizing the Lumetri Engine is the increased processing and render times.

An entire category at the bottom of the effects list is called *Lumetri Looks.* These looks are prebuilt recipes, which were built using Adobe SpeedGrade.

If you're not familiar with it, Adobe SpeedGrade is a full-color correction environment. But frankly, the interface is daunting for novices. Instead, Adobe has leveraged the Lumetri Engine from Adobe SpeedGrade into a single effect, permitting the application of Adobe SpeedGrade looks directly inside Adobe Premiere Pro.

Instead of using the Lumetri effect in the Color Correction Bin when you want to add Lumetri Looks, skip to the Lumetri Looks section (**Figure 6.60**) at the bottom of the Effects panel, because the effects in these categories already have a preset attached to them.

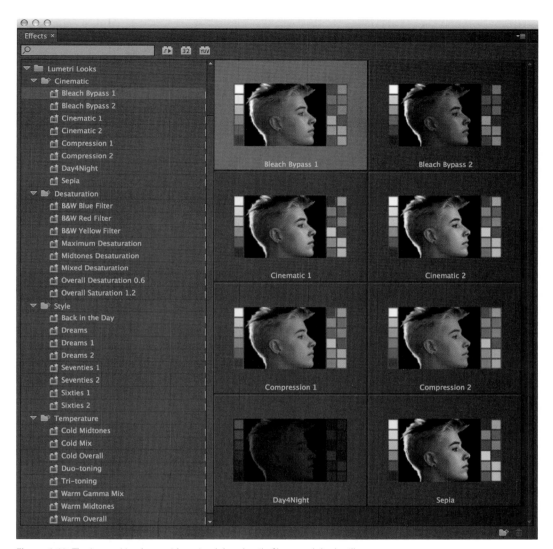

Figure 6.60 The Lumetri Looks provide a visual thumbnail of how each look will appear.

TIP

One strong suggestion is to name your adjustment layer in the Project panel based on what you intend it to do. This will make your Timeline more readable.

Applying Looks Across a Scene

Sure, it's possible to apply looks on a shot-by-shot basis. All you have to do is select one of the looks and drag it directly to a clip. But applying the looks this way can be problematic! For example, what if you (or your client) wants a change?

Instead, it's better to use one of two methods to accomplish the same goal with a single effect: adjustment layers or nesting.

Adjustment layers

Using adjustment layers to apply looks is the preferred method of most colorists in Adobe Premiere Pro. Adjustment layers are also found in Adobe Photoshop and Adobe After Effects. You can think of an adjustment layer as a clear piece of film you put effects on.

An adjustment layer was created in the project and applied to a higher video track, as shown in **Figure 6.61** on track V2. By applying the effect to the adjustment layer, Adobe Premiere Pro "adjusts" the appearance of all the clips beneath that layer.

The adjustment layer is easy to turn on or off globally by turning on or off the Track output on the Timeline. You can do this by right-clicking on the adjustment layer and choosing Enable, or by pressing Shift+Command+E (Shift+Ctrl+E).

Using the Enable command, it's also possible to build several scenic looks on several adjustment layers and enable only the one that you want to apply.

Figure 6.61 An adjustment layer is over the first half of this Timeline, and the back half is already nested. This is sequence **9 Adjustment Layers and Nesting**.

Nesting

In earlier versions of Adobe Premiere Pro, nesting was the method used to add a single look to multiple shots.

To use nesting, select the shots and choose Clip > Nest. A new sequence representing the clip(s) appears in the Project panel, and the clip(s) are replaced by the new sequence.

Adjustment layers are preferred when applying looks, because they can be easily added, removed, or modified in length, whereas nesting can't.

Nesting's major advantage is in collapsing multiple clips and/or tracks into a single element (such as collapsing the shape-based secondary corrections mentioned earlier in this chapter).

Legalizing Video

Legalizing video is often a thorny issue; it's difficult to do without dedicated hardware (such as hardware scopes and monitors, see the sidebar "Real-world Setup"), and it's specific to the broadcaster you're dealing with.

Legalization has no bearing on web delivery, because the web is very much the Wild West with no set rules.

What can further complicate legalizing video is that some broadcasters will run your work through a hardware legalizer (which will compress the way it looks, guaranteeing it'll be safe but also ruining your hard work). Some broadcasters publish detailed specifications, such as the Public Broadcasting System in the United States, which has specific guidelines available for download called the *Red Book* (www.pbs.org/producing/red-book).

Even though legalizing video mostly applies to broadcasting, it can apply to other tools in the production chain (such as online hosting or video compression headaches) when you exceed the broadcasting standards for where you live.

In essence, it's better to try to keep your video broadcast safe rather than not.

Figure 6.62 It's likely that this effect will be enough as is.

Using the Built-in Video Limiter

Whether you use an adjustment layer or nesting to apply looks, you'll need an effect to limit the video to legal levels. That effect is the Video Limiter (**Figure 6.62**).

The Video Limiter effect works by using a "Smart Limit" of luma plus chroma across all the ranges—Shadows, Midtones, and Highlights.

If you have different signal needs, you can adjust the effect's job of limiting the signal as needed for output.

Lumetri Limiters

Adobe SpeedGrade has a more intelligent set of looks to keep video legal. I've exported these looks from Adobe SpeedGrade and have included them with the project and media for this chapter.

When you apply the Lumetri effect (from the Color Correction category of effects, not the Lumetri Looks section), you'll be faced with a File Chooser dialog. Navigate and select either Legalize NTSC (US) or Legalize PAL (Europe) to take advantage of these presets that are included with the project downloads for this chapter.

Direct Link with Adobe SpeedGrade

As mentioned in Chapter 1, one of the benefits of Adobe Creative Cloud is that Adobe can easily push a bug fix or an upgrade to the Cloud users. Which is exactly what happened while we were in the middle of writing this book.

The original workflows of Adobe Premiere Pro and Adobe SpeedGrade were a little rocky, but Adobe has really listened. The developers seem to have approached the problem with fresh eyes and really got the workflow right, meeting users needs.

Now, Adobe SpeedGrade can read and write into an Adobe Premiere Pro project. Any clip that is adjusted in Adobe SpeedGrade gets a single Lumetri effect in Adobe Premiere Pro.

Unfortunately, this short section in this book cannot truly do Adobe SpeedGrade justice. It provides a minimalist crash course, a "connect the dots" to what's come prior in this chapter, and it's far from comprehensive.

Adobe SpeedGrade has a very different interface (**Figure 6.63**) than any of the other Adobe Creative Cloud applications. This section offers a great "try it" quick start to the application.

Figure 6.63 Adobe SpeedGrade's interface is very different than editorial applications and different from other Adobe applications. It's optimized for the job of color correction.

The Big Picture of Color Correction

Every concept and technique discussed earlier in this chapter *also applies* to Adobe SpeedGrade. The concepts about scopes and the three color wheels (the Three-Way Color Corrector effect) exist in *every* NLE on the market. Learning these concepts applies everywhere that you might perform color correction—Adobe Premiere Pro, Adobe SpeedGrade, and even third-party effects, such as Red Giant Colorista or Color Finesse (which happens to be included for free with Adobe After Effects).

TIP

To remove effects from multiple clips, choose Clip > Remove Effects to reset intrinsic effects, such as Position or Opacity, and/or remove video and audio effects.

CLOSE-UP

Other Adobe SpeedGrade Workflows

It's important to be aware of the other ways Adobe SpeedGrade can work with Adobe Premiere Pro and other NLEs, even if it's unlikely you'll ever use them:

▶ **Export an EDL.** You could export an edit decision list (EDL) from Adobe Premiere Pro and import the EDL to another NLE, relinking to your existing media. This always was a bit painful because EDLs contain so little information; they're really a technology from the 1980s. But this is a common way to work with other NLEs.

▶ **Export a QuickTime movie.** You could import a QuickTime movie into Adobe SpeedGrade from other NLEs. Using a feature called Scene Analysis, the QuickTime file would be separated into different shots (even though it was a single file). Quite a few workarounds are necessary to handle issues like picture-in-picture effects or any other sort of overlapping video.

▶ **Work Directly in Adobe SpeedGrade.** It's possible to create a Timeline and perform editorial tasks directly in Adobe SpeedGrade. This workflow makes sense for some uses, such as on set use for viewing material from a cinema camera—a LUT could easily be adjusted. The process of starting projects and navigating to footage is quite different compared to editorial tools like Adobe Premiere Pro.

This back-and-forth software switching process is, on the whole, a little slower than working solely in Adobe Premiere Pro. But if you decide to learn Adobe SpeedGrade on a deeper level, you will eventually be rewarded by being able do complex color corrections faster. After all, Adobe SpeedGrade is dedicated to performing this task. Yet it won't be as fast as adjusting a single shot directly in Adobe Premiere Pro.

Working with Adobe SpeedGrade

The process of getting your sequence out of Adobe Premiere Pro and into Adobe SpeedGrade consists of the following four steps.

▶ **Prepare your sequence.** It's probably a good practice to duplicate your sequence prior to doing anything else. If needed, you can "undo" any changes you make. Additionally, you might want to consider stripping any Three-Way Color Corrector effects from your sequence. If you've used any sort of stylistic effect, such as a Tint effect, decide if you want to keep it or rebuild it in Adobe SpeedGrade.

▶ **Send to Adobe SpeedGrade.** Select any sequence in Adobe Premiere Pro, choose File > Directly Link to Adobe SpeedGrade. Adobe Premiere Pro will close because both applications can't directly work on the sequence simultaneously.

▶ **Perform color corrections in Adobe SpeedGrade.** This is where you'd adjust your sequence. I'll cover the equivalents of the Three-Way Color Corrector as it relates to Adobe SpeedGrade and shot matching.

▶ **Send back to Adobe Premiere Pro.** When you're finished, you just press a button in Adobe SpeedGrade that will close down the project and reopen it in Adobe Premiere Pro. Every clip that was adjusted will now have a Lumetri effect, because that's the engine behind Adobe SpeedGrade.

Minimalist Adobe SpeedGrade

Have you launched Adobe SpeedGrade yet? If you've downloaded it, you've likely launched it once and have realized that its interface is daunting. Where are your menus? If you right-click, it doesn't seem to help, which means it's likely that you've launched it once and gave up.

The following sections contain *essential* pieces of information for Adobe SpeedGrade to actually be useful to you.

Getting Familiar with Adobe SpeedGrade

When a sequence is sent from Adobe Premiere Pro, Adobe SpeedGrade will open and look like the screen shot in **Figure 6.64**.

The top of the screen displays your footage. A Timeline is underneath it along with what looks like a Three-Way Color Corrector at the bottom.

Figure 6.64 Key areas of the Adobe SpeedGrade interface.

Because the only real effect in Adobe SpeedGrade is color grading, when you adjust the color wheels, you'll be making corrections to your footage.

To the left of the color wheels is a Layers stack showing the various adjustments that may be layered on a clip.

The panel on the right has a couple of tabs across the top that are meant for two uses, saving specific frames for reuse (Snapshots) and building masks that can be used for a secondary correction.

Returning to Adobe Premiere Pro

At the very top left of the screen is a toolbar that looks like the one in **Figure 6.65**. It has six buttons: Open, Save, Save Project As, Direct Link to Adobe Premiere Pro, Undo, Redo, and Preferences.

Figure 6.65 The toolbar in Adobe SpeedGrade.

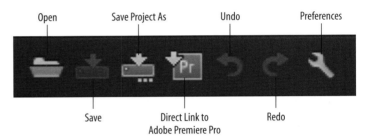

The most important button is Direct Link to Adobe Premiere Pro because you'll use it to send the Timeline back to Adobe Premiere Pro. You won't need to click Undo, Redo, or Save, because they're all the common keyboard commands you already know: Command+Z (Ctrl+Z), Command+Shift+Z (Ctrl+Shift+Z), and Command+S (Ctrl+S).

Navigating the Timeline

In many ways the Timeline is like any Timeline you've ever worked on. You can use the JKL keys to play forward and backward just like you do in Adobe Premiere Pro. The spacebar works the same as well, but that's about it.

In SpeedGrade the playhead controller (**Figure 6.66**) is *below* the clips. You can grab it at the large rectangle with the time-

Figure 6.66 It's easiest to move the playhead by clicking below in the timecode area. The green section above the Timeline represents the live cache that Adobe SpeedGrade uses for playback.

code on it. Optionally, you can click where you want it to appear above the Timeline. Notice the number "1" on it. That will become important later when we deal with shot matching. What you want to *avoid* is clicking on a clip directly.

To play the clip forward and backward, you can use the JKL keys, but the up arrow key will *also* play forward, and the down arrow key will play backward.

The left and right arrow keys play forward and back a single frame.

To move forward or backward a single clip, press Command (Ctrl) plus the left or right arrow keys.

The Home and End keys go to the In point and Out point.

Table 6.2 shows a list of some common keyboard shortcuts that are immediately valuable as you jump into Adobe SpeedGrade.

TABLE 6.2 Common Adobe SpeedGrade Shortcut Keys

	OS X	WINDOWS
Play	Spacebar	Spacebar
Play forward	Up arrow	Up arrow
Play backward	Down arrow	Down arrow
Dynamic playback	JKL	JKL
Show/hide the Grading panel	P	P
Show/hide the Analysis panel	A	A
Zoom In/Out	Numpad + / -	Numpad + / -
Zoom to 100%	Command+Shift+Home	Ctrl+Shift+Home
Zoom to fit	Command+Home	Ctrl+Home
Full screen toggle	Shift+H	Shift+H
Go to next clip	Command+right arrow	Ctrl+right arrow
Go to prior clip	Command+right arrow	Ctrl+right arrow
Copy grade below mouse	C	C
Toggle Grading on/off	0	0
Add one or more playheads	Option+1/2/3	Alt+1/2/3
Color match	Command+M	Ctrl+M

Figure 6.67 Clicking the All button zooms in and makes the six second (6s) button active. The third button zooms to the level between the In and Out points.

Zooming the Timeline

Two buttons in the top left of the Timeline are the All button and the 6s (six seconds) button (**Figure 6.67**). The All button is a toggle; the 6s button won't become active unless you've zoomed in a little. Six seconds is a *perfect* zoom level for most work because it allows you to see the shot you're working on plus a couple of other shots.

To zoom using the mouse, press Option (Alt) and the scroll wheel (a two-finger gesture on a trackpad).

Just One Shot Please

One of the major ideas when working with a dedicated color corrector is to look at a single shot repeatedly while it plays back. Adobe SpeedGrade allows you to do this by clicking two buttons.

The main button you want to use looks like the second button in **Figure 6.68** and is located above the Zoom All/6s buttons. It automatically toggles an In/Out point on the clip (versus the entire Timeline) where the playhead is. When you click play, instead of playing the entire Timeline (good in editorial, bad in color correction) only the single shot the playhead is above is shown during playback. At that point you use your next/previous shot buttons, Command (Ctrl) left/right arrows, to switch shots.

Figure 6.68 The second button represents an In/Out point, marking clips perfectly.

The other button that you *may* need to click is found with the play controls (**Figure 6.69**). The button on the far right is the Playback and Loop mode button. It has three states that you can toggle through: a play loop (default choice and best choice), play back and forth, and play once.

Figure 6.69 The Loop button is the one we're focusing on here. Truthfully, you should never be using a play button on any editorial/color correction systems. You have the keyboard for that!

Working with the Viewer

Most of your concerns with the view have to do with being able to zoom in and out to see detail. The bottom right of the screen has a pop-up menu (**Figure 6.70**) with various zoom levels.

Commonly, editors like to use zoom to Fit. But I prefer 50%, so the screen is being perfectly scaled rather than some odd scaling like 57%.

If you have a numeric keypad, the plus and minus keys zoom in and out.

To zoom using the mouse, press Command (Ctrl) and the scroll wheel (a two-finger gesture on a trackpad).

A great toggle is to press Shift+H, which shows the viewer full screen and hides the interface. Either pressing the shortcut again or pressing Esc will return you to the Adobe SpeedGrade interface.

Scope Locations

The three scopes you learned in Adobe Premiere Pro are in SpeedGrade as well along with a fourth—a Histogram. The scopes, particularly the ones you'll use regularly—the Waveform, Vectorscope, and RGB Parade—are initially hidden in Adobe SpeedGrade.

Press the A key to reveal the Analysis panel shown in **Figure 6.71**. It's also the small triangle at the top next to the left edge of the viewer. At the bottom you can choose between one and four scopes. Three is the amount you need, but there's nothing wrong with also seeing the Histogram scope, although it's generally the least-used scope.

Right-click on any scope section to choose which scope you prefer to place in that quadrant.

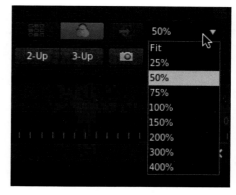

Figure 6.70 The zoom pop-up menu in the viewer.

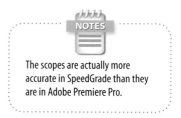

The scopes are actually more accurate in SpeedGrade than they are in Adobe Premiere Pro.

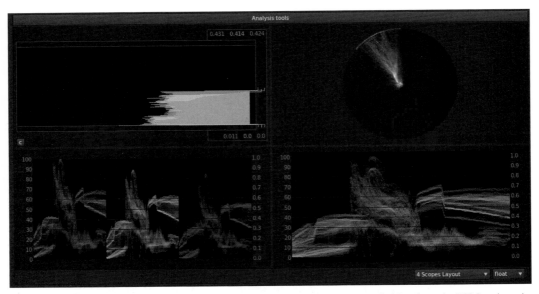

Figure 6.71 Clockwise starting in the upper right the four scopes are the Vectorscope, the Waveform, the RGB Parade, and the Histogram.

Waveform differences

The default display for the Waveform is not luma only but rather a method called *RGB* (which is also known as *Overlay*). It's called RGB because each of the three channels—R, G, and B—are displayed simultaneously.

Some colorists prefer this method, even though it's a little confusing at first. But the advantage is that it's possible to see a color cast by looking at a neutral item and then trying to adjust that section of the Waveform so the Red, Green, and Blue traces are equal, which makes it turn white (**Figure 6.72**).

If you want to turn off RGB, just right-click on the Waveform and choose Switch to Luma. Then it behaves like a Luma only Waveform monitor.

The Waveform scope doesn't read in IRE; instead, it has percentages on the left edge and a numerical setting based on the color space pop-up menu in the bottom-right corner. I suggest you change it to Float (which keeps the highest quality). Then 0 becomes Black and 1 becomes White.

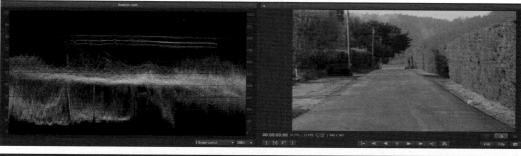

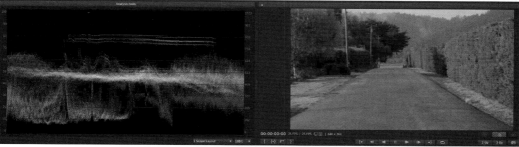

Figure 6.72 The shot on the top is before a correction. The road in the picture should be neutral; it can be found in the center of the waveform at about 50%. There's some excessive blue, which is why the blue information is higher for the road. The shot on the bottom is *after* a midtone correction has been made, reducing the blue. Notice the Waveform on the top is white—because there are equal amounts of Red, Green, and Blue—meaning that the road is now a neutral color.

Vectorscope differences

The Vectorscope (**Figure 6.73**) is very basic, which can make it difficult to tell when you're exceeding safe colors because there are no targets. This also makes it hard to find the "fleshline" between Red and Yellow.

This is a good reason to use the NTSC or PAL safe color Lumetri filter preset in Adobe Premiere Pro that's available with this chapter's media in a folder called Extras. The two .look files were saved from Adobe SpeedGrade.

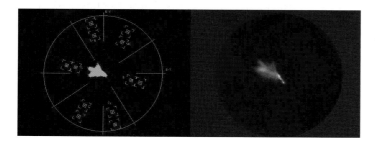

Figure 6.73 A side-by-side comparison of the Adobe Premiere Pro and the Adobe SpeedGrade Vectorscopes.

TIP

If you want to add a broadcast safe layer in Adobe SpeedGrade directly, click the large plus button at the bottom of the Layers area and choose fxLegalizeNTSC or fxLegalizePAL. Make sure it's the last adjustment (in the top of the layer stack).

Figure 6.74 The Layers panel allows you to have multiple layers for complex corrections.

Figure 6.75 Note that each wheel has a reset button on the left (reset luma) and on the right (reset chroma) that will appear *only* if there has been an adjustment.

RGB Parade differences

The only notable difference with the RGB Parade is that the scale on the left and right sides are identical to the Waveform. The left side is in percentages; the right side is based on the color space pop-up menu in the bottom right of the screen (and yes, still leave it at Float).

Primary Corrections

Adobe SpeedGrade doesn't have filters the way Adobe Premiere Pro does; rather, every shot automatically gets a Primary layer.

A Layers panel on the left shows the Primary layer (**Figure 6.74**). Yes, you can have more than one layer as well as specialized secondary layers, but for this minimal guide to SpeedGrade we'll just focus on this one layer.

Note the Reset button. It's the fastest way to reset an entire look. A trashcan is also available to delete a layer that is inactive when there is only a single layer.

How to make a luma adjustment

In Adobe Premiere Pro you adjusted the Input Black point, White point, and the Gamma value while paying attention to the Waveform. You'll work in the same order as you did with the Three-Way Color Corrector effect but you'll notice that the names have changed.

Traditionally, three-way corrections (in any tool) have a luma range where each wheel—usually called Shadows, Midtones, and Highlights—works. Adobe SpeedGrade instead calls them Offset (Shadows), Gamma (Midtones), and Gain (Highlights) as in **Figure 6.75**.

Luma adjustments are performed by clicking on the triangle (**Figure 6.76**) that sits around any of the edges of each color wheel. The adjustment order is Offset (black point), Gain (white point), and then Gamma.

To adjust luma, click the triangle icon on a wheel and drag the mouse left or right in a straight line. Don't drag the mouse in a circle. The farther left or right you drag, the larger the change.

To reset the luma adjustment of any wheel, click the triangle in the lower-left corner.

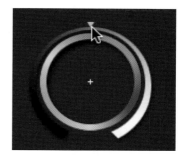

Figure 6.76 The cursor is over the triangle luma adjustment.

Let's try a luma adjustment.

1. In Adobe Premiere Pro, duplicate the sequence called 11 Direct Link to Adobe SpeedGrade. Rename it to whatever you like, and then choose File > Direct Link.

2. Move to the third shot (the first shot of an actor). Above the Timeline click the All button and then the 6s button to make sure you're zoomed in.

3. Press A for the scopes. Adjust the scopes in such a way that they feel comfortable. For these sections I tend to work with a one scope layout for each section, but normally I work with a three scope layout. Remember that you can right-click on any scope and reassign it or reconfigure it if needed.

4. In the viewer, press the Toggle In/Out button; an in/out mark should appear around the clip on the Timeline. From this point on, the best navigation method to use is to press Command (Ctrl) left/right arrows to move from shot to shot.

   Although this is a fairly full-range shot, my intention is to have you *try* using the controls.

5. Adjust the Offset triangle and crush some of the darker areas.

6. Adjust the Gain triangle. Go a little too far until the bright part of the actor's neck hits 100 and then back off until it looks good to you.

TIP

Colorists are always turning the grade on and off, checking before/after versions because their eyes adjust so fast. Clicking the 0 (zero) button turns the grade off while the button is held down.

7. Adjust the Gamma triangle. Try making the shot bright and then try making it a little darker and moodier. You may need to readjust the Offset/Gain wheels based on your Gamma changes.

Just like color grading in Adobe Premiere Pro, color grading in SpeedGrade is a combination of technique and "feel." And if the result looks terrible on your (calibrated) system, reset and try it again.

How to make a chroma adjustment

In Adobe Premiere Pro's Three-Way Color Corrector effect, you made chroma adjustments in *reverse* to luma adjustments. Again, we'll translate that to Adobe SpeedGrade.

To make a quick adjustment, click *anywhere* in the circle, and drag to adjust the chroma. For a virtual trackball, *right-click* in the wheel and move the mouse in the direction of the adjustment; then *right-click again* to accept the adjustment.

First make adjustments in the Gamma color wheel, paying attention to the Vectorscope. Then, examine the RGB Parade and adjust the Gain color wheel and the Offset color wheel.

Let's try an adjustment.

▶ Press Command (Ctrl) right arrow and move down the Timeline until you're at the third to last shot, which is called Road.

▶ Go through the Luma adjustments first by adjusting the Offset, Gain, and then the Gamma triangles.

▶ Based on the Vectorscope and the RGB Parade, the midtones have some extra blue in them. Using the right-click method, click in the middle of the Gamma color wheel, moving away from blue (toward yellow). The road becomes neutralized.

Range controls

If you need finer control, above the color wheels are buttons for Overall, Shadows, Midtones, and Highlights. Adobe SpeedGrade can *further divide* each of these ranges into a series of three ranges of their own, as shown in **Figure 6.77**.

This results in (potentially) nine ranges for minute adjustments. And because you're already familiar with how each wheel works, you can dial in adjustments precisely as needed.

If you want a challenging shot to work with to try the extra ranges, the shot prior to the Road shot, called 00020.mp4, has a severe red cast. Try removing it.

Global controls

Above the color wheels but *below* the ranges are six controls that work on the overall image. These are great for changes that might be complex in other tools that utilize a single slider.

Here's a quick overview of the global controls:

- ▶ **Input Saturation.** This adjusts the saturation before anything else happens on a shot. You'll tend to use it if a shot is too monotone at the start.

- ▶ **Final Saturation.** Whereas the Input Saturation works *before* any adjustments have been made, this adjusts the saturation *after* you've performed a color correction. You'd use this when you're happy with your grade, but you want to pull back or push all the colors in a shot.

- ▶ **Pivot + Contrast.** Yes, I've grouped these together. Contrast adjusts the difference between the lightest and darkest portions of the image. When you increase contrast, brighter pixels move toward white and darker pixels move toward black. The question becomes where should the midpoint be? At 50%? The pivot is the midpoint (default of .5). You usually contrast to make bright areas brighter and dark areas darker, and if you're unhappy with *which* pixels become brighter or darker, you adjust the pivot. Generally, it's better to make a gamma adjustment than a Contrast + Pivot because gamma leaves black/white sections alone.

- ▶ **Temperature.** This allows you to quickly cool down (add blue) or warm up (add orange tones) a shot.

TIP

If you're having a problem with a shot, most often chroma problems occur in the darkest/shadow areas. Using the Shadow tab, think about decreasing the Final Saturation control, essentially removing color in just the darkest regions.

▶ **Magenta.** You can probably skip this control, but this slider is the opposite of the Temperature control. Whereas the Temperature slider goes from Blue to Orange, this goes from Magenta to Green. If you're seeing too much magenta or green in your images, there's usually a white balance problem.

Putting It All Together

Let's look at a shot in Adobe SpeedGrade and walk through the adjustments. This example assumes that you've sent your Timeline to Adobe SpeedGrade from Adobe Premiere Pro.

You'll use the same recipe that you used in the "Three-Way Color Corrector" section earlier in this chapter.

1. Look at the Waveform and adjust the Offset (Black point). Then adjust the Gain (White point). The Gamma is subjective.

2. Looking at the Vectorscope look for the blob to include the center. Adjust the Gamma color wheel to accommodate for that. For the midrange, this is where most of a color cast tends to be visible.

3. Check the RGB Parade. Adjust the Offset wheel to balance/even the amount of color in RGB at the bottom/darkest and the top/brightest areas of the scopes. (Remember that as you approach black or white, you lose chroma.)

4. Look for neutral elements in a shot and make sure they're balanced in the RGB Parade.

Copying a Look from One Shot to Another

To copy the look from the prior shot, hover your mouse over the prior shot and press C. Commonly, you'll want to copy the grade from *two clips* prior to where you are. Why? In most narrative filmmaking, when there is a conversation between two people, you alternate between the two depending on which one is speaking. This is called a *Shot/Reverse* shot (**Figure 6.78**), which describes the pattern of cuts.

Figure 6.78 An example of a Shot/Reverse shot. One set of camera angles is primarily for Actor A and the next shot is for Actor B. This means that *every other shot* is from the same camera setup.

Yes, you could use the hover plus pressing C method. But a *great example* of how well Adobe SpeedGrade is thought out is by demonstrating the Shot/Reverse technique. A full keyboard (with a numeric keypad) is *required* for this. You must use the plus and minus and number keys on the keypad.

Set Adobe SpeedGrade to copy from *prior* shots by pressing Option+ - (Alt+ -). (The opposite, Option++ (Alt++) copies from the *next shot.*)

Press Option (Alt) and a number key to copy the look from the prior/next shot based on the number you press. So, in a Shot/Reverse shot situation where you've graded the first appearance of an actor, you'd move to the next appearance (two shots later) by pressing Option+2 (Alt+2) and *be done.*

If you tried this and ended up with a second playhead, *you didn't use the numeric keypad.* See the section "Adding a second playhead" to find out how to set your system to a single playhead again.

Color Matching

Color matching is super easy; all you have to do is press Command+M (Ctrl+M) to match two clips. But you'll need a *second playhead* (**Figure 6.79** on the next page). The shot you're working will be marked with a 1. The second playhead is marked with a 2.

Color match always matches the *first* playhead to the *second* playhead.

Figure 6.79 Two playheads permit color matching.

Figure 6.80 The buttons to the right of the 2-Up and 3-Up buttons, which look like split screen, change how multiple screens are displayed.

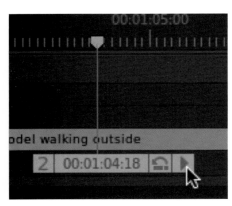

Figure 6.81 This button is a toggle between having playhead 2 "play" or stay in sync with playhead 1.

Adding a second playhead

On the right side of the screen is a button called 2-Up (**Figure 6.80**). Clicking it adds a second playhead to the Timeline and also either creates a split screen or a dual screen interface.

I prefer the dual screen interface where the second viewer appears on the left side of your screen. The viewer acts as a reference and stays in place, allowing you to quickly match several shots to the same reference shot.

The fastest way to create a second playhead is by pressing Option+2 (Alt+2). To go back to one playhead, press Option+1 (Alt+1).

If you want the second playhead to travel with the first, press the stop/play button on the edge of playhead 2 (**Figure 6.81**).

Using the color match function

Once you have two playheads, all you'll have to do to actually use the color match is press Command+M (Ctrl+M) or press the Match look to master playhead button (above the 3-Up button). When you do so, you'll see a new layer called AutoColorMatch (**Figure 6.82**).

If you want to try using AutoColorMatch with the project, you'll find the two shots you matched earlier in the section "Practical Shot Matching" are the last two shots on the Timeline.

Areas I didn't cover

Keep in mind that I've provided just a brief introduction to Adobe SpeedGrade here. It's a fantastic product that is extra useful because of its new workflow.

Some topics were just too deep to cover and keep this section as a "hit the ground running" look at Adobe Speed-Grade. You'll need to investigate the following areas on your own:

▶ **Looks.** Adobe SpeedGrade offers you the ability to save looks and recall looks from its built-in library.

▶ **Layers.** The layers stack on the left side of the screen permits multiple primary and secondary layers. This also allows for variations when clients aren't sure they want a cool or a warm look.

▶ **Secondaries.** Secondaries in Adobe SpeedGrade adjust just portions of the image based on a keyed selection. For example, you might increase the saturation of a sky or grass with a secondary layer.

▶ **Masks.** A mask adjusts part of a layer based on a circular or rectangular shape. Darkening the outside of an oval to create a vignette would be a classic use of a mask.

▶ **Tracking.** When masking, it's common to need to track a region onscreen so a mask follows something moving in the image (such as a person walking through the screen). This way a vignette would follow someone on screen.

Figure 6.82 The AutoColorMatch feature is far easier than matching via scopes (as described earlier in this chapter).

▶ **Keyframes.** Lighting situations change. It's useful to have your color adjustments vary on a single shot (similar to keyframes in Adobe Premiere Pro or Adobe After Effects).

▶ **Snapshots.** Snapshots are a great way to save a particular look for comparison.

Adobe SpeedGrade does so much that I can barely scratch the surface in a book of techniques for Adobe Premiere Pro. But the workflow made it too valuable of an application to ignore!

Exporting Strategies

Author: Jeff I. Greenberg

Give your clients the earliest delivery consistent with quality—whatever the inconvenience to us.

—Arthur C. Nielsen

Exporting Strategies

Once upon a time everyone delivered tapes to their clients. And they put two copies of the tape (usually Betacam or U-Matic tapes) on the shelf for archive. Then file-based HD cameras came along, making it possible to edit without ever owning a deck and renting decks only when absolutely needed. But those rentals became less and less frequent.

Now, it's common to spec out editorial suites without any tape-based acquisition, distribution, or archival. In other words, tape output for 99 percent of us is gone. We're expected to deliver files and be an expert in what our clients need (and want), even though they don't always have the knowledge to communicate these needs.

This chapter provides a basic primer on understanding architectures (buckets) that hold video and the codecs (math) that are used to compress files. Not every codec under the sun is covered—just the most common ones. Also discussed are the most common outputs, including a huge final output for storage, as well as a smaller MP4 h.264 file that is ideal for distribution.

I'll explain how Adobe Premiere Pro compresses video for output via the Media Export command, and I'll cover how to get video out as fast as possible (which is great for client approval copies) along with building our own presets.

Included with Creative Cloud is Adobe Media Encoder (**Figure 7.1**). It's the backend tool that Adobe Premiere Pro uses when it encodes video. It's a multipurpose encoder and has some great time-saving features, including the ability to queue video from Adobe Premiere Pro to efficiently batch video at a convenient time (or in the background). Adobe Media Encoder also can watch specific folders, permitting you to automate encoding.

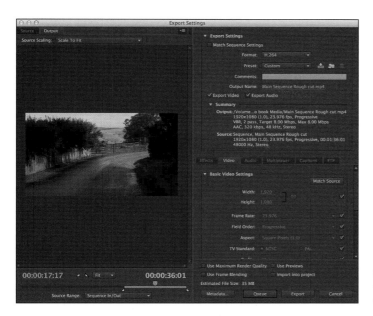

Figure 7.1 Adobe Media Encoder is the compression backend of Adobe Creative Cloud.

Let's get started by getting a primer (or just a refresh) of what architectures and codecs actually mean.

Understanding Architectures and Codecs

Video can come in many different buckets (architectures), such as XDCam, AVCHD, QuickTime, and more. The *architecture* of video, such as QuickTime, is separate from the type of compression (the math) of video, such as h.264. But why do you even need to compress video? Well, because uncompressed standard definition (SD) video requires around 1 GB a minute. Uncompressed high definition (HD) video is about 6 GB a minute *or over a half a terabyte* for a feature length video (**Figure 7.2**).

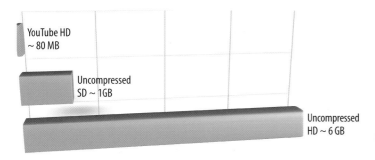

YouTube HD
~ 80 MB

Uncompressed
SD ~ 1GB

Uncompressed
HD ~ 6 GB

Figure 7.2 Uncompressed video has always been unwieldy.

The problem with all video compression is the same; it's a *lossy* compression. Information is discarded like a JPEG file, unlike a lossless compression like a ZIP file. The reason is that these techniques take advantage of the fact that the human eye can "miss" information and the picture looks the same, and partially because you need to be able to decode video in real time or else you wouldn't be able to play it back!

One of the most consistent frustrations in dealing with clients is getting them to identify exactly what it is they want (**Figure 7.3**). But it's not their fault. They're not media professionals (despite their insistence that they know what they're doing!). The job of handling video requires that editors have expertise in the area of deliverables! The only assumption you can make is that clients understand that you're shooting high definition video, either of the 1920 x 1080 variety, called 1080, or the 1280 x 720 variety, called 720 (and don't expect them to know the difference between 1080 and 720).

It's not uncommon to hear a client say:

▶ I'd like a video (and nothing more specific than that).

▶ I need a QuickTime file.

▶ I want it to work on the iPad.

Figure 7.3 Your needs dictate the outputs you must make.

- ▶ I'd like it to work on every device out there.
- ▶ I want to put it on the Internet.

None of these statements works for professional content creators. We need to know more in every case. Let's take a second look at that same list of requests.

- ▶ **I'd like a video (and nothing more specific than that).** It's crucial to find out what clients want and how they intend to play back the video. Knowing that they'd like to play it back from a Blu-ray player requires you to know a minimum of how to use Adobe Encore (and how to install it because it's not directly part of Adobe Creative Cloud), which can produce Blu-ray Discs and DVD and interactive Flash menus plus video.

- ▶ **I need a QuickTime file.** Although this statement describes that the client wants a file using the MOV Apple QuickTime architecture, it doesn't specify which *flavor* (codec) the client needs. There are some 30 plus standard codecs that are in the default QuickTime installation. Which one does your client need? Odds are it's h.264, which has become the defacto *distribution* codec.

- ▶ **I want it to work on the iPad.** The iPad has a very limited set of video formats that work on it; luckily, the presets in Adobe Premiere Pro account specifically for the iPad along with numerous other devices, including Android, TiVo, and the Nook.

- ▶ **I'd like it to work on every device out there.** Sadly, this is impossible. This would require building an infinite set of files to accommodate everything from a cellphone from five years ago to some brand new device, neither of which you own, making it difficult to test. This statement usually means you'll need to provide two or three files that cover most of the devices out there.

- ▶ **I want to put it on the Internet.** Normally, this means I'd like to use YouTube, Vimeo, Brightcove, or another hosting service. It's OK to build a larger file and deal with a long upload because the hosting services generally recompress the footage again. It's less likely (but possible) that the video will be put on your client's website, which will likely mean a file with higher compression (to be sensitive to the client's webhost/data delivery capabilities).

Common Buckets

As mentioned earlier, video can be held in a number of different architectures. It may be easier to think of these architectures as buckets because they contain the video and audio along with other information, such as copyright, timecode, and subtitles (**Figure 7.4**). Not every bucket can carry every type of video or metadata. Some of them are more flexible than others.

Figure 7.4 Each architecture has its own set of rules.

A set of common buckets include:

▶ **QuickTime.** Created by Apple, this is arguably the most flexible architecture. Its greatest advantage is that it has become the most common way to move video between different applications when Dynamic Link (which is restricted to certain Adobe products) isn't available. With its large variety of codecs and metadata, it works well for both archival and distribution needs.

▶ **MPEG-4.** The fourth revision from the Motion Picture Experts Group (MPEG) can contain over 30 different types of data, including two different video codecs, audio, subtitles, and timecode. MP4 was created to be an improvement on MPEG-2. It's more scalable (from small handheld devices through HD and beyond) at a cost of complexity: It needs more processing power to encode/decode quickly.

▶ **Flash.** This key architecture allows video to be contained but has a full-fledged interactive design engine (via Adobe Flash CC) along with a programming language.

▶ **MXF.** The Materials eXchange Format is a SMPTE standard that can contain several different codecs of video and audio along with timecode and other useful metadata. It's a *very common* architecture for file-based cameras from groups like Panasonic and Sony.

▶ **AVI.** Audio Video Interleaved is a Microsoft architecture and hasn't been developed in the last five years. At this time, it's best to avoid creating *new media* in this bucket if possible (although you may be given AVI assets, which Adobe Premiere Pro reads just fine).

Common Codecs

The word codec is short for *co*mpressor / *deco*mpressor (**Figure 7.5**). As mentioned earlier, it's crucial that you compress your video, if nothing else, to reduce the file size compared to the unwieldy uncompressed video.

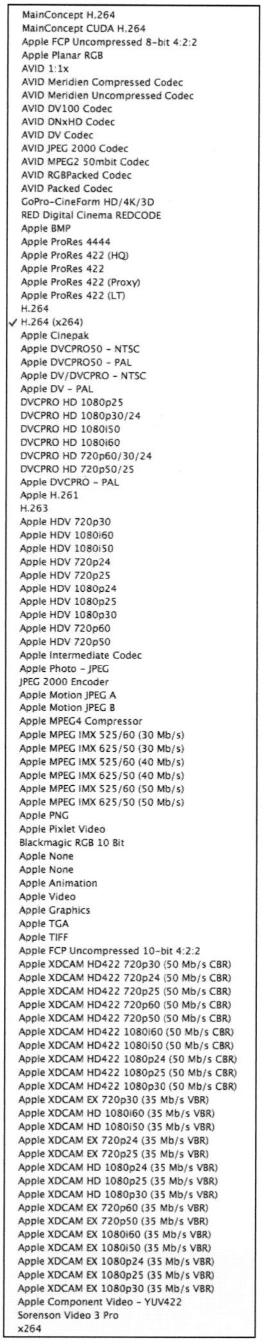

Codecs usually are one of three types:

▶ **Camera based.** These codecs are most often used by camera manufacturers. The goal of the codec is to find a balance between compressing the video for quality versus size on a storage card. XDCam and DVCPro are two camera-based codecs. Generally, the compression math merely compresses a single frame, similar to making a JPEG image; information is *lost*, but the files are still fairly large. A codec that compresses frames individually is called an I-Frame (IntraFrame) codec.

▶ **Post/Archival based.** These codecs are used either for interchange between different postproduction tools or archival uses. The goal here is to preserve quality and possibly carry an alpha (transparency) channel. Avid DNxHD and Apple ProRes are examples of postproduction codecs. Usually, these are I-Frame codecs.

▶ **Distribution based.** Ideally, the goal of distribution codecs is to make the video as small as possible, making it easier to transfer, either over the Internet or over a cable, such as USB. H.264 is a very common distribution codec and is used heavily on mobile devices.

```
MainConcept H.264
MainConcept CUDA H.264
Apple FCP Uncompressed 8-bit 4:2:2
Apple Planar RGB
AVID 1:1x
AVID Meridien Compressed Codec
AVID Meridien Uncompressed Codec
AVID DV100 Codec
AVID DNxHD Codec
AVID DV Codec
AVID JPEG 2000 Codec
AVID MPEG2 50mbit Codec
AVID RGBPacked Codec
AVID Packed Codec
GoPro-CineForm HD/4K/3D
RED Digital Cinema REDCODE
Apple BMP
Apple ProRes 4444
Apple ProRes 422 (HQ)
Apple ProRes 422
Apple ProRes 422 (Proxy)
Apple ProRes 422 (LT)
H.264
✓ H.264 (x264)
Apple Cinepak
Apple DVCPRO50 – NTSC
Apple DVCPRO50 – PAL
Apple DV/DVCPRO – NTSC
Apple DV – PAL
DVCPRO HD 1080p25
DVCPRO HD 1080p30/24
DVCPRO HD 1080i50
DVCPRO HD 1080i60
DVCPRO HD 720p60/30/24
DVCPRO HD 720p50/25
Apple DVCPRO – PAL
Apple H.261
H.263
Apple HDV 720p30
Apple HDV 1080i60
Apple HDV 1080i50
Apple HDV 720p24
Apple HDV 720p25
Apple HDV 1080p24
Apple HDV 1080p25
Apple HDV 1080p30
Apple HDV 720p60
Apple HDV 720p50
Apple Intermediate Codec
Apple Photo – JPEG
JPEG 2000 Encoder
Apple Motion JPEG A
Apple Motion JPEG B
Apple MPEG4 Compressor
Apple MPEG IMX 525/60 (30 Mb/s)
Apple MPEG IMX 625/50 (30 Mb/s)
Apple MPEG IMX 525/60 (40 Mb/s)
Apple MPEG IMX 625/50 (40 Mb/s)
Apple MPEG IMX 525/60 (50 Mb/s)
Apple MPEG IMX 625/50 (50 Mb/s)
Apple PNG
Apple Pixlet Video
Blackmagic RGB 10 Bit
Apple None
Apple None
Apple Animation
Apple Video
Apple Graphics
Apple TGA
Apple TIFF
Apple FCP Uncompressed 10-bit 4:2:2
Apple XDCAM HD422 720p30 (50 Mb/s CBR)
Apple XDCAM HD422 720p24 (50 Mb/s CBR)
Apple XDCAM HD422 720p25 (50 Mb/s CBR)
Apple XDCAM HD422 720p60 (50 Mb/s CBR)
Apple XDCAM HD422 720p50 (50 Mb/s CBR)
Apple XDCAM HD422 1080i60 (50 Mb/s CBR)
Apple XDCAM HD422 1080i50 (50 Mb/s CBR)
Apple XDCAM HD422 1080p24 (50 Mb/s CBR)
Apple XDCAM HD422 1080p25 (50 Mb/s CBR)
Apple XDCAM HD422 1080p30 (50 Mb/s CBR)
Apple XDCAM EX 720p30 (35 Mb/s VBR)
Apple XDCAM HD 1080i60 (35 Mb/s VBR)
Apple XDCAM HD 1080i50 (35 Mb/s VBR)
Apple XDCAM EX 720p24 (35 Mb/s VBR)
Apple XDCAM EX 720p25 (35 Mb/s VBR)
Apple XDCAM HD 1080p24 (35 Mb/s VBR)
Apple XDCAM HD 1080p25 (35 Mb/s VBR)
Apple XDCAM HD 1080p30 (35 Mb/s VBR)
Apple XDCAM EX 720p60 (35 Mb/s VBR)
Apple XDCAM EX 720p50 (35 Mb/s VBR)
Apple XDCAM EX 1080i60 (35 Mb/s VBR)
Apple XDCAM EX 1080i50 (35 Mb/s VBR)
Apple XDCAM EX 1080p24 (35 Mb/s VBR)
Apple XDCAM EX 1080p25 (35 Mb/s VBR)
Apple XDCAM EX 1080p30 (35 Mb/s VBR)
Apple Component Video – YUV422
Sorenson Video 3 Pro
x264
```

Figure 7.5 Knowing the codec is crucial for your media.

Distribution codecs often use a very aggressive type of compression, temporally. Instead of each frame being compressed individually, groups of pictures (GOPs)—usually about 12–15 frames long—are compressed together. The first frame has all the information; the rest of the frames have only the changes since the same full frame. When this series of pictures is 12 frames or longer, it's often referred to as a Long GOP codec.

Some codecs may have hybrid uses; for example, XDCam is used for cameras *and may* be asked for as a distribution output for a playout server for air.

Here is a basic list of codecs you should be aware of:

- ▶ **h.264.** This codec can be in several different architectures, including QuickTime, AVI, F4V (flash), and MPEG-4 (MP4, M4v). Although this codec is the best choice for mobile devices (distribution), it's also found on some cameras.

- ▶ **XDCam.** This codec from Sony is most often found in several different types of cameras in the MXF architecture. These types of MXF files are called OP1a, meaning that all the pieces (video, audio, metadata) compose a single file rather than being split up into multiple files.

- ▶ **DVCPro.** This Panasonic codec ranges from SD as DVCPro 25 (which you may be familiar with because it was also used in mini-DV), DVCPro 50, or DVCPro HD. These codecs are often found on Panasonic cameras that shoot on P2 cards.

- ▶ **AVC IntraFrame.** This codec is an implementation of h.264 by Panasonic, with better quality (at the same data rate) than DVCPro. These codecs can be found on P2 cards.

- ▶ **DNxHD.** This post codec family from Avid was recently added in Adobe Premiere Pro with the CC release. Prior to this you could find it only as a QuickTime implementation. Now it is available in the same architecture in which it's used by Avid—MXF. This codec is the postproduction codec of choice because it's included with Adobe Premiere Pro and is cross platform. There are different data rates depending on need.

- ▶ **Animation.** This post codec has traditionally been used in After Effects to generate video that has an alpha (transparency) channel, making it easy to generate a lower thirds with transparency and providing flexibility in editorial. It's used less and less because of Dynamic Linking with After Effects and because DNxHD (and Apple's ProRes) can be set up to support an alpha channel.

- ▶ **ProRes.** This family of codecs from Apple is very similar to DNxHD; there are various versions at different data rates. Only ProRes 4444 supports an alpha channel.

Getting Output Right

Before outputting your sequence, it's best to do a little preparation to get it right. The idea is to stay organized and avoid confusion. Duplicating your sequence, watermarking (optional), and separating outputs from your current sequence go a long way to keeping your sanity.

There's nothing better than fielding a call from clients asking a question about the file they're looking at and being able to call up that exact sequence quickly.

Duplicate Your Sequence

Duplicate your sequence and name it as explicitly as you can (**Figure 7.6**). There is no such thing as being too specific.

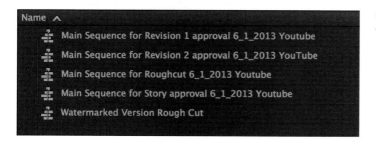

Suggested information should include the minimum of:

- ▶ Type of output (final, story approval, rough cut, etc.)
- ▶ Name of production organization (this would be your company)
- ▶ Date of generation
- ▶ Client name

Data Rates and Codecs

To describe what a codec is doing, you must also know the data rate—the amount of data necessary per second.

Some codecs, such as DNxHD, have fixed data rate sizes, such as DNxHD 36, DNxHD 145, and DNxHD 220. Other codecs, such as h.264, have an adjustable data rate; you can set any value you want.

As a rule, the higher the data rate, the *less compressed* the video is and the larger the file. The lower the data rate, the *more compressed* the video is and the smaller the file.

Here is a quick time-saver: By changing the name of the sequence to reflect the output, the file that Adobe Premiere Pro/Adobe Media Encoder creates automatically gets that name!

Figure 7.6 The more explicit it is, the easier it is to find a particular client copy.

Clip Name and Timecode

It can be advantageous to add extra information to your clips, particularly, naming individual clips and adding timecode information during the review process.

Two Mercury Accelerated effects are available in the Video category of the effects: Clip Name and Timeline:

▶ **Clip Name.** For this effect to work, it must be added to every effect. Clients can then tell you the exact name of a clip that they have comments about.

▶ **Timecode.** This effect can be added either on a nest (like watermarking; see the next section) or on a clip-by-clip basis. When it's placed on a clip, make sure that it shows the original timecode form the source clip.

Watermarking

Professional editors watermark their sequences (**Figure 7.7**). It eliminates clients' confusion of what they're looking at (the most current version) and the reason they're looking at video (rough cut, final approval, etc.). And most important, clients don't get a copy without having paid their final bill!

Figure 7.7 Use descriptive watermarks.

Some compression software has the ability to watermark with a filter. But Adobe Media Encoder doesn't have this ability. As a workaround, you can nest your sequence, and then layer any watermarking (such as a logo or a title) on the nested sequence.

The easiest method of nesting a sequence is basically to drop one sequence into another. Here are more detailed steps:

1. Find the sequence you want to watermark.

2. Create a new sequence, or faster yet, drag your sequence to the New Sequence button at the bottom of the project window. Name it appropriately and add the word watermarked to the sequence name. Open the sequence.

3. Drag your sequence from step 1 into the Timeline. The color of the sequence on the Timeline should be forest, also commonly referred to as green.

4. On V2, add the logo/title of your choice. Drag the title or logo across the entire nested sequence (**Figure 7.8**). Consider lowering the opacity.

Figure 7.8 Your original sequence doesn't have to be nested, but nesting makes it easier to handle as a single unit.

Watermarking Redux

While writing this book Adobe Premiere Pro was updated. Starting with Adobe Premiere Pro CC 7.1 (late 2013 update) Adobe expanded the features of the Effects tab, making the creation of a watermarked nested sequence discussed in the preceding section less necessary.

It's still the best way to create completely custom watermarking, but the new method probably covers the most common needs for most users.

See the section "Effects" later in this chapter to learn how to add the following types of information for output (**Figure 7.9**):

▶ **Image Overlay.** Such as logos.

▶ **Name Overlay.** Such as your company's name or other crucial identifying information (such as "for rough cut approval only")

▶ **Timecode Overlay.** Crucial for client communications of concerns

The advantage of using the Effects tab for output is that the information is quick and easy to add to the footage and can be saved to a setting.

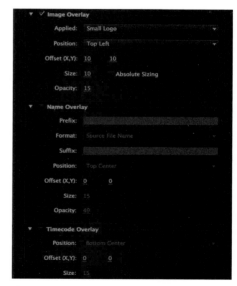

Figure 7.9 The updated Effects tab allows adjustments for client review and more.

TIP

Don't worry about how adding Bars & Tone (or other elements) can affect the output file size. In the Export Media dialog, it's possible to specify the output range and intentionally include or remove this section by selecting the In and Out point on the Timeline of only the material you want to output.

The only downside of utilizing this technique is that you can't see the finished information unless you manually open the outputted file.

Use an Output Bin

Being organized isn't accidental, and very few people are organized naturally. In this respect, you are your own worst enemy. If you don't organize and stay organized, you'll only be penalizing yourself, often at a time of need—when you're trying to identify exactly what you delivered to a client.

To stay organized, you should create a bin called Outputs (**Figure 7.10**).

Figure 7.10 An Output bin specifies exactly what you gave a client. Some projects can have multiple Output bins.

Then when a client calls asking to talk about a specific file you've generated, if you've named it explicitly, you'll have an easier time finding it.

All of your duplicate sequences should be stored in your Output bin(s). Optionally, you can create one or more bins inside your Output bin to group exports. This is particularly helpful if you have to do multiple language or other versioning of output.

Build a Bars & Tone ID Sequence

Every output sequence should have Bars & Tone along with appropriate Title cards, countdown, and other common identifiers for output.

A "best practice" is to build this as a separate sequence and nest it, adding it to your existing Timeline. It's common to make this sequence one minute in length, and it should include:

▶ Bars & Tone for at least five seconds. Choose File > New > Bars & Tone. Unique to Bars & Tone, you can type in a timecode, set an Out point (O), and set any duration you like.

▶ A slate of important information, such as client name, your production company, and any other necessary information, such as job numbers and output date.

▶ A countdown (File > New > Universal Counting Leader) that needs to end on the frame before 1;00;00. The one that Adobe Premiere Pro can automatically build lasts 11 seconds, so it's best to put it at the 49;00;00 mark.

Including all this information results in a Timeline that looks like the one shown in **Figure 7.11**.

TIP

In the ID sequence example, the Bars/Tone/Slate Timeline is exactly one minute in length. When adding it to an existing sequence, it's advisable to back up the start time of the sequence to 23:59:00;00 via the Start Time menu (right-click the name of the sequence on the Timeline tab).

Figure 7.11 The golden rule is to be consistent in using this sequence.

By putting this ID sequence at the beginning of your sequence for output, your output will be set up professionally, and with the Bars & Tone, others looking at the video will have the ability to measure and calibrate their systems.

Common Outputs

At a minimum, output needs at least two files: one to archive and one to deliver to clients. However, there are times when you may need to create three, five, or a dozen (or more!) files for clients. You might output a version for archive (MXF, DNxHD), a version for the client's iPad (MP4, h.264), a version for Vimeo (720 MP4, h.264), and a version for DVD (SD MPEG2).

The two most useful output files include a master "final" output that can be used for archival needs. If in the future other compression needs to be done, it can be done from this "digital master."

The other file is for generic devices (such as Android and iOS) and can be used for upload as well.

The Export Media Dialog

To speed along the series of outputs you'll make, it's a good idea to get a quick overview of some of the features of the Export Media dialog. It is divided into five sections: Preview, Range, Presets, Adjustments, and Fine-tuning (**Figure 7.12**).

Preview

In the Preview section at the top are two tabs: Source and Output.

The Source tab information is what Adobe Premiere Pro passes off to the compression engine (Adobe Media Encoder), whereas the Output tab information is what the compression engine returns before the file is encoded.

The Source tab gives you the ability to crop output (**Figure 7.13**). Generally, it's frowned upon to crop your output because there is no pan and scan ability on this tab (you should have done that on your Timeline). Rather, you can use the crop value to crop out black bars from your video. There's no reason to compress black bars; it's merely wasteful for compression (you'd actually have to compress the black areas!).

Preview   Presets

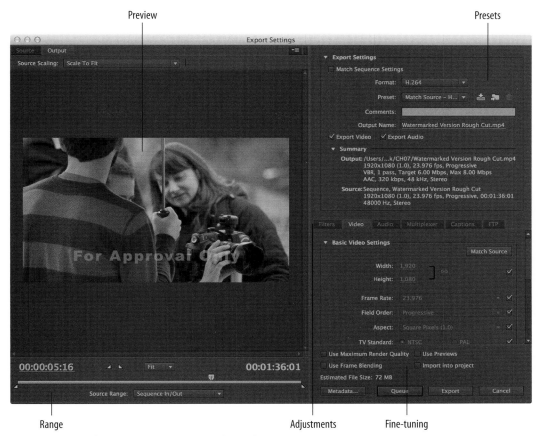

Figure 7.12 These five sections are the key to understanding output.

Figure 7.13 Although cropping is used infrequently, if needed, make sure you match the proportions for your video.

TIP

If you set an In point on the Timeline before you choose Export Media, the custom range will already be active.

The Output tab (**Figure 7.14**) shows the results of any adjustment (such as the Gaussian Blur filter) or any cropping/size changes you make. The main item to look for on this tab is the Source Scaling menu. The choices tell you what happens if you change the scale of the video or crop. Scale to fit is likely the best choice in most situations.

Range

The ability to set the range for part of the video is overlooked by many users. It's possible to use unique In and Out points, customizing which part of the video is outputted/compressed (**Figure 7.15**).

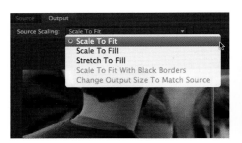

Figure 7.14 The bottom two menu choices appear only if there's a crop.

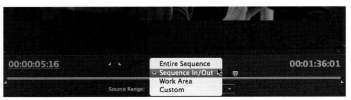

Figure 7.15 Depending on your needs, you can output the sequence just between In and Out points.

Common good practices include adding Bars & Tone along with title slates for output. See the earlier section "Build a Bars & Tone ID Sequence." Setting a custom range permits the sequence to always be treated as a whole, yet allow for selective output (for example, with or without the Bars & Tone).

Presets

Presets are the heart of the Export Media dialog. Selecting a Format and a Preset dictates what will be output. The Summary section provides a quick overview of what will be made and the destination path of where the outputted file will end up (**Figure 7.16**).

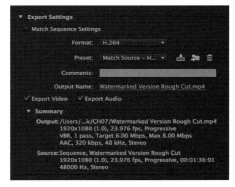

Figure 7.16 Always double-check the Summary before you output.

Adobe has been very comprehensive by including over 450 different output possibilities (not including the ones you build!).

From the Format drop-down menu (**Figure 7.17**) you can choose a file type (such as QuickTime, h.264, or MPEG-2). Then choose a preset from the Preset drop-down menu (**Figure 7.18**), which will vary based on the format you chose.

Optionally, you can save adjustments made in the adjustment tabs (discussed next) for reuse.

NOTES

Selecting the Match Sequence Settings check box causes Adobe Premiere Pro to match the codec that was used for Previews (render files). Using existing Previews creates a faster output at the cost of quality.

TIP

If you adjust anything in a preset, save a new preset and always fill out the comments.

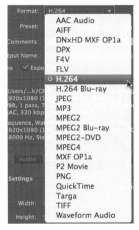

Figure 7.17 Presets range from audio only, still image sequences, and full architectures.

Figure 7.18 Hundreds of presets are prebuilt for easy access.

Figure 7.19 The new Match Source button configures h.264 output faster.

Adjustments

The adjustment tabs allow you to manipulate the output; the most important tab is the Video tab (**Figure 7.19**). On the Video tab you're be able to make any sort of codec adjustments you like, such as sizing, data rate, and color depth (not every adjustment is available for every codec).

Also worth mentioning are the abilities to embed closed-captioning information or to directly FTP video to a server.

Filtering

The initial Adobe Premiere Pro 7.0 release (and earlier releases) permitted only a Gaussian blur to be applied to video.

Starting in version 7.1 (the late 2013 release), the Effects tab becomes far more useful, allowing you to add valuable information for client reviews and other outputs.

Ideally, for client output (**Figure 7.20**), you should add your logo, a name overlay that dictates the *exact* filename, and the timecode, so clients can tell you at what points they have notes or comments for refining your cut.

Figure 7.20 The updated Effects tab permits quick addition of various overlays to watermark output.

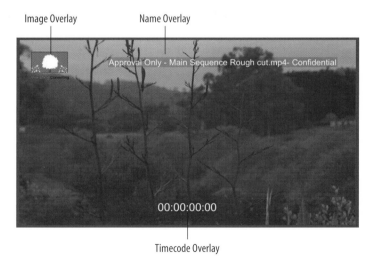

Each overlay has three common adjustments: Size (or scale), a generalized screen placement along with X,Y coordinates for fine-tuning, and an Opacity adjustment.

Let's look at each overlay in greater detail:

▶ **Image Overlay.** The Image Overlay (**Figure 7.21**) brings up a dialog that allows you to select any image file on your system. Commonly, the image will be your logo and will be set fairly small with at least a 50 percent Opacity.

▶ **Name Overlay.** For Name Overlay you'd place a text overlay based on the sequence name (**Figure 7.22**); for example: "Temp Sound for Picture approval." Instead of using the sequence name, a better choice is to use the output filename from the Format menu as a verification that the client is looking at the right file. Additionally, you could add a prefix or suffix, such as "Confidential."

▶ **Timecode Overlay.** Adding timecode (**Figure 7.23**) to the output makes it simple for clients to communicate *exactly* which frame they're looking at.

Figure 7.21 In this case, a file named J Greenberg Logo has been selected, set to the top left, offset 150 pixels to the left and 30 pixels upward at 100 percent opacity.

Figure 7.22 Added as an overlay, is the output filename (Main Sequence Rough Cut) is the prefix "Approval Only –" and the suffix " – Confidential." This has been visually offset in such a way to remain visually appealing on screen, but out of the way.

Figure 7.23 The Timecode Overlay is positioned at the bottom of the output. Using the timecode is the best way for a client to provide precise feedback.

Fine-tuning

At the bottom of the Export Media dialog are several check boxes for fine-tuning that can affect final quality (**Figure 7.24**) and rendering time if used incorrectly:

▶ **Use Maximum Render Quality.** Select this option only if you're doing loads of size conversion with different frame sizes (scaling standard definition up to high definition). Using this option increases render times.

▶ **Use Frame Blending.** It's best to use this option only when you're outputting a different frame rate than the

Figure 7.24 These switches can greatly increase output time.

actual sequence. This check box blends frames together. Plug-ins like Twixtor exist solely for higher-quality retime adjustments.

▶ **Use Previews.** See the sidebar "Adobe Premiere Pro, Preview Files, and Accelerating Output" about the advantages and disadvantages of using the Preview Files that can be created.

▶ **Import into project.** By selecting this option, the media you created is automatically imported back into the project.

Optionally, a Metadata button allows you to add metadata, such as copyright information, to your output videos.

Final Output

When you're finished editing, you should create a storage version of your sequence to put on a shelf (on two separate hard drives or on an LTO [a type of tape backup]) for permanent storage.

Although it is possible and valuable to back up all your files for future changes, it's laborious to have to grab all the assets associated with the project just to create a new output.

So which architecture and which codec will provide the easiest recall and general use? The solution is one of two choices: QuickTime and a Post codec or the new MXF output with the DNxHD codec.

Best Choice? QuickTime and a Post Codec

QuickTime is currently the most common media architecture for postproduction. It works with almost every editorial, compression, and compositing system. Creating a QuickTime file and keeping it for future needs is a very safe choice.

And only a postproduction codec should be used—one that adds minimal compression while having a larger data rate—regardless of camera codecs used. Whichever codec you choose, you'll need to build a custom output that matches your sequence's frame size and frame rate.

Adobe Premiere Pro, Preview Files, and Accelerating Output

Some people call them renders; Adobe calls them Previews. Depending on how powerful your computer is, handling effects, long GOP codecs, and other elements (that traditionally require rendering in other software) may play back in real time without needing to be rendered (**Figure 7.25**).

Those with workflows that have a quick turnaround, such as those in the news industry, may create renders as they work.

So, before you output, consider whether or not you should use your Preview files.

For the *highest quality*, you should *not* use your Preview files. Adobe Premiere Pro will ignore the existing render files and generate final output directly in the codec of choice, ensuring only one compression pass from your Timeline. The downside is a single factor: time. Leaving the Use Previews option deselected will require the maximum amount of time for compression because your system has to calculate these renders along with compression. If heavy rendering is needed, such as when there are many After Effects projects on a Timeline, output time increases.

For a *faster output*, you should render/preview as you work. In the Export Media dialog, select Use Previews. Because rendering will be occurring as you work, you end up with the only workflow being the compression time. The downside is solely quality. The fewer times you compress video, the better; compressing it once for a render/preview and a second time for output impacts the quality of the final compressed file.

For the *fastest output possible*, certain codecs permit Smart Rendering. Smart Rendering permits a copy of existing media when the camera codec, sequence codec, and outputs all match exactly. It was originally for DV and DVCPro formats. The idea was that if your media had straight cuts with no effects, Adobe Premiere Pro would copy the existing media rather than re-encoding your media.

Using Smart Rendering is very fast because it's essentially just copying media—no calculations need to be performed. The method worked because DVCPro was an I-Frame codec. Renders that were also made in DVCPro could be treated as a copy. Adobe Premiere Pro would copy the render file when an effect was added and would copy the original media on unaffected shots.

Editors planning for this type of output would "render as they go" or render during downtime (such as client phone calls, lunch, or overnight). Rendering during downtime can almost be thought of as "leisure rendering".

With renders occurring during the editorial phase, the choice of Smart Rendering codec would be a choice for the fastest output. As of this writing, Smart Rendering has been added for the following formats:

- DV
- DVCProHD
- Long Gop Op1a (XDCam)
- AVCIntraframe (MXF)
- DNxHD (MXF) Op1a
- ProRes (QuickTime)
- DNxHD (QuickTime)

When set up correctly (matching the rendering codec to the media and frame size) and rendering as you edit, output is accelerated between 4 and 12 times depending on the type of footage you're using and the rendered output.

Often, a custom sequence will need to be built that exactly matches the media format. When the sequence is built correctly and rendered during "lesuire" moments, Adobe Premiere Pro produces the fastest possible output.

Figure 7.25 If you render as you work, using Previews results in the fastest output.

NOTES

We've chosen DNxHD for this book, because it's cross platform and Adobe has licensed a form of it (in an MXF architecture). One place that DNxHD cannot be used (at this time) is for footage that is larger than HD sizes. For these, although we'd like to recommend Apple ProRes (Mac specific) or GoPro Cineform (extra purchase), there isn't an easy compressed format that works cross platform.

Common Post codecs available as of June 2013 include:

▶ **Avid DNxHD.** To get this working in Adobe Premiere Pro, you'll need to download and install the DNxHD QuickTime codecs. Depending on which frame rate you're working with, you'll get different DNxHD choices. The safest choice is to choose a large data rate (such as 145, 175, or 220—large meaning less compressed) for your footage. Choose a 10-bit version if your footage was generated from a camera that shot in 10 bits or higher. Uncompressed is always a possibility, but that will result in building a gigantic file.

▶ **Apple ProRes.** Sadly, ProRes is read-only on a Windows machine, meaning it's not truly a cross-platform codec. On a Macintosh, you have to own at least one of Apple's Professional Video Applications to be able to compress to this format. In most cases ProRes 422 (running at 145 mb/s) or ProRes HQ (running at 220mb/s) makes the best choice.

▶ **Third-party codecs.** GoPro Cineform, Lagarith, and others are third-party codecs. Just be aware that you'll need to own and install these on any machine along with QuickTime for playback. All these codecs work in Adobe Premiere Pro.

An example of a DNxHD QuickTime build for an archival file

Let's walk through building a sequence for an archival file. My main sequence (1080p, 23.98) has been duplicated and renamed to reflect its use (which is for archiving).

The system being used already has the DNxHD codecs from Avid installed (available from http://avid.force. com/pkb/articles/en_US/download/Avid-QuickTime-Codecs-LE-2-3-8). Alternatively, on a Macintosh, Apple's ProRes could be an substitute choice, but DNxHD is cross platform. The following example will not work without the DNxHD codec installed.

1. With the sequence selected, choose File > Export > Media.

2. From the Format menu, choose QuickTime, which leaves you with a very short list of prebuilt settings (**Figure 7.26**).

Figure 7.26 There aren't many QuickTime presets.

Because you'll have to build our own, the best choice is to always start off as close as possible to what you need. The starting point could be any of the HD choices (1080 25p is closest to 1080p 23.98) for this sequence. I chose the Watermarked Version Rough Cut from the project.

3. On the Video tab, adjust the codec, and check the frame size and frame rate.

Adjusting the codec to Avid DNxHD causes the Codec Settings button to become active (**Figure 7.27**).

4. Click the Codec Settings button to yield the Configuration dialog.

5. For Color Levels, the best choice is 709. This is a flag that dictates how other software interprets the Luma levels. The 709 option means that the outputted file is using the full HD gamut.

6. For Alpha, choose whether or not you want there to be an alpha channel (you probably don't want this). In After Effects you would choose to have an alpha channel, but in editorial it is less likely.

7. Choose the appropriate DNxHD resolution with the goal of matching your footage. In this case, it's 1080p, the frame rate is 23.98, 175 (megabits per second, the least compressed of the choices), and 8 bit (because the video was shot with an 8 bit camera).

With the codec set correctly (**Figure 7.28**), you then need to match the settings on the Video tab.

8. Leave the Quality slider where it is because moving it will make no difference.

9. Make sure the Width and the Height are set to 1920 x 1080, the Frame Rate is 23.976, the Field Order is Progressive, and the Aspect is Square Pixels (1.0). **Figure 7.29** shows the correct settings that match the sequence.

10. Save this preset. Because the Codec Settings and the Video tab match the sequence, it's likely you'll reuse it often.

Figure 7.27 Some codecs, such as DNxHD, will not allow any adjustments directly in Adobe Premiere Pro. You'll need to click the Codec Settings button.

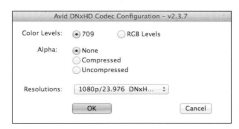

Figure 7.28 These setting are correct for this sequence. Your sequence settings will dictate your choices.

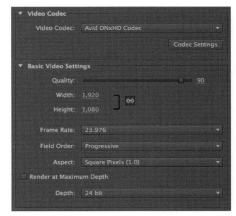

Figure 7.29 QuickTime requires you to match any codec adjustments made in the codec dialog a second time in Adobe Premiere Pro.

TIP

You can generally leave Render at Maximum Depth deselected unless you're working in a 10 bit or higher format, such as the RED Camera, Black Magic Cinema Camera, or Alexa Camera. Because these cameras shoot higher than 10 bit, it's best to choose the highest values to preserve as much of the color information as possible.

TIP

Although Adobe Premiere Pro can't export custom settings, Adobe Media Encoder can! Open the Adobe Media Encoder to save settings to put on other systems.

Figure 7.30 Saving settings saves your sanity.

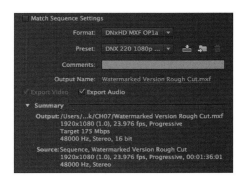

Figure 7.31 The result will be a single MXF file with DNxHD compression.

11. Click the icon to the right of the Preset setting (**Figure 7.30**) to name the setting.

It's valuable to add as much information to the setting as possible. In this case, I named it **Archival DNxHD 175 1080p 23.98 709 color space**. Add any comments as you see fit.

12. Click Export.

New in Creative Cloud: MXF DNxHD OP1a

MXF DNxHD OP1a is new in the Creative Cloud release of Adobe Premiere Pro. Adobe specifically heard the complaint from users that there was a lack of a postproduction, cross-platform SMPTE standards and licensed a way to output as such.

The sole warning about generating these files is to check which other tools in your chain need to be able to read them. Although the Adobe CC products can read these files, third-party tools are not guaranteed to do so. Also, because MXF DNxHD OP1a is a new choice, it's recommended that you test your existing needs before adopting it.

An example of a DNxHD archival build (MXF)

The MXF version of DNxHD is quite a bit easier to build than a QuickTime output, because Adobe has built a preset for your needs.

1. Choose File > Export > Media, and then choose DNxHD MXF OP1a.

2. From the Preset menu, choose DNX 220 1080p 23.98. If you're working with 10-bit video, choose DNX 220x (**Figure 7.31**).

3. Click Export or Queue.

h.264 Distribution Outputs

When it comes to distribution, aggressive choices can be made in compression. Should you sacrifice file quality for speed of output? Will the client have the codecs necessary for playback (no post production codecs here!)?

The goal is always to get a file out that is ideal for the target use, such as embedding in Microsoft PowerPoint. And the most frequent output file right now is h.264 in an MP4 architecture.

h.264 is fantastic for mobile devices and uploading to on-line hosting, and the smaller sizes can deliver decent quality output. These files have adjustable data rates (bitrates). By making the data rate larger, you'll get a larger file and generally a higher quality file. But that doesn't mean that choice is necessarily right for you!

Here are two instances in which h.264 *should not be used:*

▸ **DVDs.** MPEG-2 files are the only type of video that works on a DVD (this is different for Blu-ray where h.264 is fine.)

▸ **Playout servers.** These devices have specific needs; feeding them the wrong architecture or codec will not work. They vary through multiple formats, such as MPEG-2 Transport streams, P2 DVCPro files, XDCam OP1a MXF files, and so on.

Getting Video Out Fast (CBR h.264)

When you're working with a client in the room, it's a great idea to be able to export a file that is small, yet can be output quickly. But you have to be willing to sacrifice quality—meaning the resulting file may look crunchy/have artifacts—to improve speed of output.

As an example, let's work with an MP4 h.264 output and give it an "OK" data rate, but the crucial part is choosing a constant bit rate (CBR) with no analysis versus a variable bit rate (VBR) that takes longer to render because of the analysis needed. This setting will be the fastest encode based on your system specs.

TIP

Generally, it's best to Queue your work and later start Adobe Media Encoder and perform the compression there. Adobe Media Encoder can compress in the background, leaving you free to continue editing. If you click the Export button, it'll tie up Adobe Premiere Pro.

NOTES

Making sure you're clear about what deliverables your client needs first and testing that you can output correctly will solve 99 percent of the headaches that usually accompany deliverables.

In this example, the output will source from a 1080p 23.98 sequence.

Select and duplicate the sequence you intend to output, and add watermarking or other elements as you see fit.

Now, let's create a quick CBR output for a client.

1. Choose File > Export > Media.

2. Choose h.264 from the Format drop-down menu.

3. Choose Match Source – High bitrate to provide a good starting point.

4. On the Video tab, scroll down to the Bitrate Settings. Change the setting from VBR 1-pass to CBR. Change the Bitrate to 20, effectively tripling how much data is given to the picture. This will triple the file size compared to the original setting but still produce a small file with no analysis needed.

5. Select Use Previews. If you've been rendering your previews, you'll get an even faster output.

6. Optionally, save this preset as **CBR Client review** for faster recall in the future.

Figure 7.32 shows a finished version.

Figure 7.32 Note that little has changed beyond the CBR choice.

A Multipurpose h.264

It's time-consuming to build multiple similar outputs, especially when by making the right choices one output could serve multiple uses.

The panacea of a single file output is impossible because there are too many different devices currently on the market. But what if you could design an output to target a large majority of these devices? It might be worth sacrificing a little quality (nothing bigger than 720) for your output. And what if the same file could be used for upload to sites like YouTube and Vimeo? And what if the same file could also be embedded in PowerPoint (post 2008)?

Then you'd have one file that could handle multiple uses—a truly flexible choice.

Adjusting settings

So, to build an h.264 output, you want a file that matches the following criteria:

▶ **MP4 h.264.** This will embed in PowerPoint, cross platform.

▶ **1280 x 720.** Yes, it's a compromise but only if you're shooting 1080. By scaling the footage downward, it's still high definition and will look decent on computer screens, tablets, and phones.

▶ **Maximum hardware compatibility.** See the Note on h.264 Profile + Levels.

▶ **Frame rate.** It's crucial that you match your frame rate.

▶ **Compression.** You know the file will possibly be recompressed by an online host. The data rate that most hosts use for 720 content is around 4–5 mb/s. So, it's best to at *least double* that to provide some room for the recompression.

▶ **Highest quality.** You want to do whatever calculations are necessary for the highest quality file. A VBR 2-pass file will take longer to render but provides the best compression.

To create a multipurpose setting, follow these steps.

1. Choose File > Export > Media.

2. Choose h.264 from the Format menu.

3. Choose Match Source, High bitrate. Yes, you could dial in a closer match, but this list is full of presets!

4. Deselect Profile, deselect Level, and set level to 3.2. By doing so, you need to reset the scale to 1280 x 720 (and unlock the chain next to the sizing); the frame rate changes. Change your frame rate to match your sequence settings.

5. Change the frame rate back to 23.976.

6. Change the bitrate to VBR-2 pass. Let's favor quality!

NOTES

Although there is a category called MPEG-4 in Adobe Premiere Pro, it's really the combination of architecture plus codec optimized for older mobile devices. MP4 formats that utilize the h.264 codec are found under the h.264 format.

NOTES

The Profile + Level choices on the Video encoding tab are shortcuts for hardware maximums—size, data rate, and more. This information is much easier to check as a reference than having to spell out the specifications for every device. Level 3.2 is the lowest level that supports 720 video.

VBR compression is aggressive; not every frame has all the information. For this reason there are two numbers: the average and the amount to vary. Some frames only have the changes since the last full frame. This keyframe setting requires less full frames and allows the codec to vary more—leading to more efficient compression at the cost of complexity and taking longer to compress and decompress.

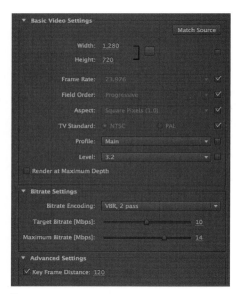

Figure 7.33 This HD preset works in many different places—on computers, all iOS devices, many android devices, and in Microsoft PowerPoint.

7. Take the Target bitrate up to 10 mb/s. Change the Maximum to 14 to permit the bitrate to vary as needed, giving more data for complex frames (fast motion and lots of detail) by stealing data from simpler ones (talking heads). If you were using a 1080 preset, you'd take the Target to 15 mb/s and the Maximum to 20.

8. Change the Key Frame distance to 120 to force a full frame every five seconds.

9. Save this preset. Name it **Multipurpose 720 23.976** (or whichever frame rate you chose).

Figure 7.33 shows a finished version of the preset.

Smart Compression Tips

Infinite sets of adjustments can be made in Adobe Premiere Pro. Just take a look at all the ones it ships with! Because it'd be impossible to cover all of them in a book, much less a chapter, the following list of suggestions might provide some guidance:

▶ **Avoid creating from scratch.** Always start from a setting *near* to what you're trying to build.

▶ **Keep h.264 as MP4 files.** Although other architectures can contain h.264, MP4 ends up being the most flexible container.

▶ **Avoid large bitrates when possible.** Larger data rates (bitrate) mean larger files.

▶ **Choose CBR for speed.** VBR builds better-looking compression at the expense of time.

▶ **Use short ranges for testing.** A short Source Range can be used for easy testing. Compress 30 to 60 seconds of a file to check the output rather than the entire piece. Is it the quality that you want? Many tests can be done quickly when you utilize this feature.

▶ **Always check specifications.** If the file is meant to play back on a hardware device, it has specifications. Pay attention to them.

Outputting a Still Frame

Although you haven't really used Adobe Premiere Pro's flexible Export outputs, it may be necessary to be able to output individual stills quickly. Often, DVD menus, website stills, or product design art for packaging need high-quality stills. In SD, the screen size is too small at 720 x 480, but in HD you can get a large enough still that will print decently at around 2 megapixels—not fantastic, but usable.

Exporting a still is straightforward. You can click the Export Frame button (**Figure 7.34**) on the bottom of both the Source and Program monitors, or press Shift+E.

The dialog (**Figure 7.35**) that appears permits you to choose the type of still you want. Here's a quick list of the ideal uses of the different file types:

▶ **DPX.** The Digital Picture Exchange format is an uncompressed file, but it's optimized for other postproduction tools, such as Adobe SpeedGrade.

▶ **JPEG.** The Joint Photograph Expert Group format is compressed, meaning it's great for transmission over the Internet and email but is less decent for print or other postproduction uses. With JPEG you have no ability to adjust the compression.

▶ **PNG.** The Portable Network Graphic format, like JPEG, is compressed but less compressed than JPEG. It's advantage is that it can carry an alpha channel (JPEG cannot).

▶ **Targa.** Targa is an uncompressed format and is often used in 3D modeling software.

▶ **TIFF.** The Tagged Image Foto Format is uncompressed (but other software like Adobe Photoshop can output compressed versions). It's ideal for print and other photographic uses.

Figure 7.34 The screen shot icon works in the Program Monitor and the Source Monitor.

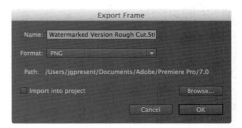

Figure 7.35 There is an option to import the still directly back into the project.

Multiple Stills

There is no easy automated way to obtain multiple stills from Adobe Premiere Pro. But at least the task can be performed faster using a four-step method.

1. Add markers to any frames you want to export. The keyboard shortcut is M for marker.

2. When all the frames are marked, go to the beginning of your sequence. Press Shift+M to move to the next Marker.

3. Press Shift+E to export the still. Choose your destination drive and format.

4. Press Return. (This often-missed, common shortcut is like clicking the OK button.)

Then all you need to do is repeat the preceding steps for each still. Press Shift+M for the next marker, press Shift+E for the next export, and then press the Return key. Adobe Premiere Pro increments each still as filename.Still001, filename.Still002, and so on.

Queue Button

Figure 7.36 Any default button, like Queue, can be clicked by pressing the Return key.

In the Export Media dialog, the Queue button may very well be the most important button, which is why it defaults to selected (**Figure 7.36.**)

How you choose to work is a question of time management; you have three choices available:

▶ **Click the Export button.** Adobe Premiere Pro will tie up all of your resources and compress your file utilizing Adobe Media Encoder in the background (headless). Just walk away from your system and let it do its job.

▶ **Click the Queue button and keep working.** This passes your sequence plus settings to Adobe Media Encoder (which launches in the background). If you start the compression in Adobe Media Encoder, you can compress *in the background* while you continue to do other work. This workflow is slightly slower than clicking the Export button but frees up Adobe Premiere Pro to do other tasks.

▶ **Click the Queue button plus batch encoding.** This passes your sequence plus settings to Adobe Media

Encoder. You can continue to work or make other adjustments in Adobe Media Encoder, such as render multiple outputs. This option allows you to continue working and choose when to compress multiple files (batch) during downtime, such as at the end of day.

When should you use each option? If the client is in the room, click Export. If the client is coming later in the day, click Queue and keep working. If there are two or more compression jobs that need to be taken care of, click Queue and batch encode.

Adobe Media Encoder

Adobe Premiere Pro really doesn't do any of your compression. It's done by Adobe Media Encoder. When you click the Export button in Adobe Premiere Pro, it launches a "headless" version of Adobe Media Encoder.

You can also launch Adobe Media Encoder independently of Adobe Premiere Pro. Aside from compression, it has some additional workflow capabilities, including powerful watch folders. Watch folders monitor a specific folder on your drives (preferably a media drive) for content and then compress that content (and possibly upload it) automatically.

Custom settings created in Adobe Media Encoder are shared by Adobe Premiere Pro and Adobe Prelude.

Overview of Adobe Media Encoder

Adobe Media Encoder has four panels devoted to compression (**Figure 7.37** on the next page): Queue, Presets, Encoding, and Watch Folders.

A source in the Queue (or Watch Folder) gets compressed by a setting chosen from the Preset Browser. During compression the status column changes to a progress gauge until the compression is complete. While the source is being compressed, the Encoding panel shows the progress of the compression.

To start compression, click the green Play button in the upper-right corner of the Queue window.

Queue

Presets

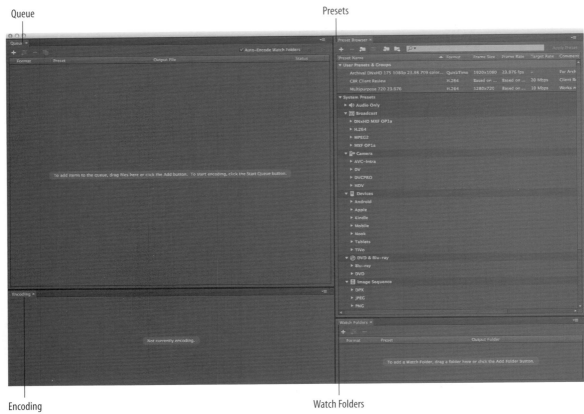

Encoding

Watch Folders

Figure 7.37 The interface has four quadrants: Queue, Encoding, Presets, and Watch Folders.

Queue

The Queue panel begins the compression process. Adobe Media Encoder can compress three types of sources:

▶ **Video media, such as QuickTime files.** Choose File > Add Source. Alternatively, you can press Command+I (Ctrl+I).

▶ **Sequences from Adobe Premiere Pro.** The most common way that sequences appear in the compression queue is by clicking the Queue button in Adobe Premiere Pro. The menu choice has the ability to *import a sequence from a closed project.*

▶ **Compositions from Adobe After Effects.** Although After Effects can generate its own outputs, doing so in Adobe Media Encoder permits easier building of multiple outputs—and as a bonus, in the background.

You read the Queue horizontally. For example, in **Figure 7.38** a source, Watermarked Version Rough Cut, will be compressed in the format DNxHD MXF OP1a using the codec DNX 220 1080p23.976 to the Output file Watermarked Version Rough Cut.mp4.

Figure 7.38 Outputs by default are stored with the original files.

Multiple outputs

When a source entry has multiple outputs, multiple files will be compressed simultaneously. Each source entry will be compressed one after the next until all are finished or one fails and has an error.

To add an output, click on the source, and choose File > Add Output (or click the Add Output button; **Figure 7.39**).

Figure 7.39 The Add Output button is located in the upper-left corner.

TIP

Make sure you have an explicit naming system in place. Opening a project and deciding which file you need among Sequence 01, Sequence 02, or Sequence 03 is difficult (or impossible). By having named the sequences (or After Effect compositions) meaningfully, using Adobe Media Encoder will be easier.

TIP

It's possible to right-click on a source and reset its status, making it easy to perform the compression a second time and make quick changes to try to improve the compression.

Encoding

During an encode, the Output Preview area (**Figure 7.40**) shows each output thumbnail while it's compressing. The thumbnail displays the elapsed time, the remaining time, and a preview of the compression.

Figure 7.40 Three outputs are being compressed simultaneously.

Preset Browser

In the Preset Browser are some 450 plus presets (**Figure 7.41**) that cover broadcast needs, phones, tablets, readers, and optical media, among others.

With so many presets, it's easy to become overwhelmed by the sheer number and variety of choices. The fastest way to find a preset is to type the intended end use into the search box.

Even with all of these choices, note that many were designed for an average need. Therefore, many presets could be refined further, perhaps by lowering the data rate (for smaller files) or increasing the data rate (for larger files). Selecting any preset and clicking the Settings button reveals the Settings dialog where you can make adjustments. See the section "Mastering Presets and Settings" later in the chapter.

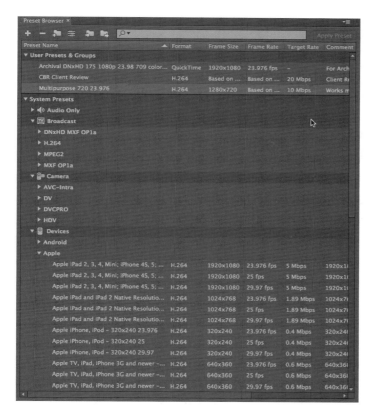

Figure 7.41 Don't forget the search box at the top to find presets easier!

Watch Folders

The Watch Folders panel (**Figure 7.42**) is conceptually identical to the Queue panel.

Figure 7.42 Once set up, watch folders "watch" for new media to be compressed automatically.

In the Queue panel, compression occurs on a source, such as a sequence. In the Watch Folders panel, compression occurs by looking inside a folder on your storage drive for media (such as QuickTime files).

Watch folders are the cornerstone to automation, because they allow the monitoring and compression of anything that gets added to a folder with zero user input.

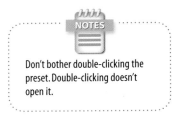

Mastering Presets and Settings

Presets (made up of different settings) are the heart of Adobe Media Encoder. These are similar to the choices in Adobe Premiere Pro but are listed a little differently. Rather than by architecture, they are listed by usage, such as for a device.

It's not enough to just be able to find and use presets; it's important to be able to adjust them for your particular needs.

For example, the DVD presets generally do a fine job until you want to author more than 100 minutes of video on a single-sided DVD-5. At that point, the data rate must be lowered to produce a file small enough to fit on the DVD.

Managing Presets

What makes one preset different from another? What sort of switches and adjustments are available? Adjusting the presets is what provides nuanced control in compression. Building your own and grouping common presets can make the handling and management of the presets easier to work with.

Figure 7.43 From left to right the icons in the Preset Browser include Add a Preset, Remove a Preset, Add a Group, Edit Settings, Import and Export.

Being able to organize (**Figure 7.43**) presets makes it easy to find a specific setting for output.

Viewing created presets

Hovering over a preset shows a summary of what the preset does. This is a quick way to see the comments about a preset (a deeper description of what the preset is for).

To actually see the controls for adjusting a preset, with a preset selected, either click the Settings button at the top or right-click and choose Preset Settings.

Exporting/Importing

Just like backing up projects, you should save any custom presets you create for future needs and to use on other systems that have Adobe Media Encoder installed. It's common in multiple editor facilities to copy (export/import) these presets to everyone's systems.

To export settings, select the settings you want to send out and click the Export Settings icon (the folder with an arrow on the *right side*).

To import settings, select the settings you want on the Adobe Media Encoder copy you're working with and click the Import Settings icon (the folder with the arrow on the *left side*). You'll get the chance to browse to the location of previously saved settings.

Creating a group (custom folder)

As you make and adjust more and more presets, it's valuable to group them together in a folder so you don't have to search for them constantly. Here are a few useful groupings:

▶ **Common outputs.** If it's probable for you to always output the same outputs, there's no need to search all the presets. Having the common presets that you use grouped together lessens the likelihood of making a mistake.

▶ **Client based.** If you're handcrafting each compression, it pays to group the custom presets, making it fast and easy to rebuild what worked most efficiently.

▶ **Output type.** Organize your presets by type, such as h.264, MPEG-2, Archival, and Device. Building a small subset of the numerous outputs provided, again, makes finding the most useful presets easy.

Creating an alias

Aliases are just pointers; they behave exactly like they do in your operating system. In Windows they're called *shortcuts* and in OS X they're called *aliases*.

If you're duplicating a preset just to have it live in two spots (such as in the h.264 group that is included by default and the common output group that you build), it makes more sense to use an alias.

A good rule of thumb is to duplicate a preset if you want to make changes to it, but create an alias if you want the same preset to live in two places.

TIP

Build a group before you import presets. With a custom group selected, Adobe Media Encoder will import directly to the group.

Understanding Presets

When you're examining presets, it's easy to get overwhelmed. The Preset Settings dialog is almost identical to the Export Settings dialog in Adobe Premiere Pro (**Figure 7.44**).

The same five tabs exist in the Export Media dialog: Filters, Video, Audio, Captions, and FTP.

See the section "The Export Media Dialog" earlier in this chapter for details about the options.

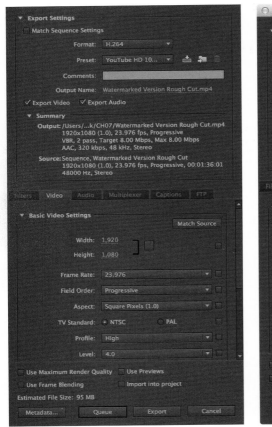
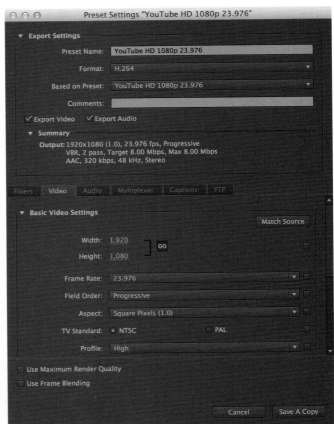

Figure 7.44 The Adobe Premiere Pro Export Settings dialog (left) compared to the Adobe Media Encoder Preset Settings dialog. They are the same, but in two different applications.

More Custom Settings

Three settings were created earlier in this chapter: an Archival QT DNxHD output, a CBR Client Review, and a Multipurpose h.264. In this section, you'll build several more settings to show you the flexibility of Adobe Media Encoder.

Building a preset for two hours on a DVD

Because DVDs have fixed sizes (DVD-5 = 4.3 GB, DVD-9 = 8.6 GB), you need to lower the data rate to accommodate more footage.

The Adobe preset you'll build for taking footage to a DVD needs to be limited in time to approximately 90 minutes.

By lowering the data rate value, you can store more footage on the DVD (resulting in more compression). The adjustments shown in **Figure 7.45** allow a DVD-5 to store 150 minutes of content.

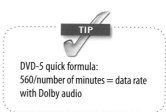

TIP

DVD-5 quick formula:
560/number of minutes = data rate with Dolby audio

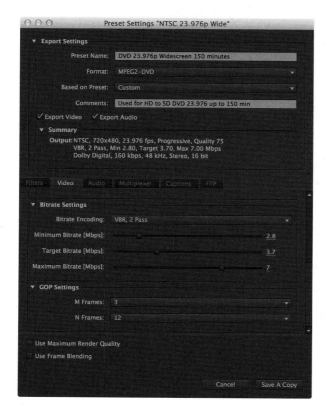

Figure 7.45 Lowering the data rate allows more footage to be stored on a DVD.

1. Open the NTSC (or PAL if your standard is PAL) widescreen setting.

2. On the Video tab, adjust the Target Bitrate to 3.7 to compress the video more aggressively.

3. Adjust the Bitrate encoding to VBR, 2 Pass. As you get more aggressive, more analysis should occur.

4. On the Audio tab, change the Audio format from PCM to Dolby Digital, which is a type of compressed, high-quality audio (see the Tip that gives you the DVD-5 formula).

5. Adjust the Bitrate to 160.

6. Save this preset as a copy called **DVD 23.976p Widescreen 150 minutes**.

Building a custom preset for Flash self-hosting

Flash video is still heavily used on the web, and although there are some great presets for it, there could be one more.

The biggest hassle in hosting your own material is finding a mix of decent quality versus data demands. There are two sets of HD settings in Adobe Media Encoder, a set of 1080 and a set of 720, which match shooting sizes.

Currently, most end users' monitors are less than 1920 x 1080. So what if you choose a custom size that is larger than SD footage (and therefore HD) with a lower data rate demand than HD, meaning easier hosting? The web (where Flash content is viewed) doesn't have any standards; for example, there is a 1024 x 576 preset that does not match any broadcast standard. A more efficient scale is exactly half of 1920 x 1080 – 960 x 545 (**Figure 7.46**). Because you've reduced the picture into a quarter of the information, you can do the same for the data rate.

Looking at the original data rate of 5,500 kilobits per second, you can reduce that number to 1,100 kb/s.

1. Under the Flash preset is a setting called Web – 1920x1080, 16x9, Project Framerate, 5500kbs. Open the F4V version of this setting (F4V is h.264 in a Flash architecture).

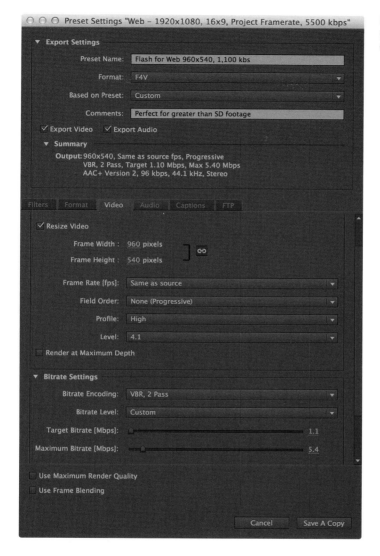

Figure 7.46 **Figure 7.46** Technically, 960 x 545 is greater than SD sizes, making it a type of HD.

2. Change the width and height to 960 x 540.

3. Change the Bitrate to 1.1 Megabits per second.

4. If output is going on a Flash *streaming* server, the bitrate encoding *must* be set to CBR. Otherwise, use VBR 1-pass for higher quality.

5. Change the level to 3.2 to provide maximal compatibility for the h.264 file with hardware devices at this size.

6. Save a copy as **Flash for Web 960x545, 1,100 kbs**.

7. Optionally, add FTP information to automatically upload it to a web server.

Building a custom preset for online hosting

Nearly identical to the preceding preset would be an h.264 preset that is a decent size for self-hosting. Generally, for self-hosting, a data rate around 1 mb/s works for all but the slowest connections. Yes, there are advantages to using services like YouTube and Vimeo, but they both recompress uploads.

You'll use the YouTube preset that matches the frame rate and then reset the size and data rate. In this case, it'll be the 1080p 23.976 setting (**Figure 7.47**).

1. Choose Web Video > Youtube settings, find the Youtube HD 1080p 23.976 setting, and open the setting.

2. On the Video Tab, change the Level to 3.2. This is the lowest level (and therefore higher compatibility) that supports your needs.

3. Unlock the chain for Width and Height, and set the values to 960 x 540.

4. Change the Frame Rate to match your footage by selecting the check box to Match Source.

5. Make sure the Bitrate encoding is set to VBR, 2 pass.

6. Adjust the Target Bitrate to 1.1 and adjust the Maximum to 2. This permits the bitrate to actually "vary" from the target value.

7. On the Audio tab, change the Bitrate setting to 128 to make the audio even smaller and still sound decent.

8. Save a copy as **Self hosting 960x545 1,100 kbs**.

9. Optionally, add FTP information to automatically upload it to a web server.

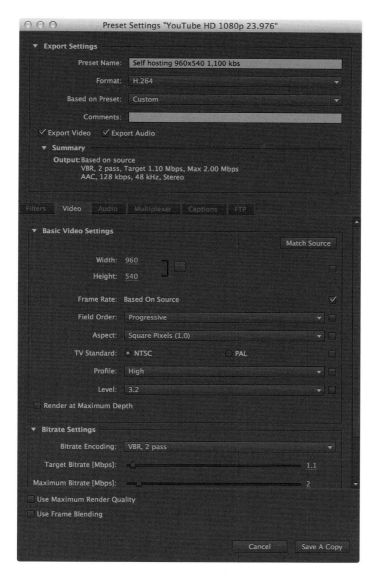

Figure 7.47 This preset works great on all but the largest screens; it's a good trade-off between size and demands for self-hosting.

Automating Adobe Media Encoder

Adobe Media Encoder helps your workflow even further by automating repetitive tasks. From simple preference adjustments to the use of watch folders, automation is the key to making your life more efficient!

Preference Adjustments

Well-designed preferences should be perfect for novices. Advanced users usually need to tweak a couple of areas to improve the user experience. You'll do some tweaking in the following sections.

Turning on the Automatic Encoding preference

In the General category is a option to "Start queue automatically when idle for 2.0 minutes." This is off by default, but turning it on allows you to click the Queue button in Adobe Premiere Pro, and after two minutes (**Figure 7.48**), Adobe Media Encoder will automatically start encoding.

Figure 7.48 Adobe Media Encoder can be set to automatically encode after a pre-set period of time.

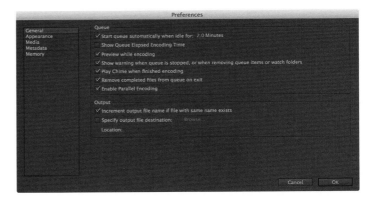

You might want to increase this number to give yourself more time to either make adjustments in Adobe Media Encoder or to cancel the job (in case you make a mistake). I set this number to 10 minutes.

Specify Output File Destination

By default, Adobe Media Encoder saves the encoded file next to the original. By selecting Specify Output File Destination, all encoding files can be saved to another destination, such as to an encode folder (**Figure 7.49**) somewhere on your system.

Turning on this preference doesn't work well for everyone. Using this preference should infer that it's twice as important to make sure you use a good naming system because encoded files from different projects will all end up at the specified location.

Appearance

Because all the Adobe CC tools ship with the same dark gray interface, it's possible to accidentally make an adjustment in the wrong application when multiple Adobe applications are open. Consider making the appearance of Adobe Media Encoder very bright to remind yourself that you're outputting files.

Metadata

Although it's possible and even advisable to add metadata to files, only software that reads XMP (eXtensible Metadata Platform) can read this information (all of the Adobe tools can read metadata). When you work with file types that cannot embed metadata, the Adobe tools will add sidecar files, which are files that exist to the "side" of the actual file.

Inputting metadata in Adobe Media Encoder's Preferences adds it to every output. If you want to add it to selective outputs, add the metadata in Adobe Premiere Pro instead.

Building a Watch Folder

Watch folders are OS level folders that are monitored by Adobe Media Encoder. When content is added into these folders, it is automatically encoded.

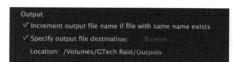

Figure 7.49 It's best to choose an obvious location on your media drives; you can still override this on an individual file basis.

Installing Adobe Encore

Disc output, like tape, is disappearing for many. No changes were made in the Adobe Creative Cloud release for Adobe Encore. In fact, Adobe Encore isn't part of the Adobe Creative Cloud release, but that doesn't mean you can't still have it!

Although the installation is a little convoluted, you can essentially install Adobe Premiere Pro CS6, uninstall Adobe Premiere Pro (but leave Encore), and then update to the latest version.

1. Install Adobe Premiere Pro CS 6. You need to install the old version to get Adobe Encore because it has no trial version.

2. (Optional) Mac users: From the Adobe Premiere Pro folder, choose Uninstall Adobe Premiere Pro CS6.

3. (Optional) Windows users: Choose Control Panels > Programs > Programs and features > Uninstall Adobe Premiere Pro.

4. Deselect Encore (only Adobe Premiere Pro CS6 will be uninstalled).

5. Launch Encore. Via the Help menu, choose Update Encore.

Using the Watch Folder functionality (**Figure 7.50**) is nearly identical to using the Queue except that instead of the source being media (a sequence, clip, or Adobe After Effects comp), it's the contents of a folder.

Figure 7.50 Here is a watch folder waiting for content to build h.264 files.

The watch folder automatically creates two subfolders:

▶ **Source.** After encoding, the source files will be moved to this folder.

▶ **Output.** After encoding, the newly created outputs will be moved to this folder.

MP3s for Transcription

An example of a common use for a watch folder would be for MP3 of raw interviews.

Getting transcription done by a service requires an MP3 file of just the audio. By building a watch folder with a prebuilt MP3 setting, it's quick and easy to dump all the interviews from a shoot into the watch folder and quickly have a series of MP3s that you could send to a transcription service.

1. Create a folder at the desktop level called **Interviews to be transcribed**.

2. In Adobe Media Encoder, click the plus icon on the Watch Folder panel and navigate to the folder "Interviews to be transcribed."

3. Change the Format drop-down menu to MP3. The specific setting of MP3 128 is fine for this use.

4. Any files added to the folder "Interviews to be transcribed" will automatically be encoded to MP3 files, ready to send off to a transcriptionist.

Workflow Management

Author: Tim Kolb

Making a movie is like going to war… (they) are always putting obstacles in your way.

—Norman Jewison

Workflow Management

With the growing variety of acquisition systems and formats used in equally diverse production projects, optimal production workflow means something different to nearly every user of Adobe's Digital Video applications. In this chapter I won't be talking as much about procedure as perspective.

Information on the functionality of Adobe applications is widely available, but it can be helpful to work through the process of evaluating how everything from what format you're shooting in to how to plan to divide tasks among colleagues and collaborators to come up with the best, most practical approach to completing your project.

This chapter is full of larger and smaller pieces of the workflow puzzle. It's not attached to a single project; instead, it's meant for you to implement in your own projects. As you think about applying some of these techniques, it is crucial that you consider doing two things: Write out your workflow from camera to delivery and then *actually test* to make sure things work the way you intend.

Protect Your Assets

You can't start postproduction if your footage is damaged or lost before it returns from the field. Although most of the following list may seem painfully basic, keep in mind that once the director calls a wrap for the day, the only product you have to show for all that expense may be a couple of gigabytes of data on a small bit of disposable media.

Consider these guidelines when handling camera data:

▶ **Have multiple versions of your raw footage** is obviously the best way to protect your considerable investment in acquiring it. Making two or, better yet, three copies on separate storage drives immediately when transferring from camera media in the field is standard practice.

▶ **Vault and maintain your camera media.** If you need to recycle camera media for continuing production, it should never be erased until the data is verified in more than one location.

▶ **Transfer media** as soon as you have the chance instead of waiting until the media is full. Every moment that you have recorded material in the camera is a moment when you have only one copy, and a camera malfunction or power glitch has the potential to wipe out whatever hasn't been transferred. If there is downtime on the set for a scene or a lighting change, why not transfer the data in the camera at that point and reduce your vulnerability?

▶ **Don't trust any digital storage,** ever. Hard drives are cheap and they fail. Most nonproprietary camera media is cheap and it fails. Your expectations of durability have to align with the cost of the device. With the cost of hard drive storage so low relative to even a modest shooting budget, there is no reason to risk your work product due to not having enough backup copies.

▶ **Store data copies in separate locations,** not in the same place. Unfortunately, luggage gets lost or damaged, equipment cases fall into rivers, and occasionally, the production assistant on your medical shoot forgets that the first letter in MRI stands for "magnetic" when he decides where to park your gear cases. Try to keep your drive copies apart from each other whenever you're not transferring, preferably in different physical locations.

▶ **Make a plan for data organization** and stick to it. Keeping the drives safe and then not being able to find the media you're looking for is more frustrating than losing the drive. Housekeeping may seem like a minor point, but maintaining some system for how the camera data will be organized on the transfer drives is critical. It doesn't need to be complex to be effective. Something as simple as saving transferred media in directories by shoot date and/or location may be all you need to be able to find the shots you need later.

NOTES

When video and audio editing on computers really started to take off in the mid 1990s, an external 9 GB hard drive was the size of a safe deposit box, weighed several pounds, and could cost as much as $4,000.00 USD, and that was still a small fraction of the value of the data it contained. It can be easy to forget that the convenience of small, inexpensive camera media like a 64 GB SDXC card at 1 percent of the cost actually holds seven times the data of that old hard drive at risk. (And those 9 GB drives couldn't be lost in a cup of coffee or left in your pocket on laundry day.)

Organizing for Post

Once you reach postproduction with your footage, you have a number of paths to choose from to create an Adobe-based workflow that makes sense for you and your project. If you set up everything right, before touching anything in Adobe Creative Cloud, and if you're organized, you'll have the greatest level of ease in post. There is no "universally optimal" process that will be right for everyone. In this section, I won't be present step-by-step procedures as much as examine your options to help you create the most efficient version of *your* workflow.

Starting in Adobe Premiere Pro

In the context of postproduction workflow, moving your field footage and other assets directly into Adobe Premiere Pro involves project setup and organization, which were outlined thoroughly in Chapter 2. Because Adobe Premiere Pro handles what may be the industry's largest list of formats, this is probably the easiest route to start postproduction.

For larger projects with multiple collaborators or even multiple editors, properly organizing your media to make each step as efficient as possible is certainly possible in Adobe Premiere Pro alone, but Adobe Prelude does fill in some gaps for many users.

Working in Adobe Prelude

Adobe Prelude, as the name implies, was designed to work at the beginning of the postproduction process or at the end of the field production process depending on your perspective. The application is designed to deal with the tasks that exist (and are often overlooked) between the camera and the edit system.

Adobe Prelude does more than just transfer and back up footage from cameras. It can add metadata (such as location), markers to help speed the editorial process, and even create a rough cut, which is fantastic for an on-set quick assembly of footage.

Transferring and transcoding footage

In the field, you can use Adobe Prelude to transfer tapeless camera footage to multiple storage destinations simultaneously. Using the Ingest function, you can specify a primary destination, and then add as many destinations as you desire for redundancy.

Adobe Prelude will also transcode your assets to a variety of different codecs if you choose to do so. Some codecs are meant to be used for "proxy" or low-quality editorial and be relinked later to high-quality footage. Some codecs (such as DNxHD) are ideal as a postproduction codec, also known as a *mezzanine* codec, and are meant to permit flexibility and are no longer dependent on highly compressed camera masters. For more on transcoding, see the "Transcode or Not to Transcode" sidebar in Chapter 1 and the section "Using Mezzanine Formats" later in this chapter.

In a new Prelude project, press Command+I (Ctrl+I) or click Ingest at the top of the interface to enter Ingest mode. The Ingest dialog opens (**Figure 8.1**). If you want to restrict the file types the dialog displays, specify the file types using the Files of Type menu at the top of the dialog (**Figure 8.2**).

Figure 8.1 Using the Adobe Prelude's Ingest dialog you can navigate to your attached camera media.

Figure 8.2 Use the Files of Type designation to sort which files are visible and speed search time.

Figure 8.3 A selected clip thumbnail showing the playhead and In and Out points.

Figure 8.4 Specify what kind of verification to use on camera media transfers.

Figure 8.5 Ingest transfer parameters are ready to transfer and transcode assets to DNxHD 36, a proxy format.

You can also designate an In and Out point on a clip using the I and O keys to do a partial ingest of a clip, although you have to choose to transcode the asset to make a new file of the selected portion (**Figure 8.3**).

Although it will take a bit more time, using the Verification feature (**Figure 8.4**) for straight camera media (nontranscoding) transfers is highly recommended to ensure that the data is being transferred completely. The bit-by-bit comparison option does a CRC check, verifying the file checksum, and is the most thorough method. If time is extremely pressing, running the File size comparison method is still better than not running verification at all

You can specify your transfer destinations and details, and add additional destinations by clicking Add Destination and providing the necessary detail of where your second copy belongs (usually a different drive). For workflows in which you will be converting camera files to a mezzanine and/or a proxy format for editing and post, Adobe Prelude can transcode assets as well.

Transcoding is likely something you would do at some point after the shoot as opposed to during your initial camera data transfers on location. Transcoding does involve more time than doing simple data transfers, depending on the source and destination formats chosen. When you need to transcode (**Figure 8.5**), you can choose the format and a preset target file specification for each destination.

TIP

Although transcoding can be done to the files targeted for each destination, keep in mind that keeping at least two versions of your camera assets in their original format is always a good idea.

Adding metadata and file renaming during ingest

Adding file metadata or file renaming during ingest requires you to create a preset. After you've set up your parameters and saved the preset, you can recall the preset during a later ingest session (**Figure 8.6**).

You have options to add metadata fields to your footage for all destinations or for just a particular destination. You could, for instance, add some sort of tag to some proxy footage that will go to the editor and leave the full-quality original footage targeted for other destinations unaltered. These presets easily can add a given set of metadata to every clip during ingest.

If you plan on using this for scene designations or something that changes frequently, you'll need to ingest only the appropriate clips for that metadata preset. Alternatively, you can add more specific shot-by-shot information after the footage is ingested.

Renaming files during ingest can also be applied to a specific destination or all destinations. Note that using renamed files will add complications when relinking media to camera originals if there is a loss of data or when moving from proxy editing to finishing. So make sure you think through your full workflow before throwing this switch.

Adding metadata and file logging

When you're ready to start assessing dailies, making log notes, and adding any further descriptors to the metadata of the footage you've ingested, you can switch the Prelude Workspace to Logging by clicking the Logging button at the top of the interface or by pressing Option+Shift+2 (Alt+Shift+2) (**Figure 8.7** on the next page).

The advantage of this logging workspace (both here in Adobe Prelude and also in Adobe Premiere Pro) is the focus on seeing all the metadata (and adding to it) that belongs to a clip.

The basic operating principle in Adobe software is to be nondestructive wherever possible; thus, Adobe Prelude does selections and notations with markers instead of making any physical changes to the source media.

TIP

The new Relink dialog is far more intelligent than it was. Once you find one element, it'll see how much of the other elements match in relative file paths. Pay close attention to the fact that you can make it ignore file extensions—meaning that it's trivial to relink from DNxHD MXF proxy files to RED R3D files with the same name but different extensions.

Figure 8.6 You can add metadata for all transfer destinations or only the primary destination.

TIP

You can ingest footage without moving it when you're starting a Prelude project to work on footage in place by deselecting the Transfer Clips to Destination check box.

NOTES

Be aware that any changes you make in a clip's metadata (markers included) will be written in an XMP "sidecar" file, which is external to the clip file in most cases (Quick-Time is one exception; it can store the metadata internally). If you need to move or reorganize media, these metadata sidecar files will need to stay next to the media files they apply to.

Figure 8.7 Adobe Prelude's Logging Workspace.

Figure 8.8 Adobe Prelude's Marker Type panel.

Using markers

When you double-click a clip in the Adobe Prelude Project panel, the interface displays the clip on a Timeline. Unlike an editing Timeline, this Timeline is strictly for one clip. To mark up the clip, you can utilize several marker types, which are listed in the Marker Type panel (**Figure 8.8**) and appear on the Timeline in corresponding colors.

By positioning the playhead on the Timeline where you want a marker to start and clicking on the marker type or typing the appropriate number (1=Subclip, 2=Comment, etc.), you set the In point for that marker. Moving the playhead where you want the marker to end and typing **O** will set an Out point for the marker. You can move any marker by dragging it right and left with the mouse or by positioning the playhead and typing **I** or **O** to move the selected marker's In or Out point to that position.

You can use several layers of various and overlapping markers as necessary. The two marker types most commonly employed for video postproduction are the Subclip and Comment types (**Figure 8.9**). You can also use custom markers.

Figure 8.9 A green Comment marker selected with the Marker Inspector shows the corresponding notes.

Here's a little more detail about some smart marker uses:

▶ **Subclips.** A Subclip marker creates a new subclip in the Project panel when you save the project. Updates and changes to the subclip's settings update at the next save.

When you send the Prelude project (or the individual subclip) to Adobe Premiere Pro, it will appear in the Adobe Premiere Pro Project panel as a subclip, and it is editable in Adobe Premiere Pro the same way a subclip created in Adobe Premiere Pro would be.

If you send the entire Prelude project to Adobe Premiere Pro, the Comment markers will be visible on any full clips and subclips, but note that subclip markers will not be visible on the original source clip.

▶ **Comments.** A Comment marker is used for any notes that you may want to make on a shot that don't fit into the other marker type categories. With the marker selected, use the Marker Inspector panel to make any appropriate notes.

► **Custom markers.** You may find that you use one type of marker repeatedly, say a Subclip marker for "Good Take" or something similar.

Save some time by saving the specific marker as a template. Select the marker you want to create the template from, and from the Marker pull-down menu, choose Save Marker as Template (**Figure 8.10**).

Figure 8.10 Click on the marker that you want to make into a template and choose Marker > Save Marker as Template.

You can make different libraries of custom markers for different types of projects and save the custom marker set using the text header at the top of the Marker Type panel (**Figure 8.11**).

Figure 8.11 After you name the custom marker, it is added to the Marker Type panel. Here, Good Take is added as number 7 in the list.

Creating rough cuts

Adobe Prelude can also help you create rough cuts of footage. An assistant can line up good takes in a sequence instead of the editor taking the time to sort out footage. The editor can then get to the work of fine-tuning faster, accelerating the editing process. You can make a new rough cut in Adobe Prelude by pressing Command+N (Ctrl+N) or just by clicking the New Rough Cut icon in the lower-right corner of the Project panel (**Figure 8.12**).

Exporting to Adobe Premiere Pro

When you've completed your work in Adobe Prelude, you can send the project to Adobe Premiere Pro directly if Adobe Premiere Pro is installed on the same machine (**Figure 8.13**). You can also export the project as an Adobe Premiere Pro project file or a Final Cut Pro XML file for use by an editor on a different system.

Figure 8.12 Right-click on the clip you want to add to the rough cut, and choose Append to Rough Cut.

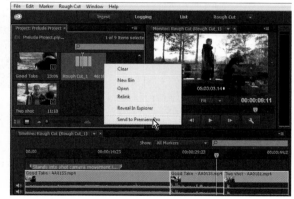

Figure 8.13 Right-click on a clip, subclip, or rough cut in the Prelude Project panel and send it to Adobe Premiere Pro.

Postproduction Planning

Adobe Premiere Pro is a very flexible application when it comes to file handling for postproduction. But flexibility is often the rope you hang yourself with. Using that flexibility wisely within Adobe Premiere Pro to set up your project appropriately to your assets and your project requirements is covered thoroughly in Chapter 2, especially in the section called "Media Setup Outside of Adobe Premiere Pro." Chapter 2 also has a section on configuring other tools in Adobe Creative Cloud to maximize performance.

Setting up a truly efficient and flexible post workflow involves anticipating not only the final needs of the finished project, but also the needs of the process along the way, and there are a few big issues that seem to keep surfacing for many editors and postproduction supervisors.

The Big Issues

Should you use a mezzanine (post) codec? Or should you use the camera's raw files? Should you optimize for Smart Rendering? What about working with any of the newer formats that are larger than HD (given that HD is the common deliverable)? Let's explore these questions.

Using mezzanine formats

Postproduction formats that utilize codecs such as Apple's ProRes, Avid's DNxHD, and GoPro's CineForm are often called mezzanine codecs. The original material, often very lossy, highly compressed h.264, is often transcoded to one of these mezzanine formats. The general trade-off is larger file size for smaller processing demands.

Because Adobe Premiere Pro is designed to load native format camera media as its primary working method, you can load most camera data file formats without excessive processing or file duplication, which of course can save time and an immense amount of storage space.

In other cases, projects where Adobe Premiere Pro interacts with other software, either collaborating on an edit with another manufacturer's nonlinear editor (NLE) or even just using various postproduction applications for effects work, knowing the optimal file formats that each application handles will help you determine if you need to use a mezzanine (or intermediate) format to make your assets more portable across multiple applications and computer platforms and operating systems.

There really isn't one best approach for every situation, and in many cases the most widely compatible formats are also the largest stored files sizes, so this decision is a significant one. Of particular concern are situations in which you're working with some type of camera raw footage. Often, these files are huge and require very fast media access. There is no single camera raw format; frequently, each camera manufacturer maintains its own raw format. Many visual effects and editing applications don't handle native camera raw formats as well as Adobe Premiere Pro (if at all).

Therefore, one solution would be to convert camera raw to some type of high-color precision format for postproduction, which would make the files more accessible to a wider variety of applications and make handling the footage a bit more "conventional." However, the trade-off in flexibility means a compromise in maintaining the original format of the clip. There will be a compromise compared to keeping the clips in their original pristine form.

If your project footage is camera raw, the consideration may not be so much "if" but "when" to transcode. The benefits to editing the camera raw footage and converting only selected segments is discussed later in this section.

Smart Rendering

One advantage to utilizing certain mezzanine codecs is Adobe Premiere Pro's ability to use Smart Rendering. Those of you who depend on codecs like DNxHD or ProRes as the backbone of your workflow can now edit the format that you export. Then, by selecting the Smart Rendering option in the Export dialog (**Figure 8.14**), you can export to that same codec without having to re-encode the frames that already exist in the proper format, saving you significant time. This is mentioned in Chapter 2 in the section "Smart Rendering codecs yield faster exports."

Figure 8.14 You may have to scroll down to reveal the Enable Smart Rendering codec check box in the Video tab in the Export dialog.

Decisions about frame size

As camera acquisition frame resolution moves from high definition past 2k to UltraHD, 4k, 5k, and beyond, acquisition formats are becoming a different frame size than the delivery spec (HD), or even the master final format for the project. A constant question is where in the process to accommodate the frame size conversion, or whether to do it all. Certainly, a 4k mastered program has more flexibility for the future than HD. But maintaining frame sizes that are four or five times larger than the specified delivery spec increases the stress on your postproduction chain at every step. There are two approaches to resolve this situation: edit at the native size and downconvert when finished or work at the delivery frame size (usually HD).

When you're shooting material for final framing and composition, you can simply edit the material in Adobe Premiere Pro in its native frame size. At the end you can then export the footage to the desired format and frame size, delaying the down conversion (and the inherent quality reduction) until the very end of the process. The edited project can then be archived with the original media and retrieved and remastered by exporting it at a different frame size in the future. So, if something was shot in 4k, it could be edited in 4k and delivered in HD with the flexibility that if 4k delivery became easy, you'd have the option to deliver the content again in 4k. Many production facilities did this with HD. They'd shoot HD and edit in SD, knowing one day they could deliver the materials again in HD.

Alternatively, using a sequence designed around the current delivery specification allows you to choose between using the original framing or "pushing in" to a larger frame to recompose the shot, which adds a significant degree of visual flexibility to the edit (**Figure 8.15**).

Figure 8.15 A 1920 x 1080 frame inside a 4096 x 2304 original camera shot.

One drawback to working in the final delivery form is that the entire project is now edited at the delivery frame spec, which is often HD. As a result, future opportunities to deploy the program at larger frame sizes (UltraHD is well on its way to a living room near you) will involve significant rework, including reframing.

Even if you don't see the need for a higher-resolution version of the project in the future, there is another issue to consider. Any compositing or effects work benefits from the highest possible resolution source images. If that effects work is designed to be downstream from the edit in your workflow, any 4k selects you send from your HD frame edit sequence will have already been reduced to a quarter of their original resolution.

The choice is to consider this question prior to entering post and try to plan for the optimal results from each link in the postproduction chain. Even if you're delivering an HD program, using 4k will provide higher-quality effects. Elements like keying will likely be easier with the extra resolution.

Using camera raw files

If you're working with a camera raw format that Adobe Premiere Pro can load in its native form, the optimal pathway through post would be to edit the material natively in Adobe Premiere Pro.

Some camera raw formats have their own primary color grading capability built in to the metadata of the file. RED R3D files can be altered in Adobe Premiere Pro by accessing each clip's Source Settings by right-clicking on the clip in the Project panel or the sequence. Changes made to RED clips in this way will stay with the clip if you choose Save to RMD (RED Metadata) in the upper right of the RED Source Settings panel (**Figure 8.16** on the next page). ARRIRAW frame sequences can also be altered using Source Settings, although the tools are basic by comparison.

Other camera raw formats may have alternate methods for making adjustments to clip metadata. GoPro's CineForm formats can be altered via an external application/utility that can run simultaneously outside of Adobe Premiere

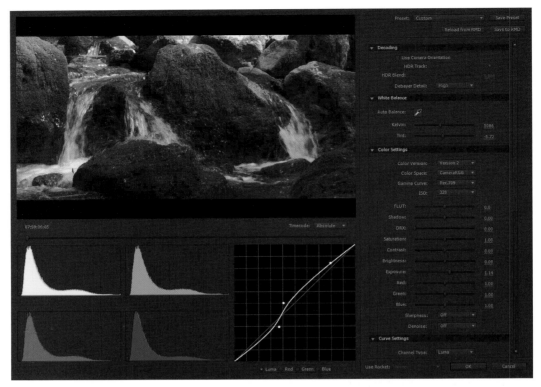

Figure 8.16 The RED metadata interface under Source Settings for RED clips in Adobe Premiere Pro.

Pro. Any changes made to a clip in metadata would then be carried with the clip, which would eliminate the need to render frames out of Adobe Premiere Pro's edit Timeline to retain the changes. The most important consideration when you're editing camera raw files is that they can't be altered and rewritten in their native form by an Adobe application in the vast majority of cases.

As discussed in the "Using Mezzanine Formats" section, the point where you convert camera raw footage to even a high-quality mezzanine format in your post process should be planned for so you can take full advantage of the flexibility of the raw format before the footage is flattened.

Working with Adobe SpeedGrade

Adobe SpeedGrade is a dedicated color grading tool that has become an integral part of the Adobe Premiere Pro editing process with the addition of Direct Link (see "Minimalist Adobe SpeedGrade" in Chapter 6). Whereas Adobe Premiere Pro is like a Swiss army knife, Adobe SpeedGrade's single job is to speed the job of the colorist.

Features such as shot-to-shot matching, Secondaries (correcting portions of an image like sky or flesh tones), and a huge library of professional "looks" are just a few advantages of working with Adobe SpeedGrade. Because it is built on the Lumetri color engine, a sequence sent to Adobe SpeedGrade via Direct Link will place a single Lumetri effect on each clip when the sequence returns to Adobe Premiere Pro.

Using SpeedGrade upstream from Adobe Premiere Pro

SpeedGrade can be used on individual clips if you want to create color lookup tables (LUTs) based on dailies prior to editing. The list of formats that SpeedGrade will load is in its manual, which is available for download at http://helpx.adobe.com/pdf/speedgrade_reference.pdf.

Adobe SpeedGrade can be used directly as Lumetri effects on clips in an Adobe Premiere Pro sequence. By first generating color LUTs (saved as .look files) saved out of Adobe SpeedGrade, the LUT can act as a basic starting point, which is particularly useful with cinema cameras.

Most cinema cameras shoot "flat"—the image looks fairly terrible until a LUT is applied. This is to maximize the amount of light captured in-camera. The LUT helps make the image look "normal" while retaining all the extra data. This technique of adding a LUT can be even applied to the raw clips and burned into transcoded clips permanently for use as mezzanine clips or for proxy files.

To save a .look file of your correction in SpeedGrade, make sure the correction layer with the settings you want to save is selected (you may want to hide any correction layers that aren't selected to ensure that the change you're seeing is the one you want to save as a .look file). In the Look Management panel at the bottom below the HSL wheels, the correction layers are shown on the left. Keep in mind that you can only select one correction layer on the Timeline; however, all the layers of correction in the

Layers list that apply to that correction layer will be part of the .look file. Below the Layers list is the Save .Look icon (**Figure 8.17**). When you click it, a new preset appears in the Look Management panel (**Figure 8.18**) to the right.

You can click on the name of the preset in the Looks Management view and type in an appropriate name. To access the .look file later, you may want to store it outside of SpeedGrade's preset library. To do this, simply right-click on the preset and choose Export Look (**Figure 8.19**).

Figure 8.19 Many of the looks are stored internally to Adobe SpeedGrade. By right-clicking on the .look file, you'll have the option to export the look and save it anywhere on your system.

Figure 8.18 If you don't see the Looks Management panel, it's probably collapsed below the correction tools. Click the icon on the bottom right of the panel to reveal it.

Figure 8.17 Select the correction layer you want to save in the Timeline, and then click the Save .Look icon at the bottom of the Layers panel in SpeedGrade.

Once you've chosen Export Look, a dialog appears (**Figure 8.20**) displaying the compatible versions that will be saved in a ZIP file. These alternative versions of the LUT can be extremely helpful to maintain maximum compatibility across a variety of software and hardware.

Figure 8.20 You can choose the LUT types that will be part of the exported file by selecting the check boxes and specifying additional types from the list.

Using .look files in Adobe Premiere Pro's Lumetri effect

In Adobe Premiere Pro, you can utilize .look files through the Lumetri effect without opening Adobe SpeedGrade to create them. You can either apply the basic Lumetri effect, which asks you to load a .look file to apply, or you can use one of the presets in the Lumetri Looks folder (**Figure 8.21**). You can use either effect with an adjustment layer to audition different looks, or toggle the track off during editing to accelerate response on laptops or less powerful systems.

Figure 8.21 The Lumetri Look Bleach Bypass preset applied to a clip in the Timeline.

If you really want to push the LUT workflow to the limit, these can be attached in Adobe Media Encoder to a preset (on the Filter tab). Presets built in Adobe Media Encoder appear in both Adobe Premiere Pro Export Media and in the Ingest dialog in Adobe Prelude. Once you've picked or adjusted a LUT, you could transfer your proxy files with the LUT "burned in" wherever you want to do the conversion: in Adobe Prelude (probably your best choice), in Adobe Media Encoder (you could even use a watch folder!), or in Adobe Premiere Pro.

Adobe Premiere Pro Direct Link to SpeedGrade

The procedure for using Direct Link to Adobe SpeedGrade is addressed in detail in "Minimalist Adobe SpeedGrade" in Chapter 6. For purposes of workflow, saving SpeedGrade changes by saving them to the Adobe Premiere Pro project as the applied Lumetri effect simplifies the workflow by creating fewer files to track. Saving your .look files into a common location is a good practice should you want to utilize them later.

Working with Adobe After Effects

Adobe After Effects has been a staple of postproduction graphics and compositing for two decades. The close relationship between Adobe Premiere Pro and After Effects is most evident when you're using Adobe's Dynamic Link. See the end of Chapter 5 for more on Dynamic Link.

Sequence vs. clip frame size considerations

After Effects compositions created through Dynamic Link are based on the frame size and rate of your current sequence, or you can replace a given clip with an After Effects composition based on the current sequence settings.

If you're editing 4k on an HD sequence, the After Effects comp created to replace the clip in that sequence will have the frame rate and size of the HD sequence instead of the source clip (**Figure 8.22**).

Figure 8.22 Right-click on a clip and select Replace with After Effects Composition.

If you need to create an After Effects composition based on a different size than the edit sequence you've set up, you can use Dynamic Link to create a new composition and set the specifications in the dialog. Of course, you can create a composition in After Effects the "old-fashioned" way, and then import the composition in Adobe Premiere Pro through Dynamic Link. You can choose any of these options from the Dynamic Link option in the pull-down menu in Adobe Premiere Pro. You can also replace a clip on the Timeline with an After Effects composition containing that clip by right-clicking on it and choosing from the menu.

When you require many Dynamic Linked After Effects compositions, you can improve your editing response in Adobe Premiere Pro by keeping the Dynamic Linked After Effects comps on their own video track. You can then switch off that track's output when you don't need to work with all the comps, or you can enable/disable individual comps on a clip-by-clip basis.

Even when edit performance is not an issue, you may want to consider rendering the After Effects comps and importing the finished clips. You can place the rendered clips on a video track above the Dynamic Linked comps. By doing so, not only will you gain some performance, but you'll also have actual media to archive with the project versus needing to restore all the After Effects projects, plug-ins, and so on to be able to complete simple changes to the project in the future (**Figure 8.23**).

Figure 8.23 Adobe Premiere Pro Timeline with V2 (containing Dynamic Linked After Effects comps) disabled and the rendered movies on V3.

Working with Adobe Audition

Adobe Audition is to audio what Adobe SpeedGrade is to color. In the course of specialized audio work on your video project (Chapter 4 covers audio in depth), there will probably be times when even Adobe Premiere Pro's competent audio capabilities may be insufficient. There are two ways to handle the migration from Adobe Premiere Pro to Adobe Audition. You can send either an individual clip you've selected to Audition for audio work or send the entire sequence (make sure the sequence is the panel with

Figure 8.24 Right-click on an audio clip in your sequence and select Edit Clip in Adobe Audition to modify a single clip.

Figure 8.25 The dialog for sending an Adobe Premiere Pro sequence to Audition has options for including a preview video, rendering any audio effects you've already applied in Adobe Premiere Pro, and choosing whether you want any volume keyframe metadata from your sequence to travel with the audio.

Figure 8.26 Audio files created when sending a clip or sequence to Audition for processing will be saved in the location designated for Captured Audio.

the focus) by choosing Edit > Edit in Audition and then choosing Clip or Sequence as appropriate. You can also select an individual clip in the sequence, right-click, and choose to edit that clip in Audition (**Figure 8.24**).

The Audition disadvantage

The big difference in how Adobe Audition works versus the video applications is that it's *destructive*. It has to render an altered file to compete its changes. For this reason, the Edit clip in Audition functions creates working copies of the audio you send to Audition so that the original media files remain untouched. These files will be labeled as "*<filename>* Audio Extracted." When you send a clip to Audition from Adobe Premiere Pro, you'll notice that the audio changes its name on the sequence. This indicates that the Audition-processed audio has replaced the original audio. Conveniently, the new extracted file is now linked to its corresponding video clip in the sequence. If you send a sequence to Audition, the audio in the existing edit sequence will not be changed (**Figure 8.25**).

These extracted audio files will be written to the directory you've identified in Project Settings (File > Project Settings) for captured audio (**Figure 8.26**). Keep this in mind for archiving purposes because these clips are now critical components of your project and will be necessary to alter your edit in the future.

If you send an entire sequence to Audition, the audio in the existing edit sequence will not be changed because a copy of all the audio is made for Audition to work on. After sending a sequence to Audition, you can make your edits and then bring back a finished audio track to insert into your sequence. Often, creating new audio tracks at the top of the sequence to accommodate the finished audio tracks and muting all the raw audio tracks underneath allows you to have the sequence ready for master output but keep the original components on the Timeline in case future changes are necessary.

Exporting Media

Most experienced users know that Adobe Premiere Pro has a rather sophisticated media export function that is a specialized link to Adobe Media Encoder. Once you've set up your export parameters, you have two choices for executing the task. You can click Export (**Figure 8.27**), which dedicates the full resources of the machine to the export process, enabling you to return to editing once the export is complete.

Figure 8.27 Click Export to encode directly from Adobe Premiere Pro, or click Queue to launch Adobe Media Encoder and send the sequence to the Adobe Media Encoder.

Alternatively, you can send the export job to the Queue. Clicking Queue opens Adobe Media Encoder and puts the export job in Adobe Media Encoder's Queue list, allowing you to continue editing or even set up additional export jobs and send them to the Queue. When planning your workflows, it's best to consider how you'll handle exporting (should you tie up your system?) and what the final archive format for the future should be.

Exporting While Editing

If you ever run Adobe Media Encoder to batch process some video files and look at the CPU activity, you'll notice that no matter how many CPU cores you have, Adobe Media Encoder uses nearly 100 percent of them to do its work. But you'll see a significant difference in system performance charting when Adobe Media Encoder is processing an Adobe Premiere Pro sequence.

Because Adobe Premiere Pro utilizes the GPU for so many functions, an Adobe Premiere Pro sequence in the Queue needs to do the same to render frames into the encoding process. Even when you continue to edit while the Adobe Media Encoder Queue is set to run, there is another version of Adobe Premiere Pro running in the background to handle the Adobe Premiere Pro sequence being encoded. When Adobe Premiere Pro is technically running in two places, it keeps resources prioritized for the editor who is continuing to work; therefore, the background version of Adobe Premiere Pro pauses every time the editor who is currently working in the foreground moves the mouse or plays back video, pausing the encoding process as well.

When Adobe Media Encoder is running processing clips from the Queue directly, it will run constantly even while Adobe Premiere Pro is editing in the foreground; however, the performance of both applications will depend on the hardware resources available.

Creating the most efficient workflow means something different to everyone. For some, completing the export as quickly as possible is worth the pause in editing necessary to do a direct export from Adobe Premiere Pro. For others, the time it takes to do the encoding in the Queue as it starts and stops is perfectly acceptable if editing progress continues. And if your project needs to be delivered in multiple distribution formats, you might consider making a master quality file. This should be a post codec such as DNxHD or Apple ProRes.

If you export a master file, you'll no longer depend on Adobe Premiere Pro, meaning less resources wasted and improved performance. And in Adobe Media Encoder you can just set up this file and have all the output profiles you require, utilizing the master file as the source for each one.

DPX Files for Ultimate Media Flexibility

The problem with outputting to architectures such as QuickTime, MXF, or AVI are the unique limitations in each type. Instead, for the greatest future flexibility, you can generate DPX files. DPX (Digital Picture eXchange) format files are huge, uncompressed still frames.

In workflows where extensive effects work is necessary, there may be a wide variety of applications playing roles in completing complex effects. Many specialized visual effects programs do not accept the wide variety of video formats of Adobe digital video applications.

Adobe Premiere Pro (and Adobe Media Encoder) has the ability to export DPX frame sequences in a wide variety of specifications and frame sizes up to 10-bit log color precision, allowing a wide variety of post effects applications to access very information-dense versions of your footage (**Figure 8.28**).

Because DPX files can have a black point set above 0 and white point below 1023, color values beyond this range can also be stored in the file, which can prove useful for effects work where maximizing the available grayscale information can aid in masking and keying operations during compositing (**Figure 8.29**). If you're working in other effects pipelines, using DPX might be the easiest *and* smartest method for interoperability.

Archiving a Project

As any editor who has had to edit out two minutes of every episode of a 1990s TV series resurrected for syndication can tell you, nothing in the industry goes away forever. Ensuring future access to your media and your project is important, and having a solid approach to archiving is critical.

Chapter 2, "Setup and Organizing," talked about organizing a project at the outset. Storing your assets where you can find them is as important at the end of the project as when you started. Multiple copies of the data are also important to have at the archiving stage, just as in the beginning of the project.

Because data storage is currently so inexpensive and disposable, not having two (or three) copies of your data is akin to not having it saved at all when that inexpensive hard drive fails (and they all do at some point). An updated version of a popular saying might be: There are only *three* things constant in this world: death, taxes, and *hard drive failure*.

Figure 8.28 The rarely seen DPX export adjustments tab permits nuanced fine-tuning of output.

Figure 8.29 Under the DPX Format setting, you'll find a wide variety of supported frame sizes and color precision settings.

If you were organized based on suggestions in Chapter 2, great. If not, the Project Manager can collect everything for you for easy backup and transfer. Or if you just want to copy part of a project, again, the Project Manager is the tool for these uses.

Using the Project Manager

Every type of editing project is a bit different. A project with a few assets isn't particularly difficult to manually archive, but archiving larger projects with hundreds or thousands of individual assets can be more challenging.

Using the Project Manager is an easy way to gather your assets in a given project and move them all to a specific destination for archive storage. When you launch the Project Manager from the File menu, a dedicated panel opens (**Figure 8.30**). At the top of the panel you'll see the sequences in your project listed. You can choose which sequences you want to archive by selecting or deselecting the corresponding check box.

Figure 8.30 The Project Manager opens in a self-contained dialog.

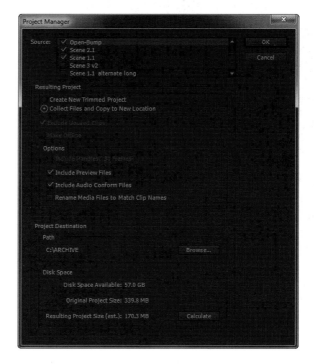

The Resulting Project options allow you to simply copy all the project assets to a specific location, or you can trim the project (**Figure 8.31**). When you trim the project, Adobe Premiere Pro trims the copies of only the parts of any video assets that you used, plus some extra frames based on the Include Handles option. You can select the Exclude Unused Clips option, and any assets inside the project that are unused will not be copied.

TIP

If you don't select all the sequences in a project for archiving, the option to Exclude Unused Clips is automatically selected whether you are trimming a project or simply moving it.

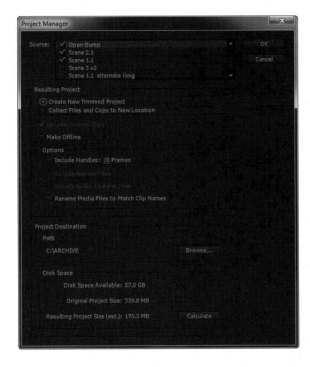

Figure 8.31 Choosing the Create New Trimmed Project option makes different options available.

The options to keep Preview and Audio Conform files are available as well. Keep in mind that Adobe Premiere Pro can rebuild the previews and conform files easily when the project is retrieved. Keeping them is rarely necessary, and they can take up considerable hard drive space in larger projects. A good reason to keep them would be for a "quick" restoration of a project. That way you could save the time in re-rendering. Everything is a trade-off.

NOTES

Not every video format can be trimmed by the Project Manager. Any proprietary media format, like RED or ARRIRAW, that can't be written by your editing workstation can't be trimmed because a new file can't be created. Many formats that use temporal compression (often referred to as "long-GOP") also can't be trimmed, although you can still elect to include or exclude individual clips. Trimmed Panasonic P2 media can be retrieved and used with Adobe Premiere Pro, but the trimmed files are not "P2 camera" compatible.

You should carefully consider whether or not to select the Rename Media Files to Match Clip Names option. In Adobe Premiere Pro, many editors will name camera data files more intuitively in the sequence, because many camera formats have clip names that are anything but intuitive to human beings. However, keep in mind that changing the names of the clips in your archived project may make the footage difficult to track down should you need to retrieve the project in a year to find a particular shot in the raw camera archive. In that situation, maintaining the original name of the media in your archive project would come in awfully handy.

After choosing a destination for the project, you can click the Calculate button to have the Project Manager show you how much disk space the resulting project will consume relative to the original.

Some files require manual backup

As convenient as the Project Manager is when consolidating and moving or archiving a project, Adobe Premiere Pro doesn't gather every file pertinent to reconstructing your entire edit project:

▶ The Dynamic Linked After Effects comp in Adobe Premiere Pro will be included in a Project Manager consolidation. But the Adobe After Effects project that contains the data for the composition exists outside the Adobe Premiere Pro project. If any media or assets were added in Adobe After Effects, they will need to be manually copied, because they weren't in the Adobe Premiere Pro project. (After Effects has its own methods for gathering project assets from inside the project.)

In After Effects you can access the project consolidation features by choosing File > Dependencies. After Effects offers several options, which range from simply collecting files to removing unused footage or finding missing footage (**Figure 8.32**).

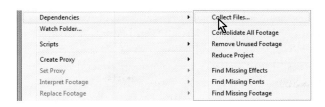

Figure 8.32 Collect and consolidate After Effects project files by using the After Effects interface.

▶ Adobe Audition projects and any audio assets you may have used in Audition but did not import into Adobe Premiere Pro directly also need to be manually collected and moved. This does not include the "Audio Extracted" (replaced) audio files because those are assets included in the Adobe Premiere Pro project and they will be included as assets in the trimmed project.

▶ Keeping all the additional audio production work and assets in one directory (the Common Media folder specified in Chapter 2 is an excellent location for this) makes moving them a simple process when the time comes.

▶ Adobe Photoshop and Illustrator assets, such as other files you reference that are not imported to Adobe Premiere Pro, will not be managed. Therefore, you'll need to keep track of them and move them as warranted.

▶ Adobe SpeedGrade corrections you applied through Direct Link will be saved within your Adobe Premiere Pro project as settings in the Lumetri effect. However, it's still a good practice to save your .look files separately in cases where you have color corrections that may be useful in the future.

One method of keeping all your files and assets organized is explained in the section "Media Setup Outside of Adobe Premiere Pro" in Chapter 2.

Index

Numbers

1:1 pixel mapping, seeing, 53
8 bits vs. 10 bits, 337
32 Bit Float Color Precision effect, 285
720p60 broadcast standard, 91

Symbols

' (accent) key, 7, 64, 138
\ (backslash) key, 138

A

accent (') key, 7, 64, 138
Activity Monitor, 31–32
Adjustment Layers bin, 99
adjustment layers, using, 292–294, 386
Adobe After Effects. *See* After Effects, 27
Adobe Audition. *See* Audition
Adobe Creative Cloud.
    See also cloud
    benefit, 17, 388
    production process, 37
    Sync, 17–21
Adobe Encore, installing, 452
Adobe Media Encoder. *See* Media Encoder
Adobe Photoshop. *See* Photoshop
Adobe Prelude. *See* Prelude
Adobe Story, 118–124
After Effects
    composition naming, 108
    Disk Cache, 108–110
    Dynamic Linking, 107
    effects, 39–40
    frame sizes, 472–473
    imported media, 110
    learning, 44–45
    Media Cache folder, 110
    presets, 39–40
    projects, 108
    rendering for performance, 110
    and SpeedGrade, 27
animating
    effects, 287–292
    stills, 37
Animation codec, 415

Animation Presets, 39
Appearance preferences, 55
Apple ProRes reset, 80
archiving projects, 478–482
audio. *See also* clipped audio; dual
    capture sound; mixing sound;
    sound
    adjusting levels, 92
    Audition, 276–282
    Clip Mixer, 260–261
    Expand Audio Track, 245
    feathering, 269
    gain and levels, 240–244
    headphones, 239–240
    listening environment, 237–240
    listening to recordings, 239
    loudness, 240–244
    matching to video, 234
    merging, 90
    nuances, 237
    overcompressing, 268
    replacing, 161–162
    sound spectrum, 269
    stereo vs. mono, 92–93
    submixes, 264–265
    syncing, 161–162
    Timeline interface, 244–250
    Track Mixer, 262–264
    unlinking from video, 183
    workspace, 240
audio channels, modifying, 93
Audio Clip Mixer, 260–261
audio clipping, 250–251
Audio FX
    DeEsser effect, 274–275
    DeHummer effect, 272–274
    EQ (equalizer), 268–270
    limiter, 268
    Loudness Radar effect, 271–272
    Multiband Compressor, 266–268
    reverb effect, 275–276
audio levels, 254–255
audio master output, 82
audio mixing, 37
Audio preferences, 52
audio previews, 71
audio repair workflow, 37
audio scrubbing, 137–138
audio setup, 237–238
audio signal, receiving, 237

audio terminology, 244
Audio Track Mixer, 262–264
audio tracks
    buttons, 246–248
    dead, 95–96
    keyframes, 248–249
    locking, 200
    naming, 250
    resizing, 245
    setting up, 81–82
    using separately, 249
audio transitions, applying, 258
audio waveforms, viewing while
    trimming, 191
Audition
    Amplitude Statistics, 281
    back to Premiere Pro, 117
    clips, 115
    DAW (Digital Audio
        Workstation), 116
    DeClipper effect, 282
    destructive disadvantage, 474
    disadvantage, 474–475
    Disk Cache, 114–115
    exporting tracks as stems, 117
    fixing clipped audio, 280–282
    learning, 43–44
    removing noise, 277–280
    restoring clipped audio, 280–282
    sample-based noise reduction, 40
    sequences, 116
auto save, 55, 72
Automate to Sequence, 155–160.
    See also sequences
AVC editing mode, 74
AVC IntraFrame codec, 414
AVCHD editing mode, 74
Avid DNxHD, 74, 414, 428, 430
Avid Media Composer
    exporting AAFs, 12
    importing from, 11
    keyboard mapping, 65
    media considerations, 12
    translation, 12

B

background encoding, 38
backing up media, 28, 69–79
backslash (\) key, 138
backup project files, 119

backups
  manual in Project Manager,
    480–482
  maximum number of, 70
Behance ProSite, 22
bin views, adjusting, 101–102
bins. *See also* projects
  common types, 98–99
  enlarging, 138
  preference, 50
  using as Source Monitor,
    155–160
black and white look, 381–382
buttons, 61

C

cache files, 56–58
caches
  configuring, 27
  directories, 105
  system setup, 119
camera data, 454–455
camera formats, 4–7
camera logs, using, 225
camera media
  maintaining, 455
  system setup, 119
  transferring, 455
  vaulting, 455
camera raw files, 467–468
cameras
  choosing for multi-camera
    editing, 234
  professional, 4–5
chroma adjustments, 354–355, 400
chroma issues
  fixing with RGB curves, 366
  fixing with Three-Way Color
    Corrector, 359–360
chroma keying, 37
clipped audio, 251, 280–282. *See
    also* audio
clips. *See also* Fit Clip panel;
    footage; Reveal Clip; shots;
    Timeline clips
  advice regarding unlinking, 50
  editing from sequences, 220
  grouping, 179
  marking on fly, 137
  merging and syncing, 89–90
  merging based on audio, 89–90
  merging based on metadata, 90
  modifying for slow motion shots,
    90–92

naming, 99
relinking, 194–195
replacing, 164, 168
scrubbing, 137
unlinking, 194–195
cloud, 28. *See also* Creative Cloud
CMY colors, 338
codecs, 78–80, 84, 413–415, 464
Color Blend mode, 327
color correction, 37, 332–334,
    351, 356–357. *See also* light;
    primary corrections; secondary
    corrections; SpeedGrade
color correction interface setup
  Combination views, 347
  customizing, 347
  full screen, 347
  keyboard remapping, 350–351
  modifying workspace, 348–350
  RGB Parade, 345–347
  tools, 340–341
  vectorscope, 343–345
  video scopes, 341
  YbCr Parade, 347
  YC Waveform, 341–343
color matching, 403, 405
Color Mattes bin, 99
color picker, using, 339
color temperature, 335
color wheel, 339
compositing and keying, 315,
    317–321
compression tips, 434
corrections vs. grades, 332
CPU, 24
crossfades, 257–258
Ctrl key. *See* keyboard shortcuts
cut points, selecting, 211–212

D

Darken Blend mode, 323
Darker Color Blend mode, 324
DeClipper effect, 282
DeEsser effect, 274–275
Default scale to frame size
    preference, 50–51
DeHummer effect, 272–274
Delete command, 172
deselection keyboard shortcut,
    65, 151
dialogue scenes, cutting, 162–163
digital storage, best practices, 455
digital-file output workflow, 37
Dissolve Blend mode, 323

distribution based codec, 413–414
Divide Blend mode, 327
DNxHD , 74, 414, 428, 430
DPX (Digital Picture Exchange),
    435, 476–477
drag-and-drop replace, 165–167
Dropped Frame indicator, 58–59.
    See also frames
dual capture sound, merging, 89.
    See also audio
DVCPro codec, 414
DVD-5 quick formula, 445
Dynamic Link, 327–330
dynamic trimming, 205–208.
    See also trimming

E

edit points, 211, 214–216
editing. *See also* multi-camera
    editing
  adding shots to sequences, 137
  Automate to Sequence, 155–160
  back-timing, 151–152
  basic assembly, 136–142
  clips from sequences, 220
  driving keyboard, 137
  four-point, 152–154
  JKL keys, 136
  key commands, 136
  keyboard as work surface,
    136–137
  marking clips on fly, 137
  modes, 74–77
  moving frames, 137
  navigating footage, 137
  panel tabs, 129–130
  Replace Edit, 168
  saving workspace presets,
    130–133
  scrubbing clips, 137
  three-point, 143–145
  Timeline, 131–135
  tracks, 146–150
  workflows, 37, 217–221
  workspace layout presets,
    127–129
  workspace setup, 127
  zoom to sequences, 138
edits. *See also* split edit
  Extract command, 170–172
  insert and overwrite, 132
  Lift, 169–170
  toggling focus, 132

effects
   adjustment layers, 292–294
   animating, 287–292
   fixed, 286
   Opacity Blend modes, 296–297
   and presets, 39–40
   reusing, 380
   Rolling Shutter Repair, 303–304
   saving, 380
   scaling height and width, 297
   standard, 286, 296
   track mattes, 294–296
   transitions, 291
   Warp Stabilizer, 300–304
Effects tab, using for output, 417
Encore, installing, 452
EQ (equalizer) effect, 268–270
Export Media dialog box,
   420–426, 436–437
exporting
   media, 475–477
   XML in Final Cut Pro, 9–10
exporting strategies
   architectures, 409–415
   AVI (Audio Video Interleaved),
      413
   buckets, 412–413
   client requests, 410–411
   codecs, 409–415
   Flash, 413
   MP4 vs. h.264, 412
   MPEG-4, 412
   MXF (Materials eXchange
      Format), 413
   needs vs. outputs, 410
   output, 413–419
   presets, 442–449
   preview files, 427
   QuickTime, 412
   rendering while working, 427
   uncompressed video, 409
   video compression, 410
Extend Edit, 188–189, 200
external ports, upgrading, 35
Extract command, 170–172

F
file naming, 104
file-based cameras, 7
Final Cut Pro, 9–10, 65
final output, 426–430.
   See also output
Fit Clip panel, 152–156.
   See also clips

Flash
   architecture, 413
   self-hosting preset, 446–448
flesh tones, adjusting, 370–372
folders, 69
fonts. See Title Designer
footage. See also clips
   ingesting, 459
   removing from Timeline,
      169–176
   replacing, 164
   transcoding, 457–458
   transferring, 457–458
four-point editing, 152–153
frame size
   decisions about, 465–467
   restoring, 139
frames, 137–138. See also Dropped
   Frame indicator

G
gain, 240–244
Gaussian Blur effect, 314
General preferences, 49–50
GPU acceleration effect, 285
GPU cards, 26, 34
grades
   vs. corrections, 332
   turning on and off, 400
Gradient filter look, 383–384
grouping clips, 179, 195–197
Group-Selecting edit points,
   214–216

H
h.264 codec, 414, 431–434. See also
   output
hardware, 23, 30, 34–36
HDV editing mode, 75
headphones, 239–240
Hue Blend mode, 327
hum, 273–274

I
import
   from Avid Media Composer, 11
   to bins, 87
   clips for slow motion shots,
      90–92
   dead audio tracks, 95–96
   dual sound, 89–90
   "generic" projects, 97
   vs. Media Browser, 86
   merge and sync clips, 89–90

Prelude, 88–89
   slow motion shots, 90–92
   stereo vs. mono audio, 92–94
Import command, 86
In and Out range, marking for
   clips, 151
In points, designating, 458
ingesting footage, 37, 459
Input tracks, setting up, 83
insert edits, source patching for,
   146–149

J
JKL keys, 136, 139–140
JPEG (Joint Photograph Expert
   Group), 435

K
Kelvin units, 335
keyboard layout presets, saving,
   142–143
keyboard mapping
   Adobe Premiere Pro, 64
   Auto Waveform, 65
   Avid Media Composer, 64
   Deselect All, 65
   Final Cut Pro 7.0, 65
   increasing speed, 140
   Media Browser, 66
   modifying pre-mapped
      shortcuts, 140
   panels, 65
   preferences, 65
   reclaiming unused keys, 140
   tips, 141–142
   Track Height Presets, 66
keyboard shortcuts
   \ (backslash) key, 138
   + (plus) and – (minus), 139
   Audio Channels option, 94
   Copy command, 150
   customizing, 140
   Cut command, 150
   deselection, 151
   Effect Controls panel, 287
   filling screen with video, 9
   jumping to markers, 171
   linking clips, 195
   Match Frame, 169
   maximize frame under cursor,
      138
   modifying, 139–140
   Paste command, 150
   Replace Clip, 169
   restore frame size, 139

search box, 66
SpeedGrade, 393
Task Manager, 32
toggle full screen, 139
toggling trims, 211
trimming in Timeline, 187
unlinking clips, 195
workspaces, 62
kéyframes, 256. *See also* track keyframes
keying, combining techniques, 321–322
keying and compositing, 315, 317–321

L

layers, 405
Lift edits, 169–170
light, 335–340. *See also* color correction
limiter, using, 268
linked selections, best practice, 50
list views with metadata, maximizing, 102–104
locking tracks, 200
.look files, 471
looks
    adjustment layers, 386
    applying across scenes, 386–387
    black and white, 381–382
    Bleach Bypass, 383
    copying between shots, 402–403
    described, 405
    developing, 334, 380–381
    filmic "S curve," 381
    Gradient filter, 383–384
    Lumetri, 384–385
    nesting, 387
    recipes, 381
    sepia, 382
    summer, 383
    summer + Grad filter, 384
looping, 44
LTO (Linear Tape Open) drive, 70
luma adjustments, 354, 397–400
luma issues, fixing, 358–359
Lumetri effect, 384–385, 388, 471

M

maintaining sync, 192–197. *See also* Sync Settings
markers, jumping to, 171
marquee-dragging, 214–216
masks, explained, 405

master tracks vs. submxes, 265
masters, 82–83
Match Frame, 160–163, 167–169
media
    exporting, 475–477
    rewrapped, 10–11
media backups, making, 69–79
Media Browser
    directory viewers, 88
    filtering by file type, 88
    vs. import, 86
    importing directly to bins, 87
    JKL keys, 88
    keyboard mapping, 66
    playing through clips, 88
    previewing media, 7–9
    Thumbnail vs. List view, 87–88
    viewing clips, 89
Media Cache folders, 57–58
Media Encoder
    Add Output button, 439
    adding metadata, 451
    appearance, 451
    Automatic Encoding preference, 450
    automating, 450–452
    automating with watch folders, 441
    background encoding, 38
    compression in Queue panel, 441
    compression process, 438–439
    custom transcode settings, 437
    encoding, 438
    interface, 438
    learning, 41
    locating media drives, 451
    log information, 440
    Media Cache folder, 111
    MP3s for transcription, 452
    naming system, 439
    Output File Destination, 451
    Output Preview area, 440
    outputs/media, 111
    overview, 437
    preference adjustments, 450
    Preset Browser, 440–442
    presets, 438, 442–449
    Queue button, 38
    Queue panel, 438–439
    resetting sources, 439
    watch folders, 438, 441, 451–452, 476
media setup, 67–69, 119–120
Memory preferences, 52
merging and syncing clips, 89

metadata views, 102–104
mezzanine formats, 464–465
mixing sound. *See also* audio
    adding keyframes, 256
    clipping, 251
    crossfades, 257–259
    DR (dynamic range), 251–254
    level adjustment in Timeline, 254–255
    noise floor/room tone, 259
    panning, 259–260
    tracking keyframes, 256
    using keyframes, 256
    VU meters, 250
mono pair, adjusting to be stereo clip, 94
mono vs. stereo audio, 92–93
moves and trims, using numeric keypad for, 216
MP3s for transcription, 452
MP4 vs. h.264, 412
MPE (Mercury Playback Engine), 14–16
MPEG-4 category, 412, 433
MTS-MPEG Transport Stream files, 13
multi-camera editing.
    See also editing
    acquiring media, 223–227
    adding sync markers, 231
    adjusting, 233–234
    building sequences, 230
    choosing cameras, 234
    keyboard mapping, 231
    multi-camera sequences, 228–232
    organizing media, 227–228
    performing, 232–233
    preparation, 228–231
    recording overlap, 226–227
    recording sync marks, 225
    selecting clips, 230
    shooting wide, 227
    sync timecode, 224–225
    using camera logs, 226
    video and matching audio, 234
    workflow, 223–227
multichannel masters, 82–83
MXF (Materials eXchange Format), 413, 430
MXF DNxHD OP1a, 430

N

nesting, using with looks, 387
Nests bin, 99
noise, removing, 277–280
noise floor/room tone, 259
noise reduction, 40
normalization methods, 244–245
numeric keypad, using for moves
    and trims, 216

O

online-hosting preset, 448–449
Opacity Blend modes, 296–297,
    323–327
Open CL architecture, 16
optimized setup. *See also* system
    setup
    Appearance, 55
    Auto Save, 55
    cache files, 55–58
    General, 49–50
    Label Colors, 55
    Memory, 52
    Playback, 53
    preferences, 48–49
    Sync Settings, 53–54
    Trim, 55
organization
    adjusting bin views, 101–102
    bins for projects, 98–99
    clip naming, 100–101
    list views and metadata, 102–104
    sequence naming, 99
Out points, designating, 458
output. *See also* final output; h.264
    codec
    accelerating, 427
    Bars & Tone ID sequence, 419
    clip names, 416
    duplicating sequences, 415
    Effects tab, 417
    file size, 418
    files, 420
    monitoring, 30
    naming sequences for, 415
    nesting sequences, 417
    timecode, 416
    watermarking, 416–418
Outputs bin, 98
Overlay Blend mode, 325
Overlays, 59–60
overwrite edits, source patching
    for, 146–149

P

P2 cards, 3
P2 editing mode, 75
panels
    enlarging, 138
    keyboard mapping, 65
    maximizing, 7
panning, 259–260
Paste Insert technique, 178–180
performance, keyboard mapping,
    65
Photoshop
    best practices, 113–114
    document setup, 112–113
    documents, 112
    documents for import, 113–114
    Files/Graphics bin, 99
    learning, 41–42
    Merge options, 114
    performance cache, 112
    window layout with Timeline, 111
pixels, measuring with color
    picker, 339
Playback preferences, 53
playhead, adding, 404
PNG (Portable Network Graphic),
    435
Post codecs, 428
post/archival based codec, 413
poster frames, setting for shots,
    156
post-faders, 265
postproduction. *See also* Prelude
    After Effects, 472–473
    Audition, 473–475
    camera raw files, 467–468
    codecs, 464
    fixing issues in, 222
    frame size, 465–467
    mezzanine formats, 464–465
    Smart Rendering, 465
    SpeedGrade, 468–473
    starting in Premiere Pro, 456
pre-faders, 265
preferences, 49–55
Prelude. *See also* postproduction
    Comment marker, 461
    exporting to Premiere Pro, 463
    features, 88–89
    file renaming during ingest, 459
    learning software, 42
    markers, 460–462
    media, 106–107
    Media Cache folder, 106

    metadata and file logging, 459
    metadata during ingest, 459
    In and Out points, 458
    project cache, 105–106
    projects, 105
    Relink dialog, 459
    rough cuts, 462
    Subclip marker, 461
    transcoding footage, 457–458
    transferring footage, 457–458
    Verification feature, 458
presets and effects, 39–40
previewing media, 7–9
previews, 119
primary colors, 336–337
primary corrections. *See also* color
    correction
    SpeedGrade, 397–398
    Three-Way Color Corrector, 352,
        357–363
production process in Adobe
    Creative Cloud, 37
Program panel, trimming in,
    187–192
project files, system setup, 119
Project Manager, 478–482
project setup
    audio previews, 71–72
    auto save, 72
    captured video, 71
    captures audio, 71
    editing modes, 74–77
    master templates, 85
    optimizing, 70–71
    sequence presets, 72–74
    sequence template preset, 77–81
    tracks, 81–85
    video previews, 71–72
projects. *See also* bins
    archiving, 477
    optimizing, 70–72
ProRes codec, 415, 428
prosumer cameras, 4–5

Q

Queue button, 436–437
QuickTime
    advantage, 412
    editing mode, 75
    and Post codec, 426, 428–430
QuickTime media, 10

R

RAID (Redundant Array of Information Disks)
  explained, 28–29
  upgrades, 35
RAID-5 backups, using, 29, 69
RAM
  recommendations, 25
  upgrades, 36
raw files, 467–468
raw footage
  bin, 98
  keeping versions of, 454–455
RED footage, maximizing performance, 26
RED Scarlet-X camera, 6
rendering, 427, 430. *See also* Smart Rendering
Replace Edit, 168
Resource Monitor, 7, 32–33
Retina MacBook, 35
Reveal Clip, 163–164. *See also* clips
reverb effect, 275–276
rewrapped media, 10–11
RGB color space, 336–337
RGB Curves, 351, 364–366
RGB Parade
  Bright/Darks, 345–346
  flesh tones, 346
  neutral items, 345
  SpeedGrade, 397
RGB processing, 364
Ripple and Roll, using in tandem, 182–186
Ripple Delete command, 172–173
Ripple Edit tool, 182
Rolling Edit tool, 181–182
room tone, 259
rough cuts, creating, 462

S

S for snapping, toggling, 50, 186
Saturation Blend mode, 327
Scale to Frame Size workflow, 217–219
scenes, combining, 220–221
script and speech technologies, 118, 120–123
scriptwriting, 120–121
scrubbing clips, 137
SDCam codec, 414
secondaries, explained, 405

secondary corrections. *See also* color correction
  eyedropper color selection, 368–369
  flesh tones, 370–372
  key-based, 368
  leaving single color, 374–375
  refining selection, 369–370
  shape-based, 375–377
  Show Mask, 369
  skies, 372–373
  Soften control, 370
  in Three-Way Color Corrector, 352–353
Selection tool, 181
sepia look, 382
sequence presets, 72–77
sequence settings, Maximum choices, 80–81
sequence template presets
  Apple ProRes, 80
  audio master output, 82
  building master template, 85
  multichannel masters, 82
  resaving presets, 77–78
  smart rendering codecs, 78–80
  split channel masters, 82–83
  tracks, 81–82
sequence types, changing, 84
sequences. *See also* Automate to Sequence
  adding shots to, 137
  dragging, 82
  editing clips from, 220
  managing, 74
  naming, 99
  naming for output, 415
  nesting, 417
  zooming in, 138
  zooming to, 138
shape-based corrections, 375–377
Shift key. *See* keyboard shortcuts
shortcuts. *See* keyboard shortcuts
shot matching, 377–379
Shot/Reverse shot, 402–403
shots. *See also* clips
  adding to sequences, 137
  replacing in timeline, 165–169
  setting poster frames for, 156
skies, adjusting, 372–373
skin tones, adjusting, 370–372
Slide tool, 189–190
Slip tool, 189–190
slots, running out of, 36
Smart Rendering, 79–80, 465.
  See also rendering

snapping, toggling, 50, 186
Sony editing mode, 75
sort buttons effect, 285
sort index, forcing, 67
sound. *See also* audio
  "brightness," 238
  "muddy," 238
  spectrum, 269
Source Monitor, using bin as, 155–160
source patching, 146–149
speakers, 237–239
speech, smoothing, 50
speech and script technologies, 118, 120–123
SpeedGrade. *See also* color correction
  Add playheads, 393
  adding playhead, 404
  and After Effects, 27
  AutoColorMatch, 405
  chroma adjustments, 400
  color correction, 390
  color matching, 393, 403 405
  Copy grade below mouse, 393
  copying looks between shots, 402–403
  Direct Link, 471
  Dynamic playback, 393
  Export Look, 470
  export options, 390
  Final Saturation control, 401
  Full screen toggle, 393
  global controls, 401–402
  Go to, 393
  grading controls, 391
  Input Saturation control, 401
  keyframes, 406
  layers, 391
  Layers panel, 398
  learning, 44–45
  .look files, 471
  Look preset filed, 118
  luma adjustments, 398–400
  LUTs (look-up tables), 118, 469–470
  Magenta control, 402
  moving playhead, 392
  navigating, 393
  navigating Timeline, 392–393
  Out points, 393
  Pivot + Contrast control, 401
  Play options, 393
  playing clips, 393
  In points, 393
  preparing sequences, 390

SpeedGrade (*continued*)
  primary corrections, 398
  range controls, 400–401
  returning to Premiere Pro, 392
  reviewing adjustments, 402
  RGB Parade, 398
  scope locations, 395–396
  Send back to Adobe Premiere
    Pro, 390
  Send to Adobe SpeedGrade, 390
  shortcut keys, 393
  Shot/Reverse shot, 402–403
  show/hide options, 393
  snapshots, 391, 406
  Temperature control, 401
  Timeline, 391
  toggle Grading, 393
  toggling In/Out points, 394
  toolbar, 391
  upstream from Premiere Pro,
    469–470
  Vectorscope, 397
  video cards, 27
  viewer, 391, 395
  Waveform, 396–397
  workflows, 390
  working directly in, 390
  Zoom options, 393
  zooming Timeline, 394
split channel masters, 82–83
split edit, creating quickly, 183. *See
  also* edits
SSD storage, 28, 35
standard effect rendering order,
  296
At Startup preference, 49
stereo vs. mono audio, 92–93
still frames, outputting, 435–436
Still Image Default preference, 50
storage
  best practices, 455
  caches, 27–28
  choosing, 27
  connections, 27
  media, 28
  OS considerations, 29–30
  projects, 28
  RAID, 28–29
  SSD, 28
Story, 118–124
subclips, using, 100–101
submixes vs. master tracks, 264
Subtract Blend mode, 327

suite relations
  After Effects, 107–110
  Audition, 114–117
  caches, 105
  file naming, 104
  media, 104–105
  Media Encoder, 110–111
  Photoshop, 111–114
  Prelude, 105–107
  SpeedGrade, 118
Swap Edit command, 176–178
sync, broken, 232
sync issues, repairing, 200
sync marks, recording, 225
Sync Replace, 167–169
Sync Settings, 53. *See also*
  maintaining sync
sync timecode, using, 224–225. *See
  also* Timecode
system design
  computer monitor, 30
  CPU, 24
  hardware monitoring cards, 30
  "minimum" configuration, 23
  performance gains, 23
  RAM, 25
  storage, 27–30
  Thunderbolt support, 23
  video card, 26
system performance, 30–34
system setup, 119. *See also*
  optimized setup

T

tails
  modified, 201–204
  removing, 173–176
tape-based cameras, 7
Task Manager, 32
three-point editing, 143–146
Three-Way Color Corrector
  fixing chroma issues, 359–360
  fixing luma issues, 358–359
  practicing with, 361–363
  primary corrections, 352,
    357–363
  ranges, 353
  vs. RGB Curves, 361–363
  secondary correction, 352–353
  Tonal Range, 353
Thunderbolt connections, 27
TIFF (Tagged Image Foto
  Format), 435

Timecode, 416. *See also* sync
  timecode
Timecode Overlay, 425
Timeline
  activating display indicators, 134
  customizing tracks, 134
  display settings, 132–133
  fly-out menu, 135
  Linked Selection, 192
  live trimming on, 208–210
  Match Frame, 160–163
  removing footage, 169–176
  removing footage from, 169–176
  replacing footage, 164–165
  replacing shots, 165–169
  repositioning clips, 176–180
  Reveal Clip, 163–164
  saving track height preferences,
    133
  scrolling, 131–132
  Show Auto Keyframes, 135
  trimming tips, 187
  zooming, 131–132
Timeline clips. *See also* clips
  Paste Insert technique, 178–180
  repositioning, 176–179
  Swap Edit command, 176–178
Timeline editing
  asymmetrical trimming, 210–216
  dynamic trimming, 205–208
  Extend Edit live, 201
  live trimming, 208
  modified tops and tails, 201–204
Timeline Playback preference, 50
Title Designer
  adjusting glow effect, 308
  BRIKZ clip, 311
  character spacing, 309–310
  Custom Style Library, 305
  effects and blends, 311–312
  explained, 304–305
  Gaussian Blur effect, 314
  gradients, 310–311
  kerning, 309–310
  Lit property, 306
  metallic styles, 305–307
  nested sequence, 312–315
  Title Properties panel, 306, 308
  track matte, 312–315
  tracking, 309–310
  Typestyle 2, 307–308
Titles bin, 99
titling workflow, 37

tools
  Ripple Edit, 182
  Rolling Edit, 181–182
  Selection, 181
  Slide, 190–191
  Slip, 189–190
tops
  modified, 201–204
  removing, 173–176
track awareness, 146
track height preferences, saving, 133
Track Height Presets, keyboard mapping, 66
track keyframes, 256.
  See also keyframes
track locks, 179
track mattes
  using, 294–296
  using with title effect, 312–315
track targeting, 150, 161
tracking, explained, 405
tracks
  adjusting to be mono pair, 93
  adjusting to ignore one, 94
  customizing in Timeline, 134
  locking, 200
  naming, 82
  setting up, 81–82
transcode settings, customizing, 437
transcoding video
  codecs, 457
  considering, 15
  vs. data transfers, 458
  explained, 12–13
  importing formats, 13
  media handling, 14
  performance, 14
  portability, 14
transferring footage, 457–458
Transform effect, 286
transitions, using as effects, 291
Transparent Video bin, 99
Trim mode, 187–188
Trim preferences, 54–55
Trim tool cheat sheet, 188

trimming. *See also* dynamic trimming
  asymmetrical, 210–214
  dynamic and live, 208–210
  Extend Edit, 188–189
  Group-Select cuts, 214–217
  maintaining sync, 192–200
  in Program panel, 187–188
  repairing sync issues, 200
  Ripple and Roll, 182–186
  Ripple Edit tool, 182
  Rolling Edit tool, 181–182
  Selection tool, 181
  Slide tool, 190–192
  Slip tool, 189–190
  Tall Trim Jim, 216
  tools, 181
trims, toggling, 211
trims and moves, using numeric keypad for, 216
TV, bins used in, 99
Typestyle 2, choosing, 307–308

U
Ultra Key, 315–319
Undo command, 179

V
VAR (Value Added Reseller), 34
VBR (variable bit rate), 431, 434
Vectorscope, 343–345, 397
Verification feature, using in Prelude, 458
video
  legalizing, 387–388
  switching with matching audio, 234
  transcoding, 12–14
  unlinking audio from, 183
Video and Audio Transition preference, 49
video cards, 26, 35
video driver, updates to, 26
Video Limiter, 388
video previews, 71
video scopes, 341
video tracks, locking, 200

visible light spectrum, 335
volume level, adjusting for clips, 254–255
VU meters, 250, 254

W
Warp Stabilizer, 300–304
watch folders. *See* Media Encoder
watermarking, 416–418
Waveform, 396–397
workflows
  animating stills, 37
  audio mixing, 37
  audio repair, 37
  Audition, 40
  background encoding, 38
  chroma keying, 37
  color correction, 37
  Default Scale to Frame Size, 51
  digital-file output, 37
  editorial, 37
  effects, 39–40
  handling camera data, 454–455
  ingest, 37
  learning curve, 38
  multi-camera, 230
  multi-camera editing, 222
  Smart Rendering, 79–80
  SpeedGrade, 390
  Story, 122–123
  titling, 37
workspaces, 61–62

X
XML, exporting in Final Cut Pro, 9–10
XMP "sidecar" file, 459

Y
YbCr Parade, 347
YC Waveform, 341–343
YCr'Cb', 339–340
YUV space, 286, 339–340

Z
zooming in sequences, 138